IFIP Advances in Information and Communication Technology 621

IFIP – The International Federation for Information Processing

IFIP was founded in 1960 under the auspices of UNESCO, following the first World Computer Congress held in Paris the previous year. A federation for societies working in information processing, IFIP's aim is two-fold: to support information processing in the countries of its members and to encourage technology transfer to developing nations. As its mission statement clearly states:

IFIP is the global non-profit federation of societies of ICT professionals that aims at achieving a worldwide professional and socially responsible development and application of information and communication technologies.

IFIP is a non-profit-making organization, run almost solely by 2500 volunteers. It operates through a number of technical committees and working groups, which organize events and publications. IFIP's events range from large international open conferences to working conferences and local seminars.

The flagship event is the IFIP World Computer Congress, at which both invited and contributed papers are presented. Contributed papers are rigorously refereed and the rejection rate is high.

As with the Congress, participation in the open conferences is open to all and papers may be invited or submitted. Again, submitted papers are stringently refereed.

The working conferences are structured differently. They are usually run by a working group and attendance is generally smaller and occasionally by invitation only. Their purpose is to create an atmosphere conducive to innovation and development. Refereeing is also rigorous and papers are subjected to extensive group discussion.

Publications arising from IFIP events vary. The papers presented at the IFIP World Computer Congress and at open conferences are published as conference proceedings, while the results of the working conferences are often published as collections of selected and edited papers.

IFIP distinguishes three types of institutional membership: Country Representative Members, Members at Large, and Associate Members. The type of organization that can apply for membership is a wide variety and includes national or international societies of individual computer scientists/ICT professionals, associations or federations of such societies, government institutions/government related organizations, national or international research institutes or consortia, universities, academies of sciences, companies, national or international associations or federations of companies.

More information about this series at http://www.springer.com/series/6102

Andrea Calimera · Pierre-Emmanuel Gaillardon ·
Kunal Korgaonkar · Shahar Kvatinsky ·
Ricardo Reis (Eds.)

VLSI-SoC:
Design Trends

28th IFIP WG 10.5/IEEE International Conference
on Very Large Scale Integration, VLSI-SoC 2020
Salt Lake City, UT, USA, October 6–9, 2020
Revised and Extended Selected Papers

 Springer

Editors
Andrea Calimera 🄳
Politecnico di Torino
Turin, Italy

Pierre-Emmanuel Gaillardon 🄳
University of Utah
Salt Lake City, UT, USA

Kunal Korgaonkar 🄳
Technion – Israel Institute of Technology
Haifa, Israel

Shahar Kvatinsky 🄳
Technion – Israel Institute of Technology
Haifa, Israel

Ricardo Reis 🄳
Universidade Federal do Rio Grande do Sul
Porto Alegre, Brazil

ISSN 1868-4238   ISSN 1868-422X (electronic)
IFIP Advances in Information and Communication Technology
ISBN 978-3-030-81643-8   ISBN 978-3-030-81641-4 (eBook)
https://doi.org/10.1007/978-3-030-81641-4

This Springer imprint is published by the registered company Springer Nature Switzerland AG
The registered company address is: Gewerbestrasse 11, 6330 Cham, Switzerland

Preface

This book contains extended and revised versions of the highest quality papers presented during the 28th edition of the IFIP/IEEE WG 10.5 International Conference on Very Large Scale Integration (VLSI-SoC 2020), a global system-on-chip design and CAD conference. The 28th edition of the conference was held during October 6–9, 2020, virtually from Salt Lake City, USA. Previous conferences have taken place in Edinburgh, Scotland (1981); Trondheim, Norway (1983); Tokyo, Japan (1985); Vancouver, Canada (1987); Munich, Germany (1989); Edinburgh, Scotland (1991); Grenoble, France (1993); Chiba, Japan (1995); Gramado, Brazil (1997); Lisbon, Portugal (1999); Montpellier, France (2001); Darmstadt, Germany (2003); Perth, Australia (2005); Nice, France (2006); Atlanta, USA (2007); Rhodes Island, Greece (2008); Florianopolis, Brazil (2009); Madrid, Spain (2010); Kowloon, Hong Kong (2011), Santa Cruz, USA (2012), Istanbul, Turkey (2013), Playa del Carmen, Mexico (2014), Daejeon, South Korea (2015), Tallin, Estonia (2016), Abu Dhabi, United Arab Emirates (2017), Verona, Italy (2018), and Cuzco, Peru (2019).

The purpose of this conference, sponsored by the IFIP TC 10 Working Group 10.5, the IEEE Council on Electronic Design Automation (CEDA), and the IEEE Circuits and Systems Society, with the in-cooperation of ACM SIGDA, is to provide a forum for the presentation and discussion of the latest academic and industrial results and developments as well as the future trends in the field of system-on-chip (SoC) design, considering the challenges of nano-scale along with state-of-the-art and emerging manufacturing technologies. In particular, VLSI-SoC 2020 addressed cutting-edge research fields like low-power design of RF, analog and mixed-signal circuits, EDA tools for the synthesis and verification of heterogenous SoCs, accelerators for cryptography and deep learning and on-chip interconnection systems, reliability and testing, and integration of 3D-ICs. The chapters of this new book in the VLSI-SoC series continue its tradition of providing an internationally acknowledged platform for scientific contributions and industrial progress in this field.

For VLSI-SoC 2020, 38 papers out of 74 submissions were selected for oral presentation, and out of those 38 full papers presented at the conference, 16 papers were chosen by a special selection committee to have an extended and revised version included in this book. The selection process for these papers considered the evaluation scores during the review process as well as the review forms provided by members of the Technical Program Committee and the session chairs as a result of the presentations.

The chapters of this book have authors from Belgium, Brazil, England, France, Germany, Israel, Italy, Japan, and USA. The Technical Program Committee for the regular tracks comprised 93 members from 23 countries.

VLSI-SoC 2020 was the culmination of the work of many dedicated volunteers: paper authors, reviewers, session chairs, invited speakers, and various committee chairs. We thank them all for their contributions.

This book is intended for the VLSI community at large, and in particular the many colleagues who did not have the chance to attend the conference. We hope that you enjoy reading this book and find it useful in your professional life and for the development of the VLSI community as a whole.

May 2021

Andrea Calimera
Pierre-Emmanuel Gaillardon
Kunal Korgaonkar
Shahar Kvatinsky
Ricardo Reis

Organization

The IFIP/IEEE International Conference on Very Large Scale Integration System-on-Chip (VLSI-SoC) 2020 took place during October 6–9, 2020, virtually from Salt Lake City, USA. VLSI-SoC 2020 was the 28th in a series of international conferences, sponsored by IFIP TC 10 Working Group 10.5 (VLSI), IEEE CEDA, and ACM SIGDA. The Organization Committee of the conference consisted of the following colleagues:

General Chair

Pierre-Emmanuel Gaillardon   University of Utah, USA

Technical Program Chairs

Shahar Kvatinsky   Technion, Israel
Andrea Calimera   Politecnico di Torino, Italy

Special Sessions Chairs

Mike Niemier   University of Notre Dame, USA
David Atienza   EPFL, Switzerland

PhD Forum Chair

Cunxi Yu   University of Utah, USA

Local Chairs

Ross Walker   University of Utah, USA
Mike Wirthlin   Brigham Young University, USA

Industrial Chair

Luca Amaru   Synopsys, USA

Publicity Chairs

Anupam Chattopadhyay   NTU, Singapore
Andre Reis   UFRGS, Brazil
Ian O'Connor   ECL, France
Joseph Friedman   UT Dallas, USA

Publication Chair

Kunal Korgaonkar   Technion, Israel

Web Chairs

Ganesh Gore   University of Utah, USA
Edouard Giacomin   University of Utah, USA

VLSI-SoC Steering Committee

Graziano Pravadelli   University of Verona, Italy
Ibrahim Elfadel   Khalifa University, UAE
Manfred Glesner   TU Darmstadt, Germany
Matthew Guthaus   UC Santa Cruz, USA
Luis Miguel Silveira   INESC ID, Portugal
Fatih Ugurdag   Ozyegin University, Turkey
Salvador Mir   TIMA, France
Ricardo Reis   UFRGS, Brazil
Chi-Ying Tsui   HKUST, Hong Kong, China
Ian O'Connor   INL, France
Masahiro Fujita   The University of Tokyo, Japan

As for the Technical Program Committee, it was composed as follows:

Technical Program Committee Track Chairs

AMS, Sensors, and RF Track

Salvador Mir   TIMA, France
Ross Walker   University of Utah, USA

VLSI Circuits and SoC Design Track

H. Fatih Ugurdag   Ozyegin University, Istanbul
Adam Teman   Bar-Ilan University, Israel

Embedded Systems Design and Software Track

Ibrahim Elfadel   Khalifa University, UAE
Michele Magno   ETH Zurich, Switzerland

CAD Tools and Methodologies for Digital IC Design and Optimization Track

Victor Grimblatt   Synopsys, Chile
Aida Todri-Sanial   University of Montpellier and CNRS, France

Verification, Modeling, and Prototyping Track

Graziano Pravadelli   Università di Verona, Italy
Yakir Vizel   Technion, Israel

Design for Testability, Reliability, and Fault Tolerance Track

Matteo Sonza Reorda   Politecnico di Torino, Italy
Leticia Bolzani Poehls   PUCRS and RWTH Aachen, Germany

Hardware Security Track

Odysseas Koufopavlou   University of Patras, Greece
Anupam Chattopadhyay   Nanyang Technological University of Singapore,
                               Singapore

Emerging Technologies and New Computing Paradigms Track

Ian O'Connor   Lyon Institute of Nanotechnology, France
Yang (Cindy) Yi   Virginia Tech, USA

Technical Program Committee

Alain Pegatoguet   University of Nice, France
Alberto Bosio   Ecole Centrale de Lyon, France
Alessandro Cimatti   Fondazione Bruno Kessler, Italy
Alexander Ivrii   IBM, Israel
Alexander Nadel   Intel, Israel
Alexandre Levisse   EPFL, Switzerland
Ali Akoglu   University of Arizona, USA
Armin Tajalli   University of Utah, USA
Arnaud Virazel   University of Montpellier, France
Avi Mendelson   Technion, Israel
Ayesha Khalid   Queen's University Belfast, Northern Ireland
Azemard Nadine   University of Montpellier, France
Bah Hwee Gwee   Nanyang Technological University of Singapore,
                               Singapore
C. Andras Moritz   University of Massachusetts, USA
Carlos Silva-Cardenas   Pontificia Universidad Catolica del Peru, Peru
Chester Rebeiro   IIT Madras, India
Christos Papachristou   Case Western Reserve University, USA
Chun-Jen Tsai   National Chiao Tung University, Taiwan
Daniele Pagliari   Politecnico di Torino, Italy
David Atienza   EPFL, Switzerland
Debdeep Mukhopadhyay   IIT Kharagpur, India
Dimitrios Soudris   National Technical University of Athens, Greece
Donatella Sciuto   Politecnico di Milano, Italy
Elena Ioana Vatajelu   TIMA, France

Contents

List of Contributors

Amin Aghighi Electrical and Computer Engineering Department, University of Utah, Salt Lake City, USA

Tutu Ajayi University of Michigan, Ann Arbor, MI, USA

Muhannad S. Bakir Georgia Institute of Technology, Atlanta, GA, USA

Rotem Ben-Hur Technion - Israel Institute of Technology, Haifa, Israel

Davide Bertozzi Department of Engineering, Universitá degli Studi di Ferrara, Ferrara, Italy

David Blaauw University of Michigan, Ann Arbor, MI, USA

Juergen Boemmels IMEC, Leuven, Belgium

Moreno Bragaglio Department of Computer Science, University of Verona, Verona, Italy

Benton Calhoun University of Virginia, Charlottesville, VA, USA

Francky Catthoor IMEC, Leuven, Belgium; KU Leuven, Leuven, Belgium

Chien-Hen Chen University of Virginia, Charlottesville, VA, USA

Yaswanth K. Cherivirala University of Michigan, Ann Arbor, MI, USA

Josie Esteban Rodriguez Condia Dip. di Automatica e Informatica (DAUIN), Politecnico di Torino, Torino, Italy

Wim Cops MACOM Technology Solutions, Sophia Antipolis, France

David Cordova MACOM Technology Solutions, Sophia Antipolis, France

Brian Crafton Georgia Institute of Technology, Atlanta, GA, USA

Shanshan Dai Brown University, Providence, RI, USA

Marina Deng University of Bordeaux, CNRS UMR 5218, Bordeaux INP Talence, Bordeaux, France

Yann Deval Laboratorie IMS, Université de of Bordeaux, Bordeaux INP, CNRS UMR 5218, Talence, France

Ronald Dreslinski Jr. University of Michigan, Ann Arbor, MI, USA

Wenbo Duan University of Michigan, Ann Arbor, MI, USA

Adi Eliahu Technion - Israel Institute of Technology, Haifa, Israel

Behrouz Farhang-Boroujeny Electrical and Computer Engineering Department, University of Utah, Salt Lake City, USA

Morteza Fayazi University of Michigan, Ann Arbor, MI, USA

Masahiro Fujita The University of Tokyo, Tokyo, Japan

Pierre-Emmanuel Gaillardon University of Utah, Salt Lake City, UT, USA

Jonas Gava Instituto de Informática, PGMicro, Universidade Federal do Rio Grande do Sul - UFRGS, 9500, Porto Alegre, Brazil

Samuele Germiniani Department of Computer Science, University of Verona, Verona, Italy

Edouard Giacomin University of Utah, Salt Lake City, UT, USA

Shourya Gupta University of Virginia, Charlottesville, VA, USA

Kangping Hu Brown University, Providence, RI, USA

Yinghua Hu University of Southern California, Los Angeles, CA, USA

Sumanth Kamineni University of Virginia, Charlottesville, VA, USA

Ankit Kaul Georgia Institute of Technology, Atlanta, GA, USA

Sumanth Kolluru University of Utah, Salt Lake City, USA

Tushar Krishna Georgia Institute of Technology, Atlanta, GA, USA

Milos Krstic IHP - Leibniz-Institut für innovative Mikroelektronik, Frankfurt Oder, Germany

Abhishek Kumar Université de Toulouse, LAAS, CNRS, INP Toulouse, Toulouse, France

Shahar Kvatinsky Technion - Israel Institute of Technology, Haifa, Israel

Kyumin Kwon University of Michigan, Ann Arbor, MI, USA

Herve Lapuyade Laboratorie IMS, Université de of Bordeaux, Bordeaux INP, CNRS UMR 5218, Talence, France

Guilhem Larrieu Université de Toulouse, LAAS, CNRS, INP Toulouse, Toulouse, France; Institute of Industrial Science, LIMMS-CNRS/IIS, The University of Tokyo, Tokyo, Japan

Sebastien Le Beux Lyon Institute of Nanotechnology, University of Lyon, CNRS UMR 5270, Lyon, France; Ecole Centrale de Lyon, Ecully, France

Aurélie Lecestre Université de Toulouse, LAAS, CNRS, INP Toulouse, Toulouse, France

Jeongsup Lee University of Michigan, Ann Arbor, MI, USA

Xiaoyu Lian Brown University, Providence, RI, USA

Sung-Kyu Lim Georgia Institute of Technology, Atlanta, GA, USA

Cristell Maneux University of Bordeaux, CNRS UMR 5218, Bordeaux INP Talence, Bordeaux, France

François Marc University of Bordeaux, CNRS UMR 5218, Bordeaux INP Talence, Bordeaux, France

Cedric Marchand Lyon Institute of Nanotechnology, University of Lyon, CNRS UMR 5270, Ecole Centrale de Lyon, Ecully, France

Alan Mishchenko UC Berkeley, Berkeley, CA, USA

Yukio Miyasaka UC Berkeley, Berkeley, CA, USA

Chhandak Mukherjee University of Bordeaux, CNRS UMR 5218, Bordeaux INP Talence, Bordeaux, France

Gauthaman Murali Georgia Institute of Technology, Atlanta, GA, USA

Shahin Nazarian University of Southern California, Los Angeles, CA, USA

Nicolas Nodenot MACOM Technology Solutions, Sophia Antipolis, France

Pierluigi Nuzzo University of Southern California, Los Angeles, CA, USA

Ian O'Connor Lyon Institute of Nanotechnology, University of Lyon, CNRS UMR 5270, Ecole Centrale de Lyon, Ecully, France

Luciano Ost Wolfson School, Loughborough University, Loughborough, England

Yohan Piccin MACOM Technology Solutions, Sophia Antipolis, France

Arnaud Poittevin Lyon Institute of Nanotechnology, University of Lyon, CNRS UMR 5270, Ecole Centrale de Lyon, Ecully, France

Graziano Pravadelli Department of Computer Science, University of Verona, Verona, Italy

Arijit Raychowdhury Georgia Institute of Technology, Atlanta, GA, USA

Sherief Reda Brown University, Providence, RI, USA

Ricardo Reis Instituto de Informática, PGMicro, Universidade Federal do Rio Grande do Sul - UFRGS, 9500, Porto Alegre, Brazil

François Rivet Laboratorie IMS, Université de of Bordeaux, Bordeaux INP, CNRS UMR 5218, Talence, France

Ronny Ronen Technion - Israel Institute of Technology, Haifa, Israel

Jacob K. Rosenstein Brown University, Providence, RI, USA

Julien Ryckaert IMEC, Leuven, Belgium

Mehdi Saligane University of Michigan, Ann Arbor, MI, USA

Rakshith Saligram Georgia Institute of Technology, Atlanta, GA, USA

Tannu Sharma University of Utah, Salt Lake City, USA

Matteo Sonza Reorda Dip. di Automatica e Informatica (DAUIN), Politecnico di Torino, Torino, Italy

Samuel Spetalnick Georgia Institute of Technology, Atlanta, GA, USA

Kenneth S. Stevens University of Utah, Salt Lake City, USA

Dennis Sylvester University of Michigan, Ann Arbor, MI, USA

Armin Tajalli Electrical and Computer Engineering Department, University of Utah, Salt Lake City, USA

Caleb R. Tulloss Columbia University, New York, NY, USA

Alessandro Veronesi IHP - Leibniz-Institut für innovative Mikroelektronik, Frankfurt Oder, Germany

John Wawrzynek UC Berkeley, Berkeley, CA, USA

David D. Wentzloff University of Michigan, Ann Arbor, MI, USA

Kaixin Yang University of Southern California, Los Angeles, CA, USA

Low-Power High-Speed ADCs
for ADC-Based Wireline Receivers
in 22 nm FDSOI

David Cordova[2(✉)], Wim Cops[2], Yann Deval[1], François Rivet[1],
Herve Lapuyade[1], Nicolas Nodenot[2], and Yohan Piccin[2]

[1] Laboratorie IMS, Université de of Bordeaux, Bordeaux INP, CNRS UMR 5218,
Talence, France
[2] MACOM Technology Solutions, Sophia Antipolis, France
`david.cordova@macom.com`

Abstract. A very low-power 875 MS/s 7b single-channel high-speed
successive approximation register (SAR) analog-to-digital converter
(ADC) that achieves a SNDR/SFDR at Nyquist rate of 41.46/55.01 dB
is presented. The use of an integer-based split CDAC combined with an
improvement for the LSB capacitor allows a substantial improvement in
the SNDR. A simple and accurate calibration procedure for the ADC is
presented thanks to back gate biasing. The ADC is designed in 22 nm
FDSOI while consuming 1.65 mW from a 0.8 V supply with a core chip
area of 0.00074 mm^2. The Walden figure-of-merit of 19.5 fJ/conversion-
step at Nyquist rate making it one of the lowest among recently published
medium resolution SAR ADCs.

Keywords: Analog-to-digital converter (ADC) · low power · single
channel · successive approximation register (SAR)

1 Introduction

The increasing demand of higher data rates in datacenters has led to new emerging standards (200–400 G Ethernet and others) in wireline communications.
These standards will favored more sophisticated encoding schemes that require
less bandwidth such as the case of PAM4. Its encoding uses 4 levels and reduces
the bandwidth by a factor of 2. But at the price to be harder to be supported
by purely analog solutions. So, a natural shift towards multi-level signaling and
mixed-signal architectures is expected.

ADC-based solutions give more opportunities for speed increase. They
present more robust solutions over channels with high losses (>20 dB) because
they can take advantage of technology scaling and most of the equalization can
be implemented in the digital domain [1,2].

Such ADCs are implemented using time-interleaving: identical sub-ADCs
multiplexed in time, operating in parallel to achieve a higher sampling rate [3].

© IFIP International Federation for Information Processing 2021
Published by Springer Nature Switzerland AG 2021
A. Calimera et al. (Eds.): VLSI-SoC 2020, IFIP AICT 621, pp. 1–19, 2021.
https://doi.org/10.1007/978-3-030-81641-4_1

A suitable sub-ADC should optimize the achievable speed, resolution, power performance and complexity [4–7]. Thus, research in this area is crucial for the next-generation of wireline communication systems.

This paper continuous the works presented in [8,9] on ADCs for high-speed wireline receivers. It explains the ADC-based receiver architecture using the speed requirements for future wireline communications standards. The ADC architecture selection based on energy efficiency and the back gate biasing calibration.

As a result of the above, a very low-power 7-bit SAR ADC is been presented. It features: an improvement for the CDAC LSB capacitor is implemented to improve the SNDR, a simple and accurate calibration procedure for the comparator and ADC using back gate biasing. The circuit was designed using the 22FDX^{TM} platform enabling a power efficient and flexible design.

Section 2 introduces the context of high-speed wireline receivers, the speed and modulation requirements for 100 Gb/s operation. Section 3 presents the sub-ADC resolution estimation based on link budget analysis. Section 4 highlights the ADC architecture selection from the energy efficiency comparison of two high-speed converters. In Sect. 5, the circuit description is presented. Simulation results are shown in Sect. 6 and Sect. 7 draws the main conclusions from this work.

2   High-Speed Wireline Receivers

Today, all datacenter managers (e.g. Google, Facebook, Amazon, ...) have implemented 100 Gb Ethernet connectivity which consists of 4 parallel signals at 25 Gb/s. The encoding of the signals is NRZ (binary modulation Non Return to Zero). The circuits in receivers and transmitters (optical or electrical) are well known and generally of an analog nature. The main disadvantage using this protocol is the high frequency bandwidth usage, especially up to (and even beyond) 12.5 GHz.

For this reason, future standards for higher bitrate transmissions will abandon NRZ in favor of more sophisticated encodings that use less frequency bandwidth. The IEEE 802.3 Ethernet Workgroup is in charge to complete the standard by fall of 2021 under the denomination IEEE 802.3ck which consists of 100, 200, and 400 GbE using 100 Gb/s lanes [10].

The Optical Internetworking Forum (OIF), a non-profit consortium, is also working on the Common Electrical I/O (CEI) 112 G standard, which targets 112 Gb/s electrical interfaces. As data rate continues to increase, 112 Gb/s over single lane is on the horizon. The feasibility certainly depends on the choice of signal modulation and channel characteristics.

4-level Pulse Amplitude Modulation (PAM4) is gaining more attention in recent years as an alternative coding scheme to NRZ. In NRZ signaling, one bit is a symbol and has two distinct amplitude levels of '0' or '1'. Symbols are expressed in terms of baud. NRZ bitrate is equal to its symbol rate where 1 Gb/s is equal to 1 Gbaud.

PAM4 signaling uses four different levels, where each level corresponds to one symbol representing two bits. With two bits per symbol, the baud rate is half the bitrate. For example, 56 Gbaud PAM4 is equal to 112 Gbaud NRZ (112 Gb/s). As such, PAM4 achieves twice as much throughput using half the bandwidth compared to NRZ.

In standard linear PAM4 signaling, it is possible for two transitions to happen at the same time. These transitions can cause two-bit errors per symbol. If standard PAM4 signaling is converted to gray code, the Bit Error Rate (BER) is reduced to one-bit per symbol and the overall bit error rate is cut in half. BER can be expressed as a function of the signal-to-noise ratio (SNR) at the decision point. The use of PAM4 signaling brings many advantages to overcome the bandwidth limitations of NRZ, but also bring new challenges in link-path analysis.

As the link's speed requirements become more stringent, pure analog architectures cannot meet them. So, a natural shift towards mixed-signal architectures is expected. ADC-based receivers give more opportunities for speed augmentation because they constitute more robust solutions due to their digital nature and they scale well with process. The high density of lower processes will allow receivers relying heavily on digital signal processing (DSP) [11]. These receivers incorporate an ADC to digitize the received signal and perform equalization in the digital domain [8,9]. A typical ADC-based receiver is shown in Fig. 1.

3   sub-ADC Resolution Estimation

The resolution of the sub-ADC will be calculated using the BER at the output of the receiver (pre-FEC or raw BER). Figure 1 corresponds to the link budget of a realistic implementation for an ADC-based receiver.

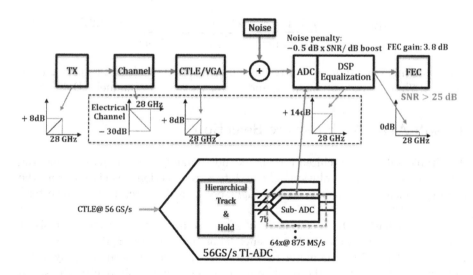

Fig. 1. sub-ADC in a Time Interleaved System

The proposed sub-ADC is designed to meet the SNR requirements for 56 GBaud PAM4 signaling. Considering the same amplitude swing for NRZ and PAM4 encodings, the SNR in PAM4 is lower than NRZ. Forward error correction (FEC) is used to improve link integrity and counteract physical layer level errors introduced by reduced SNR in PAM4 signals [8,9].

At 56 GBaud, the pre-FEC raw BER of $< 10^{-4}$ is a typical target. In our design the receiver is designed to achieve BER $= 10^{-6}$ over a 30 dB loss channel at 28 GHz. We start from the output SNR (post-FEC BER $= 10^{-15}$) and work backwards from there.

$$\text{BER}_{\text{post,FEC}} = \left(\frac{M-1}{2M}\right) \times \text{erfc}\left(\sqrt{\frac{3 \cdot \text{SNR}}{2(M^2-1)}}\right) \qquad (1)$$

where is $M = 4$, for PAM4 modulation and *erfc* is the complementary error function, which yields a SNR ≈ 25 dB.

For a FEC gain of 3.8 dB, the pre-FEC BER is

$$\underbrace{25\,\text{dB}}_{\text{BER}_{\text{post,FEC}}} - \underbrace{3.8\,\text{dB}}_{\text{Gain}_{\text{FEC}}} = \underbrace{21.2\,\text{dB}}_{\text{BER}_{\text{pre,FEC}}<10^{-6}} \qquad (2)$$

The DSP equalization boost is calculated as

$$\underbrace{30\,\text{dB}}_{\text{channel loss}} - \underbrace{8\,\text{dB}}_{\text{Tx}_{\text{gain}}} - \underbrace{8\,\text{dB}}_{\text{Rx}_{\text{gain}}} = 14\,\text{dB} \qquad (3)$$

Considering a SNR noise penalty of -0.5 dB per dB of DSP boost and a margin of 6 dB, the SNR requirement at the input of the ADC yields:

$$\text{SNR}_{\text{ADC}} = \underbrace{21.2\,\text{dB}}_{\text{BER}_{\text{pre,FEC}}<10^{-6}} + \underbrace{14 \times 0.5\,\text{dB}}_{\text{N}_{\text{o,DSP}}} + \underbrace{6\,\text{dB}}_{\text{Margin}} = 34.2\,\text{dB} \qquad (4)$$

which roughly corresponds to a resolution of ≈ 5.4b. Our design targets a resolution of 7b as a trade-off of speed and power for a single-channel ADC.

4   sub-ADC Architecture Selection

A suitable sub-ADC architecture should not magnify the complexity and the achievable speed and resolution. The architecture selection was chosen from the energy efficiency comparison of two high-speed, medium-resolution converters: the flash ADC and SAR ADC.

An N-bit flash ADC is composed of $2^N - 1$ comparators, a reference resistor ladder and a thermometer-to-binary encoder as shown in Fig. 2(a). The reference resistor ladder and thermometer-to-binary encoder energies scale roughly as 2^N but are usually less than the total comparator energy. For simplicity, the speed

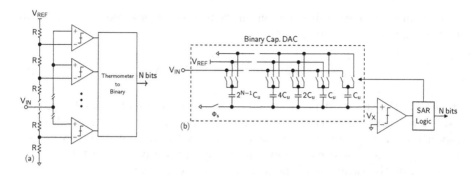

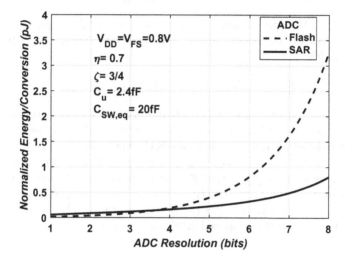

Fig. 2. (a) Flash ADC; (b) SAR ADC with binary-weighted capacitive DAC.

Fig. 3. Energy comparison between SAR and Flash ADCs as a function of resolution

and structure of the comparators used in Flash and SAR ADC are assumed to be the same. Therefore, the energy per conversion for a flash ADC is

$$
\begin{aligned}
E_{comp} &= C_{latch}V_{DD}^2 \\
E_{flash} &= (2^N - 1) \cdot E_{comp},
\end{aligned}
\tag{5}
$$

where E_{comp} is the energy of a single comparator. C_{latch} and V_{DD} represent the total switched capacitance in the comparator's latch and supply voltage, respectively. A basic SAR ADC structure is shown in Fig. 2(b). It consists of a comparator, a capacitive DAC and a SAR control logic. There are several switching schemes aiming to improve the energy efficiency in SAR ADCs [12]. For simplicity, the conventional switching scheme is used in this comparison. The energy per conversion of the comparator can be calculated similar to a flash ADC.

The capacitive DAC using the conventional switching scheme presents a total array energy for one conversion is

$$E_{DAC} = 2\eta 2^{(1+1/2\zeta)N} \frac{C'_u}{2^{N'/2\zeta}} (V_{DD} V_{FS}),\tag{6}$$

where C'_u is the process-dependent unit capacitance required for matching to the N'-bit level and is assumed to be 2.4 fF in 22FDX. V_{FS} is the ADC full scale, respectively. The η[1] and γ[2] coefficients represent the DAC energy dependence on the input-signal and capacitance mismatch, respectively. The total energy consumed by the switching of the SAR logic over one conversion is

$$E_{logic} \approx N C_{SW,eq} V_{DD}^2,\tag{7}$$

where $C_{SW,eq}$ is the total switched capacitance in the SAR logic normalized to 1-bit level. Summing the energy of the SAR blocks, the total energy per sample conversion yields

$$E_{SAR} = E_{DAC} + (N+1) \cdot E_{comp} + E_{logic}\tag{8}$$

The total energy consumption of flash and SAR ADCs are compared versus a resolution range of 1 to 8 bits, as seen in Fig. 3. At resolutions below 4 bits, a flash ADC presents lower energy compared to a SAR ADC. However, as the resolution increases the number of comparators in a flash ADC increases exponentially, while it increases linearly for a SAR ADC. Above a resolution of 6 bits, the energy efficiency of the SAR structure becomes more apparent. Based on this energy comparison, a SAR ADC is the better choice for 7-bit resolution, which is the target range for the proposed ADC-based receiver.

5   Circuit Description

This sub-ADC is designed as a building block inside a Time-Interleaved (TI) ADC. This TI-ADC is a 7-bit 56 G Sample/s with a Interleaved Sampler Ratio (ISR) of 64 [8,9]. Thus, making the sub-ADC operates at 875 MHz.

A very low-power 875 MS/s 7-bit SAR ADC that is suitable for integration into a TI-ADC is presented. The use of an integer-based split CDAC combined with an improvement for the LSB capacitor allows a substantial improvement in the SNDR. A simple and accurate calibration procedure for the ADC is presented thanks to back gate biasing.

The proposed SAR ADC uses asynchronous design to improve the speed conversion, an integer-based split capacitive DAC (CDAC) and the monotonic switching principle. Figure 4a illustrates the top-level ADC architecture. The

---

[1] $\eta = 0.7$ is a reasonable approximation [13].
[2] γ equals 3/4 or 1/2 if the mismatch is dominated by edge effects or oxide variation, respectively.

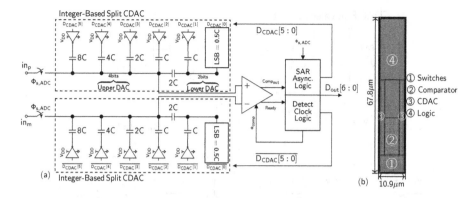

Fig. 4. (a) Architecture of the proposed single-channel 7b SAR ADC; (b) Layout

front-end T&H circuit consists of a sampling bootstrapped switch with feed-through and charge-injection compensation. The sampling clock ($\Phi_{s,ADC}$), with a 25% duty cycle, drives the T&H and triggers the asynchronous internal conversion logic, which is responsible for generating the bit-cycle phases, controlling the comparator, storing its decisions and switching the CDAC.

The ADC comprises two identical 6b CDACs to accommodate differential operation. Since the MSB decision is the sign bit, it can be decided without changing the state of the CDAC. Thus, 6b CDAC, instead of 7b CDAC, is sufficient for this 7b SAR ADC design [14].

5.1 Capacitive DAC

The 6b CDAC, depicted in Fig. 4a, is based on an integer-based split capacitive DAC. The CDAC is divided in two sides: the lower side and the higher side of 2b and 4b, respectively. The split capacitor with a value 2C (C = unit capacitor) is placed just after the smallest unit capacitor of the 4b array, thus avoiding the non-linearity issues found in the common split capacitor array [15]. In the lower side two variations for the LSB capacitor were evaluated, Fig. 5. Instead of switching a fraction of the unit capacitor (0.5C) during the LSB conversion by the full difference of the reference voltage, $V_{REF} = V_{DD}$, a C unit capacitor is switched by a fraction of the reference voltage, $V_{REF} = V_{DD}/2$, which will be referred as LSB$_1$ [5]. And the other LSB$_2$ is implemented switching two unit capacitors (1C) in series by $V_{REF} = V_{DD}$.

The unit capacitors of the CDAC are designed to achieve best area efficiency using alternate-polarity metal-finger capacitors (APMOM) which offer high density, good matching characteristics and low parasitics.

For this 7b SAR ADC, the total capacitance of this capacitor array is $(2^{7-3} + 3)\,C = 19$, [15]. A 70% area reduction compared to a conventional CDAC with

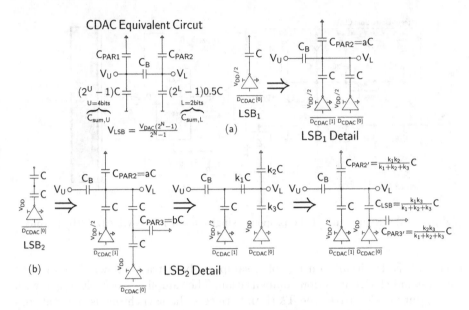

Fig. 5. LSB Capacitor Variation with parasitics: (a) LSB_1; (b) LSB_2

monotonic switching is obtained, thus reducing settling time between conversion cycles and minimizing area and power consumption.

The designed one-side total capacitance is 45.6 fF, which produces an equivalent kT/C thermal noise of 301.4 μV. The least significant bit (LSB) value for a 7b ADC at a reference voltage of 0.8 V is 6.25 mV so the thermal noise introduced by this capacitor array is not a limiting factor. Following the equivalent circuit shown in Fig. 5, the CDAC voltage (V_{DAC}) and LSB voltage (V_{LSB}) are

$$V_{DAC} = \frac{C_B(C_{VREF}^U + C_{VREF}^L) + C_{VREF}^U C_{sum,L}}{den} \cdot V_{REF}$$
$$+ \frac{C_{VREF}^U C_{PAR2}}{den} \cdot V_{REF} \quad (9)$$

$$V_{LSB} = \frac{V_{DAC}(2^N - 1)}{2^N - 1}$$
$$= \frac{C_B(C_{sum,U} + C_{sum,L}) + C_{sum,U}C_{sum,L} + C_{sum,U}C_{PAR2}}{(2^N - 1)den} \cdot V_{REF} \quad (10)$$

where $N = U + L$, $den = (C_{sum,U} + C_{PAR1})(C_{sum,L} + C_{PAR2}) + C_B(C_{sum,U} + C_{sum,L} + C_{PAR1} + C_{PAR2})$, $C_B = 2C$. $C_{sum,U-L}$ and C_{VREF}^{U-L} denotes the total capacitance and total capacitors connected to V_{REF} in the Upper and lower DACs, respectively.

The parasitic capacitance C_{PAR2} in the numerator of Eq. 10 contributes to a code dependent error, degrading the DAC linearity [16]. C_{PAR2} is defined by the

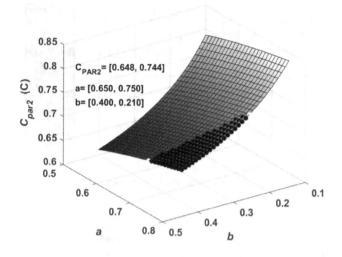

Fig. 6. C_{PAR2} grid for a,b values

total parasitic capacitance of the top plates in the Lower CDAC and the metal interconnection. Figure 5a shows the Lower DAC section for the LSB_1 capacitor. C_{PAR2} is denoted as a fraction of the unit capacitor (aC), for this condition the V_{LSB} error can be reduced by minimizing C_{PAR2} contribution.

In Fig. 5b it is shown a variation of LSB capacitor (LSB_2) to reduce the V_{LSB} error. C_{PAR2} is the same as in LSB_1, but with the addition of C_{PAR3} as the parasitic capacitance of the bottom plates of the two unit capacitors in series. C_{PAR3} is represented as a fraction of the unit capacitor (bC). Through a delta-star transformation LSB_2 is shaped with the same arrangement as for LSB_1. Figure 6 shows the new values of C_{PAR2} and C_{LSB}. A range for C_{PAR3} between [0.21 0.4]C yields the reduction of C_{LSB} and C_{PAR2} simultaneously. In 22 nm FDSOI, the APMOM capacitors present a parasitic ≈0.13C per capacitor yielding a value of b around 0.26.

5.2   Comparator and Back Gate Biasing Calibration

Since the comparator determines the accuracy and speed of the ADC, special care has to be taken for its design [17]. A strong-ARM comparator is chosen for its superior decision speed enabled by the single-stage design. It is optimized for low noise and low power. Figure 7a shows the schematic, the latch regeneration forces one of the signals, *rst* and *set*, to high and the other to low, depending on the comparison result. As a result, the output of the OR gate (*ready*) is pulled high to enable the asynchronous control clock and to facilitate the progression to the next step in the SAR conversion.

The offset voltage V_{OS} introduced by the input differential pair is calibrated using a simple and accurate procedure. The calibration operates in two phases: V_{OS} extraction and V_{OS} calibration. The offset extraction is a fast loop operating at the comparator's clock frequency Φ_{CLK} and follows the smart resettable

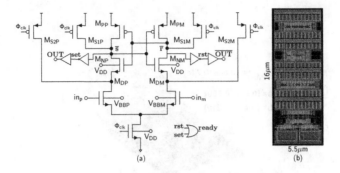

Fig. 7. Strong ARM Comparator: (a) Schematic; (b) Layout

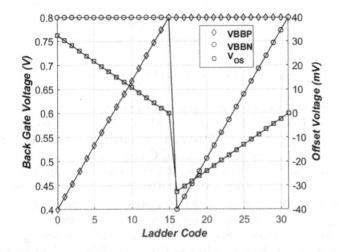

Fig. 8. Back gate biasing DAC: back gate bias and offset voltage

SAR (SR-SAR) technique presented in [18]. The SR-SAR technique is proposed as a fast and accurate alternative to the conventional linear search technique, which is simple and accurate but suffers from long simulation time. The SR-SAR uses a modified SAR algorithm to determine the comparator offset voltage in a much shorter time. The input of the comparator is modified to provide a quasi-monotonic stimulus. It allows a well defined crossing from low-to-high and high-to-low transitions. It yields to an accurate extraction of the rising offset (V_{OSR}) and falling offset (V_{OSF}) voltages.

The second phase is a slow loop (below 1 MHz), due to the low frequency nature of the transistor's back gate. After extracting the V_{OS}, the control block begins to adjust the threshold voltages (V_{TH}) of the differential pair through a back gate biasing DAC until $V_{OS} \approx 0$ or a margin is reached.

The back gate biasing DAC consists of a resistor ladder controlled by a 5-bit digital word. In order to choose the variation range of the ladder, we need

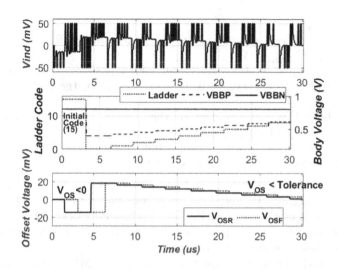

Fig. 9. Back gate biasing calibration procedure showing: input differential voltage (V_{ind}), DAC ladder code, DAC back gate voltage and offset voltage (V_{OS})

Table 1. Post-Layout V_{OS} Calibration.

Search range	−50 to 50 mV	
Resolution	0.1 mV (10 bits)	
Φ_{CLK}	10 MHz	
	Uncalibrated	Calibrated
Mean (V_{OS})	−1.61 mV	0.02 mV
σ (V_{OS})	8.86 mV	0.73 mV

to extract the V_{OS} range of the comparator. Using Monte-Carlo (MC) simulations from the schematic, a V_{OS} range ($+/-3\sigma$) of ≈45 mV was obtained for the nominal clock frequency of 875 MHz.

The nominal voltage supply for the comparator is 0.8 V, the same for the back gate bias at nominal operation. In Fig. 8 is shown the back gate bias control. The ladder was designed using a resolution of 5bits, with the back gate voltage varying between 0.4 to 0.8 V. An artificial offset voltage range of $+/-32$ mV (≈2.1 mV steps) was created. For example if a negative V_{OS} is extracted, the calibration controller will only choose from the positive range to counterbalanced the negative V_{OS} generated by the differential pair.

The V_{OS} calibration for the comparator consists of two phases:

1. V_{OS} extraction:
    - It begins with initialization of the back gate biasing DAC, ladder code $= 15 \rightarrow V_{BBP} = V_{BBN} = 0.8$ V,
    - After initialization V_{OSR} and V_{OSF} are extracted.

2. V_{OS} calibration:
  - V_{OSR} and V_{OSF} determine the iteration sequence for the ladder with $V_{OS,init} = V_{OSR} = V_{OSF}$,
  - For $V_{OS,init} < 0$, the ladder will add a positive $V_{OS,iter}[code] > 0$, with the code starting at 0. For $V_{OS,init} > 0$, the code starts at 16 ($V_{OS,iter}[code] < 0$),
  - The body-bias are switched to the current code value: $V_{BBP}[code]$, $V_{BBN}[code]$ and $V_{OS,iter}[code]$ is extracted,
  - The iteration sequence continues until $V_{OS,iter}[code] <$ tolerance, i.e. 1 mV or the code reachs its final value.

Figure 9 shows the time diagram of the comparator's V_{OS} calibration sequence for $V_{OS,init} < 0$. The code transitions had a time step of 2.5 μs and the comparator is clocked at 10 MHz (T = 100 ns). By clocking the comparator at low frequency, the time step of the transient simulation is coarse enough to allow a much faster convergence solution.

To evaluate the proposed calibration methodology, MC Post-Layout Simulations (PLS) were performed on the comparator using the same search range and resolution for V_{OS} extraction. Figure 10 shows the histogram of V_{OS} for 100 MC runs for an uncalibrated and calibrated comparator. It clearly stands out the V_{OS} mean and standard deviation reduction for the calibrated comparator. Another aspect to point out is the larger V_{OS} of the uncalibrated version, but this did not present any issues since the resistor ladder was designed with some margin. Table 1 summarizes the MC results. The V_{OS} mean was almost zeroed and the standard deviation was reduced by a factor of 12.

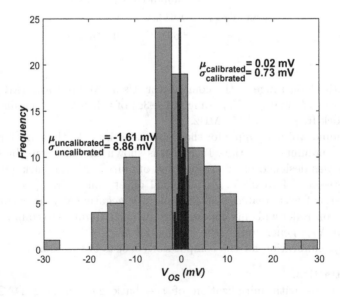

Fig. 10. Histogram Strong ARM V_{OS}: Uncalibrated, Calibrated for 100 MC runs

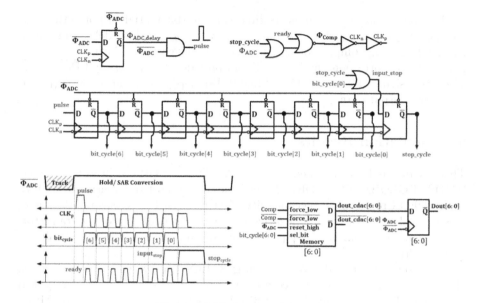

Fig. 11. SAR Logic and timing

5.3   SAR Logic

Besides the advantage of faster bit-cycle conversion, an additional benefit of asynchronous SAR logic is that it does not require an external high-frequency clock, and thus saves the power needed to generate and distribute it. This is extremely important, since this ADC will be part of a time-interleaved system.

The logic of the SAR ADC can be divided into two parts: 1) the clock generation, which provides the clock for the comparator and the bit-cycle phases and 2) the state memory, in charge of controlling the CDAC based on the comparator decision in each of the bit-cycle phases, Fig. 11. The Track duration is set at 25% of the 875 MHz clock period.

The clock generation combines the clock Φ_{ADC}, ready and stop$_{cycle}$ signals to generate the comparator clock (Φ_{Comp}) and bit-cycle clocks (CLK$_{p,n}$) with simple combinational logic. At the same time, a sampling *pulse* is generated from $\overline{\Phi_{ADC}}$ and its delay. This *pulse* propagates sequentially, as controlled by the CLK$_{p,n}$ signals, generating each of the bit-cycle phases, Fig. 11. The Track duration is set at 25% of the 875 MHz clock period. Additionally, the stopcycle signal is used to indicate the end of the conversion cycle.

The state memory part connects directly to the differential output of the comparator. A dynamic register is used as memory to optimize loop delay and enable fast settling upon comparator decision. One cell is activated during every comparison by its corresponding $bit_{cycle}[i]$ and provides $Dout_{CDAC}$ and $\overline{Dout}_{CDAC}$ as control signals for the CDAC. Finally, $Dout_{CDAC}$ is retimed by Φ_{ADC} to create the output data.

6   Simulation Results

This circuit has been designed using the 22FDX^{TM} platform in 22 nm FDSOI CMOS of GLOBALFOUNDRIES [19]. One of the most differentiated features of the 22FDX platform is the capability of effective back gate biasing. Back gate biasing applies a positive or a negative voltage to the back gate of the transistor, which allows the transistor V_{TH} to be tuned, and can be done statistically or dynamically.

The nominal full-scale ADC input is $800\,mV_{pp,diff}$ with a common mode of 400 mV. It operates from a core 0.8 V supply and simulated, under typical conditions. Power consumption is 1.65 mW based on PLS results at 875 MS/s. This overal power consists of 80 μW for the bootstrapped input switch, 40 μW for the CDAC, 0.68 mW for the comparator and 0.85 mW for the phase and SAR logic, as seen in Fig. 12.

Although, the calibration for the comparator was implemented to extract the V_{OS}, it can also be used to calibrate the ADC. Figure 13 shows the MC simulation results, the ADC was calibrated at the middle of the range (64 LSB) and a 4× reduction of the output code σ was achieved. It is worth to mention that the limiting factor for the ADC calibration is the resolution, LSB = 6.25 mV (7 bits).

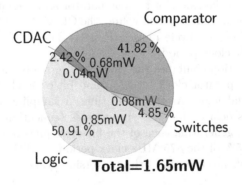

Fig. 12. sub-ADC power consumption breakdown

It is worth to mention, that the calibration procedure for the comparator and ADC was performed at low frequency, due to the time step of the transient simulation is coarse enough to allow a much faster convergence solution. For that reason, the results for static and dynamic characteristics shown are just for nominal conditions without calibration.

The simulated DNL and INL results at 875 MS/s for a ramp up input for the two LSB capacitor versions are depicted in Fig. 14. It can be seen that the second version (LSB_2) is more robust to implement the LSB capacitor of the

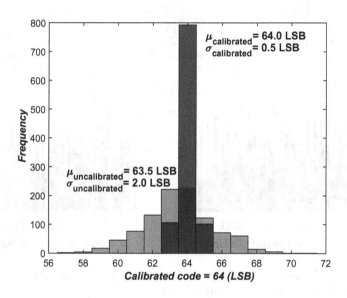

Fig. 13. Histogram of ADC Output Code: Uncalibrated, Calibrated for 1000 MC runs

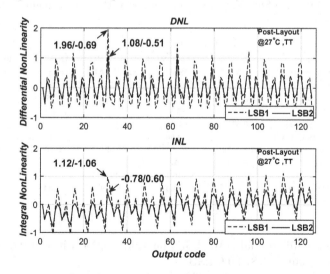

Fig. 14. DNL and INL. LSB_1 (dashed); LSB_2 (solid)

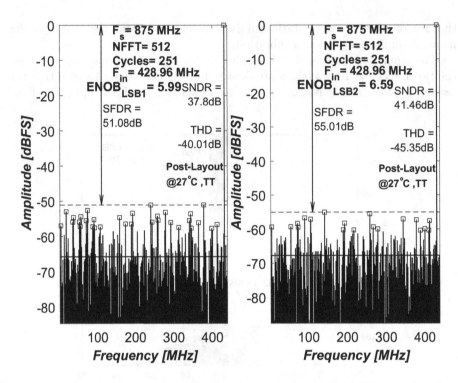

Fig. 15. Output Spectrum with 0 dBFS signal applied at 428.96 MHz, sampling frequency is 875 MHz. LSB_1 (left); LSB_2 (right)

Table 2. Performance Summary and Comparison with Single-Channel State-of-the-Art SAR ADCs

	This Work*	[7]+	[4]+	[5]+	[6]+
Technology [nm]	22 nm FDSOI	28 nm CMOS	65 nm CMOS	32 nm SOI	40 nm CMOS
Architecture	SAR	SAR	2b/c SAR	2 comp. SAR	ci-SAR
Calibration	YES	NO	YES	YES	YES
Resolution [bits]	7	7	8	8	6
Supply [Volts]	0.8	1.0	1.2	1.0	1.0
Samplig Rate [GS/s]	0.875	1.25	0.4	1.2	1
Power Consumption [mW]	1.65	3.56	4.0	3.1	1.26
Active Area [mm²]	0.00074	0.0071	0.024	0.0031	0.00058
SFDR@ Nyq. [dB]	55.01	52	53	49.8	49.7
SNDR@ Nyq. [dB]	41.46	40.1	40.4	39.3	34.6
FoM@Nyq. [fJ/conv-step]	19.5	34.4	116.9	34	28.7

+ Measured; * Post Layout

lower side of the differential DAC. LSB_2 presents a DNL within 1.08/–0.51 LSB, and the INL within –0.78/+0.6 LSB.

The output spectrum at 428.96 MHz input frequency is shown in Fig. 15. The ADC achieves a SNDR/SFDR of 41.46/55.01 dB at Nyquist frequency for the LSB_2 version, presenting an overall improvement of 0.6ENOB with respect to the LSB_1 version, showing the advantage of the proposed modification for the LSB capacitor.

Table 2 shows a performance summary and comparison with recent state-of-the-art SAR ADCs of similar performance, Fig. 16. The presented ADC achieves a comparable SNDR and lower FoM for a similar sampling rate (between 400 MS/s $\Leftrightarrow$ 1.25 GS/s) and resolution (6–8b) while having a lower complexity and a smaller area.

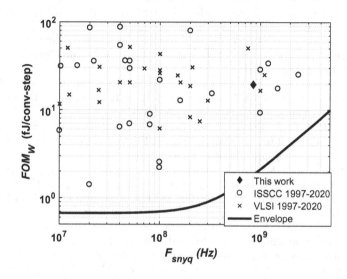

Fig. 16. Comparison with state-of-the-art single-channel SAR based on [20]

7   Conclusion

A 7b 875 MS/s single-channel SAR ADC has been presented. The integer-based split CDAC combined with an improvement for the LSB capacitor allows a substantial improvement in the SNDR. A simple and accurate calibration procedure for the ADC is presented thanks to back gate biasing. The use of a dynamic register in the SAR logic yields a shorter and more uniform settling time per cycle and therefore a faster ADC. The circuit in 22 nm FDSOI achieves a Nyquist Walden FoM of 19.5 fJ/conversion-step, which is the lowest FoM among previously medium resolution (5.5 $\Leftrightarrow$ 7.5ENOB) SAR ADCs with sampling rates greater than 0.8 GS/s/channel.

Acknowledgment. The authors thank the MACOM High-Performance-Analog design team for contributing to the circuit design and GLOBALFOUNDRIES for technology access.

References

1. Hudner, J., Carey, D., Casey, R., et al.: A 112GB/S PAM4 wireline receiver using a 64-Way time-interleaved SAR ADC in 16NM FinFET. In: 2018 IEEE Symposium on VLSI Circuits, pp. 47–48, June 2018
2. Sun, K., Wang, G., Zhang, Q., Elahmadi, S., Gui, P.: A 56-GS/s 8-bit time-interleaved ADC With ENOB and BW enhancement techniques in 28-nm CMOS. IEEE J. Solid State Circuits **54**(3), 821–833 (2019)
3. Kull, L., et al.: Implementation of low-power 6–8 b 30–90 GS/s time-interleaved ADCs with optimized input bandwidth in 32 nm CMOS. IEEE J. Solid State Circuits **51**(3), 636–648 (2016)
4. Wei, H., et al.: A 0.024mm2 8b 400MS/s SAR ADC with 2b/cycle and resistive DAC in 65nm CMOS. In: 2011 IEEE International Solid-State Circuits Conference, pp. 188–190, February 2011
5. Kull, L., et al.: A 3.1 mW 8b 1.2 GS/s single-channel asynchronous SAR ADC with alternate comparators for enhanced speed in 32 nm digital SOI CMOS. IEEE J. Solid State Circuits **48**(12), 3049–3058 (2013)
6. Choo, K.D., Bell, J., Flynn, M.P.: 27.3 area-efficient 1GS/s 6b SAR ADC with charge-injection-cell-based DAC. In: 2016 IEEE International Solid-State Circuits Conference (ISSCC), pp. 460–461, January 2016
7. Ramkaj, A.T., Strackx, M., Steyaert, M.S.J., Tavernier, F.: A 1.25-GS/s 7-b SAR ADC with 36.4-dB SNDR at 5 GHz using switch-bootstrapping, USPC DAC and triple-tail comparator in 28-nm CMOS. IEEE J. Solid State Circuits **53**(7), 1889–1901 (2018)
8. Cordova, D., et al.: A hierarchical track and hold circuit for high speed ADT-based receivers in 22nm FDSOI. In: 2019 26th IEEE International Conference on Electronics, Circuits and Systems (ICECS), pp. 358–361 (2019)
9. Cordova, D., et al.: A 0.8V 875MS/s 7b low-power SAR ADC for ADC-based Wire-line Receivers in 22nm FDSOI. In: 2020 IFIP/IEEE 28th International Conference on Very Large Scale Integration (VLSI-SoC) (2020)
10. IEEE P802.3ck: 100 Gb/s, 200 Gb/s, and 400 Gb/s Electrical Interfaces Task Force (2019). http://www.ieee802.org/3/ck/
11. Chen, E., Yousry, R., Yang, C.K.: Power optimized ADC-based serial link receiver. IEEE J. Solid State Circuits **47**(4), 938–951 (2012)
12. Rabuske, T., Fernandes, J.: Review of SAR ADC switching schemes. In: Rabuske, T., Fernandes, J. (eds.) Charge-Sharing SAR ADCs for Low-Voltage Low-Power Applications. Analog Circuits and Signal Processing, pp. 25–67. Springer, Cham (2017). https://doi.org/10.1007/978-3-319-39624-8_3
13. Ginsburg, B.P., Chandrakasan, A.P.: Dual time-interleaved successive approximation register ADCs for an ultra-wideband receiver. IEEE J. Solid-State Circuits **42**(2), 247–257 (2007)
14. Liu, C., Chang, S., Huang, G., Lin, Y.: A 10-bit 50-MS/s SAR ADC with a monotonic capacitor switching procedure. IEEE J. Solid-State Circuits **45**(4), 731–740 (2010)
15. Deng, L., Yang, C., Zhao, M., Liu, Y., Wu, X.: A 12-bit 200KS/s SAR ADC with a mixed switching scheme and integer-based split capacitor array. In: 2013 IEEE 11th International New Circuits and Systems Conference (NEWCAS), pp. 1–4, June 2013
16. Zhu, Y., et al.: A power-efficient capacitor structure for high-speed charge recycling SAR ADCs. In: 2008 15th IEEE International Conference on Electronics, Circuits and Systems, pp. 642–645 (2008)

17. Xu, H., Abidi, A.A.: Analysis and design of regenerative comparators for low offset and noise. IEEE Trans. Circuits Syst. I Regul. Papers **66**(8), 2817–2830 (2019)
18. Omran, H.: Fast and accurate technique for comparator offset voltage simulation. Microelectr. J. **89**, 91–97 (2019)
19. Carter, R., et al.: 22nm FDSOI technology for emerging mobile, Internet-of-Things, and RF applications. In: 2016 IEEE International Electron Devices Meeting (IEDM), pp. 2.2.1–2.2.4, December 2016
20. Murmann, B.: ADC Performance Survey 1997–2020. http://web.stanford.edu/~murmann/adcsurvey.html

Mixed-Mode Signal Processing for Implementing MCMC MIMO Detector

Amin Aghighi, Behrouz Farhang-Boroujeny, and Armin Tajalli[✉]

Electrical and Computer Engineering Department, University of Utah,
Salt Lake City, USA
armin.tajalli@utah.edu
https://lcas.ece.utah.edu/

Abstract. A hybrid analog/digital signal processor has been proposed
to implement energy-efficient multi-input-multi-output (MIMO) detectors. A sub-optimum MIMO detector based on Markov Chain Monte
Carlo (MCMC) algorithm for a 4 × 4 MIMO system is presented. A
careful partitioning between analog and digital domains has been made
to reduce system power consumption. The outputs of the proposed analog signal processing unit are being converted to digital using a low-
resolution analog-to-digital converter (ADC), to deliver the signals to
the digital portion of the detector system. The proposed 4 × 4 MCMC
MIMO detector is designed in a standard 45 nm CMOS technology, that
consumes 29.3 mW from 1.0 V supply. A throughput of 235.3 Mbps is
achieved, while operating at 1.0 GHz clock frequency. The design occupies a 0.11 mm² silicon area.

Keywords: Optimal detectors · sub-optimal detectors · Markov Chain
Monte Carlo (MCMC) · VLSI MIMO · Mixed-mode MIMO ·
Mixed-mode circuits

1 Introduction

Modern wireless communications use the Multi-Input Multi-Output (MIMO)
approach to improve data throughput at a lower cost. Moreover, the ever-growing
number of users makes MIMO systems even more desirable [1]. Since MIMO systems use the same frequency band for transmitting parallel data streams, data
transfer bandwidth improves with the number of transmit antennas [2]. Therefore, receiver-joint detection is crucial for exploiting the full capacity of the system. Although the optimum detectors can harness the full channel capacity, their
complexity increases exponentially with the number of transmit antennas [3]. As
a result, improving the performance of sub-optimum detectors is a demanding
research topic [4–7]. A few implementations for sub-optimum detectors operating based on the Markov-Chain Monte Carlo (MCMC) algorithm are reported

© IFIP International Federation for Information Processing 2021
Published by Springer Nature Switzerland AG 2021
A. Calimera et al. (Eds.): VLSI-SoC 2020, IFIP AICT 621, pp. 21–37, 2021.
https://doi.org/10.1007/978-3-030-81641-4_2

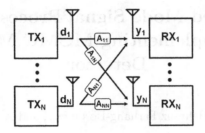

Fig. 1. MIMO system input-output description.

in [2,8–10]. Although this detector can achieve full channel capacity, the existing implementations, which are mainly based on Digital Signal Processors (DSP), result in fairly complex and power-hungry circuits.

This paper targets lowering power consumption and increasing throughput of the MCMC detectors by moving high-speed and energy-hungry operations from DSP to analog/mixed-mode domain. A set of system-level simulations are carried out to show the performance of the proposed analog/mixed-mode approach. Several analog building blocks are proposed to implement target signal processing schemes in a more energy-efficient way. The power and area cost of these blocks are calculated through simulations to have a good cost estimation of the proposed detector.

The rest of this paper is organized as follows: Sect. 2 provides a brief overview on MCMC detectors, and describes the high level implementation of the proposed MCMC detector. System level simulation results are presented in Sect. 3. Section 4 demonstrates circuit-level implementation, and Sect. 5 provides comparison between the proposed MCMC detector and the state-of-the-art.

2   System Level MCMC Detector

2.1   Conventional MCMC Detectors

Considering a flat fading channel, the input-output for each channel that is shown in Fig. 1, can be described by:

$$y = A \cdot d + n \qquad (1)$$

where, $\mathbf{y}$ is the received data vector, $\mathbf{d}$ is the transmitted data bits, $\mathbf{n}$ is the channel additive noise vector, and $\mathbf{A}$ is the channel gain matrix. The MCMC detector is based on an iterative approach. While the detection algorithm is thoroughly described in [2], a brief concept review is presented here. The MCMC detector takes a random set of initial bits, $\mathbf{b_0}$, by a Gibbs sampler [11], and calculates the error function based on:

$$e_0 = y - A \cdot b_0 \qquad (2)$$

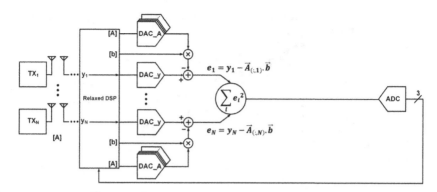

Fig. 2. The proposed MCMC detector block diagram.

where, each element of e_0 represents the initial error associated with each channel.

In other words:

$$e_{0,i} = y_{0,i} - (A_{1,i} \cdot b_{0,1} + A_{2,i} \cdot b_{0,2} + \cdots + A_{N,i} \cdot b_{0,N}) \tag{3}$$

where, i is the desired channel index and N is equal to the number of transmit antennas. When all of the e_0 elements are found, one of the bits in b_0 will be flipped in each iteration, and the error vector, e, will be recalculated. The new error vector in each iteration can be readjusted from the previous value:

$$e_k = e_{k-1} + A_{:,m} \cdot (2b_{(k-1),m}) \tag{4}$$

where, k is the index for the iteration steps, m is the index for the bit which is flipped, and $A_{:,m}$ represents the m-th column of A. In order to compare the error functions between every two consecutive iterations, and decide about the m-th bit, the summation of squared components of e is calculated and defined as:

$$E = e_1^2 + e_2^2 + \cdots + e_N^2 \tag{5}$$

Based on the E value at each iteration step, it will be decided to keep either "+1" or "−1" for the m-th bit. When the decision has been made for all the bits in b_0, the MCMC detector repeats this operation for N_{gs} times for different initial conditions. The performance (accuracy) of the MCMC detector improves when T parallel Gibbs samplers run with different initial random set of bits [2]. As including randomness to the decision process reduces the stalling problem, the MCMC detector introduced in [2] utilizes a random variable, v, and considers both E and v for making decisions.

Usually, MCMC detectors employ Forward Error Correction (FEC), in order to reduce the Bit Error Rate (BER). In this work, we will analyze only the raw BER, before applying FEC.

2.2   Proposed MCMC Detector Circuit

Figure 2 shows the proposed MCMC detector, in which most of the speed-limited operations are moved into the analog domain. In order to calculate each com-

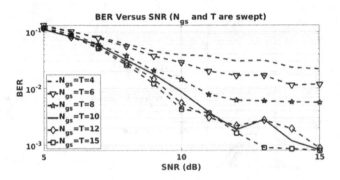

Fig. 3. BER versus SNR while sweeping $\mathbf{N_{gs}}$ and $\mathbf{T}$.

ponent of the error vector, $\mathbf{e}$, a set of digital-to-analog converters (DACs) are employed to convert the digitized received data, $\mathbf{y}$, and the channel gain matrix, $\mathbf{A}$, to the analog domain. The DACs are implemented based on very low-power and low complexity circuits. Bit-wise multiplication is implemented in the analog domain to multiply DAC_A by $\mathbf{b_0}$, and then simply subtract the result from DAC_y to produce the error vector, $\mathbf{e}$. As will be shown in Sect. 4, the summation occurs in the current domain and no extra hardware is required. There are N parallel operators in total needed to produce all the components of the $\mathbf{e}$. A square generator produces the e_i^2 for each channel separately and adds them together to estimate the updated value for $\mathbf{E}$. Finally, a low-resolution analog-to-digital converter (ADC) closes the loop by digitizing the $\mathbf{E}$ value, leaving the final step of decision, i.e., determining $\mathbf{b_0}$ to digital circuits. As will be shown later, the entire operation explained above is implemented using simple analog circuits that occupy a small area and need only one clock cycle to finish each step.

The proposed system needs one clock cycle to generate each component of $\mathbf{e}$. Therefore, considering the arrays of DAC_A and DAC_y are working in parallel, producing $\mathbf{N}$ components of $\mathbf{e_0}$ takes one clock cycle based on (2). Since all of the building blocks in Fig. 2 are synchronized and working at the same frequency, producing and digitizing $\mathbf{e_0}$ also occurs at the same clock rate. Hence, it takes one clock cycle to fulfill all the operations shown in Fig. 2. Based on (3), another clock cycle is required to calculate $\mathbf{e}_k$, and decide about k-th bit of $k > 1$. Therefore, while making decision for the first bit takes two clock cycles, the next bits require only one clock cycle to be determined. Hence, it takes $(N + 1)$ clock cycles in order to determine the polarity of all the bits in $\mathbf{b}$.

3   System Level Simulation Results

High-level simulations have been carried out to determine the performance of the circuit shown in Fig. 2, and determine the required specifications for the key building blocks in this architecture. Some design parameters, such as the number of parallel Gibbs samplers $\mathbf{T}$, the number of iterations for each Gibbs sampler $\mathbf{N_{gs}}$, and the required resolution for each data converter, will be determined based on this study. For simplicity, it is assumed that each antenna transmits bits over only one carrier, i.e., there is no sub-carrier. The number of transmit antennas is set to $\mathbf{N}$. Also, in order to have enough number of bits for calculating BER, the whole MCMC detector iterates for $N_{MC} = 500$ times, which results in $N_{MC} \times T \times N_{gs} \times N$ total number of bits. Here, $\mathbf{T}$ and $\mathbf{N_{gs}}$ are the most critical design parameters that determine the cost and the performance of the detector. This work uses the same $\mathbf{T}$ and $\mathbf{N_{gs}}$ values that have been employed in [2].

Figure 3 shows Bit-Error-Rate (BER) versus signal-to-noise ratio (SNR) for the received signal, while $\mathbf{T}$ and $\mathbf{N_{gs}}$ have been swept. As it is expected, BER improves by $\mathbf{N_{gs}}$ and $\mathbf{T}$. However, improvement for $N_{gs} = T > 10$ is marginal. It is reported in [2] that $N_{gs} = T = 6$ to 8 is a good compromise. In order to determine the right resolution for each of the data converters (DAC$_A$, DAC$_y$ and ADC), a two-step verification has been implemented. Initially, the resolution of each data converter gradually reduces, while all the other data converters are considered to be ideal. This approach prevents the other data converters to contribute to the total quantization noise and affect the system performance. In the second step, the entire system is simulated while all the data converters have been employed with their limited resolution. Figure 4(a), (b) and (c) represent the MCMC performance, while the resolution for DAC$_A$, DAC$_y$ and ADC have been swept, respectively. As it is shown in Fig. 4(a), increasing DAC$_A$ resolution higher than 6 bits, does not improve the MCMC performance. Therefore, the resolution of DAC$_A$ needs to be 6b or more, in order not to lose much performance. When the resolution of DAC$_A$ is more than 6b, the system needs to be simulated for much longer in order to produce a precise BER estimation. As can be seen in Fig. 4(a), the results for resolutions higher than 6b are not very accurate. Based on the results shown in Fig. 4(b) and (c), one can conclude that the minimum resolution for DAC$_y$ and the ADC are 6b and 3b, respectively.

Figure 5 represents the second step of our analysis, in which the resolution of all the data converters have been limited to the values discussed above. Based on these results, the performance of the proposed MCMC detector, which is utilizing a realistic model for the data converters, is very close to those reported in Figs. 4(a), (b) and (c).

4   Circuit Level Simulations

This Section demonstrates circuit-level implementations and simulation results for the proposed detector shown in Fig. 2.

Figure 6 shows the merged DAC$_A$, DAC$_y$, and the multiplier for producing the error vector, $\mathbf{e}$. Current mode logic (CML) based circuits have been used to simplify the design, and also make it possible to linearly operate at very high frequencies with a low level of consumption and complexity [12–16]. While DAC$_A$ and multiplier are shown in the right-hand side of the schematic (Fig. 6), the programmable differential pair at the left-hand side represents DAC$_y$. Current-mode

26   A. Aghighi et al.

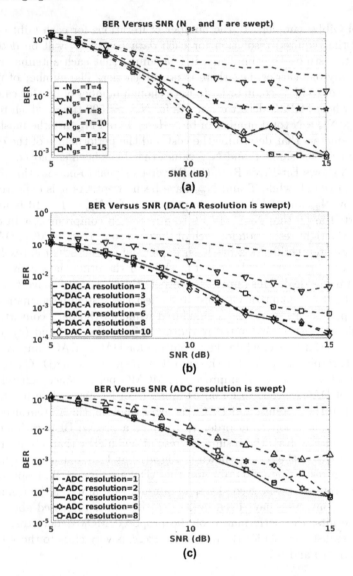

Fig. 4. BER versus SNR while sweeping (a) DAC$_A$ resolution, (b) DAC$_y$ resolution, and (c) ADC resolution.

DAC architecture has been used to simplify the multiplication and summation operations. Depending on sign of **b** values, the output of DAC$_A$ is multiplied by "+1" or "−1". The outputs of the **N** parallel DACs are shorted properly to implement a summer, as required in (3).

The consumption of the DACs depends on the resolution as well as their speed of operation. In order to make sure that the DACs can operate properly at the desired clock frequency, the time constant at the output node should be chosen carefully:

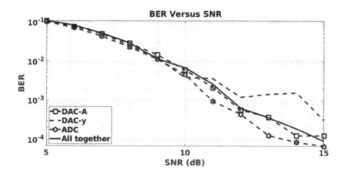

Fig. 5. BER versus SNR when including all the data converters.

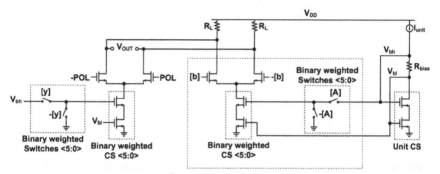

Fig. 6. DAC$_A$ merged with multiplier and DAC$_y$ for producing the e function for each channel.

$$R_L < 1/(2\pi C_{L,DAC} \times 5f_{bit}) \tag{6}$$

where C$_{L,DAC}$ is the DAC load capacitance, and f$_{bit}$ is the input bit frequency. Here, a factor of five is considered to assure settling with an error of less than 1%. The maximum DAC output swing will be achieved when all of the binary-weighted current sources are turned on in all of the N + 1 parallel DACs on each channel. Since there are a total of $2^6 - 1$ copies of the unit current source for each DAC, the minimum required unit current, I$_{unit}$, is equal to:

$$I_{unit} = \frac{V_{swing,sq}}{(2^6 - 1) \times (N + 1) \times R_{L,DAC}} \tag{7}$$

where, V$_{Swing,sq}$ is the squarer required input swing, and R$_L$ is the load resistance determined by (6). Figure 7 represents the circuit level implementation of the squarer block. Given that all of the devices work in the saturation region, and assuming ideal long channel device characteristics, it can be shown that [17]:

$$I_{SQ} = I_{D1} + I_{D2} = kV_{id}^2 + 2I_B \tag{8}$$

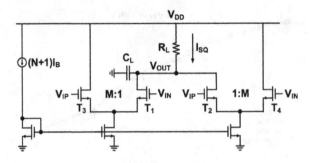

Fig. 7. Squarer circuit schematic.

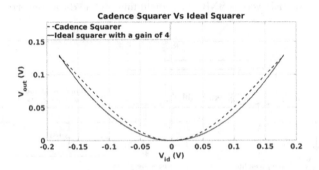

Fig. 8. Input-output transfer characteristics of the simulated squarer circuit.

where, V_{id} is the input differential voltage, $k = (W/L)\mu_n C_{ox}$ and (W/L) is the aspect ratio of T1 and T2. There should be **N** parallel squarer blocks in an N×N MIMO system, their outputs combined to produce **E**. Hence, **N** squarer output nodes have been shorted together to produce $I_{SQ,total}$:

$$I_{SQ,tot} = I_{SQ,1} + I_{SQ,2} + \ldots I_{SQ,N} \tag{9}$$

and **E**:

$$E = e_1^2 + e_2^2 + \cdots e_N^2 = I_{SQ,tot} \times R_L \tag{10}$$

While having large M as the ratio between transistors T1/T2 to T3/T4 increases the squaring accuracy [17], a ratio of M = 4 provides enough accuracy for our system. In order to prove this, the system is simulated while replacing the ideal squarer by the transistor level circuit. Figure 8 shows the input-output transfer characteristics of the squarer circuit with an ideal squarer, whose gain is 4 [V/V]. The offset introduced by the last term in (8) can be removed by comparing the output of the target circuit with a reference (replica) circuit. As can be seen in Fig. 8, the maximum error is limited to about 25%.

Figure 9 compares the expected system performance with a system that uses transistor-level squarer circuit. Here, a realistic model for all of the other building blocks including data converters has been included. Although we are using

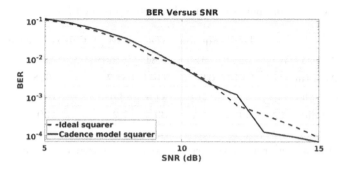

Fig. 9. System level simulation results with ideal and transistor level squarer circuit.

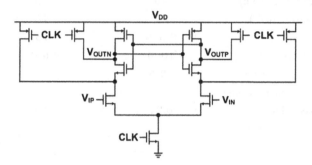

Fig. 10. StrongARM comparator used in the ADC implementation.

a replica circuit to eliminate the offset of the squarer circuit, system-level simulations show that the absolute value of the offset does not influence the system performance. Based on Fig. 9, the system performance with a transistor-level model of the squarer circuit is consistent whit that of an ideal squarer.

A careful design procedure needs to be employed to minimize the energy consumption of the circuit shown in Fig. 6, while the dynamic range is maintained. Based on this design procedure, the size of the load resistance, R_L, and the bias current of the DAC unit cells can be determined.

The 3b ADC block in Fig. 2 has been implemented using a conventional flash ADC structure, that employs StrongArm based comparator topology, shown in Fig. 10. Since PVT variations affect the output swing of the squarer, two replicas of the squarer are provided to determine the maximum and minimum reference levels for the ADC. While one of the replicas mimics the squarer when input swing is minimum, i.e., $V_{id} = 0$, the other replica produces the expected squarer output swing with $V_{id} = V_{id,max} = 180$ mV. These two voltages are then utilized to generate different reference levels for comparators using a resistor ladder.

Table 1. Area and power consumption of the proposed MCMC detector.

	DAC	Squarer	ADC	DSP	1 Gibbs iteration
Power (mW)	3.87	1.6	0.84	1.0	**7.3**
Area (mm²)	0.012	0.0026	0.011	0.002	**0.028**
Power Share (%)	53.2	21.8	11.4	13.6	**100**
Area Share (%)	43.4	9.6	39.8	7.2	**100**

Table 2. Performance comparison with synthesized version in [2].

	Proposed MCMC	Synthesized version [2]
Technology (nm)	**45**	130
Power (mW)	**7.3**	N/A
Area (mm²)	**0.028**	0.37
Clock Freq. (MHz)	**1000**	620
Throughput per Gibbs Sampler (Mbps)	**62.5**	38.75
Area Efficiency mm²/(μm × Mbps)	**0.21**	0.56

5   Comparison and Discussion

This Section provides a high-level comparison between the proposed MCMC detector and the state-of-the-art, especially synthesized version in [2], as well as other MIMO detector implementations [18–21].

Table 1 reports the detailed occupied area and power consumption of the proposed MCMC detector while considering biasing circuits and other auxiliary blocks. Pessimistic parasitic capacitance estimation is also included to account for routing and layout considerations. Based on the results in Table 1, the DAC arrays have the biggest contribution in the total power consumption. In terms of area, DACs and the ADC are the most dominant contributors. The entire system of Fig. 2 consumes 7.3 mW, while occupying a core area of 0.028 mm². It is possible to omit DAC_y to reduce area and power consumption. Since we can use the received analog data before digitizing in the RX chain prior to the DSP, DAC_y can be easily removed for the future implementations.

The MCMC presented in [2] is implemented on an FPGA, which makes it hard to have a detailed comparison with our proposed implementation. However, they have synthesized their proposed detector in a 130-nm VLSI IBM process. Therefore, we used their synthesized simulation results to compare it with that of our proposed mixed-mode MCMC detector. Table 2 compares the performance of the proposed MCMC detector with the synthesized version reported in [2]. For a fair comparison, similar system parameters have been selected (e.g., throughput per Gibbs sampler, which is defined as $f_{clk}/(N_{gs}T)$). It is assumed that

Table 3. Performance Comparison with State-of-the-Art MIMO Detectors.

MIMO detectors	[18]	[19]	[20]	[21]	Proposed detector
Detection algorithm	LMMSE	MMSE PIC	Relaxed K-best	MMF-LSD	MCMC
Technology (nm)	65	90	130	180	45
Supply (V)	1.2	1.2	1.3	1.8	1.0
Clock Freq. (MHz)	400	568	270	250	1000
Throughput (Mbps)	600	757	8.57	31.7	235.3
SNR (dB)	N/A	15	17.7	15.5	6.5^b
BER	N/A	1E-2	1E-3	1E-2	$1E\text{-}5^b$
Area (mm²)	1.4	1.5	2.38	0.31	0.11
Power (mW)	266	189.1	94	56.5	29.44
Area efficiency (mm²/(Mbps × μm²))	0.552	0.245	16.4	0.302	0.23
Power efficiency^a (pJ/b)	255.77	104.08	2920.6	247.5	125.11
Simulation (S)/ Measurement (M)	M	M	M	M	S

^{a}Normalized to 45 nm technology ^{b}After FEC

$T = N_{gs} = 4$ for both cases. In addition, the area efficiency is defined to be the ratio of the occupied area of each Gibbs sampler to the throughput per Gibbs sampler. Proper scaling factors have been employed to convert power and area between the two technologies. Based on Table 2, our proposed MCMC detector area efficiency outweigh that of [2] by a factor of about 2.66. Unfortunately, there is no power consumption reported for the implementation in [2].

Table 3 provides a performance comparison between the proposed mixed-mode MCMC detector and some of the state-of-the-art MIMO detectors with VLSI implementations. The throughput of the proposed MCMC detector is calculated based on:

$$Throughput = \frac{N_{ant} \times f_{clk}}{N_{Cycles}} \tag{11}$$

where, N_{ant} is the number of antennas, f_{clk} is the clock frequency, and N_{Cycles} is the total number of cycles which is equal to:

$$N_{Cycles} = (N_{gs} \times N_{ant}) + 1 \tag{12}$$

Also, power efficiency (PE) for each reference is normalized to 45 nm technology as calculated by:

$$PE = Power \times \frac{1(V)}{Supp.(V)} \times \frac{45(nm)}{Tech.(nm)} \times \frac{1}{Throughput} \tag{13}$$

Although a crude comparison is provided in Table 3, the following points should be considered for a more reasonable comparison:

1) **SNR:** The reported detectors in Table 3 operate at higher SNR regime which increases the throughput and reduces the achieved BER. Hence, working at the same SNR as the MCMC detector (i.e., 6.5 dB [2]) may adversely affect the throughput, power and area efficiency of such detectors.

2) **BER:** Higher BER means lower reliability of the detector and thus the system. Therefore, working at different BER affects the power and area efficiency of the system. Since the proposed MCMC detector provides soft decisions, its BER can be improved using a FEC unit. Although FEC is not implemented in this work, its power and area overhead is considered in the DSP unit. Based on [2], MCMC detector with FEC can achieve a BER of 10^{-5} while SNR is only 6.5 dB. However, the reported detectors in Table 2 are working at BER less than 10^{-3}.

3) **Adopted algorithm:** Last but not least, the intention of this paper is to introduce an alternative way for implementing MIMO detectors which reduces the cost by moving the DSP design complexity to analog/mixed mode domain circuits. In other words, this approach can be applied to other detection algorithms that are more efficient than MCMC algorithm. For instance, multiplying is considered as a complex arithmetic operation in DSP. However, it can be simply implemented in analog domain using DACs. Almost every detection algorithm includes multiplication operation. Hence, the proposed approach can be utilized to reduce their DSP complexity and thus, reduce the total system cost.

6 Future Works

The possible future works can be divided into two categories of algorithm-level improvements and circuit-level improvements.

6.1 Algorithm-Level Improvements

In this paper, the proposed approach is applied to the conventional MCMC algorithm that is discussed in [2]. However, this approach is also suitable for any other algorithm that includes multiplication operations.

For instance, stochastic iterative MIMO (SIM) detector introduced in [22] works based on the bit-flop MCMC method too. Comparing the hardware efficiency of [22] with that of [2] shows a superior performance for [22] by a factor of more than 5. While in conventional MCMC detector the Gibbs sample is updated by the conditional probabilities calculated in the DSP of the detector, SIM in [22] updates the Gibbs sampler directly using decoded bits from channel decoder. Since the SIM works based on the bit-flop method as in the conventional MCMC, the analog/mixed mode circuits working after DSP unit could be more or less the same. In other words, by applying the same approach to the DSP unit in [22] to move some of the complicated processes to the analog domain, throughput of the system significantly improves as compared with this paper.

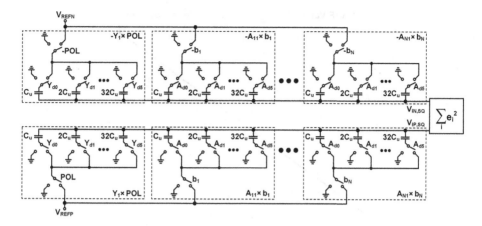

Fig. 11. Proposed charge-based architecture of the merged DAC-multiplier-summer for future implementations.

6.2   Circuit-Level Improvements

As previously discussed, a crude and very primitive circuit solution is offered here and can be improved by employing different circuit techniques and architectures. Since DAC arrays have a big contribution to both total power consumption and occupied area, more efficient DAC architectures are highly desirable. Hence, moving to a charge redistribution-based DAC which is inherently high speed, can significantly improve the efficiency of the system as compared with the current CML-based DAC implementation.

Figure 11 shows the suggested charge-based implementation of the DAC arrays to generate the **e** function for each channel. There are **N** copies of 6-bit binary weighted cap array which convert the digital [**A**] for each channel back to the analog domain. An extra switch for each capacitive bank is provided to simply take care of the multiplication function. Another capacitive bank is added to implement DAC_y in Fig. 2. Moreover, POL signal controls the summation polarity in (3) similar to the CML DAC_y in Fig. 6. Since the unit cap, Cu, can be as small as 1 or 2 fF in a 6-bit DAC, total occupied area and power consumption will be remarkably reduced as compared with the CML-based DACs. Also, as discussed earlier in Sect. 5, DAC_y array can be neglected if the received data is directly utilized before digitization prior to the DSP unit.

The currently employed CML-based architecture in Fig. 6 and the suggested charge-redistribution-based DAC in Fig. 11 are calculating the e function based on (3). As shown in both of these figures, $N + 1$ DAC arrays in each channel are operating for $N + 1$ clock cycles to perform 1 Gibbs iteration. Hence, we can define the switching activity (SA) based on the number of DACs that are operating in each Gibbs iteration:

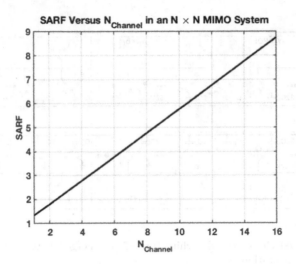

Fig. 12. Switching activity reduction factor (SARF) versus number of channels in an $N \times N$ MIMO system.

$$SA_{conv} = (N+1)_{(DAC)} \times N_{(channel)} \times (N+1)_{cycles}$$
$$= N \times (N+1)^2 \tag{14}$$

where, SA_{conv} shows the switching activity of the charge-redistribution-based DAC in Fig. 11. However, based on (4), finding $[e]_{(k)}$ with $k > 1$ is simply the addition of $[e]_{(k-1)}$ and the second term in (4). Given that generating the second term in (4) requires only one DAC per channel, it is feasible to turn off all other N DACs in each channel for K > 1 by utilizing a sample and hold (S/H) circuit. Hence, a S/H circuit which is easily compatible with charge-redistribution-based DAC, can be employed to hold the value of $[e]_{(k-1)}$ for $[e]_{(k)}$ calculation and significantly improve the system power efficiency. In other words, except for the first clock in which $N + 1$ DACs are operating in each channel, the next N cycles only need one DAC per channel to calculate the error function based on the stored value in S/H circuit. Therefore:

$$SA_{S/H}(i) = \begin{cases} (N+1)_{(DAC)} \times N_{(channel)} & \text{if } i = 1 \\ 1_{(DAC)} \times N_{(channel)} & \text{if } i = 2, 3, ..., N+1 \end{cases} \tag{15}$$

where, $SA_{S/H}(i)$ shows the switching activity of the charge-redistribution-based DAC with S/H for i_{th} clock cycle. Considering all of the $N + 1$ cycles, $SA_{S/H}$ for 1 Gibbs iteration is equal to:

$$SA_{S/H} = N \times (2N+1) \tag{16}$$

In order to compare SA_{conv} and $SA_{S/H}$, we can define the switching activity reduction factor (SARF) as follows:

$$SARF = \frac{SA_{conv}}{SA_{S/H}} = \frac{(N+1)^2}{2N+1} \tag{17}$$

As shown in Fig. 12, employing a S/H with the charge-redistribution-based DAC of Fig. 11 significantly reduces the switching activity in an $N \times N$ MIMO system by increasing the number of channels. It should be noted that the number of channels does not necessarily represent the number of antennas in a MIMO system. In fact, the effective number of channels can be increased using different types of modulations such as 16/64/256-QAM.

7 Conclusion

An analog/mixed-mode approach for designing MCMC MIMO detectors is presented. The proposed system relaxes some of the complexities in the design of conventional digital detectors, especially by moving some high-speed operations to analog domain. While the proposed system consumes 29.3 mW, the proposed detector operates at 1 GHz clock frequency. Achieving a throughput of 235.3 Mbps, the circuit occupies 0.11 mm² Silicon area (estimated). Moreover, a charge-redistribution-based implementation is presented for future works that can significantly enhance the power and area efficiency of the current implementation. The proposed approach can be applied for implementing similar processing systems in which speed and energy efficiency are the concerns.

References

1. Foschini, G.J. : Layered space-time architecture for wireless communication in a fading environment when using multi-element antennas. Bell Labs Tech. J. 1, 41–59 (1996). https://doi.org/10.1002/bltj.2015
2. Laraway, S.A., Farhang-Boroujeny, B.: Implementation of a Markov chain Monte Carlo based multiuser/MIMO detector. IEEE Trans. Circuits Syst. I Regular Papers 56(1), 246–255 (2008). https://doi.org/10.1109/TCSI.2008.925891
3. Verdu, S.: Minimum probability of error for asynchronous Gaussian multiple-access channels. IEEE Trans. Inf. Theory 32(1), 85–96 (1986). https://doi.org/10.1109/TIT.1986.1057121
4. Zhu, H., Shi, Z. and Farhang-Boroujeny, B.: MIMO detection using Markov chain Monte Carlo techniques for near-capacity performance. In: Proceedings. (ICASSP 2005). IEEE International Conference on Acoustics, Speech, and Signal Processing, vol. 3, p. 1017 (2005). https://doi.org/10.1109/ICASSP.2005.1415885
5. Farhang-Boroujeny, B., Zhu, H., Shi, Z.: Markov chain Monte Carlo algorithms for CDMA and MIMO communication systems. IEEE Trans. Sig. Process. 54(5), 1896–1909 (2006). https://doi.org/10.1109/TSP.2006.872539
6. Hedstrom, J.C., Yuen, C.H., Chen, R., Farhang-Boroujeny, B.: Achieving near MAP performance with an excited Markov chain Monte Carlo MIMO detector. IEEE Trans. Wirel. Commun. 16(12), 7718–7732 (2017). https://doi.org/10.1109/TWC.2017.2750667

7. El Gamal, H., Hammons, A.R.: A new approach to layered space-time coding and signal processing. IEEE Trans. Inf. Theory **47**(6), 2321–2334 (2001). https://doi.org/10.1109/18.945250

8. Aghighi, A., Farhang-Boroujeny, B. and Tajalli, A.: Energy and area efficient mixed-mode MCMC MIMO detector. In: 2020 IFIP/IEEE 28th International Conference on Very Large Scale Integration (VLSI-SOC), Salt Lake City, UT, USA, pp. 105–110 (2020). https://doi.org/10.1109/VLSI-SOC46417.2020.9344098

9. Auras, D., Deidersen, U., Leupers, R., Ascheid, G.: A parallel MCMC-Based MIMO detector: VLSI design and algorithm. In: Claesen, L., Sanz-Pascual, M.-T., Reis, R., Sarmiento-Reyes, A. (eds.) VLSI-SoC 2014. IAICT, vol. 464, pp. 149–169. Springer, Cham (2015). https://doi.org/10.1007/978-3-319-25279-7_9

10. Deidersen, U., Auras, D., Ascheid, G.: A parallel VLSI architecture for Markov chain Monte Carlo based MIMO detection. In: Proceedings of the 23rd ACM International Conference on Great Lakes Symposium on VLSI, pp. 167–172 (2013). https://doi.org/10.1145/2483028.2483084

11. Tribble, S.D. : Markov chain Monte Carlo algorithms using completely uniformly distributed driving sequences. Ph.D. thesis, Stanford University (2007)

12. Aghighi, A., et al.: CMOS amplifier design based on extended GM/ID methodology. In: 2019 17th IEEE Int. New Circuits and Systems Conference (NEWCAS), pp. 1–4 (2019). https://doi.org/10.1109/NEWCAS44328.2019.8961308

13. Atkinson, J., Aghighi, A., Anderson, S., Bailey, A., Crane, M., Tajalli, A.: Multi-stage current-steering amplifier design based on extended GM/ID methodology. In: 2019 IEEE 62nd International Midwest Symposium on Circuits and Systems (MWSCAS), pp. 129–132 (2019). https://doi.org/10.1109/MWSCAS.2019.8885313

14. Aghighi, A., Tabib-Azar M., Tajalli, A.: An ULP self-supplied brain interface circuit. In: 2020 IFIP/IEEE 27th International Conference on Very Large Scale Integration (VLSI-SOC), Salt Lake City, UT, USA, pp. 100–104 (2020). https://doi.org/10.1109/VLSI-SOC46417.2020.9344092

15. Aghighi, A., Alameh, A.H., Taherzadeh-Sani, M., Nabki, F.: A 10-Gb/s low-power low-voltage CTLE using gate and bulk driven transistors. In: IEEE International Conference on Electronics, Circuits and Systems (ICECS), pp. 217–220 (2016). https://doi.org/10.1109/ICECS.2016.7841171

16. Aghighi, A., Tajalli, A., Taherzadeh-Sani, M.: A low-power 10 to 15 Gb/s common-gate CTLE based on optimized active inductors. In: 2020 IFIP/IEEE 27th International Conference on Very Large Scale Integration (VLSI-SOC), Salt Lake City, UT, USA, pp. 100–104 (2020). https://doi.org/10.1109/VLSI-SOC46417.2020.9344076

17. Gerosa, A., Soldà, S., Bevilacqua, A., Vogrig, D., Neviani, A.B.: An energy-detector for noncoherent impulse-radio UWB receivers. IEEE Trans. Circuits Syst. I Regular Papers **56**(5), 1030–1040 (2009). https://doi.org/10.1109/TCSI.2009.2016125

18. Chen, X., et al.: Flexible, efficient multimode MIMO detection by using reconfigurable ASIP. IEEE Trans. Very Large Scale Integration (VLSI) Syst. **23**(10), 2173–2186 (2014). https://doi.org/10.1109/TVLSI.2014.2361206

19. Studer, C., Fateh, S., Seethaler, D.: ASIC implementation of soft-input soft-output MIMO detection using MMSE parallel interference cancellation. IEEE J. Solid-State Circuits **46**(7), 1754–1765 (2011). https://doi.org/10.1109/JSSC.2011.2144470

20. Chen, S., Zhang, T., Xin, Y.: Relaxed K-best MIMO signal detector design and VLSI implementation. IEEE Trans. Very Large Scale Integration (VLSI) Syst. Regular Papers **15**(3), 328–337 (2007). https://doi.org/10.1109/TVLSI.2007.893621

21. Myllyla, M., Cavallaro, J.R., Juntti, M.: Architecture design and implementation of the metric first list sphere detector algorithm. IEEE Trans. Very Large Scale Integration (VLSI) Syst. **19**(5), 895–899 (2010). https://doi.org/10.1109/TVLSI.2010.2041800

22. Chen, J., Hu, J., Sobelman, G.E.: Stochastic iterative MIMO detection system: algorithm and hardware design. IEEE Trans. Circuits Syst. I Regular Papers **62**(4), 1205–1214 (2015). https://doi.org/10.1109/TCSI.2015.2390558

Low Power Current-Mode Relaxation Oscillators for Temperature and Supply Voltage Monitoring

Shanshan Dai[1], Caleb R. Tulloss[2], Xiaoyu Lian[1], Kangping Hu[1],
Sherief Reda[1], and Jacob K. Rosenstein[1(✉)]

[1] Brown University, Providence, RI 02912, USA
jacob_rosenstein@brown.edu
[2] Columbia University, New York, NY 10027, USA

Abstract. This chapter presents a family of current-mode relaxation oscillators that can be designed either as a compensated digital clock source, or as an oscillator-based sensor whose frequency reports the temperature or supply voltage. One compensated timer implementation in 0.18 μm CMOS achieves a figure of merit of 120 pW/kHz, making it one of the most efficient relaxation oscillators reported to date. The oscillator design is then extended to produce a V_{DD}-controlled oscillator and a temperature-controlled oscillator. Finally, we introduce a low-power hybrid oscillator sensor, which encodes measurements of both the supply voltage and temperature into the durations of its two alternating digital clock phases. The underlying dual-phase current-mode relaxation oscillator and the resulting sensor circuits are easy to implement, are area- and energy-efficient, and offer straightforward power and speed tradeoffs for a wide range of applications.

Keywords: relaxation oscillator · low power · temperature sensor · supply voltage sensor

1 Introduction

Timers, temperature sensors, and supply voltage monitors are fundamental components of nearly all microelectronic systems. At the low-power end of the spectrum, small embedded sensors are constrained by battery capacity or unpredictable environments, and they must make the most of limited sources of energy [1,2]. At the high-performance end, servers rely on temperature and voltage monitors to maximize performance and power efficiency, while balancing computational loads, scaling voltage and frequency, and avoiding overheating.

Some of the constraints in microelectronic devices are fundamentally thermal limits. Implantable medical devices, despite their comparatively low power, are often constrained to only a few degrees of heating to avoid damaging the surrounding biological tissue [3]. In higher power CPUs and GPUs, power dissipation

© IFIP International Federation for Information Processing 2021
Published by Springer Nature Switzerland AG 2021
A. Calimera et al. (Eds.): VLSI-SoC 2020, IFIP AICT 621, pp. 39–63, 2021.
https://doi.org/10.1007/978-3-030-81641-4_3

is non-uniformly distributed, and localized hot spots can deviate significantly in temperature compared to other areas of the chip, exposing some areas of the device to potential hardware failure and reduced lifespan.

Other limitations come down to timing. Low-power devices often spend much of their time in idle modes to conserve energy, and as a result a large fraction of their total energy consumption may come from circuits like wake-up timers. There are important tradeoffs between precision, power, and area in low-power oscillators. Meeting timing specification is also clearly a main design constraint in high-performance systems, where logic timing is a function of local variations in process, supply voltage, and temperature, and there is always a tension between power efficiency and operating margin. Minimizing the area and energy associated with monitor circuits is key to supporting sensing at high spatial resolution with minimal cost and interference [4,5].

The architect and designer Frank Lloyd Wright once said, "Simplicity and repose are the qualities that measure the true value of any work of art." A similar philosophy can apply to power optimization in microelectronic circuits. Simpler circuits often use fewer transistors, reducing power. Keeping circuits in repose by minimizing their activity also improves efficiency. Although there are numerous potential strategies for performance improvements, if the aim is for straightforward design and reliability, beauty can often be found in small, simple, and low-power circuit solutions.

This chapter begins with a description of a low-power current-mode relaxation oscillator [6]. The oscillator is initially introduced with the goal of constant frequency across temperature and supply voltage. Then, we illustrate how the oscillator can be modified to use a reference voltage intentionally sensitive to either temperature or supply voltage [7]. Three sensor designs are proposed: one dedicated temperature sensor, one dedicated supply voltage sensor, and a hybrid sensor that senses both temperature and supply voltage in two alternating phases of one oscillator.

The circuits proposed here have the benefit of extremely low design complexity. There are only four key parameters (W and L of a key transistor, I_{ref}, and C) in the sensor design, which can be easily scaled to achieve speed and power trade-offs for different applications, while maintaining state-of-the-art performance. With a temperature sensor core area of 0.003 mm^2 and a supply voltage sensor core area of 0.005 mm^2, the two dedicated sensors have conversion energies of 0.28 and 0.35 nJ/conv respectively, each achieving the lowest conversion energy in its class.

Section 2 introduces the ultra-low-power and compact relaxation oscillator topology [6], and in Sect. 3 we extend the structure to design standard cells for temperature and supply-voltage monitoring. Section 4 describes two schemes for converting the analog oscillator period and duty cycle information to a digital readout. We then discuss suitable reference current generation for the oscillator, and Sect. 5 introduces a modified bandgap current reference. Section 6 highlights key design considerations, and analyzes the anticipated performance limitations. Specifically, we analyze transistor switching delays and sources of nonlinearity,

which are key to building more accurate sensor designs based on relaxation oscillators. Section 7 presents experimental results from three sensor designs implemented in a standard 0.18 μm CMOS process, and Sect. 8 concludes the chapter.

2   Dual-Phase Current-Mode Relaxation Oscillator

2.1   Operation Description

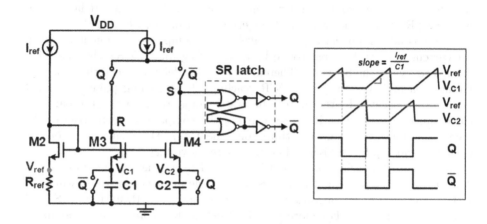

Fig. 1. A dual-phase current-mode relaxation oscillator [6].

Figure 1 shows a dual-phase current-mode relaxation oscillator described in [6].
In this circuit, M2–M4 are matched transistors. Two identical capacitors C1
and C2 are alternately charged by I_{ref} and reset to ground as dictated by the
complementary output clocks Q and $\overline{Q}$, which are generated by a set-reset (SR)
latch.

As illustrated by the timing diagram in Fig. 1, when $Q = 1$ and $\overline{Q} = 0$,
V_{C2} and node S at the drain of M4 are reset to ground. The voltage on C1 is
charged up with a slope of $(I_{ref}/C1)$. Meanwhile, biased with I_{ref}, M3 compares
V_{C1} with the reference voltage $(V_{ref} = I_{ref} \cdot R_{ref})$ and provides an amplified
difference to the R node. Once the voltage on the R node reaches the latch's
threshold voltage, the SR latch changes its state to $Q = 0$ and $\overline{Q} = 1$. In this
state, there is no current flowing through M3 and C1, and I_{ref} biases M4 while
charging C2. The oscillation period can be expressed as:

$$T = 2\left(\frac{V_{ref}}{I_{ref}/C} + t_{sw} + \tau_{SR}\right)$$
$$= 2\left(\tau_{RC} + t_{sw} + \tau_{SR}\right), \tag{1}$$

where $C1 = C2 = C$, $\tau_{RC} = R_{ref}C$. τ_{SR} stands for the digital delay of SR
latch. In low-power applications, current starving can be employed to reduce the
dynamic power consumption of the SR latch.

Power and Design Notes: Since the same devices and current are reused for both the comparator bias and capacitor charging, source-coupled comparators such as this one can be highly power and area efficient [8]. To adjust the power, area, and accuracy for different applications and/or clock speeds, one can simply modify I_{ref}, C, and the dimensions of M2-M4.

Oscillator Period Components: The first component τ_{RC} and the third component τ_{SR} are straightforward to interpret: τ_{RC} is the time required for C1 or C2 to reach V_{ref} from ground, and τ_{SR} is the digital delay of the SR latch after node S or R reaches the switching/triggering point of the SR latch.

The second component t_{sw} is relatively more complicated. In general, when the current charges the capacitor to V_{ref}, the voltage on node S or R is not high enough to switch the SR latch. Therefore t_{sw} is the delay between the capacitor voltage reaching V_{ref} and node S/R reaching the switching point of the SR latch. t_{sw} is affected by the finite comparator transistor gain and the parasitic capacitance at node S or R, so we call t_{sw} the comparator delay. Due to the second component t_{sw} and the third component τ_{SR}, the final voltage on the capacitor ends up being higher than the reference voltage V_{ref}.

In Sect. 6, the oscillation period is analyzed using the current-split model. The idea is that a portion of I_{ref} is used to charge up the capacitor C while the rest is charging up the parasitic capacitance on node S or R, until node S or R switches the SR latch. For more technique details for more accurate oscillator design, we refer the reader to Sect. 6.

2.2   Oscillator Variations and Extensions

In Fig. 1, the resistor R_{ref} creates a reference voltage that is approximately constant. For other applications, it is possible to replace this fixed reference voltage with a voltage corresponding to a measurement quantity of interest, creating a voltage-controlled oscillator.

However, one obstacle to the extension of this structure is the finite input impedance at the node V_{ref}, looking into the source of M2. Supposing that there is a voltage sampled at a capacitor, we would like to generate a voltage-controlled frequency by connecting this sampling capacitor to the source node of M2. But this voltage will be quickly corrupted by the bias current flowing into M2 due to the resistive path at its source node. Instead, we want a constant voltage at the source node of M2, regardless of the loading effect.

Figure 2 addresses this limitation by adding a high-impedance unity-gain buffer which replicates V_{IN} at V_{ref}, in an arrangement which also reuses M2's bias current. It can be viewed as an amplifier whose inputs are at the gates of M5-M6, and whose output is the drain node of M6. This amplifier is connected as a voltage follower, so that its output is regulated to be approximately equal to V_{IN}, assuming a reasonable loop gain. The open-loop gain A_0 of the amplifier made by M5-M6, M1-M2 and M7-M8 is:

$$A_0 = g_{m5/6}[r_{ds6} \parallel (1/g_{m2} + r_{ds8})], \qquad (2)$$

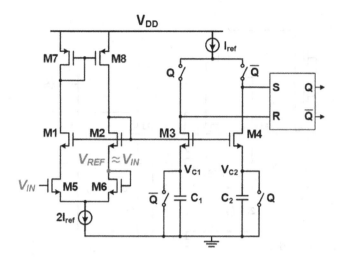

Fig. 2. Proposed voltage-controlled oscillator. V_{IN} is buffered and replicated in place of V_{ref}, producing an oscillation period proportional to V_{IN}.

where g_{m2} and $g_{m5/6}$ are the transconductances of M2 and M5/M6, and r_{ds6} and r_{ds8} are the drain-to-source resistances of M6 and M8, respectively. The static current consumption of the voltage sensor in Fig. 2 is $3 \times I_{ref}$. Thanks to the current reuse, the current addition is only one I_{ref} compared with the current-mode relaxation oscillator shown in Fig. 1.

The period of this voltage-controlled oscillator can be expressed as:

$$\tau_{V_{IN}} = 2 \left(\frac{V_{IN}}{I_{ref}/C} + t_{sw} + \tau_{SR} \right) \tag{3}$$

If t_{sw} and τ_{SR} are small, the period in (3) becomes linearly proportional to the in voltage, providing a time-encoded measurement of V_{IN}.

Now that V_{IN} is buffered, we can connect it to an arbitary sampled voltage, either from a resistive voltage divider or a sampling capacitor. Section 3 details three possible extentions realizing temperature and/or supply voltage sensing.

3   Temperature and Supply Voltage Sensing

3.1   Supply Voltage Sensing

As shown Fig. 3, a natural step towards a supply-voltage-controlled oscillator would be to create V_{IN} by a simple voltage division from V_{DD}, employing the configuration described in Fig. 2.   The period of the supply-voltage-controlled oscillator is:

$$\tau_{V_{IN}} = 2 \left(\frac{2/5 V_{DD}}{I_{ref}/C} + t_{sw} + \tau_{SR} \right) \tag{4}$$

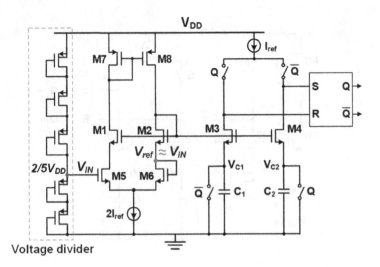

Fig. 3. Proposed voltage sensor.

The first term in (4) dominates the oscillation period because the comparator delay t_{sw} and the digital delay τ_{SR} are much faster than charging C to $2*V_{DD}/5$. The period in (4) becomes linearly proportional to the supply voltage, providing a time-encoded measurement of V_{DD}.

Design Notes and Example: To trade off between power, area, and accuracy, the circuit designer can tune the three key parameters in this supply voltage sensor, I_{ref}, C, and the dimensions of M1-M4, to meet different specifications. Taking a μW supply-voltage sensor operating around 10 MHz for example, I_{ref} is 2.1 μA and C is 50 fF. Transistors M2-M4 have W/L = 3 μm/1 μm, operating in the subthreshold region for high g_m/I_D (transconductance efficiency). For the other design parameters, M5-M6 have W/L = 5 μm/1 μm, and operate in subthreshold, while M7-M8 have W/L = 2 μm/4 μm and operate in strong inversion.

3.2   Temperature Sensing

Biased with a constant current I_{ref}, a forward-biased diode has a voltage V_{diode} with a complementary to absolute temperature (CTAT) coefficient, due to the exponential temperature dependence of its reverse saturation current I_s:

$$V_{diode}(T) = \frac{kT}{q} \ln\left(\frac{I_{ref}}{I_s(T)}\right),\qquad(5)$$

where T is the absolute temperature, k is Boltzmann's constant, and V_{diode} is on the order of several hundred millivolts.

Considering the fact that both the diode and M2 can be biased by the same reference current, a low-power temperature sensor can be readily implemented

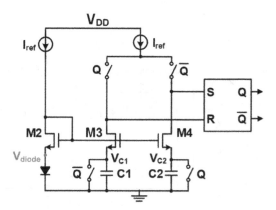

Fig. 4. Proposed temperature sensor. By replacing V_{ref} with V_{diode}, a temperature-dependent oscillation is obtained.

by replacing R_{ref} with a forward-biased diode from Fig. 1, as redrawn in Fig. 4. Now the period of this relaxation oscillator becomes:

$$\tau_{temp} = 2 \left(\frac{V_{diode}}{I_{ref}/C} + t_{sw} + \tau_{SR} \right) \tag{6}$$

Since the first term in (6) dominates the oscillation period, the oscillation period will reflect the diode's sensitivity to temperature. Excluding bias generation, the static current consumption of this temperature sensor is $2I_{ref}$.

Design Example: To implement a µW temperature sensor operating at a speed around 10 MHz, I_{ref}, C, and the M2-M4 dimensions can be assigned the same values as those in the supply-voltage sensor design.

3.3 Hybrid Oscillator Sensing both Temperature and Supply Voltage

For ultra-low power applications like radio-frequency identification (RFID) tags which need both temperature and supply voltage monitoring, we can save power by combining the two sensors into one.

Figure 5(a) presents a conceptual diagram, containing two halves: the left half has an input of $1/4V_{DD}$ generated from a voltage divider, and the input to the right half comes from the complementary-to-absolute-temperature (CTAT) voltage of a forward-biased diode. As a result, the digital output Q will be modulated by both the temperature and the supply voltage. The detailed transistor-level schematic is drawn in Fig. 5(b). Four identical PMOS transistors in series from V_{DD} to ground form a supply voltage divider. To minimize power, a small W/L ratio is chosen for these four devices, which ensures that the current of the voltage divider is much less than I_{ref}; additionally, the high impedance combined with the gate capacitance of M5 helps to filter out high-frequency supply noise.

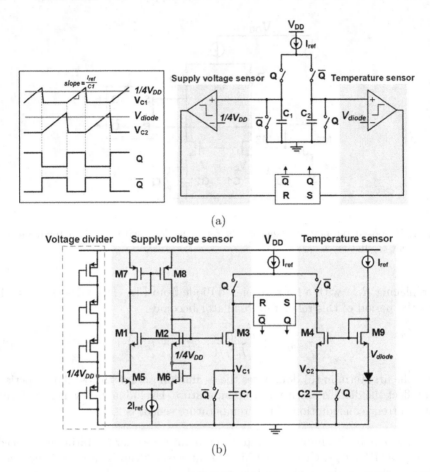

Fig. 5. Proposed structure for a hybrid oscillator which senses both supply voltage and temperature (a) conceptual and its timing diagram, (b) transistor-level schematic.

Compared with two separate temperature and V_{DD} sensors, this hybrid oscillator saves half of the dynamic power and reduces static current consumption by I_{ref}.

The logic "high" and "low" durations of the digital output Q are linearly proportional to V_{DD} and temperature, respectively. If t_{sw} and τ_{SR} are negligible, then

$$\tau_{high} \approx \frac{1/4\ V_{DD}}{I_{ref}/C} \tag{7}$$

$$\tau_{low} \approx \frac{V_{diode}}{I_{ref}/C} \tag{8}$$

Design Notes: Some very careful readers may ask: why is the gate voltage of M5 $1/4V_{DD}$ in Fig. 5 but $2/5V_{DD}$ in Fig. 3? In order to make the unity-gain operational amplifier work, the gate voltage of M5 has to provide a gate-to-source voltage drop for M5, plus enough headroom for the $2I_{ref}$ current source beneath M5, which operates in the saturation region. We apply the circuit described in Fig. 5 to the ultra-low power domain. With I_{ref} on the nA level, the gate-to-source voltage of M5 is lower than with a µA level bias current, so the required M5 gate voltage is lower.

As a parameter example for a nanowatt hybrid sensor operating at several tens of kHz and nanowatts, I_{ref} is set to be 6 nA and C to be 50 fF. Transistors M2-M4 have a dimension of W/L = 1 µm/3 µm.

4   Readout Circuit

When integrating the sensors in a System-on-Chip (SoC), a readout circuit is required to digitize the analog time information using a reference clock. There are two approaches to the frequency-to-digital conversion, depending on the relative reference clock speed.

With a reference clock faster than the sensor clock, the first approach is to count the fast reference clock cycles during N slow sensor cycles (N = 256). As depicted in Fig. 6, after N slow sensor cycles, the time-to-digital converter sends a DONE signal to latch the reference clock counting for DATA readout. Meanwhile, it clears the reference clock counter for the next round of conversion. This approach has a quick conversion time at the expense of high dynamic power due to the fast reference clock.

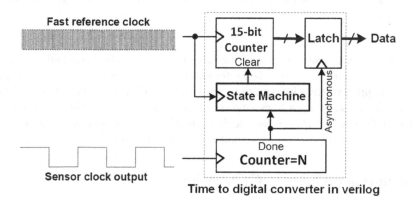

Fig. 6. Frequency-to-digital conversion scheme used to digitize the sensor outputs, when the reference clock is much faster than the sensor clock.

The second approach is to count the sensor cycles during a fixed number (N) of reference clock cycles, when the reference clock is slower than the sensor clock.

To implement this method, we can just swap the connections of the reference and sensor clock in Fig. 6. This approach is generally applied to ultra low power systems, where the reference clock is typically slow to reduce the power budget.

One similarity shared by the two approaches is that between the sensor clock and reference clock, a faster clock is counted during a fixed number (N) of the slower clock cycles. For the dedicated supply voltage and temperature sensors in Fig. 3 and Fig. 4, we can use either fast or slow reference clocks, depending on the data-conversion speed requirement.

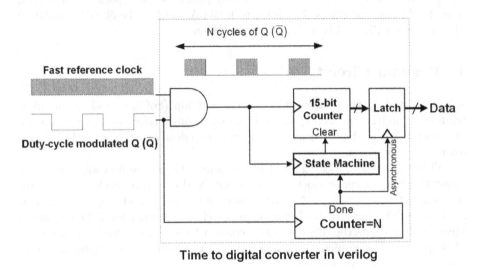

Fig. 7. Modification of the frequency-to-digital conversion scheme to digitize the hybrid sensor output.

For the hybrid sensor in Fig. 5, we have to measure the logic high and logic low duration separately with a fast reference clock, in order to obtain the temperature or supply voltage information, respectively. Figure 7 illustrates measurement of the sensor clock's logic phase. An AND gate enables the fast reference clock counting only during sensor logic high. Similarly, to measure the logic low duration, we can replace the AND gate with an OR gate.

5   Reference Current Generation

In Fig. 1, 2, 3, 4 and 5, does I_{ref} have to be a bandgap reference current insensitive to supply voltage and temperature (PVT)? Let us only consider the dominant term in each oscillation period, with the assumption that the comparator delay t_{sw} and the SR latch delay τ_{SR} are much smaller.

For a Resistor-Capacitor (RC) relaxation oscillator, its linear component is:

$$T_{relx\_osc,linear} = 2 \times \frac{V_{ref}}{I_{ref}/C} = 2 \times \frac{I_{ref} \cdot R}{I_{ref}/C} = 2 \times RC \qquad (9)$$

We can see that the reference current I_{ref} is cancelled out, leaving only RC. In other words, I_{ref} does not have to be a PVT insensitive current to keep the linear dominant period components constant. In fact, a proportional-to-absolute-temperature (PTAT) current can bias the RC relaxation oscillator, while keeping a constant oscillation frequency over temperature and supply voltage, as in [6].

When it comes to the supply voltage and temperature sensor, Eq. (7) and (8) tell us that a constant reference current I_{ref} is required in order to make the period component linear with V_{DD} or V_{diode}.

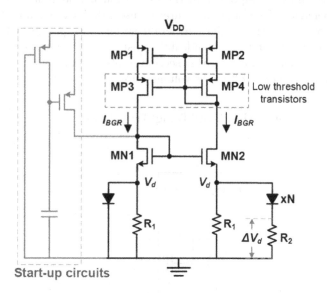

Fig. 8. A compact and easy-to-design bandgap current reference modified from [9] with removal of the operational amplifier. Copies of the reference current are created with mirrors from MP2.

Figure 8 depicts a compact and easy-to-design bandgap current reference circuit. This circuit is modified from [9] with removal of the operational amplifier. It places a resistor R_1 in parallel with the diodes in order to reduce the minimum supply voltage compared to a classical bandgap configuration. The identical NMOS pair MN1-MN2 will regulate their source voltages to be equal. By selecting a proper ratio of R_1 to R_2 and a diode area ratio of N, one can generate a temperature-independent current I_{BGR},

$$I_{BGR} = \frac{V_d}{R_1} + \frac{\Delta V_d}{R_2} = \frac{1}{R_1}\left(V_d + \frac{R_1}{R_2}\frac{kT}{q}\ln N\right), \qquad (10)$$

where V_d is the voltage across the P+/N-well junction diodes, and ΔV_d is the difference between the two diodes' forward voltages, which appears across R_2. V_d has a CTAT coefficient, while the second term is PTAT. Similar to other bandgap circuits, the basic principle is to compensate a CTAT coefficient with a weighted PTAT coefficient, by choosing the correct value of $(R_1/R_2 \times \ln N)$ in (10).

It is worth noting that the resistor temperature coefficient can affect the temperature variation of I_{BGR}. This could be addressed by implementing R_1 and R_2 with two series resistors having opposite temperature coefficients.

6   Design Considerations

The dominant linear component in the oscillation period represents the ideal oscillation behavior. To design an accurate sensor, we have to suppress the non-linear components in the oscillation period as much as possible. This section takes a detailed look at these nonidealities, using the current-split model. The expressions and delay model in this section apply to both constant frequency oscillators and extended voltage or voltage sensors.

6.1   Delay Model of the Amplifying Transistor

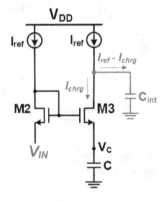

Fig. 9. Current splitting when both the drain and source of M3 are ramping up.

As illustrated in Fig. 9, I_{ref} splits into two branches. One branch I_{chrg} flows into M3 to charge up the capacitor C while the remainder charges the parasitic capacitance at the drain node of M3. The voltage change at the drain node of M3, $\Delta(V_{d,M3})$, can be written in terms of its charging current $(I_{ref} - I_{chrg})$ and the internal parasitic capacitance C_{int}:

$$\Delta(V_{d,M3}) = \frac{I_{ref} - I_{chrg}}{C_{int}} \Delta t \tag{11}$$

If M3 has a gain of A_{M3}, the voltage change at the drain node of M3, $\Delta(V_{d,M3})$, also equals the ramping rate on C amplified with A_{M3},

$$\Delta(V_{d,M3}) = A_{M3} \times \frac{I_{chrg}}{C} \Delta t, \tag{12}$$

we can use (11) and (12) to solve for I_{chrg}:

$$I_{chrg} = \frac{I_{ref}}{1 + A_{M3}C_{int}/C} \tag{13}$$

Equation (13) tells us that the gain of M3 affects the current splitting. When M3 works in the linear region, $A_{M3,lin}$ is small, and the denominator is approximately 1. Thus almost all the I_{ref} flows into M3 to charge up C ($I_{ref} \approx I_{chrg}$). As M3 enters the saturation region, or $A_{M3,sat}$ is large, $A_{M3,sat}C_{int}$ becomes comparable to C, and a fraction of I_{ref} begins to charge up C_{int}. At this phase, we could also say that C_{int} requires more current than C, since M3 is amplifying the changes in V_C. From the small-signal perspective, dV/dt at the output of M3 could approach ($A_{M3,sat} \times I_{ref}/C$) only if M3 had infinite bandwidth (no C_{int}, and thus no current splitting). But in practice, C_{int} limits the bandwidth.

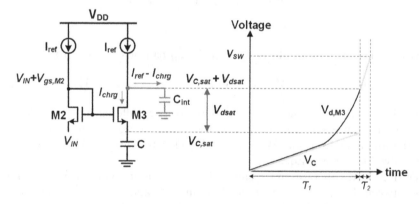

Fig. 10. The delay model and illustrated transition of the source-coupled amplifier transistors (M3 and M4).

As shown in Fig. 10, the source voltage of M3 ramps up from zero until its drain voltage reaches V_{SW}, the switching threshold of the SR latch. We divide the total period into two phases τ_1 and τ_2 based on the operation of M3 (linear and saturation). We use the capacitor ramping voltage V_C and M3 drain voltage $V_{d,M3}$, to calculate τ_1 and τ_2 respectively, as illustrated by the two yellow segments in Fig. 10. We use $V_{d,M3}$ rather than V_C to derive τ_2, because it is simpler to obtain the initial and final voltages of $V_{d,M3}$ during τ_2.

During τ_1, M3 is in the linear region, with its drain-to-source voltage below V_{dsat}. Here M3 operates as a resistor, and initially the drain of M3 ($V_{d,M3}$)

directly follows the capacitor voltage V_C. The gain $A_{M3,linear}$ is small, and the voltage is charging at a rate of I_{ref}/C based on (13).

This first phase ends when the drain-to-source voltage of M3 equals V_{dsat}, which corresponds to a capacitor voltage $V_{C,sat}$. The duration of the first phase τ_1 can be derived as:

$$\tau_1 = \frac{V_{C,sat}}{I_{ref}/C} \tag{14}$$

In order to derive τ_1, we need to find $V_{C,sat}$, the capacitor voltage at which M3 enters saturation.

At the end of τ_1, M2 and M3 form a differential amplifier, whose input voltage is the difference between the two source voltages and whose output is the difference between the two drain voltages. Their source and drain node voltages at the end of τ_1 are described in Table 1.

Table 1. Node voltages at the end of τ_1.

Transistor	Source	Drain
M2	V_{IN}	$V_{IN} + V_{gs,M2}$
M3	$V_{C,sat}$	$V_{C,sat} + V_{dsat}$

Given that the gain of M3 is $A_{M3,sat}$, $V_{C,sat}$ can be obtained from:

$$A_{M3,sat}(V_{IN} - V_{C,sat}) = V_{IN} + V_{gs,M2} - V_{C,sat} - V_{dsat}, \tag{15}$$

where $(V_{IN} - V_{C,sat})$ on the left is the source voltage difference between M2 and M3, and the expression on the right is the drain voltage difference of M2 and M3, the amplifier's output. We can use Eq. (15) to solve for $V_{C,sat}$, and from there solve for τ_1 using Eq. (14).

During τ_2, M3 operates in the saturation region, amplifying the voltage difference between the two source voltages V_{IN} and V_C, and current splitting occurs. The drain voltage of M3, $V_{d,M3}$, is $(V_{dsat} + V_{C,sat})$ at the start of τ_2 and slews to V_{SW}, at a rate of $(A_{M3,sat}I_{chrg}/C)$, to trigger the SR latch, as illustrated by the second yellow segment line in Fig. 10. From (13), the total time of the second phase τ_2 is:

$$\tau_2 = \frac{V_{SW} - (V_{dsat} + V_{C,sat})}{A_{M3,sat}I_{chrg}/C}$$

$$= \frac{V_{SW} - (V_{dsat} + V_{C,sat})}{A_{M3,sat}I_{ref}/(C + A_{M3,sat}C_{int})} \tag{16}$$

Substituting the expression of $V_{C,sat}$ obtained from (15) into τ_1 and τ_2 in (14) and (16), we can reach to the overall oscillation half-period:

$$\tau_1 + \tau_2 = \frac{V_{IN}}{I_{ref}/C} + \frac{V_{SW} - V_{dsat} - V_{IN}}{I_{ref}/C_{int}}$$
$$+ \frac{V_{SW} - V_{gs,M2} - V_{IN}}{A_{M3,sat}I_{ref}/C} + \frac{V_{gs,M2} - V_{dsat}}{(A_{M3,sat} - 1)I_{ref}/C_{int}} \quad (17)$$

The last term in (17) is negligible, because its ratio to the first term is on the order of $(\frac{1}{A_{M3,sat}} \cdot \frac{C_{int}}{C})$ assuming V_{IN} and $(V_{gs,M2} - V_{dsat})$ have the same order of magnitude. In a sensor design example at the $0.18\,\mu m$ CMOS process node, $A_{M3,sat}$ is about 100, C is 50 fF and C_{int} is <5 fF. Thus, the last term contributes less than 0.1% to the overall conversion time. Similarly, the contributions of the second and third terms can be justified numerically by substituting $A_{M3,sat}$ and C_{int} into their ratios to the first term. Moreover, the contribution of the second term can be further reduced by decreasing $|V_{SW} - V_{dsat} - V_{IN}|$. We can achieve this reduction by adjusting the transistor dimensions of NOR gates in the SR latch (V_{SW} adjustment).

6.2 Curvature Error/Nonlinearity

In (17), the first term describes the ideal behavior, in which the oscillation period $\tau_1 + \tau_2$ is linear with V_{IN}, and V_{IN} can represent a resistor voltage, temperature or supply voltage. The second and third terms highlight important sources of nonlinearity.

In this subsection, we can begin to understand the nonlinearity of the oscillation period by building an expression for errors in (17) in terms of several partial derivatives, and then considering the magnitude and temperature dependence of each term, assuming that V_{IN} is ideal:

$$\Delta(\tau_1 + \tau_2) \approx \frac{-V_{IN}}{I_{ref}^2/C} \cdot \Delta I_{ref}$$
$$+ \frac{1}{I_{ref}/C_{int}} \cdot \Delta(V_{SW} - V_{dsat} - V_{IN})$$
$$+ \frac{1}{I_{ref}/C} \cdot \Delta \left[\frac{V_{SW} - V_{gs,M2} - V_{IN}}{A_{M3,sat}}\right] \quad (18)$$

The first term in this expansion approximates the sensitivity to errors in I_{ref}. When analyzing the other terms in (18), I_{ref} is assumed constant.

Since C_{int} has minimal temperature and voltage dependences [8], the second error term will vary primarily with the switching threshold V_{SW}. For the SR latch design, we suggest adding current sources (mI_{ref}) on top of the PMOS devices in series with V_{DD} to limit the peak dynamic current, which is also called current starvation. Using this technique will make V_{SW} more robust to the supply voltage variation. Assuming subthreshold operation near the switching threshold, V_{SW} can thus be formulated as:

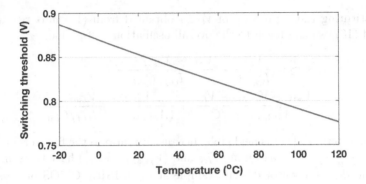

Fig. 11. Simulated switching threshold of the SR latch versus temperature.

$$V_{SW} = \eta V_T \ln \left(\frac{mI_{ref}}{V_T^2 \mu C_{ox}(W/L)_{n,SR}} \right) + V_{TH,n} \qquad (19)$$

This expression predicts that V_{SW} will be complementary to absolute temperature, as plotted in Fig. 11. Assuming M2 and M3 are also subthreshold, $V_{gs,M2}$ follows (19) and the gain of M3 is:

$$A_{M3,sat} = g_{m3}r_{ds,m3} = \frac{V_A}{\eta V_T}, \qquad (20)$$

where V_A is the early voltage (which has minimal temperature dependence), η is the subthreshold slope factor, and $V_T = kT/q$ is the thermal voltage.

Substituting (19) and (20) into (18), one can observe that the second term scales linearly with temperature. The third term introduces second-order temperature curvature error.

Based on this analysis, we can recognize the importance of minimizing C_{int} to reduce the second term in (18), and maximizing $A_{M3,sat}$ to reduce the third term. Therefore, in our designs, we increased the lengths of the amplifying transistors, and minimized the sizes of the transistors in the SR latch. The importance of minimizing C_{int} indicates that the proposed circuit can continue to benefit from CMOS technology scaling.

7 Measured Performance

Sensing circuits based on relaxation oscillators can be applied across a wide range of applications, from low-power sensor nodes to high-performance thermal monitors on multicore processors.

This section gives three oscillator-based sensor examples: one nW hybrid oscillator (Fig. 5), one µW V_{DD} sensor (Fig. 3), and one µW temperature sensor (Fig. 4), in a standard 0.18µm CMOS process. A micrograph of the fabricated chip is shown in Fig. 12. One bandgap reference circuit based on Fig. 8 is also

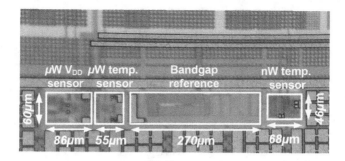

Fig. 12. Die photo of the proposed temperature and voltage sensors, fabricated in 0.18 μm CMOS.

included. The bandgap draws 2.0 μA and occupies 0.0156 mm², including several current mirrors to distribute I_{ref} to multiple sensors.

As depicted in Fig. 6 and Fig. 7, the experimental sensor readout is performed using a time-to-digital converter (TDC) implemented on an FPGA module (Opal Kelly XEM6310). The TDC counts reference clock cycles during N sensor cycles (N = 256 in the μW sensors and N = 10 in the nW hybrid sensor), which is the equivalent conversion time.

7.1   State of the Art

Before we introduce the current-mode relaxation oscillator-based supply voltage and temperature sensors, let us first briefly review the state-of-the-art in each category.

There are several options for producing digital outputs that represent the supply voltage. One of the simplest arrangements is a voltage-controlled oscillator, which is often used for supply monitoring [10,11]. Digital critical path monitors (CPMs) [12,13] have very low latency and can be used to respond to power supply transients, but they are less precise for continuous monitoring, and CPMs are often combined with other complementary sensors.

Temperature sensors use a wider variety of approaches. Resistive [15–17] and thermal-diffusivity [18] temperature sensors are able to achieve high resolution (often <0.1 °C), but demand sophisticated frequency-locked loops or ΣΔ-ADCs to digitize the temperature-dependent information. Their area, power consumption, and design complexity increase accordingly. Oscillator-based temperature sensors, which employ frequency [4,19–21] or duty cycle modulation [22], are appealing for thermal monitoring as they are straightforward to implement.

Low-latency temperature measurements are important to track thermal transients, which can swing 10–20 °C within 2–3 ms in smartphone SoCs [23]. Ultimately, a monitor circuit must be evaluated by a combination of factors [14] including its area, power, resolution, conversion time, and accuracy. Some of these metrics are quantified for a survey of temperature sensors in Fig. 13.

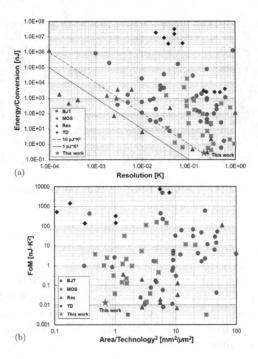

Fig. 13. CMOS smart temperature sensors [14] are compared by plotting (a) energy per conversion versus temperature resolution, and (b) an energy-resolution figure-of-merit (FoM, with unit of nJ·K²) versus normalized circuit area.

7.2   Hybrid nW Temperature/V_{DD} Sensor

The hybrid nW oscillator has an active area of 46 μm × 68 μm in a standard 0.18 μm CMOS process. At room temperature, with a supply voltage of 1.3 V, the circuit oscillates at 35.7 kHz while consuming 40 nA. The duration of the temperature phase (τ_{low}) is 16.0 μs, and the V_{DD} sensing phase (τ_{high}) is 12.0 μs.

The time-to-digital converter (TDC) described in Fig. 7 is also simulated in 0.18 μm CMOS. Its simulated power is 1.2 μW for the temperature phase data readout, and is 0.9 μW for the V_{DD} phase data readout, under a 0.8 V digital supply. Its estimated area is 3000 μm², using low-power D-flip-flops based on [24]. In more advanced process nodes, the TDC power and area would decrease further.

Figure 14(a) shows a temperature sweep of the hybrid sensor measured across five chips when V_{DD} is 1.3 V. The duration of the temperature phase is linear with temperature, while the V_{DD} phase has minimal temperature dependence. The peak-to-peak temperature nonlinearity error is +0.68/−0.51°C after two-point linear calibration, as plotted in Fig. 14(b). In Fig. 14(c), measured on five chips, the mean voltage sensitivity of the temperature phase is 2.03 °C/V without calibration when V_{DD} varies from 1.2 V to 1.8 V. Based on the time-to-digital converter described in Fig. 7, each reading was conducted by counting

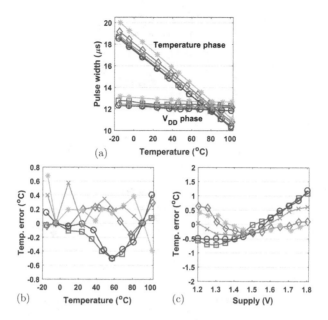

Fig. 14. Measurements of the temperature-sensitive phase of five hybrid sensor samples, showing (a) pulse width versus temperature, (b) nonlinearity error after 2-point trimming, and (c) supply sensitivity.

a 100 MHz reference clock only during the temperature sensitive phase for 10 sensor cycles, yielding a conversion time of 280 μs. The corresponding root-mean-squared (RMS) temperature resolution is 0.17 °C.

Figure 15(a) shows a supply voltage sweep for the hybrid sensor from 1.2 V to 1.8 V at room temperature. The duration of the V_{DD} phase has a peak-to-peak nonlinearity error of +9.73/−13.98 mV after two-point calibration. In Fig. 15(c), from −15 °C to 100 °C, the duration of the V_{DD} phase shows an average temperature dependence of 0.54 mV/°C without any calibration. The RMS V_{DD} resolution is 1.8 mV via 100 consecutive V_{DD} readings at 1.3 V V_{DD}. Each reading was conducted by counting a 100 MHz reference clock only during the V_{DD} sensitive phase for 10 sensor cycles, corresponding to a conversion time of 280 μs.

7.3   Dedicated μW Temperature Sensor

The μW temperature sensor has an active area of 60 μm × 55 μm. It consumes 6.57 μA and operates at 12.0 MHz with $V_{DD} = 1.3$ V at room temperature. Figure 16(a) shows a temperature sweep of the temperature sensor measured across 15 sample test chips when V_{DD} is 1.3 V, in which the periods are linear with temperature. The peak-to-peak temperature nonlinearity error is +0.85/−0.94°C after two-point linear calibration, as plotted in the upper panel of Fig. 16(b). In the lower panel of Fig. 16(b), measured on 15 samples, the mean

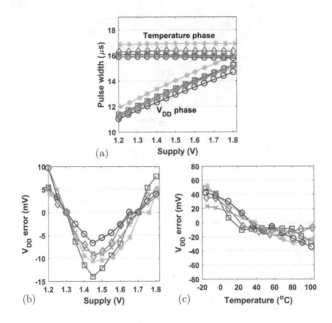

Fig. 15. Measurements of the V_{DD}-sensitive phase of five hybrid sensor samples, showing (a) pulse width versus V_{DD}, (b) nonlinearity error after 2-point trimming, and (c) temperature sensitivity.

voltage sensitivity is 2.28 °C/V after the removal of the systematic non-linearity when V_{DD} varies from 1.2 V to 1.8 V. The RMS temperature resolution is 210 mK via 1000 consecutive temperature readings at room temperature. Each reading was conducted by counting a 100 MHz reference clock for 256 sensor cycles as shown in Fig. 6, yielding a conversion time of 21.4 μs. The simulated power of the time-to-digital converter described by Fig. 6 is 2.1 μW in 0.18 μm CMOS.

7.4   Dedicated μW V_{DD} Sensor

The V_{DD} sensor core occupies an area of 60 μm × 86 μm. Its current consumption is 8.34 μA, measured with $V_{DD} = 1.3$ V at room temperature. Figure 17(a) shows a supply voltage sweep for the V_{DD} sensor from 1.2 V to 1.8 V at room temperature. As shown in the lower panel of Fig. 17(b), the period has a peak-to-peak nonlinearity error of +28.7/−30.0 mV after two-point calibration. Based on 1000 consecutive V_{DD} readings at 1.3 V V_{DD}, with a conversion time of 256 sensor cycles (22.4 μs), the corresponding RMS V_{DD} resolution is 0.94 mV.

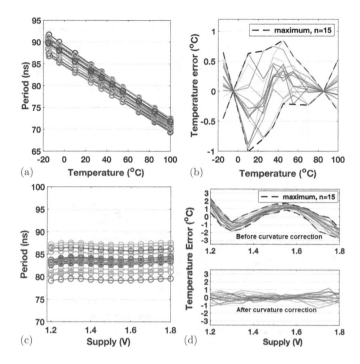

Fig. 16. Measurements of the μW temperature sensor, illustrating (a) oscillation period versus temperature, (b) temperature nonlinearity error after two-point calibration with 15 samples, (c) oscillation period versus V_{DD}, and (d) supply sensitivity without calibration (upper) and supply sensitivity after curvature correction (lower).

7.5   Performance Summary

Table 2 summarizes the nW and μW temperature sensor performance, and Table 3 summarizes the performance of the two V_{DD} sensors. When we evaluate the energy per conversion, the power consumption of the bandgap reference and the time-to-digital converter are also taken into account. In particular, the time-to-digital converter consumes more power than the nW sensor itself, due to the fast reference clock.

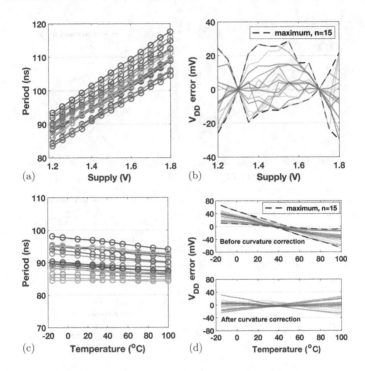

Fig. 17. Measurements of the μW V_{DD} sensor, showing (a) oscillation period versus V_{DD}, (b) V_{DD} nonlinearity error, (c) oscillation period versus temperature, (d) temperature sensitivity before (upper) and after curvature correction (lower).

Table 2. Temperature sensor specifications

Temperature sensor	nW sensor/μW sensor
Technology node	0.18 μm
Supply voltage range (V)	1.2–1.8
Temp. range (°C)	−15–100
Sensor core area (mm^2)	0.0031/0.0033
Frequency at room temp. (MHz)	0.0357/12.0
Power (μW)	0.052/8.54
Supply sensitivity (°C/V)	2.03/2.28
Peak-to-peak error (°C)	(+0.68/−0.51)/(+0.85/−0.94)
Calibration	2-point
Resolution (mK)	168/210
Conv. time (μs)	280/21.4
Simulated TDC power (μW)	1.2/2.1
Energy/Conversion (nJ)	1.08/0.35

Table 3. Supply voltage sensor specifications

V_{DD} sensor	nW sensor/µW sensor
Technology node	0.18 µm
Supply voltage range (V)	1.2–1.8
Temp. range (°C)	−15–100
Sensor core area (mm^2)	0.0031/0.0052
Frequency at room temp. (MHz)	0.0357/11.3
Power (µW)	0.052/10.84
Temp. sensitivity (mV/°C)	0.54/0.79
Peak-to-peak error (mV)	(+9.73/−13.98)/(+28.7/−30.0)
Calibration	2-point
Resolution (mV)	1.8/2.1
Conv. time (µs)	280/22.4
Simulated TDC power (µW)	0.9/2.1
Energy/Conversion (nJ)	0.99/0.28

8 Conclusion

Before we conclude, perhaps we can take a broader perspective, and ask what
the current-mode relaxation oscillator and the bandgap circuit structure have
in common, which enables their power efficiency. One feature they share is that
they save power by obviating the operational amplifiers used in the conventional
oscillator and bandgap. In most operational amplifiers, signal amplification is
obtained by sharing a common source node and comparing the differential gate
voltages between two transistors. In the oscillator and proposed bandgap, the
amplifying transistors share a common gate voltage but compare their source
nodes, allowing current reuse in the capacitor charging or bias branches. Recog-
nizing that voltage amplification is not constrained to gate comparison is essential to understanding the performance of the designs in this chapter.

Acknowledgements. This work was funded in part by grant FA8650-18-2-7851 from
the Defense Advanced Research Projects Agency (DARPA). C. R. Tulloss is also grate-
ful for support from the Jayakumar Undergraduate Summer Research Fellowship.

References

1. Ferro, E., Brea, V.M., López, P., Cabello, D.: Micro-energy harvesting system
   including a pmu and a solar cell on the same substrate with cold startup from 2.38
   nw and input power range up to 10 µW using continuous MPPT. IEEE Trans.
   Power Electron. **34**(6), 5105–5116 (2018)

2. Sadagopan, K.R., Kang, J., Ramadass, Y., Natarajan, A.: A cm-scale 2.4-GHz wireless energy harvester with nanowatt boost converter and antenna-rectifier resonance for WiFi powering of sensor nodes. IEEE J. Solid-State Circuits **53**(12), 3396–3406 (2018)
3. Jia, Y., et al.: Wireless opto-electro neural interface for experiments with small freely behaving animals. J. Neural Eng. **154**, 046032 (2018)
4. Anand, T., Makinwa, K.A., Hanumolu, P.K.: A VCO based highly digital temperature sensor with 0.034 °/mV supply sensitivity. IEEE J. Solid-State Circuits **51**(11), 2651–2663 (2016)
5. Mordakhay, A., Shor, J.: Miniaturized, 0.01 mm^2, resistor-based thermal sensor with an energy consumption of 0.9 nJ and a conversion time of 80 μs for processor applications. IEEE J. Solid-State Circuits **53**(10), 2958–2969 (2018)
6. Dai, S., Rosenstein, J.K.: A 14.4 nW 122 kHz dual-phase current-mode relaxation oscillator for near-zero-power sensors. In: IEEE Custom Integrated Circuits Conference (CICC) (2015)
7. Dai, S., Tulloss, C.R., Lian, X., Hu, K., Reda, S., Rosenstein, J.K.: Temperature and supply voltage monitoring with current-mode relaxation oscillators. In: IFIP/IEEE International Conference on Very Large Scale Integration (VLSI-SoC) (2020)
8. Jiang, H., Wang, P.H.P., Mercier, P.P., Hall, D.A.: A 0.4-V 0.93-nW/kHz relaxation oscillator exploiting comparator temperature-dependent delay to achieve 94-ppm/°C stability. IEEE J. Solid-State Circuits **53**(10), 3004–3011 (2018)
9. Banba, H., et al.: A CMOS bandgap reference circuit with sub-1-V operation. IEEE J. Solid-State Circuits **34**(5), 670–674 (1999)
10. Chen, S.W., Chang, M.H., Hsieh, W.C. Hwang, W.: Fully on-chip temperature, process, and voltage sensors. In: IEEE International Symposium on Circuits and Systems (ISCAS) (2010)
11. Kobayashi, A., Hayashi, K., Arata, S., Murakami, S., Xu, G., Niitsu, K.: A 65-nm CMOS 1.4-nW self-controlled dual-oscillator-based supply voltage monitor for biofuel-cell-combined biosensing systems. In: IEEE International Symposium on Circuits and Systems (ISCAS), pp. 1–5 (2019)
12. Vezyrtzis, C., et al.: Droop mitigation using critical-path sensors and an on-chip distributed power supply estimation engine in the z14^{TM} enterprise processor. In: IEEE International Solid-State Circuits Conference (ISSCC) (2018)
13. Hsu, C.-H., Huang, S.-Y., Kwai, D.-M., Chou, Y.-F.: Worst-case IR-drop monitoring with 1 GHz sampling rate. In: International Symposium on VLSI Design, Automation, and Test, VLSI-DAT, pp. 1–4 (2013)
14. Makinwa, K.A.A.: Smart Temperature Sensor Survey. https://ei.ewi.tudelft.nl/docs/TSensor_survey.xls
15. Pan, S., Luo, Y., Shalmany, S.H., Makinwa, K.A.: A resistor-based temperature sensor with a 0.13 pJ · K^2 resolution FoM. IEEE J. Solid-State Circuits **53**(1), 164–173 (2018)
16. Park, H., Kim, J.: A 0.8-V resistor-based temperature sensor in 65-nm CMOS with supply sensitivity of 0.28 °C/V. IEEE J. Solid-State Circuits **53**(3), 906–912 (2018)
17. Choi, W., et al.: A compact resistor-based CMOS temperature sensor with an inaccuracy of 0.12°C (3σ) and a resolution FoM of 0.43 pJ · K^2 in 65-nm CMOS. IEEE J. Solid-State Circuits **53**, 3356 (2018)
18. Sonmez, U., Sebastiano, F., Makinwa, K.A.: Compact thermal-diffusivity-based temperature sensors in 40 nm CMOS for SoC thermal monitoring. IEEE J. Solid-State Circuits **52**(3), 834–843 (2017)

19. Yang, K., et al.: A 0.6 nJ −0.22/+0.19 °C inaccuracy temperature sensor using exponential subthreshold oscillation dependence. In: IEEE International Solid-State Circuits Conference (ISSCC), pp. 160–161 (2017)
20. Wang, X., Wang, P.H.P., Cao, Y., Mercier, P.P.: A 0.6 V 75 nW all-CMOS temperature sensor with 1.67 m°/mV supply sensitivity. IEEE Trans. Circuits Syst. I Regular Papers (TCASi) 64(9), 2274–2283 (2017)
21. Someya, Teruki, Mahfuzul Islam, A.K.M., Sakurai, T., Takamiya, M.: An 11-nW CMOS temperature-to-digital converter utilizing sub-threshold current at sub-thermal drain voltage. IEEE J. Solid-State Circuits 54(3), 613–622 (2019)
22. Wang, B., Law, M.K., Tsui, C.Y., Bermak, A.: A 10.6 pJ·K^2 resolution FoM temperature sensor using a stable multi vibrator. IEEE Trans. Circuits Syst. II Express Briefs (TCASII) 65(7), 869–873 (2018)
23. Said, M., Chetoui, S., Belouchrani, A., Reda, S.: Understanding the sources of power consumption in mobile SoCs. In: IEEE Ninth International Green and Sustainable Computing Conference (IGSC) (2018)
24. Piguet, C.: Logic synthesis of race-free asynchronous CMOS circuits. IEEE J. Solid-State Circuits 26(3), 371–380 (1991)

Fully-Autonomous SoC Synthesis Using Customizable Cell-Based Analog and Mixed-Signal Circuits Generation

Tutu Ajayi[1]([✉]), Sumanth Kamineni[2], Morteza Fayazi[1],
Yaswanth K. Cherivirala[1], Kyumin Kwon[1], Shourya Gupta[2], Wenbo Duan[1],
Jeongsup Lee[1], Chien-Hen Chen[2], Mehdi Saligane[1], Dennis Sylvester[1],
David Blaauw[1], Ronald Dreslinski Jr[1], Benton Calhoun[2],
and David D. Wentzloff[1]

[1] University of Michigan, Ann Arbor, MI, USA
ajayi@umich.edu
[2] University of Virginia, Charlottesville, VA, USA

Abstract. This chapter presents the world's first autonomous mixed-signal SoC framework, driven entirely by user constraints, along with a suite of automated generators for analog blocks. The process-agnostic framework takes high-level user intent as inputs to generate optimized and fully verified analog and mixed-signal blocks using a cell-based design methodology.

The approach is highly scalable and silicon-proven by an SoC prototype which includes 2 PLLs, 3 LDOs, 1 SRAM, and 2 temperature sensors fully integrated with a processor in a 65 nm CMOS process. The physical design of all blocks, including analog, is achieved using optimized synthesis and APR flows in commercially available tools. The framework is portable across different planar and FinFET CMOS processes and requires no-human-in-the-loop, dramatically accelerating design time.

Keywords: analog synthesis · analog generator · SoC generator

1 Introduction

There is an ever-growing need for automation in analog circuit design, validation, and integration to meet modern-day SoC requirements. Time-to-market constraints have become tighter, design complexity has increased and more functional blocks (in number and variety) are being integrated into SoCs. These challenges often translate to increased manual engineering efforts and non-recurring engineering (NRE) costs. FASoC is an open-source[1] framework for Fully-Autonomous SoC design [1,2]. Coupled with a suite of analog generators,

---

[1] Source code for the framework and all generators developed as part of this work can be downloaded from https://github.com/idea-fasoc/fasoc.

© IFIP International Federation for Information Processing 2021
Published by Springer Nature Switzerland AG 2021
A. Calimera et al. (Eds.): VLSI-SoC 2020, IFIP AICT 621, pp. 65–85, 2021.
https://doi.org/10.1007/978-3-030-81641-4_4

FASoC can generate complete mixed-signal system-on-chip (SoC) designs from the high-level user specifications. The framework leverages differentiating techniques to automatically synthesize correct-by-construction RTL descriptions for both analog and digital circuits, enabling a technology-agnostic, no-human-in-the-loop implementation flow.

Analog blocks like PLLs, LDOs, ADCs, DC-DC converters, and sensor interfaces are recasted as structures composed largely of digital components while maintaining analog performance. They are then expressed as synthesizable Verilog blocks composed of digital standard cells and auxiliary cells (aux-cells). The framework employs novel techniques to automatically characterize aux-cells and develop models required for generating bespoke analog blocks. The framework is portable across processes and scalable in terms of analog performance, layout, and other figures of merit.

The SoC generation tool translates user intent to low-level specifications required by the analog generators. The IP-XACT [3] standard is leveraged to achieve full SoC integration. Added vendor extensions capture additional metadata relating to the generated blocks. This enables the composition of vast numbers of digital and analog components into a single correct-by-construction design. The fully composed SoC design is finally realized by running the Verilog through synthesis and automatic place-and-route (APR) tools to realize full design automation.

2   Overview

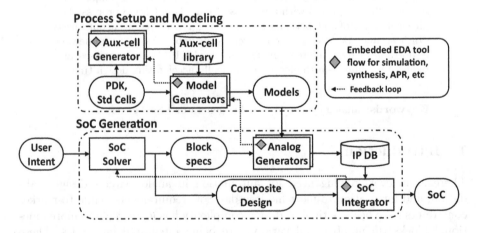

Fig. 1. FASoC Framework Overview [1]

A high-level representation of the framework is shown in Fig. 1. The *Process setup and modeling* phase is performed once for the process design kit (PDK), and it involves the generation of the aux-cells and models for the generator. The setup process is largely dominated by simulations using the design templates in combination with the characterization scripts. The automation of aux-cell and model generation significantly reduces porting effort across PDKs.

The *SoC generation* phase begins by invoking the *SoC solver* repetitively to translate the high-level user-intent into analog specifications that satisfy the user constraints. The *SoC solver* explores the SoC design space through a combination of mathematical and heuristic system models, to determine the necessary system blocks and their specifications. For instance, it can determine the operating frequency of the PLL to be generated based on the target application, SoC. If targeting a neural network application, it considers parameters such as the supported pipelines, instructions per operation, inference per second and operations per inference. The block generators are invoked as needed and the SoC integrator stitches the composed design and walks it through a synthesis and APR flow to create the final SoC layout. The FASoC framework is tightly integrated with analog generators for PLL, LDO, temperature sensor, SAR ADC, switched-capacitor DC-DC converter and SRAM blocks. Section 4 describes the circuit architecture adopted by the different generators.

3   Process Setup and Modeling

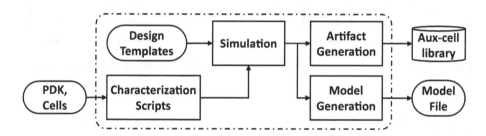

Fig. 2. Aux-cell and model file generation flow [1]

FASoC employs a synthesizable cell-based approach for generating analog blocks, significantly cutting back on manual layout and verification efforts. Aux-cells are small analog circuits that buttress the standard cell library and provide specific analog functionality required by the generators. Each cell is no larger than a D flip-flop and can be placed on the standard cell rows. The creation of aux-cells is simplified by using a suite of design templates in tandem with PDK characterization scripts. The templates capture the aux-cell's precise circuit behavior without including any PDK-specific information. The characterization scripts operate on the PDK to derive technology-specific parameters required to set knobs within the templates. Example parameters extracted from the PDK include threshold voltage, metal parasitics, MOSFET behavior, and Fan-out of 4. The knobs set within the template include device type, transistor sizing, and other circuit design options. The results from aux-cell generation include the netlist, layout, timing library, and other files required to proceed with conventional synthesis and APR. Presently, the layouts for the aux-cells are manually created, however, there is an expanding array of tools [4–6] for layout automation that show promising results. The template-based methodology for creating aux-cells enhances process-portability and significantly cuts down on design time. All of the generators presented in this work leverage a suite of aux-cells that are depicted in Fig. 3. The template-based methodology enables users to extend the aux-cell library by creating a design template that captures the respective aux-cell precise behavior without including the PDK information.

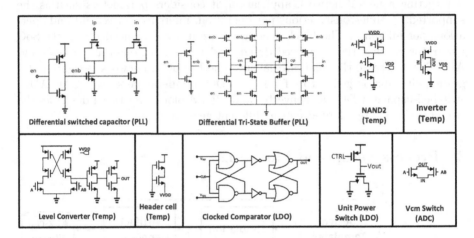

Fig. 3. Schematic for aux-cells used across PLL, LDO and temperature sensor generators [1]

The analog generators use models to predict performance and select design parameters to create optimized block designs that satisfy the input specifications. The models are derived from the parameterized templates that incorporate the aux-cells. The models for each generator vary and are developed from a combination of mathematical equations, machine learning, and design space exploration. The modeling exercise is also performed once per PDK and the results are saved into a model file. Section 4 briefly describes the modeling approach adopted by each generator integrated into the framework.

4   Analog Generator Architecture

Synthesizable analog blocks [7] were introduced a few decades ago and have continued to evolve, closely matching the performance obtainable by full custom designs. Prior works have described techniques for synthesizing analog blocks for UWB transmitters [8], PLLs [9], DACs [10], and other types of analog blocks [11–13]. This approach lowers engineering design costs, increases robustness, eases portability across PDKs, and continues to show promise even at advanced process nodes [14–16]. The analog generators developed as part of this work can be

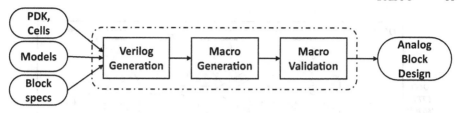

Fig. 4. Analog generator flow [1]

likened to ASIC memory compilers that take in a specification file and produce results in industry-standard file formats, which can then be used in standard synthesis and APR tools. Unlike typical memory compilers, the generators are open-source, process agnostic, and share a scalable framework amenable to different types of blocks. The framework is modular and share a similar process as depicted in Fig. 4. The full generation process is broken down into three steps:

Verilog Generation: This step leverages models to produce a synthesizable Verilog description of the block that conforms to the input specifications. It also generates guidance information in a vendor-agnostic format. The guidance includes synthesis constraints, placement instructions, and other information that may be required by the synthesis and/or APR tool to generate blocks that achieve the desired performance. In addition, this step also reports early estimates on performance and the characteristics of the block to be created.

Macro Generation: The Verilog and guidance information is passed to a digital flow to create macros that can be embedded into larger SoC designs. The digital flow in this step performs synthesis, APR, DRC, and LVS verification. The digital flow includes an adapter to translate the guidance into vendor-specific commands used in synthesis and APR. The adapter abstraction allows us to (1) express additional design intent without exposing protected vendor-specific commands and (2) easily support multiple EDA tools including open-source alternatives [17–19].

Macro Validation: The last step is a comprehensive verification and reporting of the generated block. The full circuit goes through parasitic extraction, SPICE simulations, requirement checks, and other verification to culminate in a detailed datasheet report.

The generators can be invoked standalone, outside of the full SoC generator flow. To simplify the system integration, the AMBA™ APB protocol was adopted as the register interface to all blocks.

The following subsections briefly describe the analog generators currently integrated into the FASoC framework.

4.1   PLL

The generated PLLs (Fig. 5) share the same base architecture as ADPLL [20]. The phase difference of the reference and output clocks are captured by the

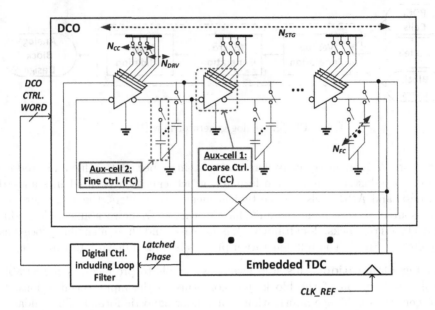

Fig. 5. DCO architecture indicating the aux-cells and designs parameters [1]

embedded time-to-digital converter (TDC), while the digital filter calculates the frequency control word for the digitally controlled oscillator (DCO). The input specification to the generator defines the nominal frequency range and in-band phase noise (PN). The PLL generator uses a physics-based mathematical model [21] for characterization. The first step is building a mathematical relationship between DCO design parameters (number of aux-cells and stages) and the required DCO specifications. Using simulation results from a parametric sweep, the effective ratio of drive strength and capacitance can be derived for each aux-cell. This ratio enables us to predict frequency and power results (frequency range, frequency resolution, frequency gain factor, and power consumption) given a set of input design parameters.

4.2 LDO

The generated LDOs (Fig. 6) share the same base architecture as DLDO [22]. The LDO leverages an array of small power transistors that operate as switches for power management. Based on design requirements, the generator can swap the clocked comparator with a synthesizable stochastic flash ADC [23] to improve transient response. The input specifications to the LDO generator are the V_{IN} range, $I_{load,max}$ range, and the dropout voltage. The generator uses a poly-fit model of the load current ($I_{load,max}$) performance for various combinations of aux-cell connections (connected in parallel and for different VDD inputs) in both ON and OFF states. The model is created by simulating various test circuits after parasitic extraction.

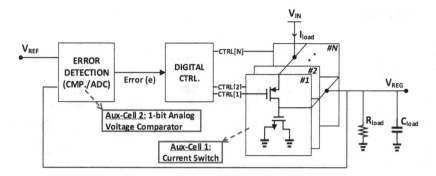

Fig. 6. LDO architecture indicating the aux-cells and design parameters derived from input specifications of V_{IN}, I_{load} and desired transients [1]

4.3   Temperature Sensor

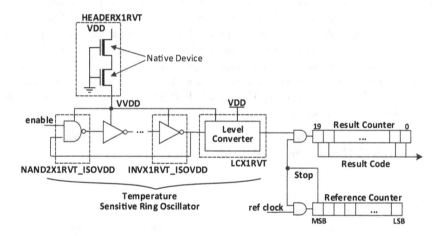

Fig. 7. Temperature sensor architecture indicating the aux-cells [1]

The generated sensors (Fig. 7) share the same base architecture as [24]. The sensor relies on a temperature-sensitive ring oscillator and stacked zero-VT devices for better line sensitivity. The input specifications include the temperature range and optimization strategy, for either error or power. For a given temperature range, the generator first checks a modeling file to select an optimized design model. If the modeling file is not already present, the generator will sweep the design parameters and start the internal simulations. The results are then utilized to train a predictive Bayesian neural network model. Doing this can considerably reduce the total simulation time and predict the best design parameters that can match the input specifications.

4.4 SAR ADC

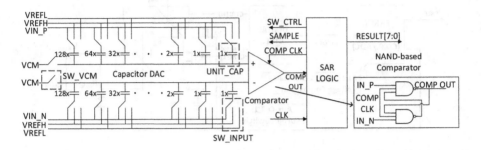

Fig. 8. SAR ADC architecture indicating the aux-cells

The generated SAR ADC (Fig. 8) utilizes the same base architecture as [25], which consists of capacitors, switches, a comparator, and a SAR controller. The Capacitor DAC includes the capacitor arrays and switches, it samples the differential signals at the input. The comparator uses a NAND-based structure, which is more suitable for design synthesis. The SAR controller generates the control signals for switches in the Capacitor DAC and the comparing clock for the NAND-based comparator. The input specification includes the sampling frequency, the target effective number of bits (ENOB), and the optimization method (for either power or area). For a given ENOB value, the generator selects the optimal number of switches that can satisfy the target sampling frequency.

4.5 Switched-Capacitor DC-DC Converter

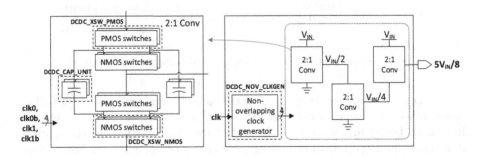

Fig. 9. Switched-Capacitor DC-DC converter architecture indicating the aux-cells

The generated switched-capacitor DC-DC converter (Fig. 9) utilizes the same base architecture as [26], which consists of multiple stages of 2:1 converters. The conversion ratio of the DC-DC converter is determined by the number of 2:1 converter stages and their configuration. The 2:1 converters are composed of 3 different aux-cells: DCDC_CAP_UNIT, DCDC_XSW_PMOS, and DCDC_XSW_NMOS. One additional aux-cell, i.e. DCDC_NOV_CLKGEN, is also required to generate two non-overlapping clock signals and their inverted signals for the 2:1 converters. Based on the input specifications (V_{IN}, V_{out}, I_{load}, and f_{clk}), the generator finds the optimal number of aux-cells in the 2:1 converters as well as determining the number of stages and their configuration.

4.6 SRAM

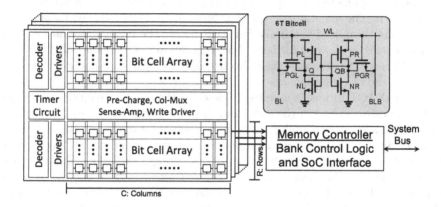

Fig. 10. SRAM architecture showing macros and bank strategy

A third party Commercial memory compilers (CMCs) [27–29] can generate an SRAM for a given PDK. However, they are the outcome of a human-driven design effort for each PDK and cover a fixed design space that usually emphasizes high performance. Such limitations restrict compilers' usage for applications such as ultra-low-power systems, which often operate in the nW to µW space. More importantly, the CMCs are not open source and may not be readily available due to cost or licensing issues, especially for newer technologies. Hence, a memory macro generation framework [30] is developed to address these issues and allow easy and autonomous generation of optimized memory macros in the design space where CMCs can not be used.

The memory generator creates fully-functional tapeout-ready integrated memories across a broad range of user specifications. The compiled SRAMs (Fig. 10) follow a standard multi-bank memory architecture. The memory generator uses a 6T bitcell, a row decoder, column mux, wordline driver, sense amplifier, write driver, and a pre-charge circuit as the aux-cells. The aux-cells are stitched together, bottom-up, to form a bank, and then a multi-bank memory. The user input specifications are capacity, word size, operating voltage, and operating frequency. The generator adopts a hierarchical memory model to determine the optimal row and column periphery. The model helps to select the SRAM architecture and the leaf-level components that best satisfy the user specifications while minimizing energy consumption and delay.

5   SoC Generation

The top-level SoC generation begins with an iterative *SoC solver* to determine the optimal *composite design* which is a combination of blocks, analog specifications, and module connectivity. The strategy is guided by high-level user intent (i.e. target application and power/area budgets), available analog block generators, and a database of IPs. Analog generators are then invoked as necessary to generate bespoke blocks required to satisfy the specifications within the composite design. The generator outputs include all artifacts required to push the block through standard synthesis and APR tools. The outputs are also cached in an *IP database*, allowing for faster SoC generation if a matching entry already exists. Entries in the database can also be populated with 3rd party IPs such as processors and other peripherals.

The IP-XACT format is adopted to describe the composite design as well as the block designs stored in the database. Added Vendor extensions [31] capture additional analog data, simulation, and verification information. The *SoC integrator* begins by stitching the composite design together and translating it to its structural Verilog equivalent that can be run through digital simulation tools. The structural Verilog, along with all required artifacts from the database, is then passed through the embedded EDA tool flow to generate the final verified GDS. This same flow is pervasive across the framework and is also used by all generators (aux-cell, model, and analog). Tools within the flow cover all aspects of chip design including SPICE simulations, digital simulations, synthesis, APR, DRC, LVS, and extraction.

The rest of this section describes key components that make up the SoC generation stage.

5.1   SoC Solver

The primary task of the SoC solver is to derive a feasible solution to the supplied user intent and further derive an optimal solution that satisfies the intent. The user intent provides a basic sketch of the target application and includes minimal information relating to the performance, power, and area requirements. The solver takes an iterative approach to perform targeted design space exploration based on predictions learned from prior executions of the analog generators. It essentially builds a correlation between the user intent, analog block specifications (of all supported generators), and the generated block results.

Although the solver relies on a database of existing IP for faster iteration, it can quickly start from a cold cache to narrow down to an optimal solution. The run-time of the solver is based on the number of blocks in the design, supplied budget, and how warm the cache is. The solver employs a heuristic algorithm to optimize the overall SoC metrics including power, performance, area, and other figures of merit.

The primary result of this process is a composite design in the form of a structural netlist. The netlist includes all specific module instances and information describing the ports and connectivity of all modules that constitute the design. The stitching process employs standard Arm AMBA protocols (e.g. APB and AHB) and includes all necessary interconnects and multiplexers.

5.2 IP-XACT and Database

The database entries are implemented using IP-XACT++, an extended version of IP-XACT. The added vendor extension catalogs supplemental meta-data relating to the IP. This non-tabular format allows for the storage of the PPA metrics as well as other figures of merits specific to each generator. This is in addition to the traditional IP information like ports, interfaces, memory maps, and validation data. The information associated with each generated instance of the IP allows the SoC Solver to quickly search the database for specific parameters and eases the stitching process to create the final netlist.

5.3 Embedded EDA Flow

The framework relies on an embedded EDA tool flow to accelerate the RTL-to-GDS process. It is a set of scripts and methodologies that leverage commercial EDA tools to accomplish the task of walking arbitrary designs through the synthesis and implementation process as quickly as possible. It builds on several modular abstractions to provide a PDK agnostic flow. Figure 11 shows the main abstractions inherent within the tool flow.

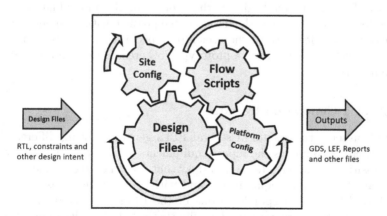

Fig. 11. Embedded EDA tool flow abstractions

Flow scripts: These are robust reference scripts for all the steps in the flow. It is collection of scripts span several EDA vendors used throughout the steps. It contains the *best practices* and recommendations from the tool providers and has been stitched together to form a generic end-to-end flow that can easily be customized based on several factors.

Platform Configuration: These constitute the PDK specific information, configurations, rules, and requirements for a specific technology node. There is a one-time effort to create this customization for newly supported technologies, however, subsequent designs can re-use that effort transparently

Site Configuration: These are configuration parameters that establish pointers to the required site-specific information. These are file paths to the PDK, standard cells, tool binaries, and license information for the EDA tools.

Design Files: This is the design-specific information that contains significantly less information about the EDA tools, PDK, and Site location since those have mostly been abstracted away and are expressed as customization to the generic flow in the EDA scripts. It is intended to express the actual design intent with little reference to the other abstractions.

Combined, these modular abstractions can be customized and combined together to form a block or chip specific flow. The various steps supported in the flow are simulation, synthesis, APR, LVS, DRC and extraction. It has support for 13 PDKs and has been validated with 6 different tape-outs across different PDKs. The flow is used at various levels and steps within the FASoC framework and has also been leveraged for other projects.

6   Evaluation

The framework has been fully verified in a planar 65 nm and FinFET 12 nm processes. The evaluation begins with a focus on the individual generators. The results presented explore the design-space possible with each generator and demonstrate full adherence to the user input specification in a 65 nm process. Results are then presented from a prototype SoC created in 65 nm process using this framework.

6.1   Analog Generation Results

Figure 12 presents the results of several PLLs generated using different input specifications. It compares the input requirements against the simulated results after parasitic extraction. The results show that the generated frequency ranges cover that of the input requirements and with better phase noise levels. The highlighted PLL 8, corresponds to one of the PLLs integrated into the SoC prototype and also shows measured results that satisfy the given specifications

Figure 13 shows the spice simulation results of multiple LDO designs after parasitic extraction. The graph shows the maximum load current at different

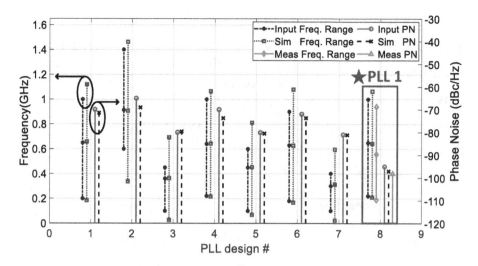

Fig. 12. Generated PLL designs for eight different input specifications. PLL1 is taped-out in the SoC prototype [1]

input voltages corresponding to the input parameter array size for a dropout voltage of 50 mV. The highlighted measurements correspond to the input specification for blocks integrated into the SoC prototype with $V_{IN} = 1.3$ V and $V_{REG} = 1.2$ V.

Figure 14 presents the simulation results of various memory capacities across a broad range of architectural options and operating voltages (VDD). Each point on the curve corresponds to an energy-delay pair specific to an architecture (rows, columns, and banks) and VDD combination. The generator selects the Pareto-optimal design that satisfies the user requirements. The highlighted point on the 16 KB curve corresponds to the memory block integrated into the SoC prototype.

Figure 15 shows the spice simulation results of multiple temperature sensor designs after parasitic extraction.

Figure 16 presents the simulation results of various numbers of V_{cm} switches. The generator selects the optimized value to satisfy the input specifications. By using a common-centroid placement strategy on the capacitors, the generator can also reduce the systematic mismatch which affects the accuracy of capacitance ratios. Table 1 shows the spice simulation results of cdl and pex netlists that closely match the input specifications with an area optimization.

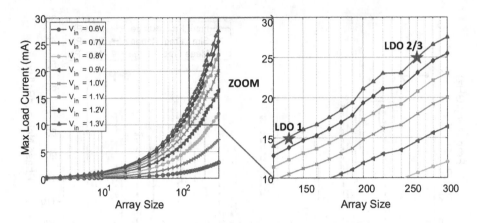

Fig. 13. $I_{load,max}$ vs. array size, for multiple LDO designs generated [1]

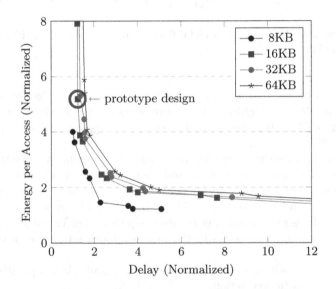

Fig. 14. Normalized energy and delay plots for various memory sizes while sweeping VDD. The results are normalized with respect to the 8 KB memory [1].

Table 1. ADC Simulation Results

Output Specifications	CDL	PEX
Sampling Freq (MHz)	1	
Unit Cap Value (fF)	2.6	
Area (mm^2)	-	0.04
Power dissipation (µW)	6.72	11.2
Effective Number of Bits	7.86	7.75

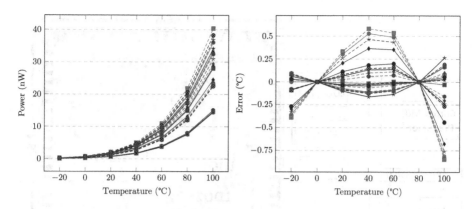

Fig. 15. Power and Error results against temperature for various temperature sensor designs (each fitted plot represents a unique design) [1]

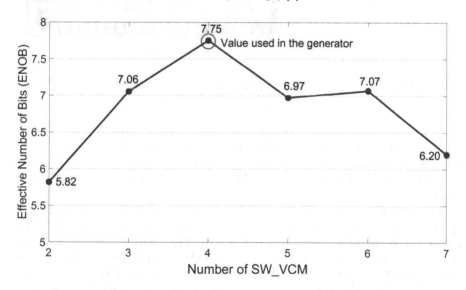

Fig. 16. Effective number of bits vs. Number of switches for V_{cm}

6.2 Prototype Chip Results

The 65 nm prototype SoC design (Fig. 17) features 2 PLLs, 3 LDOs, a 16 KB SRAM, and 2 temperature sensors fully integrated with an Arm® Cortex™-M0 in a 65 nm CMOS process. Using off-chip connections, the entire SoC can be powered using one of the LDOs and clocked using the PLLs while monitoring the temperature of the chip.

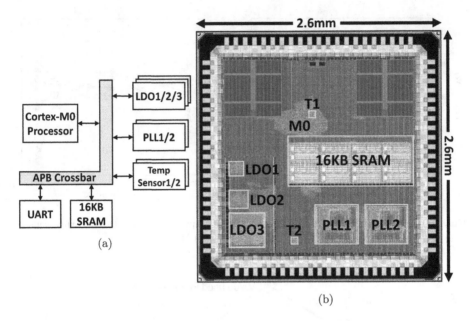

Fig. 17. Simplified block diagram (a) and annotated die photo (b) for the 65 nm prototype SoC [1]

A similar 12 nm prototype SoC (Fig. 18) features a PLL, 2 LDOs, a 64 KB SRAM, 3 temperature sensors, a bluetooth transmitter, 2 SAR ADCs, a switched-capacitor DC-DC converter fully integrated with an Arm Cortex-M0 processor.

Figure 12 presents results for 8 PLL designs generated from different input specifications, including one from the prototype, and the results show output performances in-line with the input specifications. The measured frequency is 10% slower while the phase noise matches the simulation and specification requirement. Table 2 summarizes the results for all PLLs in the prototype.

Table 3 shows the LDO $I_{load,max}$ measurements closely matching the input specification requirements. Compared to the comparator-based architecture (LDO1/2), the ADC based controller architecture (LDO3) achieves better transient performance with a $10\times$ and $7\times$ improvement in settling time and undershoot voltage respectively. The line and load regulation values are measured at $V_{IN} = 1.3$ V, $V_{REF} = 1.2$ V, and $I_{load} = 10$ mA. LDO3 load regulation is comparatively worse due to the high gain of the ADC based controller. While

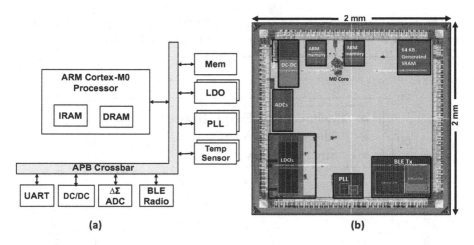

Fig. 18. Simplified block diagram (a) and annotated die photo (b) for the 12 nm prototype SoC

Table 2. PLL Simulation vs Measurement Results [1]

Output Specifications	PLL1		PLL2	
	Sim	Meas	Sim	Meas
Min Freq (MHz)	200	190	170	150
Max Freq (MHz)	1,060	920	1,080	930
F_{nom} (MHz)	643	558	627	548
Power@F_{nom} (mW)	7.20	6.90	8.06	7.70
Area (μm^2)	167,639.04		167,639.04	

Table 3. LDO Simulation vs Measurement Results @ 200 MHz control clock [1]

Output Specifications	LDO1		LDO2		LDO3	
	Sim	Meas	Sim	Meas	Sim	Meas
Dropout Voltage (mV)	50	70	50	80	50	80
$I_{load,max}$ (mA)	15.00	15.38	25.00	24.84	25.00	23.72
Settling Time - Ts (μs)	1.1	1.8	2.1	2.9	0.12	0.19
Max Undershoot (V)	0.35	0.98	0.57	0.98	0.38	0.14
Max Current Eff. (%)	94.2	96.4	95.7	94.5	81.9	74.0
Load Regulation (mV/mA)	-	−1.00	-	−0.35	-	−3.6
Line Regulation (V/V)	-	0.180	-	0.004	-	0.950
Area (μm^2)	17,318.56		31,187.56		127,163.56	

operating at lower V_{REF} and I_{load} conditions, the line/load regulation degrades for all the LDOs because of the increase in relative switch strength.

The temperature sensor has an area of 2,620 μm². A 2-pt calibration is performed at 0 °C and 80 °C. Measured results show a sensing range between −20 °C and 100 °C with an accuracy of ±4 °C.

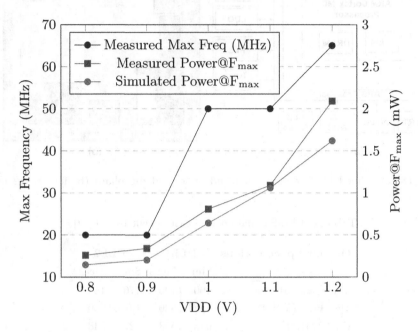

Fig. 19. Measured and simulated performance and power results of SRAM across VDD [1]

Figure 19 summarizes the SRAM measured and simulated performance across the input operating voltage range of 0.8 V to 1.2 V. The SRAM peak performance is at 65 MHz with the power consumption of 2.09 mW at 1.2 V, which exceeds the targeted frequency of 50 MHz. The measured power for the SRAM also include the leakage power of the processor and peripheral interface. The generated SRAM has an area of 0.68 mm² with the custom bitcell area occupying 0.4 mm².

7   Conclusion

This chapter presented an autonomous framework that generates a completely integrated SoC design based on user input specifications. The framework is PDK agnostic and allows for faster turn-around times when building custom analog blocks and integrating them into larger SoC designs. The framework includes generators for PLL, LDO, temperature sensor, SAR ADC, switched-capacitor DC-DC, and SRAM blocks. The framework can easily be extended to support more generators and different PDKs. The framework's validation was performed by creating and fabricating SoC prototypes in 12 nm and 65 nm processes. Silicon measurements for the analog blocks were inline with user requirements and simulation results. This work establishes a new milestone in creating a silicon compiler [32] that further reduces the complexity of realizing modern SoCs and cuts down on design time.

Acknowledgment. This material is based on research sponsored by Air Force Research Laboratory (AFRL) and Defense Advanced Research Projects Agency (DARPA) under agreement number FA8650-18-2-7844. The U.S. Government is authorized to reproduce and distribute reprints for Governmental purposes notwithstanding any copyright notation thereon.

References

1. Ajayi, T., et al.: An open-source framework for autonomous SoC design with analog block generation. In: 2020 IFIP/IEEE 28th International Conference on Very Large Scale Integration (VLSI-SOC), pp. 141–146. IEEE (2020)
2. Ajayi, T., et al.: Fully autonomous mixed signal SoC design and layout generation platform (2020)
3. Accellera, "IP-XACT - Accellera". https://www.accellera.org/downloads/standards/ip-xact. Accessed 03 May 2020
4. Wu, C.-Y., Graeb, H., Hu, J.: A pre-search assisted ILP approach to analog integrated circuit routing. In: 2015 33rd IEEE International Conference on Computer Design (ICCD), pp. 244–250. IEEE (2015)
5. Kunal, K., et al.: ALIGN: open-source analog layout automation from the ground up. In: Proceedings of the 56th Annual Design Automation Conference 2019, pp. 1–4 (2019)
6. Xu, B., et al.: MAGICAL: toward fully automated analog IC layout leveraging human and machine intelligence. In: 2019 IEEE/ACM International Conference on Computer-Aided Design (ICCAD), pp. 1–8. IEEE (2019)
7. Vladimirescu, A., Zlatanovici, R., Jespers, P.: Analog circuit synthesis using standard EDA tools. In: 2006 IEEE International Symposium on Circuits and Systems, p. 4 (2006)
8. Park, Y., Wentzloff, D.D.: An all-digital 12pj/pulse 3.1–6.0 GHz IR-UWB transmitter in 65 nm CMOS. In: 2010 IEEE International Conference on Ultra-Wideband, vol. 1, pp. 1–4. IEEE (2010)
9. Park, Y., Wentzloff, D.D.: An all-digital PLL synthesized from a digital standard cell library in 65 nm CMOS. In: 2011 IEEE Custom Integrated Circuits Conference (CICC), pp. 1–4. IEEE (2011)
10. Ansari, E., Wentzloff, D.D.: A 5 mw 250 ms/s 12-bit synthesized digital to analog converter. In: Proceedings of the IEEE 2014 Custom Integrated Circuits Conference, pp. 1–4. IEEE (2014)
11. Bang, S., Wang, A., Giridhar, B., Blaauw, D., Sylvester, D.D.: A fully integrated successive-approximation switched-capacitor DC-DC converter with 31 mv output voltage resolution. In: 2013 IEEE International Solid-State Circuits Conference Digest of Technical Papers, pp. 370–371. IEEE (2013)
12. Jung, W., Jeong, S., Oh, S., Sylvester, D., Blaauw, D.: A 0.7 pf-to-10 nf fully digital capacitance-to-digital converter using iterative delay-chain discharge. In: 2015 IEEE International Solid-State Circuits Conference-(ISSCC) Digest of Technical Papers, pp. 1–3. IEEE (2015)

13. Shim, M., et al.: An oscillator collapse-based comparator with application in a 74.1 db SNDR, 20ks/s 15b SAR ADC. In: 2016 IEEE Symposium on VLSI Circuits (VLSI-Circuits), pp. 1–2. IEEE (2016)
14. Bang, S., et al.: A fully synthesizable distributed and scalable all-digital LDO in 10 nm CMOS. In: 2020 IEEE International Solid-State Circuits Conference-(ISSCC), pp. 380–382. IEEE (2020)
15. Kundu, S., Chai, L., Chandrashekar, K., Pellerano, S., Carlton, B.: A self-calibrated 1.2-to-3.8 ghz 0.0052 mm^2 synthesized fractional-n MDLL using a 2b time-period comparator in 22 nm finfet CMOS. In: 2020 IEEE International Solid-State Circuits Conference-(ISSCC), pp. 276–278. IEEE (2020)
16. Rovinski, A., et al.: A 1.4 GHz 695 giga risc-v inst/s 496-core manycore processor with mesh on-chip network and an all-digital synthesized PLL in 16 nm CMOS. In: 2019 Symposium on VLSI Circuits, pp. C30–C31. IEEE (2019)
17. Wolf, C.: Yosys open synthesis suite. http://www.clifford.at/yosys/. Accessed 08 May 2020
18. Ngspice: the open source spice circuit simulator. http://ngspice.sourceforge.net/. Accessed 08 2020
19. S. N. Laboratories: Xyce parallel electronic simulator (xyce). https://xyce.sandia.gov/. Accessed 08 May 2020
20. Moore, D.M., Xanthopoulos, T., Meninger, S., Wentzloff, D.D.: A 0.009 mm^2 wide-tuning range automatically placed-and-routed ADPLL in 14-nm finfet CMOS. IEEE Solid-State Circuits Lett. 1(3), 74–77 (2018)
21. Perrott, M.H., Trott, M.D., Sodini, C.G.: A modeling approach for Σ-Δ fractional-N frequency synthesizers allowing straightforward noise analysis. IEEE J. Solid-State Circuits 37(8), 1028–1038 (2002)
22. Okuma, Y., et al.: 0.5-v input digital LDO with 98.7% current efficiency and 2.7-μa quiescent current in 65 nm CMOS. In: IEEE Custom Integrated Circuits Conference 2010, pp. 1–4. IEEE (2010)
23. Weaver, S., Hershberg, B., Kurahashi, P., Knierim, D., Moon, U.-K.: Stochastic flash analog-to-digital conversion. IEEE Trans. Circuits Syst. I Regular Papers 57(11), 2825–2833 (2010)
24. Saligane, M., Khayatzadeh, M., Zhang, Y., Jeong, S., Blaauw, D., Sylvester, D.: All-digital SoC thermal sensor using on-chip high order temperature curvature correction. In: 2015 IEEE Custom Integrated Circuits Conference (CICC), pp. 1–4. IEEE (2015)
25. Jeong, S.: A 120 nw 8b sub-ranging SAR ADC with signal-dependent charge recycling for biomedical applications. In: 2015 Symposium on VLSI Circuits (VLSI Circuits), pp. C60–C61 (2015)
26. Salem, L.G., Mercier, P.P.: A recursive switched-capacitor DC-DC converter achieving $2^N - 1$ ratios with high efficiency over a wide output voltage range. IEEE J. Solid-State Circuits 49(12), 2773–2787 (2014)
27. ARM: Artisan memory compilers. https://developer.arm.com/ip-products/physical-ip/embedded-memory. Accessed 18 Jan 2021
28. Synopsys: Designware memory compilers. https://www.synopsys.com/dw/ipdir.php?ds=dwc_sram_memory_compilers. Accessed 18 Jan 2021
29. D. Technology: Memory products. http://dolphin-ic.com/memory-products.html. Accessed 18 Jan 2021
30. Kamineni, S., Gupta, S., Calhoun, B.H.: Memgen: an open-source framework for autonomous generation of memory macros. In: 2021 IEEE Custom Integrated Circuits Conference (CICC), pp. 3–2. IEEE (2021)

31. Dreslinski, R., et al.: Fully-autonomous SoC synthesis using customizable cell-based synthesizable analog circuits. Technical Report, University of Michigan Ann Arbor United States (2019)
32. Johannsen, D.: Bristle blocks: a silicon compiler. In: 16th Design Automation Conference, pp. 310–313. IEEE (1979)

Assessing the Configuration Space of the Open Source NVDLA Deep Learning Accelerator on a Mainstream MPSoC Platform

Alessandro Veronesi[1](✉), Davide Bertozzi[2](✉), and Milos Krstic[1](✉)

[1] IHP - Leibniz-Institut für innovative Mikroelektronik,
15236 Frankfurt Oder, Germany
{veronesi,krstic}@ihp-microelectronics.com
[2] Department of Engineering, Universitá degli Studi di Ferrara, 44122 Ferrara, Italy
davide.bertozzi@unife.it

Abstract. Deep neural networks (DNNs) are computationally and memory intensive, which makes them difficult to deploy on traditional hardware environments. Therefore, many dedicated solutions have been proposed in the literature and market. However, most of them remain proprietary or lack maturity, thus preventing the adoption of deep-learning (DL) based software in new application domains. The Nvidia Deep-Learning Accelerator (NVDLA) is a free and open architecture that aims at promoting a standard way of designing deep neural network (DNN) inference engines. Following an analogy with open-source software, which is downloaded and executed, open hardware is likely to use FPGAs as reference implementation platform. However, tailoring accelerator configuration to the capacity of cost-effective reconfigurable logic remains a fundamental challenge for their actual deployment in system-level designs. This chapter presents an overview of the hardware and software components of the NVDLA inference framework, and reports on the exploration of its configuration space. It explores the resource utilization-performance trade-offs spanned by the main precompiled NVDLA accelerator configurations on top of the mainstream Zynq UltraScale+ MPSoC. For the sake of comprehensive end-to-end performance characterization, the inference rate of the software stack and of the accelerator hardware are matched, thus identifying current bottlenecks and promising optimization directions.

Keywords: Deep-Learning · Reconfigurable Logic · Bare-Metal Software · Open Hardware · Configurable Accelerator

1 Introduction

In recent years, the market request for efficient hardware supporting deep-learning inference and training is increasing. As a result, computing accelerators

© IFIP International Federation for Information Processing 2021
Published by Springer Nature Switzerland AG 2021
A. Calimera et al. (Eds.): VLSI-SoC 2020, IFIP AICT 621, pp. 87–112, 2021.
https://doi.org/10.1007/978-3-030-81641-4_5

in the context of heterogeneous hardware platforms are becoming key enablers for the large-scale adoption of Artificial Intelligence (AI)-based solutions. While graphics processing units (GPUs) are still the most commonly used platform for accelerating deep neural networks (DNNs), more specialized hardware may enhance the overall power and time execution budget [1,17].

Among the several options that are currently investigated, Field-Programmable Gate Arrays (FPGAs) are gathering momentum because of their capability to fit the tight power budgets of embedded applications [15] and to shorten the development cycle. Unlike their ASIC counterparts, they can be reconfigured on-the-field, which plays a fundamental role in modern context-sensitive IoT scenarios with changing input datasets over time and frequent model updates. As a result, FPGAs are gaining ground in assisting CPUs for deep neural network (DNN) acceleration [14,26].

The growing popularity of FPGAs well beyond their traditional prototyping function as mainstream computing platforms well matches another emerging trend: open hardware. Inspired by the successful trajectory of open-source software, open hardware typically refers to the publicly availability of RTL models of IP components, so that interested users can feed them to a physical implementation flow. The industry itself may leverage open hardware as a means of speeding up the adoption of disruptive technologies, thus triggering a virtuous cycle that potentially results in broader market opportunities. This paradigm enables companies and academia to reduce development times and to take advantage of emerging technologies without massive investments. It is the case of the RISC-V Foundation, which aims at promoting the free and open RISC-V instruction set architecture, together with its hardware and software ecosystem [34].

There is a strong parallelism between open hardware and open software at various level of development and deployment process. In particular, as open software can be easily downloaded and compiled for a general-purpose CPU, an open hardware IP can be easily synthesized for an FPGA target, with a number of additional benefits. First, the released hardware models undergo an intensive customization effort by developers, either to specialize them for the application at hand or to augment the level of security of the hardware realization, since anybody can inspect and test the design. Second, prototyping on specific FPGA platforms may be an integral part of the business model for open hardware, to enable its validation on the field. Third, the resulting implementation on reconfigurable logic may already hit the desired compromise between performance, power and development cost to make it the target platform for deployment.

From the above brief observations, it is possible to assess how open hardware may play a central role in deep-learning-based ecosystems. Besides the availability of various commercial deep-learning accelerator (DLA) designs, closed DLA solutions' reserved nature and demanding license cost prevent broad adoption of those architectures and, more generally, of AI in new application domains. Therefore, the availability of open hardware DLA may be a key enabler for future innovative AI-based applications.

The more relevant examples in this sense are represented by the Nvidia Deep-Learning Accelerator (NVDLA) [32] and the agile systolic array generator Gemmini [4]. NVDLA is an open-source industry-grade inference engine that has also been integrated into the Jetson Xavier SoC platform [30]. NVDLA is an end-to-end software-hardware stack from the high-level deep-learning framework to the actual hardware implementation through the Runtime environment. The accelerator is highly configurable to adapt to various computing applications with different resource budgets.

On the other hand, Gemmini is an academic design implementing a parametric systolic array architecture for general matrix-to-matrix multiplication (GEMM) acceleration. In Gemmini, the systolic array hardware is expanded with some elementary post-processing units and a scratchpad memory. Given their open source nature, both NVDLA and Gemmini are influential contributions to the abundance of new machine learning accelerators, which raises interest in their comparison against state-of-the-art common benchmarks. The work in [5] has proven NVDLA to be 3.77× faster than Gemmini on an equivalently sized configuration running ResNet-50. Due to its promising performance and to its industry-proven nature, the focus of this chapter will be on the NVDLA accelerator and on its concrete FPGA deployment.

Each target FPGA platform can impose a different resource budget, which forces developers to trade architectural complexity and performance for lower resource utilization to some extent. On the one hand, hardware and algorithm optimizations for performance are pursued to make up for the inherently limited reconfigurable fabric speed. On the other hand, the limited programming density of such fabrics may cause full-featured hardware architectures not to fit the FPGA resources at hand. These conflicting requirements are exacerbated by the recent advancements of DNN algorithms (e.g. Winograd and FFT convolutions, weight compression), which come with their associated hardware extensions [2,11,28].

This chapter moves from the observation that the flexible NVDLA accelerator has mainly undergone virtual or physical prototyping so far while validating only single design points. Moreover, although the accelerator gained ample popularity since its initial release, the active support received from the community remains below expectations. One of the main reasons is the design complexity and poor software documentation. Moreover, few works correlate its wide configuration space to the capacity of mainstream reconfigurable fabrics and achievable performance. At the same time, like many other open hardware cores, NVDLA comes with testbenches for direct hardware performance evaluation. However, they may turn out to be misleading since they ignore the overhead of the software stack, including user-mode and kernel-mode drivers, the Runtime environment and portability layers for compatibility across computing platforms.

In order to facilitate the assessment, the further development and the concrete deployment of NVDLA, this chapter expands our previous work [20] by providing a more detailed introductory guide to the hardware and software stack of this DLA and an accurate in-sight of the available NVDLA Compiler's workflow and capabilities. This chapter will analyze the Compiler's workflow and functional capabilities (Sect. 4), the Runtime environment and its inference performance (Sect. 5), and will correlate hardware configurations to the resource capacity of a mainstream FPGA platform (Sect. 6).

The Xilinx's Zynq UltraScale+ MPSoC family (more precisely, the ZCU102 board) has been considered as implementation target. A bare-metal porting guide on top of the board is described in Sect. 5.1. On the other hand, Sect. 6.2 describes the synthesis results of available pre-compiled configurations on top of the board's programmable logic. Last, Sect. 7 provides a comparison between software and hardware throughput, thus, identifying major bottlenecks and pointing to some easily affordable optimizations to enhance the architectural support for FPGA targets.

2   Related Work

There is a surge of interest in FPGAs as implementation platforms for DNN accelerators [14,25,26]. The availability of high-level synthesis (HLS) tools from FPGA vendors lowers the programming hurdle and allows sophisticated end-to-end hardware-software co-design flows [13,21]. Flexibility of reconfigurable logic is typically exploited to directly map hardwired DNN models for better performance [16,25,26].

A more general approach consists of supporting the mathematical operations at the core of deep-learning inference in the accelerator hardware. This approach is better suited for virtualized environments and frequent model updates. Along this direction, the NVIDIA deep-learning accelerator project promotes interoperability with the majority of modern deep-learning networks [32]. Early works on this architecture mainly resulted in extensive prototyping effort: some of them targeted virtual platforms [8,27], while others targeted FPGAs [29]. However, none of them initially have gone beyond a functional verification of the design or the straightforward reporting of FPGA resource utilization, thus lacking of in-depth analysis.

Only the work in [12] provides performance evaluation. For instance, assuming the YOLO-v1 neural-network model as a benchmark, with a 256-MAC NVDLA at 150 MHz, they reach 8 frames per second. Unfortunately, a single design point is investigated (e.g., there is no discussion on the feasibility of fitting larger NVDLA configurations into the target board) and the Runtime overhead was not taken into account. To date, the most informative parametric study is still the one reported on the NVDLA website [32], which is however referred to ASIC technology, is far from exhaustive, and ignores the overhead of the software stack.

More recently, the focus has shifted on system integration and customization. NVDLA has in fact been synthesized and combined with different MCU architectures [3,6]. For instance, in work [6], authors have integrated NVDLA with a RISC-V processor core, while keeping under control the power consumption of the accelerator. In the works [22,23], the NVDLA's convolutional core has been extended with additional hardware to implement an error detection routine working in parallel to the standard convolution operation. With only 30% of extra hardware and power consumption in the convolutional core, they can identify up to 99% of the injected faults during convolutions.

Udupa et al. [19] noticed that the NVDLA's dataflow is not optimal for 2D Convolutions and Pooling operations, which are quite common in mobile-oriented CNNs. Therefore, they propose a modification of the baseline MAC cells to enhance resource usage during those operations.

While the hardware architecture has been the focus of explorative research only since recently, the NVDLA Compiler has been targeted for optimization since the original release. An Open-Source tool enabling both the compilation of a broader range of neural networks than initially supported and their mapping onto different NVDLA configurations is presented in Ref. [9].

Last, the scalable SIMBA deep-learning accelerator [24] is based on an array of processing elements that are directly derived from the NVDLA architecture. The SIMBA DLA targets the provisioning of scalable compute power within package-level integration through multi-chip modules rather than large monolithic dies.

This chapter provides an introduction to the NVDLA architecture and aims to correlate the configuration space of the accelerator to the configuration space of the NVDLA accelerator to the performance-resource utilization trade-offs spanned on a commercial FPGA platform. In particular, this work has a distinctive focus on the interplay between hardware and software layers in determining inference performance, and investigating the NVDLA's synthesis outcome on a mainstream FPGA platform.

3   The NVDLA Architecture

The NVDLA project is composed of three main GitHub repositories, providing the source code of:

- The Virtual Prototyping platform;
- The Software Stack, composed of two Runtime Drivers and a Neural Network Compiler;
- The Hardware RTL and SystemC models.

The *Virtual Prototyping* repository is mainly composed by an NVDLA SystemC model and by a Linux Kernel image running on a QEMU platform and containing both drivers and Compiler. It is worth highlighting that the available SystemC model is an RTL model. Therefore, more complex networks may have a long simulation time.

The *Software* repository contains the Runtime environment, composed of a User-Mode Driver (UMD) and a Kernel-Mode Driver (KMD). The NVDLA's Compiler is released as part of the UMD code, since the two software components share many data structures. Both User-Mode and Kernel-Mode Drivers

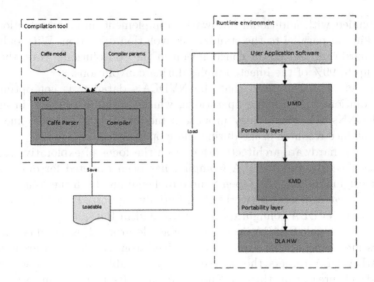

Fig. 1. NVDLA software stack.

are largely hardware-independent, and the needed modifications to make them run with different NVDLA configurations are few and simple.

The *Hardware* repository is structured into three different branches: the *"nvdla v1"* contains the "Full" configuration, entirely supported by the Compiler and containing all NVDLA functional units; the *"nv_small"* branch contains two "Small" and one "Large" configurations, suitable for more scaled applications; last, the *"master"* branch contains several custom configurations, most of them only partially verified or not mature for an ASIC implementation. All the available branches contain both a SystemC and a Verilog source code of the accelerator instances. Those descriptions are dynamically generated by a script-based environment which revolves around a *".spec"* Specification File of the configuration.

For our purpose, we focus on the software stack and the Verilog RTL model.

3.1 Software Environment

The software environment is composed by a Network Compiler and by a Runtime Environment. The Compiler acquires a pre-trained Neural Network written in *Caffe* as well as an NVDLA configuration and produces a *".loadable"* file, containing the list of hardware layers to be executed (see Fig. 1). A hardware layer is a set of operations to be scheduled on each functional unit of the NVDLA architecture. The current baseline Compiler fully supports only the "Full" configuration (also referred as *"NVDLA_v1"* online), while other configurations are only partially supported (see Sect. 4.2).

The loadable file is given to the Runtime Environment, which is composed by a *User Mode Driver (UMD)* and a *Kernel Mode Driver (KMD)*. The former loads the network into the main memory (which has to be shared between the two drivers and the hardware), reads and unpackages the image file and executes data preparation, which mainly consists of re-interpreting the input pixel format into an accelerator-specific memory mapping. The KMD contains the functional unit scheduler and the hardware abstraction layer.

Instead, the network's weights are already prepared by the Compiler, which also takes care of their memory reservation. Network's execution information are thus serialized and packed into the *".loadlable"* file. More precisely, the "load-able" file consists of a byte sequence, containing network's data and a network's compiled model description structured as a list of executable hardware layers.

UMD starts its execution copying in DRAM the loadable file content. Together with the pre-processed input image, the loadable file's data are used by the UMD to prepare and send an "NVDLA Task" to the KMD. Thus, the inference is performed in a single NVDLA Task, through a layer-by-layer execution.

The OS-driver interactions are wrapped into a Portability Layer structure and hidden to the drivers' main routines. Currently, no actively supported bare-metal implementations exist for the NVDLA drivers, a gap that the work reported in this chapter will bridge not to include the OS overhead into the NVDLA performance evaluation. Both the UMD and the KMD are originally written for Linux and only support *JPEG* and *PGM* image formats.

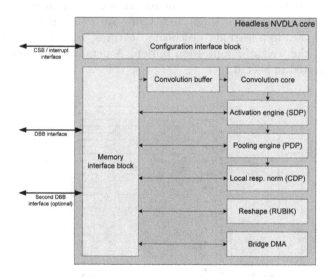

Fig. 2. NVDLA hardware block diagram.

3.2 Hardware Architecture

The NVDLA architecture is composed of several functional units. As shown in Fig. 2, NVDLA revolves around a sophisticated Convolution Pipeline (CONV), which is augmented by an activation engine (Single-Point Data Processor, SDP) and a pooling engine (Planar Data Processor, PDP). There are also more specialized hardware units to extend the range of compatible deep-learning applications. They include a Cross-Channel Data Processor (CDP) for local response normalization and a Reshape Engine (RUBIK) for simple image manipulation.

The accelerator has two interfaces to the outside world. On the one hand, the Configuration Space Bus (CSB) is a slave interface connected to the host processor and is used for accelerator configuration together with an interrupt signal. On the other hand, the data backbone (DBB) is a link with the main system memory, which is shared with the host processor. The CSB is a simple, memory-like interface, thought to be easily connected to a different standard bus. As an instance, the NVDLA's GitHub hardware repository already contains a CSB-to-AMBA APB bridge. Last, it is possible to instantiate an optional DBB interface, which typically consists of a high-speed, dedicated SRAM, onto which a Bridge DMA moves data from the main memory in a software-controlled way.

Beyond supporting the processing of a wide range of DNNs, NVDLA targets instantiation flexibility: in fact, most of the above hardware units are optional and highly configurable (e.g., number of MACs, convolution buffer size, batch size, number of operations per convolution round, activation function, etc.). Even when all functional units are supported, there are still significant degrees of freedom as to the deep-learning processing features, such as the convolution algorithm and the weight compression option. A detailed list of configuration options is reported in Sect. 6.1.

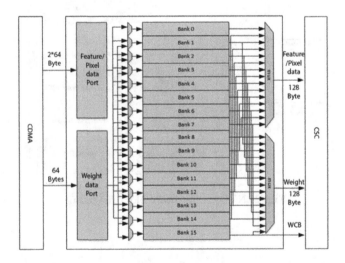

Fig. 3. NVDLA CBUF block diagram in the "Full" configuration.

The Convolutional Pipeline (CONV unit) is composed of five stages: Convolution DMA (CDMA), Convolution Buffer (CBUF), Convolution Sequence Controller (CSC), Convolution MAC array (CMAC), and Convolution Accumulator (CACC). The system designer can configure the CONV pipeline by enabling optional extra features (Winograd convolution support, Multi-Batch size and weight compression support) and choosing CBUF and CMAC sizes.

CBUF block comprises several SRAM banks (see Fig. 3) which can be configured in number and size. Each bank acts as a circular buffer, where new data has incremental entry address, and if the address reaches the end, it wraps to zero and starts increasing again.

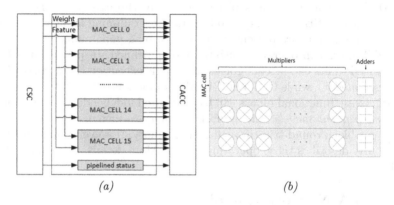

Fig. 4. NVDLA CMAC unit. An array of MAC cells shares a broadcast input (a). Each MAC cell is composed of an array of multipliers and the result is sent to the adder tree in CACC (b).

The computing core of the CONV unit is the CMAC. The CMAC unit is structured as an array of $Atomic\_K$ MAC_cells, where each cell is composed of an $Atomic\_C$ number of multipliers (see Fig. 4). Data are fed from the CBUF and broadcast among different MAC cells. The two above parameters define the simplest atomic convolution supported, where $Atomic\_C$ is the maximum number of accepted input tensor channels and $Atomic\_K$ is the maximum number of accepted kernels in a single layer. Multiplication results are sent to the accumulation unit (CACC) and summed thanks to an adder tree. Last, it is essential to remember that the CONV unit output has no direct access to the memory interface. Instead, CONV results are sent to the SDP unit as inputs.

In NVDLA "Full", the Single-Point Data Processor (SDP) can perform bias addition, batch normalization, element-wise operations among different input tensors and non-linear functions applications, mainly to perform activations. Non-linear functions may be both natively supported by SDP hardware (like ReLU and PReLU) or emulated through a Look-Up Table unit (like Sigmoid and Tanh in the "Full" configuration). Other configurations differ per type of supported operations and sub-units throughput (see Sect. 4.2 and Sect. 6.1).

The Planar Data Processor (PDP) is capable of *min*, *max* and *mean* pooling operations. The PDP engine operates on different planes of the input feature data cube. No interferences are present on different channels of the same feature data cube. PDP can acquire data both from the memory interface and the SDP output (also referred to as *"fused"* mode or *"on-the-fly"* mode).

The Cross-Channel Data Processor (CDP) is specifically designed to implement those functions that need to cross-combine values coming from separate channels. To perform them, CDP uses a LUT-based engine. In the "Full" configuration the Compiler can configure it to perform Local-Response Normalization (LRN) functions. LRN layers are present in models like AlexNet [7] and GoogLeNet [18], but are becoming less and less popular in recent DNN models.

NVDLA configuration takes place exclusively through the CSB interface. Every unit has a CSB slave where, to hide the programming latency, two sets of configuration registers are present, handled in a ping-pong manner.

NVDLA units can operate sequentially or pipelined. In particular, CONV, SDP and PDP units can be configurred as a single execution chain (also referred to as *"fused mode"*), while CDP and RUBIK cannot, since they differ in data format. Otherwise, functional blocks can be configured independently (also referred to as *"independent mode"*) and perform memory-to-memory operations. This causes a per-block round-trip through main memory. However, online documentation poorly describes those operating modes. More details will be provided in Sect. 4.2.

4   NVDLA Network Compiler

The NVDLA's *Compiler* takes care of the Neural Network (NN) framework interpretation and of the operations for functional units mapping. Its routine revolves around two primary operations: input files parsing and execution code generation. An NVDLA environment refers to the compiled file containing the information for the complete execution of a Deep-Learning model as *".loadable"* file.

It is worth noticing that the NVDLA's original Compiler is compatible only with the *Caffe* Neural Network Framework. Nevertheless, different alternative solutions are available online. Talking about the direct support by NVIDIA, the TensorRT library [31] is an open-source AI toolchain and runtime software developed for Jetson boards. It fully supports the ONNX framework and is capable of advanced NN compiling features (e.g., kernel auto-tuning, layers and tensors fusion, etc.). Although, it natively targets NVIDIA Jetson boards, thanks to its open-source availability, it may be adapted to different NVDLA-based SoCs.

Regarding the third parties support, Skymizer developed an ONNX Compiler with a dedicated NVDLA backend [9]. The Open Neural Network Compiler (ONNC) is capable of the same features of the initially developed Compiler by NVIDIA, but with a greater focus on customization simplicity and flexibility. Additionally, it has been reported to support more networks than the original NVIDIA Compiler (see Ref. [8]).

4.1 Compiler Workflow

The NVDLA Compiler is released as a set of APIs available in the UMD source code. The Compiler is structured into a frontend and a backend. The frontend coincides with the NN model parser, the backend instead implements compiling routines, which are composed, among other things, of the network model-to-hardware units assignment procedure, the memory allocation routine and the graph optimization. NVIDIA provides a Compiler executable for *Caffe*-based Neural Network models which relies on Google's Protocol Buffer library.

The NVDLA Compiler execution always starts with the parsing operation. The Compiler takes a pre-trained *Caffe* network (composed of a *".prototxt"* file containing the model description and a *".caffemodel"* file containing the trained weights), and produces a first intermediate representation of the network. This first representation consists of an oriented graph where nodes are network layers, and edges are features and weights data cubes. Next, the Compiler realizes a second inspection of this graph and associates to every network layer a different hardware unit to perform it, compliant to the layer behaviour. Last, several optimization cycles are performed on top of this graph to resolve data and control dependencies.

During the optimization cycles mentioned above, many essential routines take place. One relevant example is the convolutions splitting process. Since NVDLA's CMAC unit size is user-defined, it is expected that bigger convolutions are not fitting it. Thus, the Compiler separates them in several different hardware layers to be processed in sequence (see Fig. 5).

As stated in Sect. 3, the convolution engine has no write-dedicated DMA, and every convolution operation result is sent to the SDP engine. Since data coming from the CONV engine are not automatically retrieved from the SDP, the Compiler appends to every CONV layer an SDP "no-operation" (NOP), to make it write out its input. Since most of the convolutions in NNs are followed by activations, the Compiler then optimizes the graph by merging adjacent SDP operations, whenever possible. As a result, the number of scheduled SDP operations is always equal or bigger than the number of convolutions performed (see Fig. 5).

NVIDIA chose to make its DLA compatible with the FP16 and INT8 data types. However, many NN frameworks (and *Caffe* as well) rely on a 32-bit Floating-Point data type (FP32) to improve training precision.

The conversion between the original FP32 data and an FP16 or even INT8 data is automatically handled by the Compiler. However, a calibration table should be used to simplify the work that may not turn out successful in the most complex transformations (i.e., from FP32 to INT8, see Ref. [33]). Finally, when the entire network's data are converted, the Compiler reserves memory entries for them in a virtualized memory environment.

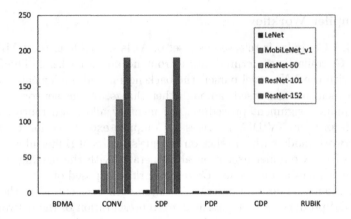

Fig. 5. Hardware Layers programmed for each functional unit (hereby compiled for the "Full" configuration). The CONV operations number is always equal or bigger than the network's convolutions number because of the splitting mechanism. The number of SDP is never less than the CONV operations, due to the NOPs appended to every CONV operation performed.

Together with the above operations, the Compiler performs additional transformations. Among them, this software updates the tensors sizes for optimizing element-wise operations in the SDP engine or pre-processes the network's auxiliary data.

Last, the Compiler can also support operations that are not natively accelerated by the NVDLA's hardware. This feature is mainly available for the *"SoftMax"* non-linear function. To achieve the SoftMax support, the Compiler produces a particular hardware layer labelled as "emulator-dedicated". EMU-dedicated hardware layers are network operations not supported by the hardware that must be executed by the Runtime environment instead and, thus, by the CPU where the software is running on.

When all the above operations are successfully performed, the Compiler serializes the network's graph representation and translates the whole data structure into a list of addresses and configuration values. The whole memory stack containing the network compiled information is finally saved into the loadable file.

4.2 Supported Features

The original NVDLA Compiler supports only the "Full", "Large" and "Small" configurations, but can be extended to additional configurations by customizing the proper data structure present in the source code. However, NVIDIA fully verified all the three available configurations ("Full", "Large" and "Small") only for the MNIST, ResNet-18 and ResNet-50 models, providing an INT8 calibration table only for ResNet-50.

Table 1. NVDLA's Compiler supported features per data path (a) and supported functional units per configuration backend (b)

Functional Unit	Feature	FP16	INT8
CONV	Direct Conv.	Yes	Yes
	Dilatation Conv.	Yes	Yes
	Winograd Conv.	Yes	Yes
	Deconvolution	Yes	Yes
	Fully Connected	Yes	Yes
	Group Conv.	Yes	No
	Winograd Group Conv.	Yes	No
PDP	Pooling (min/max/avg)	Yes	Yes
SDP	Bias Addition	Yes	Yes
	Batch Norm.	Yes	Yes
	Scale	Yes	Yes
	Sigmoid	Yes	No
	Tanh	Yes	No
	EltWise SUM	Yes	Yes
	EltWise SUB	No	No
	EltWise MIN	Yes	No
	EltWise MAX	Yes	No
CDP	LRN	Yes	No

Unit	Full	Large	Small
Winograd	No	No	No
Compress Weights	No	No	No
PDP	Yes	Yes	Yes
CDP	Yes	Yes	Yes
SDP Bias	Yes	Yes	Yes
SDP BatchNorm	Yes	Yes	Yes
SDP EW	Yes	Yes	No
SDP LUT	Yes	Yes	No
BDMA	Yes	No	No
RUBIK	Yes	No	No

(a) *(b)*

Even if the Compiler can support a vast amount of different features, not all of them are implemented in practice (see Table 1). For example, the procedures to perform Winograd Convolutions are available in both the presented data path, but to date none of the available Compiler's backends can produce a loadable file supporting this algorithm. The same happens for the weight compression capability.

Different considerations hold for the LUT sub-engines in SDP and CDP units. The software must configure those units in order to use non-linear activation functions on them. To offload the Runtime and speed-up the execution, the Compiler already determines the configuration register values for the LUT programming.

Therefore, to implement a non-linear function in the LUT engines, the Compiler must contain a quantized version of the selected function and a dedicated subset of routines determining the configuration registers' values to program it into the hardware. Even if the Compiler supports LUT engines in both the "Full" and "Large" configurations, the functions' quantized descriptions are not available for all the datapaths (see Table 1). More precisely, *Sigmoid* and *Tanh* activations functions are available for the "Full" configuration, but not for the "Large" configuration.

The same happens with the LRN operations in the CDP engine. Since this unit is LUT-based, a quantized version of the non-linear function must be provided and programmed into the hardware. Like Sigmoid and Tanh, a quantized version of the LRN is available in the Compiler's code for the FP16 data path, but not for the INT8 data path, thus no LRN support is available in the "Large" configuration.

Another Compiler's duty consists of serializing the network's graph representation. That means the Compiler determines the precise functional units' execution order and optimizes it. Since NVDLA can combine the CONV, SDP and PDP engines, the Compiler decides if those units are operating independently (*independent mode*) or in a single pipelined chain (*fused mode*, or "on-the-fly* *processing"* in the online programming guide). Independent and fused modes are always available and supported since all the provided NVDLA configurations contain the involved units.

The CONV and SDP pipelining is always available since the CONV unit has no direct write back to the memory interface but always passes through the SDP engine. Nevertheless, currently the fused mode is only supported for *"ReLU"* activations, while executing a *"No Operation"* in SDP to write back the convolution result in other cases.

Last, if CONV and SDP units are pipelined, the Compiler always tries to append the PDP operations whenever possible. However, this is possible only when the PDP buffer size is compliant to the SDP output size. This means that if the software splits a convolution layer into more hardware layers, PDP pipelining is not possible.

5   Software Runtime Analysis

NVDLA's Runtime is composed of two drivers, named UMD and KMD. While UMD mainly takes care of data preparation, KMD contains the functional unit scheduler and the hardware abstraction layer.

UMD is available to the developer as a set of C++ APIs. NVIDIA provides a sample main routine for image recognition tasks, containing the input image pre-processing and basic routines calling the UMD APIs for network loading and task submission.

User-Mode Driver contains an *"Emulator"*, a software extension to DLA's capabilities. Thanks to the Emulator, the UMD can offload the execution of specific layers to the CPU. In the original UMD and Compiler, this is used to perform *SoftMax* activation functions.

Kernel-Mode Driver contains the functional units scheduler and the hardware abstraction layer. Since the network model interpretation and resource assignment have already been made by the Compiler, the functional unit scheduling restrict itself to a temporal assignment of the hardware layers to free units.

One of the main goals of this chapter is to shed light on the performance of the Runtime environment. A porting of the whole software stack on the industry-standard Zynq UltraScale+ MPSoC (ZCU102) is presented to assess it, including a bare-metal implementation of the Runtime software in order to hide the additional overheads introduced by the Operating System.

5.1   Bare-Metal Implementation

A bare-metal version of the NVDLA firmware can be derived and ported to one core of the 64-bit ARM Cortex A53 host processor on this platform, running at 1.2 GHz. The board's DRAM memory sub-system revolves around a 4 GB Micron MTA4ATF51264HZ device configured to reach a peak bandwidth of 21.3 GB/s. This speed is enough for the requirements of the DNNs that will be tested later [32]. Without a lack of generality, the board SD Card is used as the repository for the input loadable file and for the images to be processed.

According to NVDLA's drivers' structure, the porting must be accomplished mainly by re-writing their portability layers. To simplify the hardware management, Xilinx provides a group of software libraries (named "standalone" in case of bare-metal software) for the Zynq UltraScale+ MPSoC boards family. Thus, those libraries were exploited to achieve the file system support (to read images and loadable file from the I/O unit), interrupt control (to interact with NVDLA hardware) and dynamic memory management (extensively used by the UMD). The file system support is not essential, but allows to reuse a big part of the available software without strongly patching the Compiler and the Runtime.

Since the focus is on the performance assessment of UMD essential routines, the Emulator code section is not ported, containing the SoftMax non-linear function implementation. This even simplifies the UMD porting since no half-precision Floating-Point (FP16) support is required anymore.

The original Linux drivers implementation relies on file descriptors to manage the communication between the two drivers, using virtualized memory regions for data exchange. As a workaround, specific data structures are instantiated as an exchange area between UMD and KMD. The actual exchange routines take place via *memcpy()* operations.

The NVDLA's original drivers communicate with each other through an *ioctl()* mechanism. Therefore, the original *ioctl()* methods have to be converted into lightweight standard C routines, which can be invoked by the UMD-to-KMD interface functions.

Last, since the UMD hadn't been initially developed for a bare-metal environment, many routines in the UMD portability layer (that largely correspond to the UMD-to-KMD interface) are thought to be invoked during the UMD associated process creation and closure. Those procedures are mainly unnecessary for a single-process environment like the one considered in this chapter, while the memory reservation mechanism (easily replaced by a *malloc()*) and the initialization procedures (to initialize the interrupt handler and the hardware-related parameters like the NVDLA's address) can be relevant for other contexts.

After the Runtime's bare-metal porting, the latter consists of a unified execution flow where the developer can focus on key Runtime operations rather than on the driver entities that perform them. Therefore, key Runtime operations include:

- **Network loading.** It transfers a pre-compiled loadable file from an I/O device (in our case, the SD Card) to main memory.
- **Test operation.** It performs image reading, data preparation and fills up a data structure with task scheduling information.
- **Submit operation.** It schedules operations to the accelerator's functional units, with which interaction takes place through the hardware abstraction layer.

In order to assess the software stack of the NVDLA framework in isolation, the hardware execution should be assumed to occur in zero time. This can be achieved by disabling write/read operations to/from the accelerator registers in the KMD, and by virtually driving interrupt responses of the accelerator to the hardware abstraction layer, under the assumption of instantaneous execution of scheduled commands.

Achieving the latter object is relatively easy. The inference always starts with the UMD sending an "NVDLA task" to the KMD. The task is a decompressed version of the loadable file, containing a list of hardware layers to be performed, their dependencies and a set of memory addresses pointing to the weights data allocated in main memory. The KMD performs the task in a functional unit scheduling wheel, where at each cycle, a new operation is programmed in the NVDLA's registers, then a "wait for interrupt" statement is performed. At the arrival of the interrupt, the KMD reads the functional units' status and determines which operations have completed. With this information, the KMD updates the task dependencies and programs the next operation to be executed.

To virtually drive the interrupts, the registers interactions are hidden and the operation programmed data saved directly in a variable. Then, the interrupt handler function is manually called, and the correct flag is set according to the saved data.

5.2 Runtime Performance

To evaluate the Runtime performance, Zynq Cortex's APU Global Counter can be used. If clocked at 100 MHz, Runtime execution time measurement turn out to have a precision of 10 ns.

Regarding the tested DNNs, their Caffe models have been compiled with the baseline NVDLA Compiler provided by NVIDIA. According to what presented in Sect. 4.2, compiling for different NVDLA configurations mainly results in different functional units availability, different data path precision and convolutional pipeline characteristics. In order to characterize the software stack, all the DNNs under test have to be compiled for the NVDLA "Large" configuration of the accelerator hardware, with a batch size of 1.

As anticipated in Sect. 5.1, the key Runtime operations include compiled Network Loading, Test operation and task Submit. Next, the assessment of the performance of these operations is provided.

As shown in Fig. 6, the network Loading time dominates over that of other operations, due to reading of the loadable file from SD Card. On the target board, the loading time turns out to be slightly better than a similar operation performed from Flash memory, given the bandwidths of the devices under test: 100 MByte/s for the SD card vs. a peak bandwidth of up to 90 MByte/s for the Flash memory. It is worth recalling that network loading occurs only occasionally for DNN model update, while Test operation and Submit are performed at each inference. Therefore, from now on, our focus will be only on Test and Submit.

In contrast, the scheduler and the hardware abstraction layers (see "Submit" column) run much faster, mainly because the DNN interpretation has already been realized during the compilation phase. Thus, Runtime scheduling restricts only to task-to-functional unit assignment over time. As a result, the "Submit" time grows with the number of schedulable "hardware layers" the DNN is broken into by the Compiler, and that the KMD scheduler will process.

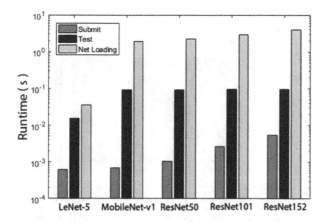

Fig. 6. Execution time of the key operations of the NVDLA Runtime for different DNNs under test. Image format: 28 × 28 pixels for LeNet-5, 224 × 224 pixels for the others.

While the "Submit" time scales with the computational cost of the DNN under test, the Test operation time shows a tighter correlation with the format of the input dataset (MNIST for LeNet-5 vs. ImageNet for the remaining DNNs). This results from the breakdown in Fig. 7, which shows the contribution of the image loading time from SD card (in yellow). Clearly, the Test execution time is dominated by data preparation on the ARM and DRAM subsystems, and not by the I/O unit.

Next, under the assumption of instantaneous hardware execution, it is possible to characterize sustainable software throughput. In order to get realistic performance estimates, the assumption is that the image to be processed is already in DRAM. As a result, the Test routine remains the throughput bottleneck and does not enable a frame rate higher than roughly 20 frames-per-second for ImageNet-processing DNN models, and 120 fps for LeNet-5. The Submit operation alone would enable up to 1600 fps for LeNet-5 and slightly more than 200 fps for the most complex Resnet152.

It is important to observe that the Test operation is hardware-independent and memory-centric, thus the NVDLA Runtime environment gives rise to a significant software overhead. Therefore, using NVIDIA precompiled testbenches to project accelerator frame rate may be misleading, since limitations dictated by the software stack are not accounted for.

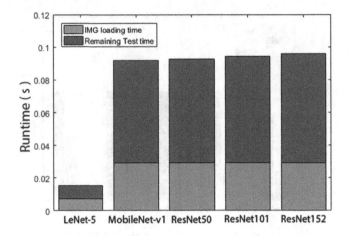

Fig. 7. Breakdown of the test execution time.

6   Hardware Synthesis

One of the distinctive features of NVDLA is hardware configurability. For the sake of coherent analysis, the Xilinx's Zynq UltraScale+ MPSoC is also used as target platform as already done for the software stack. More in detail, NVDLA model was synthesized and mapped for the Programmable Logic (PL) of the ZCU102 board.

In all tested configurations, the accelerator is inferred as a single clock domain. No specific mapping optimization to heterogeneous FPGA resources was applied. Thus, absolute performance measurements reported in this chapter have to be considered as pessimistic.

6.1   Inspected Hardware Configurations

NVDLA currently comes with several pre-compiled hardware configurations. All the main stable configurations for an FPGA synthesis will be tested. A detailed description can be found in Table 2. They encompass "Small", "Medium" and "Large" or even "Full" instances. All of them share a common baseline feature: they instantiate all the functional units of the accelerator, except for RUBIK. Moreover, the usage of the SRAM interface is configuration-specific.

Instead, they mainly differ by the target data type, the number of instantiated MACs and the buffer size in the convolutional unit, batch size, and by DNN algorithmic features such as weight compression or Winograd convolution (which correspond to matching hardware units).

The "Full" version includes, among the other things, Winograd convolution, weight compression, a batch size of 32, 2048 MACs (organized as 16 MAC cells, 64 multipliers each), INT8/FP16 data path and a dedicated SRAM interface. In this configuration, internal optimizations are enabled in the SDP, PDP and

CDP in order to maximize throughput. The 16 FP16 MAC cells can be re-configured to support multiple data path as 32 INT8 MAC cells. Overall, it is a high-end instantiation of a deep-learning accelerator aiming at memory-efficient high-performance inference. The "Large" configuration is directly retrieved from the "Full" configuration while relying only on an INT8 data path.

The "Small" configuration exhibits a baseline convolutional pipeline without the optional memory interface, and a tighter resource budget for reduced area and power requirements, including 64 MACs (organized as 8 MAC cells, 8 multipliers each), INT8 data path, and a batch size of 1. To further diminish the area foot-print, the SDP engine cannot perform element-wise operations between two input feature data cubes and its LUT-based activation unit is not present (see Table 2 for all details). The "Medium" configuration directly enhances the "Small" con-figurations, enlarging the MAC array size and the other units' throughput.

Table 2. Tested hardware configurations. *Atomic_K* is always referred to INT8 data precision

	Data Type	Total MACs	Atomic C	Atomic K	CBUF (KB)	SDP	PDP	CDP	Winograd Support	Weight Compression	Batch Size
nv_small	Int8	64	8	8	128	Yes	Yes	Yes	No	No	1
nv_small_256	Int8	256	32	8	128	Yes	Yes	Yes	No	No	1
nv_medium_512	Int8	512	32	16	512	Yes	Yes	Yes	No	No	1
nv_large	Int8	2048	64	32	512	Yes	Yes	Yes	Yes	Yes	32
nv_full	Int8/Fp16	2048	64	32	512	Yes	Yes	Yes	Yes	Yes	32

	SDP E-W Support	SDP LUT Support	SDP Throughput (op/cycle)	SDP E-W Throughput (op/cycle)	PDP Throughput (op/cycle)	CDP Throughput (op/cycle)	RUBIK Support	SRAM Mem. If.
nv_small	No	No	1	-	1	1	No	No
nv_small_256	No	No	1	-	1	1	No	No
nv_medium_512	No	No	4	-	2	2	No	No
nv_large	Yes	Yes	16	4	8	8	Yes	Yes
nv_full	Yes	Yes	16	4	8	8	Yes	Yes

6.2 Implementation Synthesis Results

Table 3 reports FPGA resource utilization for the configurations under test. Interestingly, even the smallest accelerator instance ("Small" configuration) takes already 43% of available CLBs, an utilization that grows to 84% for the "Medium" configuration. From these tests, the "Large" and "Full" architectures are so overprovisioned that they do not fit the Programmable Logic of the Zynq UltraScale+ platform, which questions their deployment in cost-sensitive appli-cation domains.

More in detail, the second column of Table 3 shows an extensive logic LUT utilization, which grows from 25% in the "Small" configuration to 47% in the "Medium" one. MAC units occupy only 10% of the LUTs in the "Small" baseline configuration and roughly add from 60 to 90 additional LUTs for each increment in the number of MACs, which depends on the specific configurations.

Table 3. Synthesized hardware resource utilization

	LUTs	LUTRAMs	FFs	BRAMs	DSP slices	CLB occupation
nv_small	68927	196	69347	100	41	43%
nv_small_256	90871	196	92830	165	41	57%
nv_medium_512	130532	200	116364	187	75	84%

Simultaneously, the number of instantiated DSP slices is quite limited: from 1.63% in "Small" to 2.98% in "Medium". This points to an inherent limitation of the released source code of the accelerator: it natively targets ASIC implementation and is not optimized to make extensive use of DSP slices of the target FPGA. The root cause for such inefficient use of DSPs may be identified in the logic-level specification of convolutional's unit multipliers. In facts, MAC cells multipliers' gate-level description biases the synthesis tool interpreter toward a LUT-based implementation of those hardware elements.

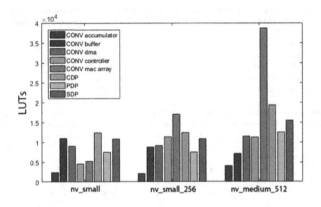

Fig. 8. LUT occupation for each NVDLA functional unit.

Allocated DSP slices are in the Convolution DMA, which uses them for address manipulation, and especially in the CDP engine. In those units, multiplications are described as arithmetic operations and modelled with a more abstract behavioural syntax, thus mapping to DSP slices is straightforward for the synthesis tool. As a result, when target CDP performance is boosted in the transition from "Small 256" to "Medium" configurations, hardware redundancy is used to meet the requirement, which results in a doubled allocation of DSP slices. Source code optimizations for better use of DSP slices in the convolutional pipeline is an active research and development area.

For each hardware configuration under test, Fig. 8 illustrates a breakdown of LUT occupation into the individual functional units. Only interfaces to external busses are omitted since constant throughout the configurations and lightweight with respect to reported results (e.g., 300 LUTs for the CSB interface).

We can first notice that the LUT occupation of the MAC array significantly changes across configurations. In the "Small" one, the MAC array area is irrelevant compared to contributions of other functional units, while in the "Medium" configuration it becomes as large as 30% of the total LUT count.

Besides the MAC array, the CDP makes the most extensive usage of LUTs, followed by the SDP engine. In particular, the number of LUTs in both CDP, PDP, and SDP increases from "Small 256" to "Medium" due to the boost in these functional units' throughput requirements.

(a)   *(b)*   *(c)*

Fig. 9. NVDLA CBUF bank structure in three different configurations. nv_small, SRAM macros = 8-Byte × 256 each (a); nv_small_256, SRAM macros = 8-Byte × 128 each (b); nv_medium, SRAM macros = 16-Byte × 128 each (c)

Observing the Convolutional Buffer (CBUF), we can notice a counterintuitive trend in LUT (Fig. 8) and BRAM allocation (Table 3). Starting from the "Small" configuration, the CBUF LUT utilization decreases with the growth of the CBUF size (from 128 kB to 512 kB). At the same time, the BRAM utilization has a significant increase in the transition from "Small" to "Small 256" architectures (i.e., from 64 to 128 BRAMs, which determines a similar trend also for the total number of BRAMs allocated by the design as a whole). However, the allocated BRAMs remain stable in the transition from "Small 256" to "Medium" configurations.

This synthesis result is apparently unjustified observing the CBUF total size, which does not change between the "Small" configurations, but increases in the "Medium" one. The explanation can be found in the way the CBUF is organized. In all the tested configurations, NVDLA comes with 32 SRAM banks, but in the "Small" one they have a width of 8-Byte, which grows to 32-Byte data in the "Small 256" and "Medium" configurations.

The single buffer bank organization consists of a set of SRAM macros with a bitwidth of 64 in the two "Small" architectures (see Fig. 9). Therefore, when the MAC array needs to be fed with a 64-bit input ("Small" case), one macro would be enough. However, in order to increase the buffer depth, the "Small" configuration combines two SRAMs into a unique aggregate macro, while leaving the output bitwidth unaffected.

When the bitwidth increases to 256 bits ("Small 256" and "Medium" cases), the CBUF aggregates 4 64-bit macros to provide it in "Small 256", and 2 128-bit macros in "Medium".

The mapping of these convolution buffer configurations to FPGA turns out to be sub-optimal. In fact, both the 16 kb SRAM macros in the "Small" configuration and the 8 kb macros of the "Small 256" configuration are exclusively mapped to 36 kb BRAMs of the FPGA. The result is twofold. On the one hand, this explains the increase in allocated BRAMs in Table 3 when moving from "Small" to "Small 256" despite the convolutional buffer size stays the same. On the other hand, this mapping results in a total of 2304 Kb occupied memory for the "Small" and 4608 Kb for the "Small 256" instances versus a request of only 1024 Kb in both cases.

When moving to the "Medium" configuration, the SRAM macro size grows to 64 Kb, which exceeds the BRAM size, hence justifying the FPGA synthesis and mapping tools (Vivado) choice to map each macro to two different 36 Kb BRAMs. Thus, the number of occupied BRAMs is the same as in "Small 256" (see Table 3). However, memory utilization efficiency is better: 4608 Kb of memory is occupied versus the requested 4096 Kb. Overall, the "Medium" configuration makes more efficient use of memory resources than the lower-end ones.

Finally, the different convolution buffer organization leads to different complexity of the multiplexing and control logic. From Fig. 8, the "Small" configuration takes more LUTs in its CBUF due to an additional multiplexing layer to aggregate SRAM macros. Moreover, "Medium" reduces the used LUTs in CBUF with respect to "Small 256" because only two SRAM macros have to be combined to provide the target bitwidth instead of 4.

Table 4. Synthesized hardware timing

	Clock speed	ResNet-50 (frame/sec)
nv_small	130 MHz	0.95
nv_small_256	130 MHz	5.98
nv_medium_512	80 MHz	7.44

Moving the discussion to the hardware execution time, we can observe the clock speed and inference performance results reported in Table 4. We observe a 38% reduction of the clock speed only for the "Medium" configuration.

In order to factor in the clock speed to assess inference performance, we assume the ResNet-50 DNN as a benchmark. From the "Small" to the "Small 256" configuration, an allocation of 4× the number of MACs results in an inference rate improvement by 6×.

When we move from "Small 256" to "Medium", the benefits of doubling the number of MACs, improving the convolutional buffer size and speeding up the functional unit throughput are partly offset by the more complex hardware and the lower operating speed. Therefore, the inference rate speedup is only 1.2× (instead of the theoretical 2×), achieved with a number of CLBs which is 1.4×, thus giving rise to an unbalanced cost-benefit trade-off for "Medium".

7   End-to-End HW/SW Performance and Optimizations

For a single inference of the ResNet-50 DNN, the hardware and software execution times have been combined. The software stack has been characterized for the "Large" configuration, but it is matched to the performance of a "Medium" accelerator instance since the only difference, i.e., the Submit time, would be negligible. Assuming a batch size of 1 (which is the only possible in the "Medium" and smaller configurations), 63 ms have to be budgeted for the software stack (the Test operation takes two orders of magnitude longer than Submit) and 134 ms for hardware inference in the "Medium" configuration. Overall, the resulting frame rate amounts to 5.13 fps. For the "Small" configuration, the frame rate can be as small as 1 fps.

As a future optimization, it is conceivable to parallelize data preparation with hardware operation. Since the total frame rate is currently hardware-dominated, the expected upper bound consists of the 7.44 fps derived in Table 4 for "Medium", while no noticeable improvement is expected for "Small". One way to quickly achieve this modification may be to restore the original UMD and KMD software entities and make them work in parallel on two different processing cores. Since original drivers act independently, their execution can be pipelined.

As far as hardware is concerned, future performance optimizations may come from better FPGA heterogeneous resource utilization. A significant re-writing of the MAC cells source code may involve DSP slices in the convolutional pipeline, enhancing the CMAC throughput. Second, onboard BRAMs can be better exploited to implement both CBUF's and other units' memories. Moreover, since those modifications reduce the LUT occupation and better use the already available FPGA resources, the total CLB usage will likely be reduced. Thus, this would enable smaller NVDLA configurations to fit the programmable logic of low-end devices as well.

Last but not least, since not all NVDLA functional units are always addressed (as seen in Sect. 4.2) and the Runtime is mainly configuration-independent, many NVDLA sub-units can be removed from the hardware "spec" file, without significant modifications of the hardware/software stack (e.g., CDP unit in "Small" configuration). This will lead to even smaller hardware footprints, without loss in performance or functionalities.

8   Conclusions

The NVIDIA Deep-Learning Accelerator is a promising project bringing an industrial-grade design to the open-source community. However, even if a rich hardware architecture has been released, the software's available support and documentation are reduced and must be enhanced by the community.

The exploration of the software stack reported in this chapter revealed the Compiler not to be optimized for hardware configurations different from "Full". At the same time, not all the functionalities available in hardware are adequately exploited in the software stack. LUTs engines are fully supported only for the FP16-capable architectures, while the Compiler support for INT8-based architectures is reduced. Moreover, additional functionalities such as Winograd convolutions, weight compression or the additional memory interface for the "Large" configuration are unsupported even when available in the instantiated hardware.

Moving to the hardware implementation, this chapter reports on the DNN accelerator mapping onto the commercial Xilinx UltraScale+ MPSoC and its integrated reconfigurable logic. The analysis revealed that the pre-compiled "Large" and "Full" configurations are overprovisioned for cost-effective Edge computing platforms. The "Medium" configuration makes effective use of FPGA memory resources and provides the best performance, but exhibits an unfavourable cost-benefit trade-off with respect to the "Small 256" configuration.

Finally, the chapter projects some optimization possibilities from the observation of the more evident bottlenecks. For instance, the frame rate on the target platform is currently hardware-dominated: it achieves roughly 5 fps for ResNet-50, potentially extended up to 8 fps, while future optimizations of hardware performance (including synthesis for ASIC) will bring a software-limited throughput of 20 fps to the forefront.

References

1. Chen, J., Ran, X.: Deep learning with edge computing: a review. Proc. IEEE **107**(8), 1655–16674 (2019). https://doi.org/10.1109/JPROC.2019.2921977
2. DiCecco, R., Lacey, G., Vasiljevic, J., Chow, P., Taylor, G., Areibi, S.: Caffeinated FPGAs: FPGA framework for convolutional neural networks. In: Proceedings of the 2016 International Conference on FPT, pp. 265–268 (2016). https://doi.org/10.1109/FPT.2016.7929549
3. Farshchi, F., Huang, Q., Yun, H.: Integrating NVIDIA deep learning accelerator (NVDLA) with RISC-V SoC on FireSim. arXiv preprint (2019). arXiv:1903.06495v2
4. Genc, H., et al.: Gemmini: an agile systolic array generator enabling systematic evaluations of deep-learning architectures. arXiv preprint (2019). arXiv:1911.09925
5. Gonzalez, A., Hong, C.: A Chipyard Comparison of NVDLA and Gemmini. http://charleshong3.github.io/projects/nvdla_v_gemmini.pdf
6. Guoyu, C., Zhenjiang, P., Shanggong, F., Dawei, W., Jingwen, C., Shengang, Z.: Research on the architecture of edge computing SoC with ultra-low power. In: Proceedings of the 2020 IEEE 3rd International Conference on Electronics Technology (ICET), pp. 54–57 (2020). https://doi.org/10.1109/ICET49382.2020.9119600
7. Krizhevsky, A., Sutskever, I., Hinton, G.E.: ImageNet classification with deep convolutional neural networks. In: Proceedings of Advances in Neural Information Processing Systems, pp. 84–90 (2012). https://doi.org/10.1145/3065386
8. Lin, W., Hsieh, C., Chou, C.: ONNC-based software development platform for configurable NVDLA designs. In: Proceedings of the 2019 International Symposium on VLSI Design, Automation and Test (VLSI-DAT), pp. 1–2 (2019). https://doi.org/10.1109/VLSI-DAT.2019.8741778

9. Lin, W., et al.: ONNC: a compilation framework connecting ONNX to proprietary deep learning accelerators. In: Proceedings of the 2019 IEEE International Conference on AICAS, pp. 214–218 (2019). https://doi.org/10.1109/AICAS.2019.8771510
10. Liu, S.-M., Tang, L., Huang, N.-C., Tsai, D.-Y., Yang, M.-X., Wu, K.-C.: Fault-tolerance mechanism analysis on NVDLA-based design using open neural network compiler and quantization calibrator. In: Proceedings of the 2020 International Symposium on VLSI Design, Automation and Test (VLSI-DAT), pp. 1–3 (2020). https://doi.org/10.1109/VLSI-DAT49148.2020.9196335
11. Lu, L., Liang, Y., Xiao, Q., Yan, S.: Evaluating fast algorithms for convolutional neural networks on FPGAs. In: Proceedings of the 25th IEEE International Symposium on FCCM, pp. 101–108 (2017). https://doi.org/10.1109/FCCM.2017.64
12. Luo, S.: Customization of a deep learning accelerator. In: Proceedings of the 2019 International Symposium on VLSI-DAT, pp. 1–2 (2019). https://doi.org/10.1109/VLSI-DAT.2019.8741855
13. Moreau, T., Chen, T., Jiang, Z., Ceze, L., Guestrin, C., Krishnamurthy, A.: VTA: an open hardware-software stack for deep learning. arXiv preprint abs/1807.04188 (2018)
14. Qiu, J., et al.: Going deeper with embedded FPGA platform for convolutional neural network. In: Proceedings of the 2016 ACM/SIGDA International Symposium on Field-Programmable Gate Arrays, pp. 26–35 (2016). https://doi.org/10.1145/2847263.2847265
15. Shawahna, A., Sait, S.M., El-Maleh, A.: FPGA-based accelerators of deep learning networks for learning and classification: a review. IEEE Access 7, 7823–7859 (2019). https://doi.org/10.1109/ACCESS.2018.2890150
16. Suda, N., et al.: Throughput-optimized OpenCL-based FPGA accelerator for large-scale convolutional neural networks. In: Proceedings of the 2016 ACM/SIGDA International Symposium on Field-Programmable Gate Arrays, pp. 16–25 (2016). https://doi.org/10.1145/2847263.2847276
17. Sze, V., Chen, Y.H., Yang, T.J., Emer, J.S.: Efficient processing of deep neural networks: a tutorial and survey. Proc. IEEE 105(12), 2295–2329 (2017). https://doi.org/10.1109/JPROC.2017.2761740
18. Szegedy, C., et al.: Going deeper with convolutions. In: Proceedings of 2015 IEEE Conference on Computer Vision and Pattern Recognition (CVPR), pp. 1–9 (2014). https://doi.org/10.1109/CVPR.2015.7298594
19. Udupa, P., Mahale, G., Chandrasekharan, K.K., Lee, S.: Accelerating depthwise convolution and pooling operations on z-first storage CNN architectures. In: Proceedings of the 2020 IEEE International Symposium on Circuits and Systems (ISCAS), pp. 1–5 (2020). https://doi.org/10.1109/ISCAS45731.2020.9180863
20. Veronesi, A., Krstic, M., Bertozzi, D.: Cross-layer hardware/software assessment of the open-source NVDLA configurable deep learning accelerator. In: Proceedings of the 28th IFIP/IEEE International Conference on Very Large Scale Integration (VLSI-SoC), pp. 1–6 (2020). https://doi.org/10.1109/VLSI-SOC46417.2020.9344109
21. Wang, D., Xu, K., Jiang, D.: PipeCNN: an OpenCL-based open-source FPGA accelerator for convolution neural networks. In: Proceedings of the 2017 International Conference on FPT, pp. 279–282 (2017). https://doi.org/10.1109/FPT.2017.8280160
22. Xu, Z., Abraham, J.: Design of a safe convolutional neural network accelerator. In: Proceedings of the 2019 IEEE Computer Society Annual Symposium on VLSI (ISVLSI), pp. 247–252 (2019). https://doi.org/10.1109/ISVLSI.2019.00053

23. Xu, Z., Abraham, J.: Safety design of a convolutional neural network accelerator with error localization and correction. In: Proceedings of the 2019 IEEE International Test Conference (ITC), pp. 1–10 (2019). https://doi.org/10.1109/ITC44170.2019.9000149
24. Yakun, S.S., et al.: Simba: scaling deep-learning inference with multi-chip-module-based architecture. In: Proceedings of the 52nd Annual IEEE/ACM International Symposium on Microarchitecture, pp. 14–27 (2019). https://doi.org/10.1145/3352460.3358302
25. Zhang, J., Li, J.: Improving the performance of OpenCL-based FPGA accelerator for convolutional neural network. In: Proceedings of the 2017 ACM/SIGDA International Symposium on Field-Programmable Gate Arrays, pp. 25–34 (2017). https://doi.org/10.1145/3020078.3021698
26. Zhang, X., et al.: DNNBuilder: an automated tool for building high-performance DNN hardware accelerators for FPGAs. In: Proceedings of the 2018 International Conference on Computer-Aided Design, pp. 1–8 (2018). https://doi.org/10.1145/3240765.3240801
27. Zhou, G., Zhou, J., Lin, H.: Research on NVIDIA deep learning accelerator. In: Proceedings of 12th IEEE International Conference on Anti-counterfeiting, Security, and Identification, pp. 192–195 (2018). https://doi.org/10.1109/ICASID.2018.8693202
28. Zhuge, C., Liu, X., Zhang, X., Gummadi, S., Xiong, J., Chen, D.: Face recognition with hybrid efficient convolution algorithms on FPGAs. In: Proceedings of the 2018 GLSVLSI Great Lakes Symposium on VLSI, pp. 123–128 (2018). https://doi.org/10.1145/3194554.3194597
29. Internet: GitHub issue #110: NVDLA running on a FPGA platform. github.com/nvdla/hw/issues
30. Internet: NVIDIA Jetson modules. https://www.nvidia.com/en-us/autonomous-machines/embedded-systems/
31. Internet: NVIDIA TensorRT library. developer.nvidia.com/tensorrt
32. Internet: NVDLA open source project. nvdla.org
33. Internet: NVDLA low precision support. github.com/nvdla/sw/blob/v1.2.0-OC/LowPrecision.md
34. Internet: RISC-V Foundation. riscv.org

SAT-Based Mapping of Data-Flow Graphs onto Coarse-Grained Reconfigurable Arrays

Yukio Miyasaka[1]([⊠]), Masahiro Fujita[2], Alan Mishchenko[1],
and John Wawrzynek[1]

[1] UC Berkeley, Berkeley, CA, USA
yukio_miyasaka@berkeley.edu
[2] The University of Tokyo, Tokyo, Japan

Abstract. Recently, it has been common to use parallel processing for machine learning. CGRAs are drawing attention in terms of reconfigurability and high performance. We propose a method to map data-flow graphs onto CGRAs by SAT solving. The proposed method can perform the automatic transformation which changes the order of operations in data-flow graphs to obtain more efficient schedules. It also accommodates mapping of multi-node operations like MAC operation. We have solved mapping problems of matrix-vector multiplication. In our experiment, a SAT solver outperformed an ILP solver. Our method successfully processed a data-flow graph of more than a hundred nodes. The automatic transformation under the associative and commutative laws was not as much scalable but successfully reduced the number of cycles, where the XBTree-based method worked faster than the enumeration-based method. As another direction, we tried to optimize a CGRA architecture according to a data-flow graph and were able to reduce its PEs and connections through incremental SAT solving.

Keywords: SAT problem · mapping · data-flow graph · CGRA

1 Introduction

Neural networks are used for machine learning in many fields including image recognition [1]. The calculation of neural network involves numerous MAC operations, and there have been many accelerators developed. For example, TPU [2] has a square mesh of MAC operation units and efficiently performs matrix multiplication in a pipelined manner.

On the other hand, fabricating an ASIC for each application is costly, and reconfigurable devices such as FPGAs attract attention these days. A CGRA (Coarse-Grained Reconfigurable Array) is a reconfigurable device that consists of ALU-like units, whereas an FPGA consists of LUTs. It has been shown that

© IFIP International Federation for Information Processing 2021
Published by Springer Nature Switzerland AG 2021
A. Calimera et al. (Eds.): VLSI-SoC 2020, IFIP AICT 621, pp. 113–131, 2021.
https://doi.org/10.1007/978-3-030-81641-4_6

CGRAs achieve higher performance and better energy-efficiency than FPGAs for domain-specific applications [3].

This paper proposes a SAT-based method for mapping data-flow graphs onto CGRAs. The optimality of the obtained schedule in terms of the number of cycles can be proved by checking the mapping problem with one less number of cycles is unsatisfiable. The proposed method can apply transformations to data-flow graphs during the mapping process by using XBTrees [4] that can implicitly express all possible orders of operations under the associative and commutative laws. Our method also supports mapping of multi-node operations.

In the experiments, we compared the XBTree-based transformation method with the enumeration-based method on mapping problems of matrix-vector multiplication. The XBTree-based method was able to solve the problems that cannot be solved in time by the enumeration-based method. Furthermore, as an additional attempt, we tried to optimize a CGRA architecture according to a data-flow graph. Through iterative synthesis with incremental SAT solving [5], we were able to remove several PEs and connections in a 3×3 square mesh architecture without degrading the performance for an AES data-flow graph.

This paper is organized as follows. Section 2 reviews related work and contrasts our approach. Section 3 explains the basics of SAT problem. Section 4 defines the mapping problem, explains the core of our SAT-based mapping method, and compares a SAT solver and an ILP solver. Section 5 explains the enumeration-based transformation methods proposed in our previous work and shows mapping results for sparse matrix multiplication as an example. Section 6 proposes the XBTree-based transformation method and compares it with the enumeration-based method on mapping of matrix vector multiplication. Section 7 explains a CGRA optimization method and shows a result for a mesh CGRA and an AES data-flow graph. Section 8 concludes the paper.

2   Related Work

There have been many studies on mapping onto CGRAs. A study [6] proposed MRRG (Modulo Routing Resource Graph), where the computational resources are duplicated by the number of cycles as the time-frame expansion, and performed simulated annealing under the law of causality. Recent studies replaced simulated annealing by ILP (Integer Linear Programming), which can prove the possibility of mapping in the given number of cycles [7]. We use a SAT solver instead of an ILP solver because the SAT solver worked faster than the ILP solver as shown in our preliminary experiment.

The studies above and others, as far as we know, did not modify the data-flow graphs generated by architecture-agnostic compilers. A study [8] proposed an approach using an encoding like an SMT (Satisfiability Modulo Theories) solver to map linear functions and optimize them during the mapping process, but it was limited to linear functions. Our method can automatically optimize data-flow graphs according to the architectures of CGRAs.

Some studies [9] mapped data-flow graphs at the level of assembly language, but we target high-level data-flow graphs where nodes correspond to arithmetic operations [10] or subroutines. Such a high-level description makes it easy for the mapper to optimize the calculation by changing the order of operations.

Our previous work [11] used a table to enumerate all possible orders of operations for the automatic transformation. That caused a combinational explosion where the number of intermediate values increases exponentially over the number of contiguous associative (and commutative) operations. To improve the scalability, this work adopts XBTrees and sorters. An XBTree is a binary tree with exchangers and can implicitly express all possible structures of binary trees with a specific number of leaf nodes. Besides, this paper extends the mapping method to optimization of CGRA architectures.

3 SAT Problem

A SAT (Satisfiability) problem is a problem to find an assignment to the variables that makes the given logic formula evaluate to true. If there is such an assignment, the logic formula is satisfiable (SAT); otherwise, it is unsatisfiable (UNSAT). The modern SAT solvers take a CNF (Conjunctive Normal Form) formula as an input. A CNF formula is a conjunction of clauses, a clause is a disjunction of literals, and a literal is a boolean variable or its negation.

For example, the CNF formula (1) consists of clauses a, $(\overline{a} \vee \overline{c})$, and $(\overline{a} \vee b \vee c)$, where a, $\overline{a}$, b, c, and $\overline{c}$ are the literals, and a, b, and c are the variables. This CNF formula is satisfiable with the assignment $(a, b, c) = (\text{true}, \text{true}, \text{false})$. If we add a clause $\overline{b}$ to it as shown in the CNF formula (2), it becomes unsatisfiable.

In many applications, we need to impose a constraint that more than K of the specified literals cannot be true at the same time. (3) is a typical representation of the constraint on N literals $\{a_0, a_1, ..., a_{N-1}\}$ with integer addition $(+)$, where it is assumed that true is 1 and false is 0 as an integer. This constraint is called an at most K constraint. In this paper, we used the bimander encoding [12] (with two literals in each group) if $K = 1$, and the sequential unary counter encoding [13] otherwise.

$$a \wedge (\overline{a} \vee \overline{c}) \wedge (\overline{a} \vee b \vee c) \tag{1}$$

$$a \wedge (\overline{a} \vee \overline{c}) \wedge (\overline{a} \vee b \vee c) \wedge \overline{b} \tag{2}$$

$$a_0 + a_1 + ... + a_{N-1} \leq K \tag{3}$$

4 Mapping Problem

4.1 Data-Flow Graph

A data-flow graph in this paper is a directed acyclic graph that represents calculation as trees of operations. We call the leaf nodes as input-nodes as they correspond to the input variables of the calculation. The internal nodes are called operator-nodes, and each of them represents one operation. The edges pass the values of nodes: the input variables of input-nodes, and the results

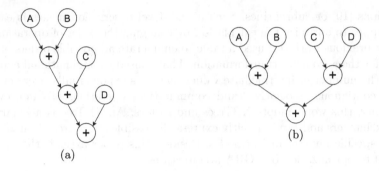

Fig. 1. Data-flow graphs for sum of four variables: A, B, C, and D.

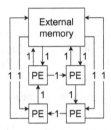

Fig. 2. A CGRA consisting of four PEs connected in a one-way ring.

of the operations of operator-nodes. An operator-node uses the received values as the operands of the operation. The incoming edges to an operator-node are labeled to specify the order of the operands when the operation is not commutative. The operator-nodes whose results are the outputs of the calculation are also called as result-nodes.

A data-flow graph is not a canonical representation. For example, there are multiple data-flow graphs for sum of four variables as shown in Fig. 1. The order of the operations is fixed in a data-flow graph even if it is arbitrary in nature. In this case, one can be transformed to the other under the associative law.

4.2   CGRA

We represent a CGRA as a directed graph. We call nodes and edges in CGRAs as components and paths respectively to distinguish those from those in data-flow graphs. There are three kinds of components: PE (Processing Element), memory, and external memory. Each PE has a given number of operation-units and registers. A memory holds the values received from other components, and its size is unlimited unless specified. For each memory, a user can specify the input variables that are stored in the memory in advance of the calculation, and even use it as a ROM by removing its incoming edges. The external memory is a memory that supplies the specified input variables and collects the outputs. It can store and pass intermediate values by a user setting. Each path is labeled by the number of values it can pass in one cycle. An example of CGRA is shown at Fig. 2.

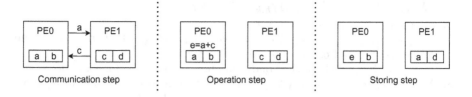

Fig. 3. An example of cycle.

We assume that all components in a CGRA are synchronized. We divide one cycle into three steps: communication step, operation step, and storing step as shown in Fig. 3. First, some of the values in the registers in PEs and the values in memories are passed to other components in the communication step. Next, each operation-unit performs at most one operation in the operation step. An operation-unit can use as the operands the values in the registers in the same PE and the values communicated to that PE in that cycle. Finally, in the storing step, the registers and memories store the values. A register stores one value from the values in the registers in the same PE, the results of the operations in that PE, and the values communicated to that PE in that cycle. A memory, if the number of residing values exceeds a specified limit, selects the values to discard.

4.3 SAT-Based Mapping

We create a CNF formula using three kinds of boolean variables shown below. Let i, j, k, and h be integers. We number (zero-based) the nodes in a data-flow graph and the components and the paths in a CGRA. Let node i denote the i-th node, component j denote the j-th component, path h denote the h-th path, and cycle k denote the k-th cycle. The range of k is from 0 to $N - 1$, where N is the number of cycles. In the following, node i also means the value of the node.

- $X_{i,j,k}$ ... node i exists in component j at the end of cycle k
- $Y_{i,h,k}$ ... node i is communicated in path h at cycle k
- $Z_{i,j,k}$ ... node i is calculated in component j at cycle k

$X_{i,j,k}$ means node i is stored (in the registers) in component j at cycle k.

The CNF is composed of the following clauses. Let H_j denote the set of incoming paths to component j, s_h denote the component at the origin of path h, component e denote the external memory, D_i denote the set of the nodes which are the operands (the nodes at the origins of the incoming edges) of node i, and O denote the set of the result-nodes.

1. $X_{i,j,0}$ for $\forall(i,j)$ where component j is a memory or external memory storing node i, which is an input-node, in advance of the calculation
2. $\neg X_{i,j,0}$ for $\forall(i,j)$ where the condition above is not met
3. $X_{i,e,N-1}$ for $\forall i \in O$

4. $\neg X_{i,j,k} \vee X_{i,j,k-1} \vee \bigvee_{h \in H_j} Y_{i,h,k} \vee Z_{i,j,k}$ for $\forall (i, j, k \neq 0)$
5. $\neg Y_{i,h,k} \vee X_{i,s_h,k-1}$ for $\forall (i, h, k \neq 0)$
6. $\neg Z_{i,j,k} \vee X_{d,j,k-1} \vee \bigvee_{h \in H_j} Y_{d,h,k}$ for $\forall d \in D_i$, for $\forall (i, j)$ where node i is an operator-node and component j is a PE, for $\forall k \neq 0$
7. $\neg Z_{i,j,k}$ for $\forall (i, j)$ where the condition above is not met, for $\forall k \neq 0$
8. At most K constraint on $\{X_{i,j,k}$ for $\forall i\}$ where K is the number of registers in component j, for $\forall j$ where component j is a PE, for $\forall k$
9. At most K constraint on $\{Y_{i,h,k}$ for $\forall i\}$ where K is the label of path h, for $\forall (h, k \neq 0)$
10. At most K constraint on $\{Z_{i,j,k}$ for $\forall i\}$ where K is the number of operation-units in component j, for $\forall j$ where component j is a PE, for $\forall k \neq 0$

The clauses 1 and 2 set the initial condition and the clause 3 sets the condition at the end of the computation. The clause 4 imposes the constraints that the existence of a node in a component infers its existence in the component at the previous cycle, its communication to the component at the same cycle, or its calculation in the component at the same cycle (if the node is an operator-node and the component is a PE). The clause 5 imposes the constraint that the communication of a node in a path infers its existence in the component at the origin of the path. The clauses 6 and 7 impose the constraint that the calculation of a node in a component infers that the node is an operator-node, the component is a PE, and all of its operands are available there. The clause 8 limits the number of nodes in a PE to the number of registers in the PE, the clause 9 limits the number of nodes communicated in a path to the label of the path, and the clause 10 limits the number of the operations performed simultaneously in a PE to the number of operation-units in the PE. Additional clauses are necessary if a user limits the size of memories or forbids the external memory to store and pass the intermediate values.

It is assumed that an operation-unit can process one operator-node in a cycle. On condition that an operation-unit can process two or more operator-nodes at the same time, MAC operation for example, we need to use a different formulation. Fortunately, the formulation for the enumeration-based transformation method also works for that purpose.

The formulation above does not consider pipelining. To be pipelined, a schedule must not use the same resource in multiple cycles that are congruent modulo T, where T is the number of contexts. This constraint can be imposed by modifying the clauses 8, 9, and 10. Let t be an integer. The modification to the clause 8 is shown below, where the changes are written in a bold font. The same modification must be applied to the clauses 9 and 10.

8. At most K constraint on $\{X_{i,j,k}$ for $\forall i$, **for $\forall k$ where $k \bmod T = t$**$\}$ where K is the number of the registers in component j, for $\forall j$ where component j is a PE, for $\forall t \in [\mathbf{0}, \boldsymbol{T-1}]$

4.4   Preliminary Experiment

As a preliminary experiment, we compared a SAT solver (KISSAT) and an ILP solver (CPLEX v20.1), each running in a single thread. In the ILP problems, the

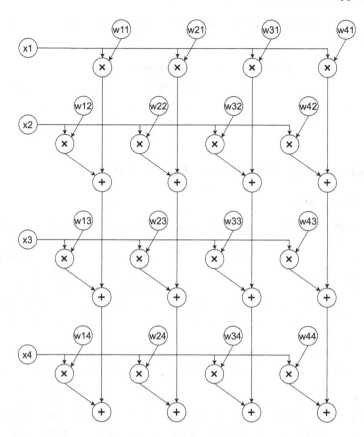

Fig. 4. A data-flow graph of 4 × 4 matrix-vector multiplication.

at most K constraints were directly expressed without encoding. A parameter "emphasis mip" was set at one for the ILP solver to focus on the satisfiability.

We mapped a data-flow graph of 4 × 4 matrix-vector multiplication shown at Fig. 4 and a CGRA consisting of four PEs connected in a one-way ring shown at Fig. 2. The number of operation-units and the number of registers in each PE were set at 1 and 2 respectively. No pipelining was done. The external memory was not allowed to store the intermediate values.

The runtime is shown in Table 1. The mapping problem was UNSAT when the number of cycles was 9 and SAT when it was 10. It means that 10 is the minimum possible number of cycles. The SAT solver solved the problems more than a hundred times faster than the ILP solver. The runtime of ILP solver is reasonable because several studies [7, 14, 15] showed that an ILP solver got timeout (one day) just in mapping a data-flow graph consisting of dozens of nodes.

Table 1. The results and runtime in seconds for mapping 4×4 matrix-vector multiplication onto the CGRA of four PEs in a one-way ring.

Cycle	Result	Runtime	
		SAT solver	ILP solver
9	UNSAT	8.9	3567.8
10	SAT	1.2	767.1

5   Enumeration-Based Transformation

5.1   CNF Formulation

The enumeration-based automatic transformation method was proposed in our previous work [11]. It enumerates all possible operations that calculate each node and modifies the CNF formula so that the node can be calculated by any of those operations. For example, the value $A + B + C$ can be calculated as $(A+B)+C$, $(B+C)+A$, or $(C+A)+B$, but one data-flow graph can represent only one of them. The method enumerates all of them from one data-flow graph by traversing it and uses the modified CNF formula where any of them can be used in mapping.

The enumeration of all possible operations under the associative and commutative laws is performed as follows. First, we create cluster-nodes by merging all contiguous operator-nodes of the same associative operator. An example is shown at Fig. 5. Next, we enumerate all candidates for the last operation for each cluster-node, taking the commutativity of the operator into account. For example, for multiplication of four variables, there are seven candidates: four candidates are the multiplication between one variable and the product of the other three variables, and three candidates are the multiplication between the product of two variables and the product of the other two variables. Finally, for each intermediate value we encountered, we create a new node, called an intermediate-node, and enumerate all candidates for its last operation. This final step is recursively done until every intermediate value corresponds to one intermediate-node. Intermediate-nodes are virtual and not located in data-flow graphs. We create a table, as shown in Table 2 for example, to avoid duplication of intermediate-nodes.

The CNF formula is modified to enable each node to be calculated by any of the enumerated candidates. Here, the cluster-nodes and intermediate-nodes are treated as operator-nodes. Let l be an integer, L_i be the number of candidates to calculate node i, and $D_{i,l}$ be the set of the nodes which are the operands in the l-th candidate to calculate node i. We use a new kind of boolean variable, $Z_{i,j,k,l}$, which means all the operands in the l-th candidate to calculate node i are available in component j at cycle k. The clause 6 is replaced by the following clauses:

6.1. $\neg Z_{i,j,k,l} \vee X_{d,j,k-1} \vee \bigvee_{h \in H_j} Y_{d,h,k}$ for $\forall d \in D_{i,l}$, for $\forall l \in [0, L_i - 1]$, for $\forall (i, j)$
where node i is an operator-node and component j is a PE, for $\forall k \neq 0$

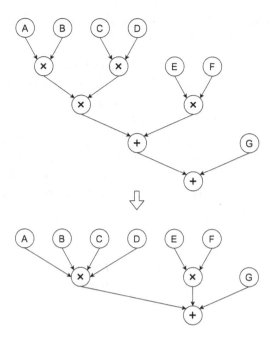

Fig. 5. Creation of cluster-nodes by merging contiguous operator-nodes of the same associative operator.

6.2. $\neg Z_{i,j,k} \vee \bigvee_{l \in [0, L_i - 1]} Z_{i,j,k,l}$ for $\forall (i, j)$ where node i is an operator-node and component j is a PE, for $\forall k \neq 0$

   This formulation also makes mapping of multi-node operations possible. A multi-node operation is an operation that simultaneously processes multiple nodes in data-flow graphs. For example, MAC operation, which processes contiguous multiplication and addition, can be mapped as follows. For each node i that is an operator-node of addition, for each candidate to calculate node i, let node a be the first operand and node b be the second operand. If node a is an operator-node of multiplication, for each candidate D (a pair of operands) to calculate node a, we add $D \cup \{b\}$ to the candidates to calculate node i. The same for node b. By doing this, we can map MAC operation using the same CNF formula. Note that the addition of candidates is actually performed after all new candidates are enumerated for all nodes and for all multi-node operations in order to prevent the new candidates from interfering each other,

5.2 Example: Sparse Matrix Multiplication

As an example, we synthesized sparse matrix multiplication algorithms based on TPU [2] using our mapping method. We can obtain the fastest algorithm exploiting the sparsity for each sparse matrix. Figure 6 shows the original algorithm for $A = W \cdot X$ where W, X, and A are 3×3 matrices. Each element of W

Table 2. A table from a node to its candidates after processing a cluster-node of multiplication of four variables: A, B, C, and D.

Node	Candidates
$A \times B \times C \times D$	$(A \times B \times C) \times D, (A \times B \times D) \times C,$ $(A \times C \times D) \times B, (B \times C \times D) \times A,$ $(A \times B) \times (C \times D), (A \times C) \times (B \times D), (A \times D) \times (B \times C)$
$A \times B \times C$	$(A \times B) \times C, (A \times C) \times B, (B \times C) \times A$
$A \times B \times D$	$(A \times B) \times D, (A \times D) \times B, (B \times D) \times A$
$A \times C \times D$	$(A \times C) \times D, (A \times D) \times C, (C \times D) \times A$
$B \times C \times D$	$(B \times C) \times D, (B \times D) \times C, (C \times D) \times B$
$A \times B$	$A \times B$
$A \times C$	$A \times C$
$A \times D$	$A \times D$
$B \times C$	$B \times C$
$B \times D$	$B \times D$
$C \times D$	$C \times D$

is assigned to one PE. The elements of X are passed to the right, and the partial sums are passed down in the figure. Each PE multiplies a received element of X and the assigned element of W and adds the result and a received partial sum. It takes eight cycles to calculate A, where the number of contexts is 3. The figure also shows the beginning of the next matrix multiplication $B = W \cdot Y$.

We solved the problems mapping sparse matrix multiplication where some elements of W are zero and the corresponding multiplications can be skipped. We used a CGRA of the same topology with each path labeled by one. The number of operation-units and the number of registers in each PE are 1 and 2 respectively, and MAC operation was enabled. The inputs come from the external memory, to which the outputs are returned. We put a ROM for each PE and connected the ROM to the PE. At most one none-zero element of W can be assigned to each ROM. Because of the automatic transformation, permutations of rows and columns of W can be done automatically with swapping output-columns and input-rows, so we only have to consider permutationally inequivalent matrices. There are 36 permutationally inequivalent matrices in 3×3 matrices [16].

We tried to reduce the number of cycles and the number of contexts for each matrix except an all zero matrix. We fixed the number of contexts at 3 when changing the number of cycles. On the other hand, we fixed the number of cycles at 9 when changing the number of contexts. Note that there is one extra cycle required for the initial condition. Table 3 shows the results. The minimum possible number of cycles was reduced in proportion to the number of zeros. Only when the number of zeros was 3 or 6, the number of required cycles changed depending on the places of zeros. The number of required contexts reduced by one for one matrix when the number of zeros was 5 or 6. For lager number of

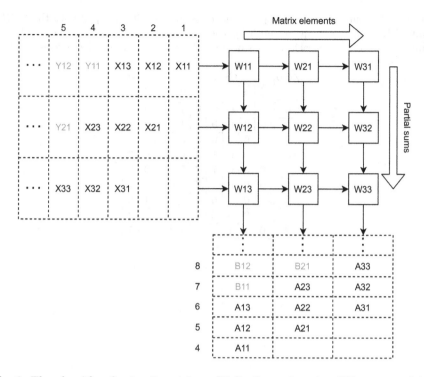

Fig. 6. The algorithm for 3×3 matrix multiplication using nine PEs connected in a 3×3 square mesh.

zeros, the minimum possible number of contexts was 2 when it was 7, and 1 when it was 8.

6   XBTree-Based Transformation

6.1   CNF Formulation

In this work, we implemented another transformation method based on XBTrees, which is originally used for logic factoring of logic circuits [4]. This method can perform the same transformation as the enumeration-based method if the transformation is done for associative and commutative two-input operators.

An XBTree is a binary tree with exchangers that rotate the order of inputs according to the control signals. It can efficiently enumerate all possible structures of binary trees with a specific number of leaf nodes. For an exchanger of size S, let $x_0, ..., x_{S-1}$ and $y_0, ..., y_{S-1}$ be the inputs and outputs respectively. The control signal of the exchanger, c, is an integer in the range from 0 to $S-1$. The function of the exchanger is shown at (4). For example, an XBTree with four leaf nodes is shown at Fig. 7. Depending on the control signal of the exchanger,

Table 3. The number of 3×3 sparse matrices successfully mapped onto the CGRA of nine PEs in a 3×3 square mesh for each number of cycles (when the number of contexts was 3) and for each number of contexts (when the number of cycles was 9).

Zero	Cycle						Context		
	4	5	6	7	8	9	1	2	3
0	0	0	0	0	0	1	0	0	1
1	0	0	0	0	1	1	0	0	1
2	0	0	0	0	3	3	0	0	3
3	0	0	0	1	6	6	0	0	6
4	0	0	0	7	7	7	0	0	7
5	0	0	0	7	7	7	0	1	7
6	0	0	1	6	6	6	0	1	6
7	0	0	3	3	3	3	0	3	3
8	0	1	1	1	1	1	1	1	1

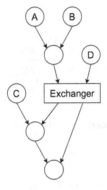

Fig. 7. An XBTree with four leaf nodes: A, B, C, and D.

it is either Fig. 1(a) or (b), assuming the internal nodes are operator-nodes of addition.

$$\forall n.y_n = x_{n+c \bmod S} \qquad (4)$$

We can apply the XBTree-based transformation to two-input operators that are both associative and commutative. We create cluster-nodes as described in the previous section and replace each cluster-node by an XBTree and a sorter instead of enumerating all possible orders of operations. For example, a cluster node of multiplication of four variables is replaced by the data-flow graph shown at Fig. 8. The XBTree has as many leaf nodes as the number of inputs to the cluster-node, while the leaf nodes are the outputs of the sorter that reorders the inputs to the order designated by its control signal. The sorter is required to fully search the variants under the commutative law. We implement a sorter as a set of one-output multiplexers, where each multiplexer exclusively selects one from the inputs of the sorter.

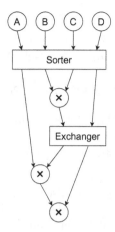

Fig. 8. A data-flow graph implicitly enumerating all possible orders of operations for multiplication of four variables: A, B, C, and D.

The CNF formula needs to be modified to accommodate exchangers and sorters, which are called blocks and not treated as nodes. We introduce new kinds of boolean variables shown below. Let p, q, and r be integers. We number the blocks in a data-flow graph and denote the p-th block by block p and its size (the number of its inputs) by S_p.

- $P_{p,q,j,k}$ ... the q-th output of block p exists in component j at cycle k ($q \in [0, S_p - 1]$)
- $P_{p,q,r,j,k}$ ... the q-th output is the r-th input in block p, and the r-th input of block p exists in component j at cycle k ($q, r \in [0, S_p - 1]$)
- $Q_{p,q}$ or $Q_{p,q,r}$ ... control signal of block p ($q, r \in [0, S_p - 1]$)

We adopt the one-hot encoding for control signals. The variables $\{Q_{p,q}$ for $\forall q \in [0, S_p - 1]\}$ are used as a control signal for block p that is an exchanger, and the variables $\{Q_{p,q,r}$ for $\forall q \in [0, S_p - 1]\}$ are used as a control signal for the multiplexer generating the r-th output of block p that is a sorter.

We add the following four types of clauses to the CNF. Let $d_{p,r}$ denote the r-th input of block p. It can be a node or an output of another block. In the latter case, where it is the q'-th output of block p', $d_{p,r}$ is a pair (p', q'). For simplicity, when d is (p', q'), $X_{d,j,k-1}$ is regarded as $P_{p',q',j,k}$, and $Y_{d,h,k}$ is constant-false (excluded from clauses). The same applies for the elements in D_i, a set of operands, used in the clause 6, and the elements in $D_{i,l}$ in the clause 6.1. A one-hot constraint is a combination of an at most 1 constraint and a large clause containing all literals in the set to make at least one of them true.

11. $\neg P_{p,q,r,j,k} \lor Q_{p,r-q \bmod S_p}$ for $\forall (q,r) \in [0, S_p - 1]^2$, for $\forall p$ where block p is an exchanger, for $\forall j$ where component j is a PE, for $\forall k \neq 0$
12. $\neg P_{p,q,r,j,k} \lor Q_{p,q,r}$ for $\forall (q,r) \in [0, S_p - 1]^2$, for $\forall p$ where block p is a sorter, for $\forall j$ where component j is a PE, for $\forall k \neq 0$

13. $\neg P_{p,q,r,j,k} \vee X_{d_{p,r},j,k-1} \vee \bigvee_{h \in H_j} Y_{d_{p,r},h,k}$ for $\forall (q,r) \in [0, S_p - 1]^2$, for $\forall j$ where component j is a PE, for $\forall (p, k \neq 0)$

14. $\neg P_{p,q,j,k} \vee \bigvee_{r \in [0,S_p-1]} P_{p,q,r,j,k}$ for $\forall q \in [0, S_p - 1]$, for $\forall j$ where component j is a PE, for $\forall (p, k \neq 0)$

15. One-hot constraint on $\{Q_{p,q}$ for $\forall q \in [0, S_p - 1]\}$, for $\forall p$ where block p is an exchanger

16. One-hot constraint on $\{Q_{p,q,r}$ for $\forall q \in [0, S_p - 1]\}$, for $\forall r \in [0, S_p - 1]$, for $\forall p$ where block p is a sorter

17. At most 1 constraint on $\{Q_{p,q,r}$ for $\forall r \in [0, S_p - 1]\}$, for $\forall q \in [0, S_p - 1]$, for $\forall p$ where block p is a sorter

The clauses 11 and 12 make $P_{p,q,r,j,k}$ false when the q-th output is not the r-th input in block p according to the control signal. The clause 13 then ensures that the r-th input of block p is available in component j at cycle k. The clause 14 finally determines the presence of the q-th output of block p in each component at each cycle. Note that we do not care the cases where component j is not a PE because such $P_{p,q,j,k}$ will never be used (especially in the clause 6 or 6.1). The clauses 15 and 16 make the control signals one-hot. The clause 17 prohibits any two multiplexers in a sorter from selecting the same input.

A minor difference from the enumeration-based method is that intermediate values cannot be shared. For example, when we calculate $A + B + C$ and $A + B + D$, it might be good to calculate $A + B$ and use it to calculate both $(A + B) + C$ and $(A + B) + D$. The enumeration-based method can do that by sharing a table among the cluster-nodes, but the XBTree-based method cannot because it creates an XBTree separately for each cluster-node.

The multi-node operation can be supported by using the clauses 6.1 and 6.2 even if we use the XBTree-based method. After inserting XBTrees, we traverse the data-flow graph to find nodes that match a multi-node operation. During this process, we may encounter the places where nodes are separated by blocks but match a multi-node operation if the control signals for the blocks take a particular value. In this case, we create $R_{i,l}$, a set of control signal variables ($Q_{p,q}$ and $Q_{p,q,r}$) that are true when the control signals take that particular value, while adding the set of operands as a new (l-th) candidate to calculate node i. Then, we disable that candidate unless the control signals take that value by adding the following clause. Note that we do not care the control signal variables that are false because the control signals are one-hot encoded.

6.3. $\neg Z_{i,j,k,l} \vee Q$ for $\forall Q \in R_{i,l}$, for $\forall l \in [0, L_i - 1]$ where $R_{i,l}$ exists, for $\forall (i,j)$ where node i is an operator-node and component j is a PE, for $\forall k \neq 0$

6.2   Comparison: Matrix-Vector Multiplication

We solved the same problem as in the preliminary experiment in Sect. 3 to compare the automatic transformation methods. We enabled MAC operation in this comparison. We also changed the size of the problem (the size of matrix and the number of PEs) to see the scalability of the methods. We used KISSAT.

Table 4. The results and runtime in seconds for mapping matrix-vector multiplication using MAC operation with or without the automatic transformation under the associative and commutative laws which was performed by the enumeration-based method (Enum) or the XBTree-based method (XBTree).

Size	Node (Block)			Cycle	Result (Runtime)		
	w/o	Enum	XBTree		w/o	Enum	XBTree
4	48 (0)	80 (0)	48 (8)	6	UNSAT (<0.1)	UNSAT (0.2)	UNSAT (0.1)
				7	UNSAT (0.5)	SAT (1.2)	SAT (0.8)
				8	SAT (0.1)	SAT (0.3)	SAT (0.5)
5	75 (0)	185 (0)	75 (12)	7	UNSAT (0.2)	UNSAT (3.7)	UNSAT (0.8)
				8	UNSAT (2.8)	SAT (761.1)	SAT (109.8)
				9	SAT (1.8)	SAT (61.0)	SAT (4.2)
6	108 (0)	420 (0)	108 (16)	8	UNSAT (0.3)	TO (>10800)	UNSAT (2879.8)
				9	UNSAT (45.7)	TO (>10800)	SAT (3284.0)
				10	SAT (54.0)	SAT (4248.2)	SAT (92.8)

The results and runtime are shown at Table 4. TO (Timeout) was set at three hours. When the problem size was 4, the minimum possible number of cycles was 8 (two cycles reduced) just by using MAC operation. This number cannot be more than the number of cycles required to map the data-flow graph where each set of addition and multiplication is manually converted into a three-input operator-node of MAC operation. When the automatic transformation under the associative and commutative laws was done, the minimum possible number of cycles became 7. It spends one cycle for the initial condition, one cycle just loading inputs, another cycle loading inputs and calculating initial products, three cycles loading inputs and performing MAC operations, and one cycle storing the outputs. The number of cycles also reduced by 1 for the problems of size 5 and 6 by the automatic transformation.

Regarding the comparison between the enumeration-based method and the XBTree-based method, some problems ended up in TO in the enumeration-based method when the problem size was 6 probably because of the exponential increase in the number of intermediate-nodes. On the other hand, the XBTree-based method was able to solve those problems and worked faster than the enumeration-based method for most of the other problems.

7   CGRA Optimization

We conducted another experiment to optimize an architecture of CGRA with incremental SAT solving [5]. Up to here, we have considered the methods to adapt data-flow graphs to CGRAs, but we can also optimize CGRAs through iterative synthesis. After getting a minimum cycle schedule, we try to reduce the components and paths one by one without increasing the number of cycles. In this process, we utilize incremental SAT solving, which can reuse the clauses added and learned in the previous calls. Specifically, we solve the CNF, where we obtained a minimum cycle schedule, again with the assumptions (a set of literals that are forced to be true) to disable one component or path. If it is SAT, we

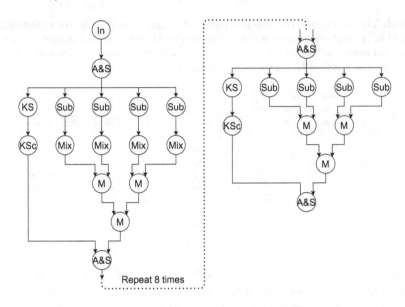

Fig. 9. A data-flow graph for AES.

add those assumptions to the CNF as clauses, then the component or path will never be used in mapping. Otherwise, we give up removing that component or path. We repeat this for each component and path in the CGRA.

We targeted a data-flow graph generated for AES [17] shown at Fig. 9. It consists of 138 nodes where each operator-node corresponds to a subroutine. We used a CGRA of 3 × 3 square mesh PEs shown at Fig. 10. Each PE has one operation-unit and two registers. The mapping was done with no pipelining and no transformation. We used another SAT solver, Glucose v4.1, which supports incremental SAT solving.

The original mapping problem was solved with 52 cycles in 0.5 s. It is the theoretical minimum number of cycles because the data-flow graph has 50 levels of operator-nodes and we need one cycle for the initial condition and another cycle for storing the result. Compared to the mapping problem of matrix vector multiplication onto a ring architecture, this problem was solved very fast even though the data-flow graph has more than a hundred nodes. It means that the mapping difficulty comes from not only the number of nodes but also the capacity of the architecture.

Next, we ran incremental SAT solving to optimize the CGRA. We first removed as many PEs as possible, and then removed as many paths as possible. The result is shown at Fig. 11. The optimization took only 1.8 s. It turned out that we can sequentially map the data-flow graph onto four PEs connected in a ring, where some PEs are connected in two-way, but others are in one-way. Note that we checked redundancy of PEs (and paths) in a specific order, and it may be better to explore different orders.

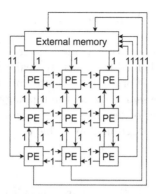

Fig. 10. A CGRA consisting of nine PEs connected in a 3 × 3 square mesh.

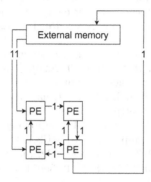

Fig. 11. The CGRA optimized through incremental SAT solving.

8   Conclusion

We proposed a SAT-based data-flow graph mapping method for CGRAs. It performs the automatic transformation under the associative and commutative laws using XBTrees and sorters. We compared the XBTree-based transformation method with the enumeration-based method, and the XBTree-based method worked faster and solved more problems than the enumeration-based method. In another experiment, we optimized an architecture of CGRA through incremental SAT solving.

Regarding the ILP solver, it was slower than the SAT solver probably because the mapping problem contained few at most K constraints and K was small. If K is large (each PE has a large number of registers for example), the ILP solver might work faster than the SAT solver. Also, we used incremental SAT solving for optimization, but one can use the ILP solver instead.

Our method using SAT solver is not as scalable as the heuristic methods like simulated annealing. We are considering decomposing a data-flow graph or imposing some heuristic constraints by generalizing small mapping results. We are currently working on a hierarchical mapping method, which maps nodes while partitioning the array.

We are also considering adopting a rule base transformation, where a rule is a possible transformation defined by a user, to deal with other than the associative and commutative laws. For CGRA architecture optimization, it might be good to further explore the search space: the topology of CGRA, the number of operation-units, the number of registers, and the bandwidth of paths.

The source code of our program is available at [18].

References

1. Krizhevsky, A., Sutskever, I., Hinton, G.E.: ImageNet classification with deep convolutional neural networks. In: Proceedings of International Conference on Neural Information Processing Systems, pp. 1097–1105 (2012)
2. Jouppi, N.P., et al.: In-datacenter performance analysis of a tensor processing unit. ACM SIGARCH Comput. Archit. News **45**(2), 1–12 (2017). https://doi.org/10.1145/3140659.3080246
3. Liu, L., et al.: A survey of coarse-grained reconfigurable architecture and design. ACM Comput. Surv. (CSUR) **52**(6), 1–39 (2020). https://doi.org/10.1145/3357375
4. Yoshida, H., Fujita, M.: Exact minimum factoring of incompletely specified logic functions via quantified Boolean satisfiability. IPSJ Trans. Syst. LSI Des. Methodol. **4**, 70–79 (2011). https://doi.org/10.2197/ipsjtsldm.4.70
5. Audemard, G., Lagniez, J.-M., Simon, L.: Improving glucose for incremental SAT solving with assumptions: application to MUS extraction. In: Järvisalo, M., Van Gelder, A. (eds.) SAT 2013. LNCS, vol. 7962, pp. 309–317. Springer, Heidelberg (2013). https://doi.org/10.1007/978-3-642-39071-5_23
6. Mei, B., Vernalde, S., Verkest, D., De Man, H., Lauwereins, R.: Exploiting loop-level parallelism on coarse-grained reconfigurable architectures using modulo scheduling. IEE Proc. Comput. Digit. Tech. **150**(5), 255 (2003). https://doi.org/10.1049/ip-cdt:20030833
7. Chin, S.A., Anderson, J.H.: An architecture-agnostic integer linear programming approach to CGRA mapping. In: Proceedings of Design Automation Conference (DAC), pp. 1–6 (2018). https://doi.org/10.1145/3195970.3195986
8. Greene, J.W.: Exact mapping of rewritten linear functions to configurable logic. In: Proceedings of International Workshop on FPGAs for Software Programmers (FSP), pp. 11–18 (2019)
9. Chin, S.A., et al.: CGRA-ME: a unified framework for CGRA modelling and exploration. In: Proceedings of International Conference on Application-specific Systems, Architectures and Processors (ASAP), pp. 184–189 (2017). https://doi.org/10.1109/ASAP.2017.7995277
10. Flynn, M.J., Pell, O., Mencer, O.: Dataflow supercomputing. In: Proceedings of International Conference on Field Programmable Logic and Applications (FPL), pp. 1–3 (2012). https://doi.org/10.1109/FPL.2012.6339170
11. Miyasaka, Y., Fujita, M.: SAT-based mapping of data-flow onto array processor. In: 2020 IFIP/IEEE International Conference on Very Large Scale Integration (VLSI-SoC) (2020)
12. Nguyen, V.H., Mai, S.T.: A new method to encode the at-most-one constraint into SAT. In: Proceedings of International Symposium on Information and Communication Technology (SoICT), 03–04 December, pp. 1–8 (2015). https://doi.org/10.1145/2833258.2833293

13. Sinz, C.: Towards an optimal CNF encoding of Boolean cardinality constraints. In: van Beek, P. (ed.) CP 2005. LNCS, vol. 3709, pp. 827–831. Springer, Heidelberg (2005). https://doi.org/10.1007/11564751_73
14. Lee, G., Choi, K., Dutt, N.D.: Mapping multi-domain applications onto coarse-grained reconfigurable architectures. IEEE Trans. Comput. Aided Design Integr. Circuits Syst. **30**(5), 637–650 (2011). https://doi.org/10.1109/TCAD.2010.2098571
15. Yoon, J., Shrivastava, A., Park, S., Ahn, M., Paek, Y.: A graph drawing based spatial mapping algorithm for coarse-grained reconfigurable architectures. IEEE Trans. Very Large Scale Integr. (VLSI) Syst. **17**(11), 1565–1578 (2009). https://doi.org/10.1109/TVLSI.2008.2001746
16. Živković, M.: Classification of small (0,1) matrices. Linear Algebra Appl. **414**(1), 310–346 (2006). https://doi.org/10.1016/j.laa.2005.10.010
17. Liu, B., Baas, B.M.: Parallel AES encryption engines for many-core processor arrays. IEEE Trans. Comput. **62**(3), 536–547 (2013). https://doi.org/10.1109/TC.2011.251
18. https://github.com/MyskYko/dfgmap

Learning Based Timing Closure
on Relative Timed Design

Tannu Sharma$^{(\boxtimes)}$, Sumanth Kolluru, and Kenneth S. Stevens$^{(\boxtimes)}$

University of Utah, Salt Lake City, USA
`tannu.sharma@utah.edu, kstevens@ece.utah.edu`

Abstract. Relative timed circuits leverage formal timing specifications
to design and optimize integrated circuits. Relative timing can be applied
to specify design correctness and performance properties of digital circuits in the form of a set of timing constraints. These circuits often show
significant performance and power advantages over other approaches,
but require assistance to automate timing driven synthesis and place
and route in commercial electronic design automation (EDA) tools. A
machine learning based automatic timing closure solution for relative
timed circuits is presented. The machine learning implementation is
expected to speed-up the process by learning from the features during
each iteration, minimizing the overall run-time to timing close a design. A
comparative study between regression model based and gradient boosting tree based solutions with an algorithmic approach is presented. Power
and performance of the circuits are improved while reducing overall runtime required to timing close a relative timed design with commercial
EDA tools.

Keywords: relative timing · timing closure · heuristic · greedy ·
machine learning · gradient descent · boosting · regression · EDA

1 Introduction

Time delays are manifested in the components and wires of an integrated circuit
(IC). Delays are evaluated based on a timing path between two points in a
circuit, which consist of a sequence of components a signal must pass through.
Time delays dictate the robustness, performance, and power of a system. Static
timing analysis is employed to evaluate and optimize delays and to close timing
during synthesis and layout [1].

Traditional techniques employed by commercial electronic design automation
(EDA) tools are insufficient to close timing on a relative timed (RT) design. RT
timing paths can be cyclical, and may be controlled by state bits in sequential
logic implemented as combinational gates with feedback. To improve quality of
relative timed designs, an engine that understands relative timing is required
to obtain delay target values and sign-off timing in the current commercial
framework.

© IFIP International Federation for Information Processing 2021
Published by Springer Nature Switzerland AG 2021
A. Calimera et al. (Eds.): VLSI-SoC 2020, IFIP AICT 621, pp. 133–148, 2021.
https://doi.org/10.1007/978-3-030-81641-4_7

1.1 Relative Timing

Relative timing (RT) is a universal representation of the sequencing property of time [2]. Sequencing in the time domain is a common correctness requirement used in integrated circuits. An example of a critical well known correctness requirement in the time domain is the storing of data in a flip-flop. Data must arrive at a flop earlier than the clock.

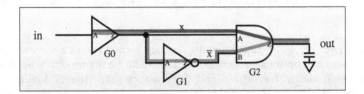

Fig. 1. Pulse generator circuit. The maximum delay path from the rising edge of in (poc$_0$) to the rising edge of out (poc$_0$) of Eq. 2 is highlighted in red, and the minimum delay path from the rising edge of in (pod) to the falling edge of out (poc$_1$) is highlighted in blue. The capacitor models wire and gate capacitance of a latch array. (Color figure online)

The simplified universal specification of a relative timing constraint is shown in Eq. 1 [2]. Relative timing constraints require there must be a common timing start point called a point of divergence (pod) which has causal paths to two timing endpoints called points of convergence (poc$_0$, poc$_1$). To ensure delay of the early path of the constraint is always less than the delay of the late path requires taking the maximum delay from pod to poc$_0$ (plus margin m) and the minimum delay from pod to poc$_1$. RT expressions employ unbounded delays, and thus are a property of the circuit structure. Therefore, RT constraints are agnostic to specific implementation details of a design which affect circuit delays such as technology node, device sizes, or standard cell layout. Specific path delays are not known until design instantiation and timing closure.

$$\text{pod} \mapsto \text{poc}_0 + m \prec \text{poc}_1 \tag{1}$$

Assume one needs to synthesize and verify a circuit that generates a pulse. Such a circuit could be used to pulse clock a latch bank. The circuit in Fig. 1 generates a pulse on the out net upon a rising edge of the in net when proper circuit delays are employed. The delay path through the inverter can be designed to generate the required minimum pulse width. The relative timing constraint (RTC) to correctly realize the pulse generator of Fig. 1 is shown in Eq. 2. This produces a pulse on net out with a minimum width m. The '+' or '−' appended to each net name indicates a rising or falling transition respectively on the net. The causal path through the circuitwhich creates a rising edge on out transitions through pin A of gate G2; the causal path for the falling edge is through pin B.

$$\text{in+} \mapsto \text{out+} + m \prec \text{out-} \tag{2}$$

A relative timed design can contain as many as several million RT constraints. Many of these paths conflict, because maximum and minimum delay path segments can partially or completely overlap [3]. Manually converging timing by modifying the timing constraints on individual paths is not a feasible option for such designs, and it may not be possible to resolve the large number of violating paths through mere post-layout ECO [4]. As such, an automated aid to produce timing closed designs is required.

The timing on a relative timed design is complex, where the optimization of one path may affect timing of other paths (associated or non-associated). The entire problem is an interaction of non-convex optimization algorithms across often competing timing path constraints. In order to model the delay target value for each path, the algorithms consider device sizes, drive strength, transition capacitance, fanout, derating factors, and EDA uncertainty along with the affects of other paths.

This chapter discusses timing closure methodologies for relative timed design. The key contribution of this work describes a machine learning based timing closure engine (MLTC) developed to minimize the number of iterations required to converge timing on complex relative timed designs. Machine learning timing closure results are compared with a heuristic based timing closure (HBTC) CAD tool that automatically generates functional delay targets for a complete RT constraint set [5].

The MLTC engine is capable of generating a timing closed design with arbitrary initial delay targets, including initial maximum delay targets as zero (0 ps). The tool is usually able to produce a completely closed set of constraints with no negative slack violations.

The machine learning based timing closure tool is evaluated on a variety of designs for run-time (number of iterations), power, performance, and design robustness. Several types of RT constraints are employed in these designs. Pipelined designs employ the bundle data design style with handshake controllers [6].

2   Background

Relative timing passes a large set of overlapping maximum and minimum path delay constraints to the EDA tools for timing driven optimization. The interaction between these constraints in commercial timing driven EDA optimization algorithms is complicated and non-convex. A small variation in one maximum or minimum path delay constraint can create a large perturbation in slacks on seemingly unrelated paths. This unexpected variation is based on physical placement among other factors in the EDA algorithms.

While the HBTC algorithm produces solutions of reasonable quality, a number of factors encouraged us to search for better algorithmic solutions. In order to obtain good results, the heuristic based approach requires many iterations through the synthesis or place and route (PnR) tools resulting in very large run times. Assessing and configuring the heuristic tool to include a number of second order factors was difficult. These optimizations include important aspects such as competing maximum and minimum delay paths, whether the path is a timing critical delay path, determining when performance improvements are coming at the cost of too much power, and other interdependent factors.

Multiple gradient descent based algorithms were implemented and tested while exploring the algorithmic solution space to solve the relative timing closure problem. Because the search space is a non-convex optimization problem, none of the gradient descent solutions were able to generate a timing closed design with quality of results similar to those achieved by the greedy heuristic based timing closure engine. Therefore we investigated algorithms that employ a supervised learning based framework.

Machine learning (ML) algorithms are an excellent application to this problem space if data is carefully prepared. The ML based approach is not used to replace the current EDA tools but to improve the quality of RT design flow with commercial EDA tools. The timing constraints and their associated paths are unique to each design, so our initial work is not generalized by training on sample designs. Rather this work employs the more flexible and programmable search properties of ML algorithms to achieve better solutions than heuristic or gradient descent based approaches.

Data plays an important role for any machine learning problem, especially when there may not exist a direct correlation between data among designs or data paths. Due to this ML has already carved its niche in the EDA industry to find design or timing solutions [7–14]. In our approach two supervised learning based regression models were implemented for a given set of input and outputs. One to handle smaller designs with a basic algorithm and second for complex relative timed designs with a more sophisticated algorithm. Both the approach works well on all designs (small and large), with a better run-time on complex relative timed designs with the later.

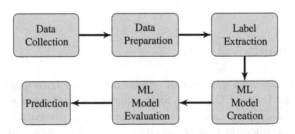

Fig. 2. General Approach to use Machine Learning in RT timing driven optimizations.

3   Approach

The general approach to use machine learning in relative timing driven EDA optimizations is shown in Fig. 2. The timing closure algorithm proceeds by using an ML algorithm to update path delay values for relative timing constraints.

The updated path delays are passed to commercial EDA tools to perform timing driven synthesis or place and route (PnR) of the design. Each iteration with ML includes a synthesis or PnR run and timing analysis with PrimeTime. The results generated by the ML algorithm are also validated to ensure the RT constraints are obeyed with each new prediction.

3.1   Data Collection and Preparation

A careful selection of both timing and physical design parameters, is necessary during data collection. It is equally important to discard irrelevant/overlapping features to maintain the quality of data during data preparation. After extracting the relevant features, it is also important to adjust the hyper-parameters to improve the quality of the predictive model during model evaluation.

3.2   Machine Learning Algorithms

A tree based gradient boosting framework and a polynomial regression based algorithm were tested for RT timing closure.

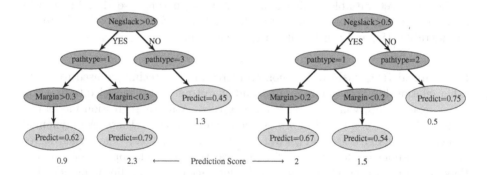

Fig. 3. Decision tree Example

Gradient Boosting Decision Trees. Decision tree ensembles create a gradient boosted decision tree (gbdt) model [15]. The problem of estimating accurate delay target values with no negative slack is modeled here. The model created from the training data consists of an ensemble of trees, where each tree makes a prediction. All the predictions are taken into account by the ensemble model to make the final prediction. The prediction scores of each individual tree are summed up to get the final score. In Eq. 3, K is the number of trees, $\overline{y_i}$ is the prediction, x_i is the input, f is a function, and F is all the possible decision trees.

$$\sum_{k=1}^{K} \overline{y_i} = f_k(x_i), f_k \in F \tag{3}$$

Based on the extracted features, decision trees are created to establish a relationship between inputs x_i and output y_i. The objective function and various tree pruning techniques are utilized to optimize the model. Based on the prediction scores and weights assigned to the leaf nodes, the final prediction value is calculated. A model similar to Fig. 3 is created during each iteration. In our case, the inputs are the timing constraint parameters and path characteristics. In Fig. 3 two such trees are illustrated. In practice, many such trees are constructed by the gradient boosting decision tree based learning algorithm.

The initial experiments were performed using extreme gradient boosting (*xgboost*) algorithm. However, it was observed, that the delay predictions of the *xgboost* model were inaccurate due to improper inclusion of encoded categorical features during each prediction. With the *xgboost* model, no timing closure could be achieved after +500 iterations on a small design and +100 iterations on a large design. The light gradient boosting model *lgbm* implementation can handle encoded categorical features well. It allows to establish a relationship between paths that are dependent on each other (especially in a complex design).

LightGBM (*lgbm*) is a gradient boosting model that can also use a tree based learning algorithm [16]. The framework is capable of handling large data sets. It performs supervised learning on data with multiple features in order to predict a target variable, which is a delay value in this case [17]. LightGBM is faster, outperforms other algorithms like extreme gradient boosting (*xgboost*) considerably [18], and can handle categorical data.

Polynomial Regression. Polynomial regression is a technique used to establish a relationship between an input x and an output y. It is modeled to fit a non linear relationship, which means x has degree n. A linear regression model can be formulated as $y = \beta_0 + \beta_1 x$ where the β_i values are constants. A polynomial regression is modeled as $y = \beta_0 + \beta_1 x + \beta_2 x^2 + ... + \beta_n x^n$ [19]. The higher degree model is responsible for the raised non-linearity in the relationship of x and y. Polynomial regression models are much more accurate than linear models, but they tend to over-fit the input data. The model is more suitable to minimize variance in unbiased estimators of the coefficients.

3.3   Models

It is worth noting that inclusion of the right features as part of the data set is more important in this problem than the choice of algorithm to implement the learning based model. The behavior of the model is directly driven by the quality of the data provided to the model.

Different RT constraints have varying impact on timing driven optimization of a design. Most, if not all, of the relative timing constraints must hold for design correctness. Some of these correctness constraints have large margins and easily hold (e.g. the early path has two gates and the late path passes through nine gates). Other correctness constraints drive the overall performance of the design, such as paths that pass through pipeline registers. The quality of results can be improved if timing closure focuses on these performance driven constraints. Therefore, path types as well as their constraints need to be included in the feature set. Path types identify the performance criticality of RT constraints are passed to the ML algorithms.

EDA tools require the timing graph of a circuit to be represented as a directed acyclic graph (DAG). This is critical when relative timing is applied to asynchronous circuits with sequential functions implemented as combinational gates with feedback. Representing the graph as a DAG necessitates utilizing a subset of the full set of RT path constraints. In addition, many included paths are cut in producing the DAG, resulting in timing paths that are subsets of the full RT constraint path. The current implementation only employs a subset of the RT paths for both synthesis and validation, not the full RTC path. Thus, after timing closure as reported in this paper some timing paths may have violations, even though the path segments used for timing closure have all met timing. These are reported in Sect. 6.

Uniformity of the delay in performance driven paths is very important. Common designs which require such uniformity include dependent cycles (e.g. linear pipelines) and signals with large fan out (e.g. driving a large register bank). Uniformity of delay targets can be achieved in this tool by using a common tcl variables for the delay values. Another method for creating uniform delay targets is to use wild cards in the design based on design hierarchy. For example, the presence of the wildcard "*" in the sample constraint in Eq. 4 indicates applicability of defined delay of 0.2 to all the paths between register clock pin to another register data pin as defined by the start and end point. A similar situation is applicable while extracting path delays using Synopsys PrimeTime. Thus, it helps in reducing physical design variation due to EDA on the connected paths [4].

$$\text{set\_max\_delay } 0.2 \text{ -from ctlreg0/qreg} * /\text{G -to doutl/qreg} * /\text{D} \qquad (4)$$

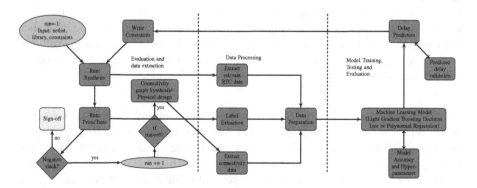

Fig. 4. Workflow of machine learning based delay evaluation to sign-off timing on a RT design with commercial EDA tools in the inner loop of the implementation.

4 Implementation

The flow diagram in Fig. 4 shows the basic framework of the implementation. The complete timing closure system is powered by small sub-programs to interface with synthesis or PnR tools, to process data, to validate quality of predictions and to extract required data at various stages of the flow using timing tools.

The end goal of the ML workflow is to generate delay target values for the subsets of RT constrained paths while ensuring timing closure of the design with no negative slack. The ML based framework always ensures that delay margin is obeyed between associated minimum and maximum delay constraints during the predicted delay validation step.

The prediction of the model produces targets with the intent of generating a solution with positive slack. Timing closure is obtained when no negative slack exists on any timing path. The program terminates with non-convergence when three subsequent iterations have the exact same values of the negative slack on the exact same relative timing paths. At this moment, no upper bound is added to the number of iterations, however, the time-frame is restricted based on the allowed run-time of a program on a machine.

It is imperative to have a uniquely trained model for each design. The constraints and their paths are unique to each design netlist and iteration. The constraints remain relevant for a design unless there is a change in the netlist. If there is a change in netlist, discarding the old model and restarting timing closure run from the beginning will ensure the timing paths and the model are not outdated.

4.1 Learning

The data set passed to the ML workflow varies depending on the size of the design. Run time to converge timing on a complex design can extend up to many hours. Nearly all the run time is spent in the synthesis and/or PnR runs to reach converged delay values with no negative slack. Therefore our process focuses on minimizing the number of iterations required to reach a converged set of design constraints by learning from both positive slack and negative slack data generated during each iteration. The results of the model are evaluated during subsequent iterations to ensure the model is moving towards convergence in each iteration.

Feature Selection. The selected feature set or columns in the data set currently includes the following. (a) Design connectivity data including timing end points for RT constraints such as: start point (pod) and end point (poc), and path type information identifying whether the path is a data path (register-to-register) or control path (controller-to-controller or controller-to-register). (b) Timing constraint data including margin, delay value, delay type (minimum delay or maximum delay), slack (positive or negative), and whether a path is a performance path or a design correctness path.

Algorithm 1. Light Gradient Boosting

1: **Data:** $data_i$
2: current run = i
3: **if** column_type is 'object' **then**
4:     data encoding = encode($\sum_{k=1}^{i} data_k[column\_name]$)
5: **end if**
6: $train.data \leftarrow \sum_{k=1}^{i} data_k$
7: $x.train.data \leftarrow train.data-$ [column with cost function delay value]
8: $y.train.data \leftarrow train.data$[cost function delay value column]
9: $test.data \leftarrow data_i$
10: lgb_train = Create GBDT Model with data set ($x.train.data$, $y.train.data$, $test.data$)
11: $gbm = lgb.train(lgb\_train)$ in iterations
12: **if** $test.data$ not empty **then**
13:     $gbm.predict(test.data)$
14: **end if**

Certain features are categorical features. These are required to build a relationship between the data and/or prioritize certain paths over others. The cost function is composed of a negative slack value, delay, and margin. The results of the cost function i.e. *target feature* (y_i) is predicted by the model. Eqs. 5 and 6 define the basic estimated delay for maximum and minimum paths, respectively.

$$CF_{max}(\text{target delay max}) < delay - negslack \tag{5}$$

$$CF_{min}(\text{target delay min}) > delay + negslack \tag{6}$$

The cost function changes based on the margin values defined for minimum and maximum delay paths. If the margin is not maintained during estimated delay calculation, the difference is calculated and added to the cost function to maintain margin. The maximum delay is decreased (or minimum delay is raised) based on the positive slack on each path. A performance constraint in the form of a maximum delay constraint is present on minimum delay paths of performance type to reduce variability and more tightly constrain cycle times. The estimated maximum delay is raised to maintain the margin between minimum and maximum delay constraint on paths with the same start point and end point, which minimizes energy consumption but allows more variation. The algorithm learns from the data set in order to achieve optimized predictions. The data set increases over time, which leads to improved prediction accuracy. The predicted delay values replace the delay values in the constraints file for next synthesis or PnR run.

Training. The training data includes all the extracted features and labeled data. The data set grows with each iteration while learning between subsequent iterations. Data with consistent trends simplifies the training of a machine learning algorithm. That luxury is generally not observed in this application as the identical delay value on a path can return vastly different slack values on different runs due to a change caused on a totally different path or different synthesis run. Often such variations are caused by a path becoming an outlier as optimizations on other paths take priority. Such unpredictable changes tend to be itinerant, so by incrementally updating the training data set progress is made towards an accurate and consistent model.

Testing. The test data set consists of data with a negative slack. The supervised learning model created from the training data set is used to predict delay for all the failing timing paths. The delay target is updated in the constraints for next iteration. The test data set is also updated between iterations.

4.2 Machine Learning Algorithms

A comparative analysis is performed between the results obtained from gradient boosting decision tree based model and polynomial regression based model. The later implements separate models for minimum and maximum delay paths.

There exists n relative time constraint sub-paths in each design. On iteration i, a path n has delay target tn_i and delay dn_i where $dn_i \geq 0$, and a slack sn_i. In the event of a negative slack ($sn_i < 0$) on path n, maximum delay fixing is prioritized over minimum delay. The cost function estimates the delay tn_i for each constraint path to be $dn_i - sn_i$ if it is a maximum delay path, and $dn_i + sn_i$ if it is minimum delay path. The estimated delay value data set is input into a machine learning algorithm to obtain predicted delay values based on the feature set and relationship built over iterations. In the event of non-convergence, slack on same paths between subsequent iterations is compared. If there is no change in slack for three iterations, the program terminates with non-convergence.

4.3 Light Gradient Boosting (LightGBM)

The pseudo code of the implementation is in Algorithm 1. The features were extracted and an input data set was created using commercial EDA tools. The data set generated for each iteration i with negative slack present on one or more delay paths is given by $data_i$. There exists categorical features in the data set, so data encoding is performed to convert them to numerical values. Training data *train.data* and test data *test.data* are separated. A check is added to exclude paths with negative slack that are being tested during an iteration from the training data set of that iteration. The created model is used to predict new delay values that would fit the design better. The process is repeated until the design converges with no negative slack.

Algorithm 2. Polynomial Regression Model

1: **Data:** $data_i$
2: current run = i
3: $train.data \leftarrow \sum_{k=1}^{i} data_k$
4: $test.data \leftarrow data_i$
5: $train.min \leftarrow \sum_{k=1}^{i} data_k$, when column 'delay_type' is 'min'
6: $train.max \leftarrow \sum_{k=1}^{i} data_k$, when column 'delay_type' is 'max'
7: $test.data\_pos \leftarrow test.data$, when column 'negslack' value is 0
8: $test.data\_neg \leftarrow test.data$, when column 'negslack' value is less than 0
9: $test.min \leftarrow test.data\_neg$, when column 'delay_type' is 'min'
10: $test.max \leftarrow test.data\_neg$, when column 'delay_type' is 'max'
11: $x.train.min.data \leftarrow train.min-$[column with cost function delay value]
12: $x.train.max.data \leftarrow train.max-$[column with cost function delay value]
13: $y.train.min.data \leftarrow train.min$[cost function delay value column]
14: $y.train.max.data \leftarrow train.max$[cost function delay value column]
15: $model.min$ = create pipeline with polynomial features ($x.train.min.data$, $y.train.min.data$)
16: $model.max$ = create pipeline with polynomial features ($x.train.max.data$, $y.train.max.data$)
17: $min\_pred = model.min.predict(test.min)$
18: $max\_pred = model.max.predict(test.max)$
19: $pred$ = append(min_pred, max_pred)

4.4   Polynomial Regression Model

The polynomial model was chosen over the linear regression package provided by the scikit-learn package [20] to better fit the data outliers. A linear regression model looks for a linear relationship between the features, which does not exist in our case. No linear model would serve the problem appropriately since this is a non-convex optimization problem. A polynomial regression establishes a non linear relationship between the feature set to obtain the predicted delay value. On a large complex design, too high of a model degree will result in memory out errors. We found that a polynomial of the order of four works well to predict the delay target values from the feature set. Pseudo-code for this implementation is shown in Algorithm 2.

5   Designs

The machine learning based timing closure (MLTC) tool and HBTC have been applied to converge timing on a number of designs implemented in the 40 nm technology node. Designs with varying complexity are used to test the convergence engine: linear pipeline, watchdog timer, wakeup timer, timer, and FFT-64 design. The designs implemented here are hierarchical designs containing soft macros of asynchronous linear controllers and register banks, as well as free form RT constraints in the counters.

The pipeline design is a retimed 10-stage linear pipeline design implementing $dout = 2x^2 + 2x + 2$. This design can be scaled to arbitrary pipeline depth, but here contains 179 unique RT constraint sub-paths.

The general, wakeup, and watchdog timers are small designs contain 121, 86, and 108 RTCs respectively. They contain 16 bit programmable timers including multiple clocked and asynchronous time sampled inputs and prescale dividers. These designs all show a power reduction of 30× or more in common operational modes compared to a clocked design.

The FFT design is a 32-bit, 64-point multirate fast Fourier transform (FFT) design that is hierarchically decomposed at the top level to operate at multiple frequencies [21]. This is a large design that contains over 50,000 RTCs, that takes approximately 40 min to synthesize with Design Compiler.

6 Results

Synopsys Design Compiler is used for synthesis. Synopsys PrimeTime for timing analysis, power analysis, and slack output. Modelsim is used for simulation. The results are compared for power, performance, and simulation errors that occur after the timing closure run due to the partial paths used in synthesis and timing analysis. The same starting point is employed for all the designs during the two machine learning models by assigning zero maximum delay targets.

The maximum delay targets for all of the designs in Table 1 and 2 are set to zero to start the timing closure optimization. This allows the ML algorithms to optimize the designs targeting maximum achievable frequency. Table 1 shows results obtained from light gradient boosting decision tree model, and Table 2 shows results for polynomial regression model. Each iteration includes synthesis/Primetime/ML runs and one PnR run. The number of iterations are identified.

Table 1. Results with light gradient boosting model (lgbm)

Designs	No. of iterations	sim. errors	avg cycle time (ns)	Power (uW)	Energy (fJ)	$e\tau^2$
Pipeline	5	0	0.945	0.27	0.26	0.023
Wakeup	8	0	0.548	51.23	28.07	0.843
Watchdog	13	0	1.247	46.72	58.26	9.06
Timer	22	6	1.903	57.71	106.02	38.39
FFT-64	4	0	1.692	17,300	$29.27e^3$	$8.38e^3$

For small designs like the wakeup and watchdog controllers, the overall runtime was 20 min with lgbm and convergence with prm was much quicker. The largest design example, FFT-64, took 16 h to converge with lgbm implementation whereas prm took 23 h to converge on the same design. Most of the run-time is

Table 2. Results with polynomial regression model (prm)

Designs	No. of iterations	sim. errors	avg cycle time (ns)	Power (uW)	Energy (pJ)	eτ^2
Pipeline	1	0	0.945	0.27	0.26	0.023
Wakeup	6	0	0.548	50.39	27.61	0.830
Watchdog	7	1	1.247	44.31	55.25	8.59
Timer	7	6	1.903	57.44	109.31	39.59
FFT-64	6	0	1.690	18,400	$31.10e^3$	$8.88e^3$

spent running commercial EDA tool, whereas machine learning data-set generation, feature and label extraction, model training and testing takes a few seconds
to a few minutes based on the complexity of the design.

Table 3. Comparison between LGBM and PRM.

Designs	No. of iterations	Energy	eτ^2
Pipeline	5.00	1.00	1.00
Wakeup	1.33	1.02	1.01
Watchdog	1.86	1.05	1.05
Timer	3.14	0.97	0.97
FFT-64	0.67	0.94	0.94

6.1   Comparative Analysis

LGBM vs PRM. A comparison of results from the polynomial regression
model (prm) and light gradient boosting model (lgbm) learning algorithms is
presented in Table 3. Both designs produce results with nearly identical cycle
times for the small and large designs. They produce equivalent results for the
simple pipeline design with prm converging in one iteration. The polynomial
regression model performs better in both run time and energy efficiency on the
small designs. The opposite is true for large designs, where lgbm model converges
more quickly with better energy results. The prm model is better trained with
positive slack data in comparison to including the complete data set for light
gradient boosting model. Also, the train data set needs to be substantial to run
light gradient boosting model which is achieved in subsequent iterations for a
small design. This also makes lgbm model a better choice for complex relative
timed designs.

MLTC vs HBTC. Table 4 compares the results obtained from two machine learning models: light gradient boosting (lgbm) and polynomial regression model (prm) with respect to the heuristics based timing closure (HBTC) engine [5]. Both the machine learning algorithms perform better in comparison to HBTC based engine in terms of number of iterations (shown in Fig. 5), power, energy and performance on the smaller designs. The HBTC algorithm produces improved results over the lgbm model, but requires 4.5× more run time.

Table 4. Power and performance contrast between ML and HBTC results.

Design	Cycle Time (lgbm)	Cycle Time (prm)	Cycle Time (hbtc)	Energy (fJ) (lgbm)	Energy (fJ) (prm)	Energy (fJ) (hbtc)
Wakeup	0.548	0.548	0.550	28.07	27.61	28.80
Watchdog	1.247	1.247	1.238	58.26	55.25	64.87
Timer	1.903	1.903	2.115	109.82	109.31	85.55
FFT-64	1.692	1.690	1.688	$29.27e^3$	$31.10e^3$	$20.93e^3$

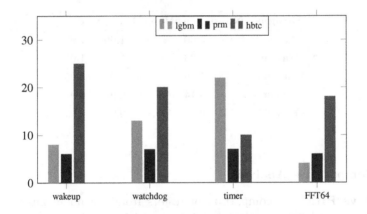

Fig. 5. Number of iterations, ML vs HBTC

7   Conclusion

Machine learning is employed to implement gradient descent algorithms in combination with boosting to solve the non-convex timing closure problem for relative timed circuits. These algorithms drive synthesis or place and route to produce a full timing closed design. The designs are started in a state where maximum delay values are set to zero, and convergence is reached when there are no negative slacks in the designs.

Various ML algorithms were investigated and the results were compared to heuristics based timing closure (HBTC) method. The better version of gradient boosting algorithms in the form of light gradient boosting algorithm is implemented which is faster and works well with the desired encoded features. The polynomial regression model was also implemented. Timing data generated during synthesis or place and route is incorporated while implementing the two machine learning models.

The algorithms were compared using a set of five designs, ranging from a simple linear pipeline using retiming to solve a polynomial function, to a complex 64-point fast Fourier transform function. Both machine learning algorithms converged to produce results of similar quality in terms of circuit cycle time. The *lgbm* models use many weak learners like the decision trees shown in Fig. 3, so, the learning process is slower than polynomial regression which is mainly numerical based relationship to learn and predict. This makes LGBM model best suited for complex designs where one path delay/slack is intertwined with other paths and polynomial regression is best suited for smaller/simpler designs.

The polynomial regression model showed 5.4% better energy results on the small design, whereas the light gradient boosting model showed 6% better energy efficiency on the large 64 point FFT design. The machine learning algorithms served as a solution to build a relative timing closure tool when other gradient descent based approaches failed. The contrast with HBTC approach shows scope of improvement in ML approaches by making them power aware. At the same time, applying ML based timing closure on a small hierarchical blocks serves to improve the quality of top level design. Finally, by implementing learning based timing closure, we could minimize the number of iterations required to generate a timing closed relative timed design.

References

1. Nair, R., Berman, C.L., Hauge, P.S., Yoffa, E.J.: Generation of performance constraints for layout. IEEE Trans. Comput. Aided Des. **8**(8), 860–874 (1989)
2. Stevens, K.S., Ginosar, R., Rotem, S.: Relative timing. IEEE Trans. Very Large Scale Integr. Syst. **1**(11), 129–140 (2003)
3. Manoranjan, J.V., Stevens, K.S.: Qualifying relative timing constraints for asynchronous circuits. in: International Symposium on Asynchronous Circuits and Systems, pp. 91–98 (2016)
4. Sharma, T., Stevens, K.S.: Physical design variation in relative timed asynchronous circuits. In: IEEE Computer Society Annual Symposium on VLSI (ISVLSI), pp. 278–283 (2017)
5. Sharma, T., Stevens, K.S.: Automatic timing closure for relative timed designs. In: 28th IFIP International Conference on Very Large Scale Integration, IEEE (2020)
6. Sutherland, I.E.: Micropipelines. Commun. ACM **32**(6), 720–738 (1989)
7. Bao, W., Cao, P., Cai, H., Bu, A.: A learning-based timing prediction framework for wide supply voltage design. In: Proceedings of the 2020 on Great Lakes Symposium on VLSI, Series (GLSVLSI 2020), New York, USA, pp. 309–314 (2020)
8. Turtletaub, I., Li, G., Ibrahim, M., Franzon, P.: Application of Quantum Machine Learning to VLSI Placement, pp. 61–66 (2020)

9. Kapre, N., Chandrashekaran, B., Ng, H., Teo, K.: Driving timing convergence of FPGA designs through machine learning and cloud computing. In: 2015 IEEE 23rd Annual International Symposium on Field-Programmable Custom Computing Machines, pp. 119–126 (2015)

10. Kahng, A.B.: Machine learning applications in physical design: recent results and directions. In: Proceedings of the 2018 International Symposium on Physical Design, Series (ISPD 2018), pp. 68–73 (2018)

11. Airani, K., Guttal, R.: A machine learning framework for register placement optimization in digital circuit design. CoRR vol. abs/1801.02620 (2018)

12. Yanghua, Q., Ng, H., Kapre, N.: Boosting convergence of timing closure using feature selection in a learning-driven approach. In: 2016 26th International Conference on Field Programmable Logic and Applications (FPL), pp. 1–9 (2016)

13. Elfadel, I.A.M., Boning, D.S., Li, X.: Machine Learning in VLSI Computer-Aided Design. Springer, Cham (2019). https://doi.org/10.1007/978-3-030-04666-8

14. Beerel, P.A., Pedram, M.: Opportunities for machine learning in electronic design automation. In: 2018 IEEE International Symposium on Circuits and Systems (ISCAS), pp. 1–5 (2018)

15. Ke, G., et al.: LightGBM: a highly efficient gradient boosting decision tree. In: Proceedings of the 31st International Conference on Neural Information Processing Systems, Series (NIPS 2017) (2017)

16. Welcome to LightGBM's documentation! - LightGBM 2.2.4 documentation

17. Sun, X., Liu, M., Sima, Z.: A novel cryptocurrency price trend forecasting model based on LightGBM. Fin. Res. Lett. **32**, 101084 (2018)

18. Light GBM vs XGBOOST: which algorithm takes the crown

19. Huang, L., Jia, J., Yu, B., gon Chun, B., Maniatis, P., Naik, M.: Predicting execution time of computer programs using sparse polynomial regression. In: Advances in Neural Information Processing Systems (2010)

20. sklearn.preprocessing.PolynomialFeatures - scikit-learn 0.21.3 documentation

21. Lee, W., Vij, V.S., Thatcher, A.R., Stevens, K.S.: Design of Low energy, high performance synchronous and asynchronous 64-Point FFT. In: Design, Automation and Test in Europe (DATE). pp. 242–247. IEEE (2013)

Multilevel Signaling for High-Speed Chiplet-to-Chiplet Communication

Rakshith Saligram[✉], Ankit Kaul, Muhannad S. Bakir, and Arijit Raychowdhury

Georgia Institute of Technology, Atlanta, GA 30332, USA
rakshith.saligram@gatech.edu

Abstract. Increasing memory bandwidth bottleneck, die cost, lower yields at scaled nodes and need for more compact and power efficient devices have led to sustained innovations in integration methodologies. While the semiconductor market has already started witnessing some of these in product forms, many other techniques are currently under investigation in both academia and industry. In this chapter, we explore a 2.5D integrated system where the interconnects are modelled in the form of coplanar microstrip lines. A model is developed to understand the behavior of these wireline structures and is used to study their signaling characteristics. Generally, the conventional NRZ signaling is used to transmit data. As an alternative, we explore a higher order modulation scheme, namely, PAM4. Through the simulation study, we demonstrate that PAM4 can provide up to 63% better energy efficiency and 27% higher bandwidth density than NRZ.

Keywords: Heterogeneous Integration · Coplanar Microstrip · NRZ · PAM4 · Channel Operating Margin

1 Introduction

The power, performance, area, and cost (PPAC) benefits of semiconductor-based electronic systems have traditionally been addressed via conventional scaling. With the slowing down of Moore's Law-an empirical rule which predicted that the number of transistor densities doubles every two years, both the computing performance and the DRAM capacity have plateaued in the last couple of years as depicted in Fig. 1 [1]. The feature size which was once defined as the gate length (but no longer is) has shrunk and in the past few years, a node actually encompasses several consecutive technology generations and has been enabled by process optimizations and circuit redesign. The unstated assumption of Moore's Law is that the die size remains unchanged so that doubling of the number of transistors will lead to doubling of performance. However, at nodes 10 nm and lower, this assumption fails to hold due to the yield issues and costs. The cost of the dies continues to increase at lower technology nodes indicating that increasing die size are not economically viable (Fig. 2 [2]), Fig. 3 [3].

© IFIP International Federation for Information Processing 2021
Published by Springer Nature Switzerland AG 2021
A. Calimera et al. (Eds.): VLSI-SoC 2020, IFIP AICT 621, pp. 149–178, 2021.
https://doi.org/10.1007/978-3-030-81641-4_8

Performance scaling can be achieved through solutions like heterogeneous integration where instead of fabricating large single die, multiple smaller dies will be tessellated. These smaller dies will communicate in order to achieve same functionality and achieve same performance as the single large die. This appears to address the two main issues of lower yield and higher manufacturing cost. But we need to make sure that the cost of "putting together" or integrating the smaller dies is reasonable and the connections between these dies will be as efficient as it were a single die in terms of speed and quality of the signals. We henceforth call these smaller dies as chiplets and is defined as any die which is integrated with such other dies (or chiplets).

Heterogeneous Integration can be defined as the assembly and packaging of multiple separately manufactured components onto a single chip in order to improve functionality and enhance operating characteristics. It allows for components of different functionalities, different process technologies (that may be incompatible otherwise), and many times separate manufacturers to operate as a single entity. It also offers ways to continue the use of dies that are not performance critical with high performance dies from newer generation.

The idea of assembling dies is well-known in the industry. Multiple chips like power regulators, transceivers, processors, memories have been interconnected to form a system using printed circuit boards (PCBs). Typically, several PCBs are connected through a back plane. For the PCBs, we need to have a packaged chip which even though has been the mainstay, has disadvantages like low structural integrity due to chip-package-interactions [4] and low IO density. The large bump pitches limit the number of IOs that emanate from the chip. The board level latencies also become prominent in high performance systems. The dimensions of the package features have scaled by 3-5× while silicon has scaled by 1000× [5] over the last 50 years. Also, with an increasing need for high-performance and high-efficiency computing, due to increasing cloud, mobile, and edge-based devices, the PPAC targets are increasingly challenged by interconnect bandwidth demands between the dies (mainly CPU and memory), which require low-power, high bandwidth interconnects [6]. Thus, the PCB based SOC approach has been replaced with many technologies like EMIB, CoWoS, HIST, Foveros etc., which are discussed in next section.

1.1 Overview

A general prototype of a heterogeneous integrated system is shown in Fig. 4. One of the constraints for such a system is that the chiplets must be able to communicate as if they were a single entity. Hence, there is a huge demand for the bandwidth (BW) of such systems. The BW depends directly on the number of interconnects that are connected between two chiplets. While the size of the chiplets (the amount of surface area available for interconnect connections) dictates the number of interconnects, it is a natural tendency to pack as many interconnects as possible in the given area. However, this is not possible, as the number of interconnects that can be drawn depends on (i) the technology which governs the interconnect pitch and (ii) cross-talk interference

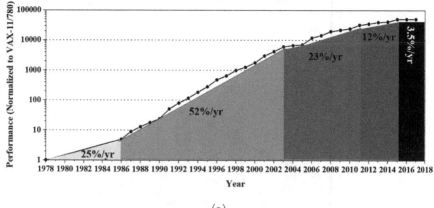

(a)

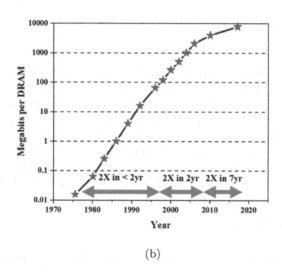

(b)

Fig. 1. (a) Uniprocessor Performance Scaling and (b) DRAM Capacity Scaling.

factors which increase as more interconnects are crammed together in a smaller area. Thus, in a heterogeneously integrated system, as pitch (distance of separation between two interconnects) decreases, more physical IO get packed in a much smaller area leading to higher shoreline -BW-density albeit with increased cross-talk and interference. One way to increase the bandwidth is to explore alternative signaling techniques which can transmit more information in a given clock period. This is the key idea presented in this work where higher order signaling scheme like PAM4 is systematically studied.

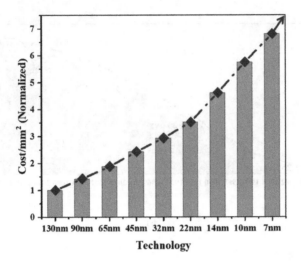

Fig. 2. Die Cost per mm^2 across technology nodes

First, a sample system is modelled to understand the channel characteristics of inter-chiplet communication systems. After analysis of the system, we apply two types of signals viz., conventional NRZ and PAM4 to determine the highest operating frequency of the system. We vary the channel length and pitch to study the behavior of fine pitch and long length interconnect systems and understand how the frequency of operation varies. In order to quantify the performance, we use two metrics namely shoreline-BW density and energy per bit transmitted. Simple transceiver models are used to estimate energy efficiency of transmission.

2   Literature Survey

The need for high bandwidth and low energy chip-to-chip signal interconnections can be addressed with multi-die heterogeneous integration (HI) schemes, such as 2.5D and 3D integration, to enable opportunities in low-power and high performance mobile and server computing [7]. This approach involves partitioning large SoCs into smaller dice, improving yield, hence reducing cost, and subsequently aggregating the partitioned known good dice (KGD). KGD from different nodes or technologies (e.g. silicon CMOS and emerging non-volatile memories) can be integrated together to enable HI, thus supporting flexible product migration to advanced nodes further reducing cost. HI can also facilitate packing more silicon than traditional approaches enable.

There are multiple types of die integration architectures that can be used to enable HI of disparate active dice. While the objective of this work is to explore

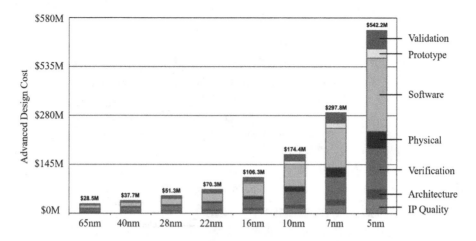

Fig. 3. IC Design Cost Breakdown

coplanar microstrip based channels as a model for die to die interconnects for 2.5D integration, and evaluate the use of higher order modulation schemes for die-to-die signaling, in this section we provide a summary of different multi-die integration techniques, their potential applications, and associated technical tradeoffs.

2.1 2D and 2D Enhanced Architectures

The Heterogeneous Integration Roadmap (HIR) 2019 [8] describes a 2D architecture as one where two or more active silicon dice are arranged laterally on an underlying package and are interconnected on the package. An example of a conventional 2D architecture where interconnection is accomplished using an organic package, as shown in Fig. 5b. However, any form of integration with an enhancement in interconnect density over mainstream organic packages, and with interconnection achieved through an underlying substrate can be termed as a 2D enhanced architecture. The choice of underlying substrates for 2D enhanced architectures can include silicon/ceramic/glass interposers, bridges (both embedded and non-embedded), and organic material. As noted in [8], architectures with significant interconnection enhancements over conventional 2D architectures (such as two or more dice integrated with flip-chip technology on an organic package substrate (Fig. 5b)) are typically referred to as 2.x architectures.

Figure 6 illustrates four common types of 2D enhanced (or 2.5D) integration architectures. The first approach (Fig. 6a) represents a bridge-based integration where a silicon"bridge chip" is embedded within an organic package substrate. Dense interconnects on the Si-bridge along with fine-pitch μ-bumps are used for

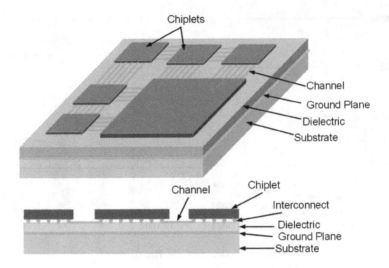

Fig. 4. Generic Prototype of Heterogeneous Integrated System

die-to-die interconnection. Figure 6b represents a traditional interposer-based integration which uses through silicon vias (TSV) for signaling and power delivery to the interconnected dice. The third approach (Fig. 6c) de-embeds the silicon bridge chip and places it between the active chips and the package. The fourth approach, typically referred to as wafer-level packaging (WLP), is a method of packaging dice while they are still on a silicon wafer or on a reconstituted wafer, post singulation. There are primarily two kinds of WLP: fan-in and fan-out. In fan-in WLP the I/O density is limited to the die size, whereas with a fan-out WLP the redistribution layer (RDL) is processed on the wafer, and the interconnect area can be larger than the die area, thus, I/O distribution is not limited by die size. An illustration example of a fan-out WLP cross-section is shown in Fig. 6d.

Silicon interposer-based integration is capable of supporting higher interconnect densities (0.5–1.0 μm line/space) than organic substrates (2–5 μm) along with less thermal coupling and lower package power densities compared to 3D integration [9]. However, Si-interposers are more expensive compared to organic substrates, highlighting a tradeoff between cost and density. Moreover, interposer-based links can also have higher energy-per-bit (EPB) and latency for die-to-die connections compared to 3D integration due to the potentially longer interconnects leading to higher parasitics.

2.5D integration of field-programmable gate arrays (FPGA) based on silicon interposers can achieve an aggregate BW in excess of 400 Gb/s [10]. The 3D processor-on-memory integration using through silicon vias (TSVs) exhibits a maximum memory BW of 510.4 Gb/s at 277 MHz [11]. Recent demonstrations using passive interposer technology include TSMC's CoWoS used to integrate two chiplets on a silicon interposer [12]. One of the first demonstrations

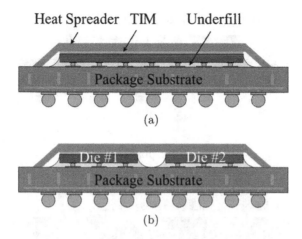

Fig. 5. (a) Conventional flip-chip and (b) multi-chip module (MCM) integration using controlled collapse chip connection (C4) and ball grid arrays (BGA).

of 2.5D integration of chiplets on an active interposer include the work from Vivet et al. [13]. There have also been multiple demonstrations of multi-die packages using bridge-chip technology, including embedded multi-interconnect bridge technology [14] and heterogeneous interconnection stitching technology [15] to enable 2.5D microsystems. In its simplest form, bridge-chip technology utilizes a silicon die with high-density interconnects for inter-die communication. The performance metrics of these 2.5D integration technologies are comparable to interposer-based 2.5D solutions, but many other benefits are offered, including the elimination of TSVs. The Kaby Lake G from Intel [9] is an example of a consumer-end product which integrates silicon from different process nodes and providers: intel 8th Gen core CPUs, AMD Radeon discrete GPU, and high bandwidth memory (HBM) using the EMIB bridge technology.

2.2 3D Architectures

An architecture where two or more active dice are vertically arranged and interconnected without the means of a package is defined as a 3D architecture, according to the HIR [8]. 3D integration can be broadly classified into two types. First is monolithic 3D integration, where two or more active device layers and interconnects are sequentially processed using standard lithography tools. The other type is TSV-based 3D, which utilizes TSVs along with either solder capped copper pillars (or μ-bumps) or wafer-level hybrid bonds to establish vertical interconnections between stacked KGDs.

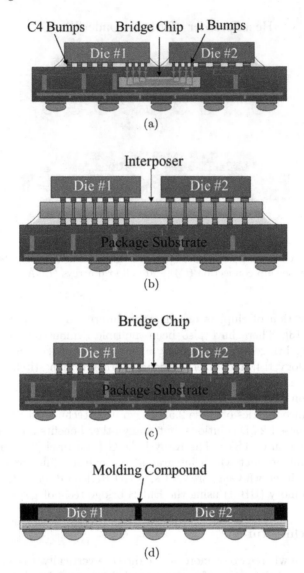

Fig. 6. 2.5D chip stack using (a) bridge-chip technology, (b) interposer technology, (c) Non-embedded bridge-chip using multi-height microbumps technology, and (d) fan-out wafer level packaging.

Compared to single die system-on-chips (Fig. 5a), 3D integration architectures such as TSV-based 3D 7a and Monolithic 3D 7b can provide certain benefits. TSV-based 3D enables diverse heterogeneity in device integration from different technology nodes and improves overall yield through splitting larger monolithic dice into multiple smaller dice [16]. Monolithic 3D integration [17],

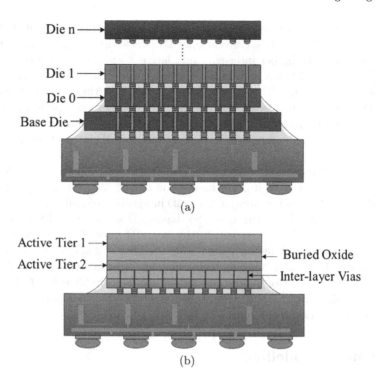

Fig. 7. 3D chip stack. (a) TSV-based and (b) monolithic inter-layer via-based integration.

enabled through fabrication of high-density fine-pitch inter layer vias (ILVs), can enable higher inter-layer connectivity compared to both conventional 2D and TSV-based 3D and higher interconnect density than TSV-based 3D [18], [19]. Based on these studies, there exists a performance gap between TSV-based 3D and monolithic 3D ICs in terms of energy, bandwidth, and interconnect density.

With conventional air-cooling, 3D integration of logic-on-logic tiers can lead to a worst case 73% higher maximum junction temperature ($T_{j,max}$) compared to an equivalent 2.5D case [20]. This difference in $T_{j,max}$ can be attributed to increased volumetric power in 3D ICs, which can lead to higher inter-tier steady state temperatures and transient thermal coupling. However, 3D integration technologies present significant electrical benefits including lower signaling EPB, lower interconnect latency, and higher interconnect density compared to 2.5D integration schemes such as interposers and bridge-based integration [9,21,22].

A few benefits of TSV-based 3D integration include lower signaling EPB, lower link latency, and higher interconnect density compared to other enhanced-2D integration schemes such as interposers and bridge-based integration. However, relative to monolithic 3D ICs, conventional TSV-based 3D integration is expected to have higher EPB, higher inter-chip link latency, and lower interconnect density [21]. Monolithic 3D integration is a promising option for increased BW, which achieves higher BW than TSV-based 3D integration resulting from the utilization of shorter and denser nanoscale vertical vias [23]. Owing to this performance gap, there is a significant interest in monolithic 3D fabrication. However, limitations in devices, materials, and temperatures make monolithic 3D integration challenging and limiting.

A number of recent 3D integration demonstrations have been explored to enable opportunities in high-performance computing [24], imaging [25,26], and gas sensing [27]. In these demonstrations, 3D integration of multiple active device layers is realized primarily through TSV-based 3D stacking [22,28,29] or fabrication of multiple active layers within the same IC (monolithic 3D integration) [30,31]. Sinha et al. [22] demonstrated a 3D stacking of 2 active dice using high-density face-to-face wafer-bonding technology at 5.76 µm pitch and TSVs. They demonstrated an order-of-magnitude better bandwidth (204–307 GB/s), BW (2276–3413 GB/s/mm^2), and EPB (0.013–0.021 pJ/bit) compared to existing 2.5D/3D bump-based techniques.

3   Channel Modelling

The prototype model shown in Fig. 4 electrically resembles the coplanar microstrip lines. A close-up figure focusing on the interconnects is depicted in Fig. 8. In our case, we keep the structure symmetrical i.e., the spacing between the microstrips (referred to as the pitch) is uniform and all the channels are of equal width. In this system, we transmit signals on all channels textit(SSS) as compared to others where it can be either an interleaving of signal and ground signals *(SG-SG-SG)* or multiple grounds with a signal *(GSG-GSG-GSG)* which can possibly use asymmetric signal-ground pitches and different widths for signal and ground interconnects. Here, the ground signal will be a common plane beneath the channel and a dielectric material of height h. The microstrip lines have the benefits as they are planar in nature, easily fabricable, have good heat sinking and good mechanical support. It is a wire over a ground plane structure and thus tends to radiate as the spacing between the channel and the ground plane increases. The two-media nature or the substrate discontinuity of the coplanar microstrip causes the dominant mode of transmission to be quasi-TEM (hybrid) which means it has non-zero electric and magnetic fields in the direction of propagation.

Due to the quasi-TEM mode of propagation, the phase velocity, characteristic impedance, and the field variation across the channel become frequency dependent. One of the guiding criteria for stipulating the physical dimension of the coplanar microstrip lines is provided by [32] which are used mainly for

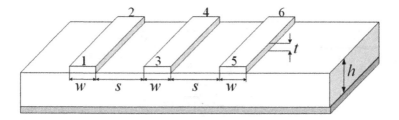

Fig. 8. Coplanar Microstrip Channel Model

Table 1. Coplanar Microstrip Channel Model Dimensions

Dimension	Symbol	Value
Channel Width	w	5 μm
Channel Thickness	t	2 μm
Substrate Height	h	10 μm
Channel Pitch	s	5 μm–50 μm (5 μm steps)
Channel Length	l	100 μm–1000 μm (100 μm steps)

developing closed form equations for effective dielectric constants, characteristic impedance etc., The physical dimensions should satisfy:

$$0.1 \leq w/h \leq 10 \tag{1}$$
$$0.1 \leq s/h \leq 10 \tag{2}$$
$$1 \leq \epsilon_r \leq 18 \tag{3}$$

where s is the spacing between the conductors (channels) or the pitch, h is the thickness of the dielectric, w is the width of the channel, t is the thickness of the channel and the ground plane. $s/h = g$ denotes the normalized gap factor and $w/h = u$ denotes the normalized channel width. Table 1 shows the various parameters used in the model building. The concept of effective dielectric constant was introduced to account to the fact that most of the electric fields are constrained within the dielectric substrate but, a fraction of the total energy exists within the air above. The variation of effective dielectric constant with the pitch is depicted in Fig. 9 and that for intrinsic impedance with pitch is shown in Fig. 10 [33–37].

The analytic expressions for the same are given by [38]

$$\epsilon_{eff} = \frac{1 + \epsilon_r \cdot \frac{K(k')}{K(k)} \cdot \frac{K(k_3)}{K(k_3')}}{1 + \frac{K(k')}{K(k)} \cdot \frac{K(k_3)}{K(k_3')}} \tag{4}$$

$$Z_0 = \frac{60\pi}{\sqrt{\epsilon_{eff}}} \cdot \frac{1}{\frac{K(k)}{K(k')} + \frac{K(k_3)}{K(k_3')}} \tag{5}$$

where

$$k = \frac{w}{2s + w} \tag{6}$$

$$k' = \sqrt{1 - k^2} \tag{7}$$

$$k_3 = \frac{tanh(\pi s/4h)}{tanh(\pi(2s + w)/4h)} \tag{8}$$

$$k_3' = \sqrt{1 - k_3^2} \tag{9}$$

and $K(x)$ denotes Complete Elliptic Integral of First Kind

$$K(x) = \int_0^{\frac{\pi}{2}} \frac{d\theta}{\sqrt{1 - x^2 sin^2\theta}} \tag{10}$$

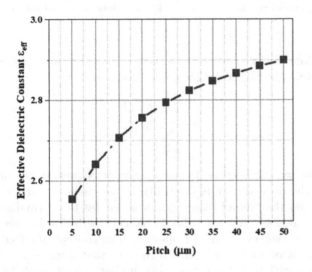

Fig. 9. Variation of Effective Dielectric Constant with Channel Pitch

A coplanar microstrip model has been designed in HFSS. Each terminal of the channel acting as a port yielding frequency dependent 6 port scattering parameters in the form of touchstone files. The microstrip lines show higher radiation

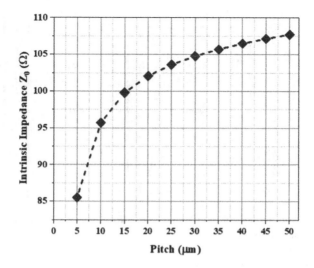

Fig. 10. Variation of Intrinsic Impedance with Channel Pitch

due to lower isolation and thus more cross-talk. The cross-talk experienced by a channel due to the adjacent channels depends on the pitch while the amount of signal attenuation depends on how far the signal has to travel which is the length of the channel. Thus, pitch and length are the two factors that dictate the quality of the received signal. In order to study their effects on the system performance, we parametrically vary them: the pitch is changed from 5 μm to 50 μm in steps of 5 μ and the length is varied from 100 μm to 1 mm in increments of 100 μ. The effect of E-field coupling can be observed in Fig. 11 with three cases that show the variation of magnitude of electric field on the victim channel with (a) no aggressors, (b) one aggressor and (c) two aggressors. Noting this, we use the generated touchstone files for performing the channel simulation. But, before applying signals to the channel, it is recommended that the models be checked for passivity.

The Passivity theorem states that the Scattering matrix S(s) represents a passive linear system iff

1. $S(s^*) = S^*(s)$ where * denotes complex conjugate operator.
2. Each element of $S(s)$ is analytic in $Re\{s\} > 0$
3. $[1 - S^H(s)S(s)] \geq 0$ for all ω

The S parameters have been verified in ADS to be passive.

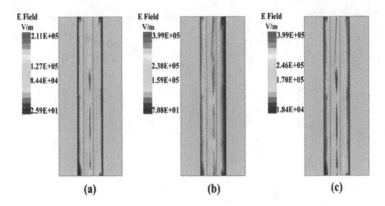

Fig. 11. E field coupling for different Scenario (a) No Aggressor Active, (b) One Aggressor Active (c) Both Aggressor Active

4 Transceiver System Architecture

4.1 Bundle Data Clock Forwarded Channels

Each of the coplanar microstrip lines act as a channel transmitting data from the transmitter to the receiver in the form of voltage signals. As mentioned earlier, the BW of the interconnects is critical. Thus, in order to improve the useful BW, and to enhance the area utilization, we propose single ended transmission as opposed to differential mode which uses two links to transmit one signal, though differential signaling offers lesser crosstalk and higher signal swings. Meanwhile, the negative effects of single ended data transmission like simultaneous switching and reference offset can be mitigated by adjusting the voltage amplitude of the signal. In order to minimize the energy per bit, we propose not to use any equalization at both transmitter and receiver side. We also try to eliminate other sources of link power consumption like clock data recovery circuits at the receiver side by using clock forwarding.

This essentially allows a fully parallel IO design. This is a distinguishing factor in the design of current parallel chiplet to chiplet communication technologies and is simpler to design than traditional SERDES. This is effective because in the target designs the channel lengths are short. Thus, there can be one additional clock signal for a bundle of few data signals (8 or 16) which can be used to forward the reference clock generated on the transmitter to the receiver as shown in Fig. 12.

4.2 Signaling

Here we evaluate two types of signaling schemes.

Non-Return to Zero (NRZ). Here the data is represented in the form of single 0's and 1's. When signaling a "0" bit, a voltage of 0V is sent on the channel and for transmitting a "1" bit, a voltage of V_{dd} is sent. A sample waveform for a given stream of bits is shown in the Fig. 13.

4 Level Pulse Amplitude Modulated (PAM4). In this scheme, two bits of data are grouped to signal a voltage value. Since 4 combinations of 2-bit sequence are possible, we have 4 voltage levels. $00 \longrightarrow 0V$, $01 \longrightarrow V_{dd}/3$, $10 \longrightarrow 2V_{dd}/3$ and $11 \longrightarrow V_{dd}$. The sample waveform of PAM4 for the same bit stream is shown in Fig. 13. The symbol rate in PAM4 is half that of the NRZ or the data rate is twice that of the NRZ.

With two different signaling schemes, we have the corresponding transmitter and receivers.

4.3 Transmitter

NRZ. Since we do not use pre-emphasis or equalization, the transmitter can be a simple buffer which transmits voltages on to the channel. The only design constraint for these buffers is that they must be suitably sized to be able to drive the pad capacitance of the receiver along with that of the channel.

PAM4. Here, two bits need to be transmitted as one value of voltage. The input data is passed through a serializer which is then input to a simple 2-bit Digital to Analog Converter (DAC). The DAC will convert it to a mapped voltage and is transmitted on to the channel by a current mode driver.

4.4 Receiver

NRZ. Similar to the transmitter, the receiver is a simple buffer which will detect the voltage on the channel and decode it as a 0 or a 1. Thus, the buffer acts as a high gain voltage comparator which will compare the signal value to the trip-point voltage of the buffer in order to make the decision.

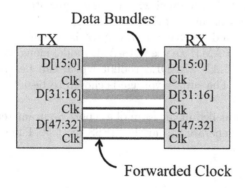

Fig. 12. Bundle Data Clock Forwarded Channel

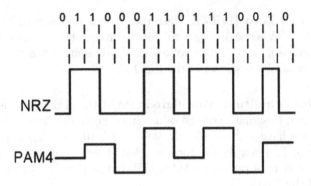

Fig. 13. NRZ and PAM4 waveforms for an arbitrary bit stream

PAM4. The four voltage levels on the channel need to decoded back to two bits. Here, we use a simple 2-bit Analog to Digital Converter (ADC) to do the conversion. Due to its high speed of operation, a flash-ADC is best suitable for the purpose. The Flash-ADC in-turn comprises of three high gain comparators which compare the signal value against the external reference voltage. The ADC output is then encoded to binary.

The NRZ and PAM4 systems are shown in Fig. 14.

5   Channel Simulation

5.1   Setup

The simulation is performed in Keysight Advanced Digital System (ADS) platform for a 28 nm technology node and the simulation setup is as shown in Fig. 15. The transmitter is a Pseudo-Random Bit Sequence (PRBS) generator with the bits being electrically encoded to voltage signals. In this study, a PRBS-7 system is used for which the sequence generating monic polynomial is given by $x^7 + x^6 + 1$. The transmitter has a transmit resistance denoted by R-TX which is typically around 50Ω in parallel with the pad capacitance (C_{pad}) which for a typical 28 nm node is around 5 pF.

The transmitter and receiver for the NRZ is a buffer as explained in the previous section. For PAM4, we use IBIS-AMI model along with the executables generated from MATLAB SERDES toolkit which can be used in conjunction with the ADS setup. The supply voltage is chosen to be 1 V for both NRZ and PAM4.

The channel is modelled in the form of a 6 port S-parameter network. We use the touchstone files generated from the HFSS models. The six ports represent

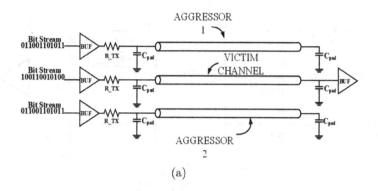

(a)

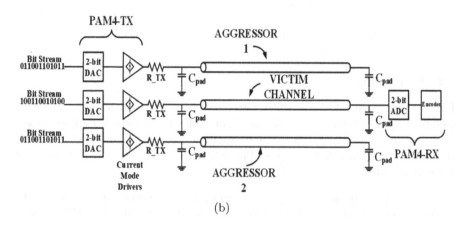

(b)

Fig. 14. Circuits of (a) NRZ and (b) PAM4 Systems.

the three transmitter and three receiver ports which constitute the three channels. The middle channel is the victim channel that needs to carry the required data signal under the influence of the two aggressor channels on the side which contribute to the crosstalk. To emulate the worst-case crosstalk scenario, we have the crosstalk generators ("XTalk" Transmitter) which are configured to operate at the same data rate as the main transmitter but generate out of phase signals.

On the receiver side, we have the pad capacitance. The termination resistance used in most of communication channels will impact power as it causes the received signals to attenuate. Thus, in order to reduce the power consumption, short links typically eliminate the legacy termination resistance. This will make the load on the receiver side to be purely capacitive which will cause the received signal to be reflected back to the transmitter affecting the quality of the transmitted signal and increasing inter-symbol interference (ISI). With the channel length being considerably small, the lack of termination resistance does not affect the bit error rate (BER) significantly.

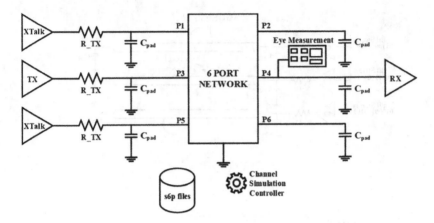

Fig. 15. Channel Simulation Setup in ADS Platform

5.2 Simulation

The channel simulation controller performs statistical convolution of channel impulse response with that of the data transmitted and the eye-diagram is generated at the receiver side. The channel simulation is performed for different pitch and channel length configurations. The following is the trend that is desirable to be observed:

1. At a constant data rate, as the channel pitch decreases, the opening of the eye diagram decreases. This is due to the fact that the channels will get closer and the crosstalk increases.
2. At a constant data rate, as the channel length increases, the opening of eye diagram decreases because the signals suffer more attenuation when it travels longer distance on the dissipative media.
3. With constant dimensions, the eye-opening decreases with the increase in data rate due to higher inter-symbol interference.

Figures 16 and 17 show the eye diagrams for a sample of four pitch-length configurations at a constant data rate. In an ideal case, the eye-opening must be minimum for 1000 μm length-5 μm pitch channel due to highest attenuation and crosstalk and maximum for 100 μm length-50 μm pitch channel due to lowest attenuation and crosstalk. However, we note that the electromagnetics of the coplanar microstrip line is much more complex than simple linear relationships between frequency of operation and channel dimensions.

5.3 Role of Termination Resistance

As mentioned earlier, the termination resistance at the receiver side is the major cause of signal attenuation and power dissipation. But, the main role of using a termination resistance is to avoid signal reflection back to the transmitter

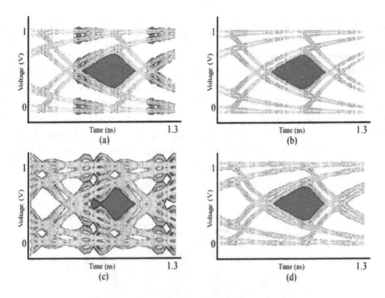

Fig. 16. NRZ Eye for (a) L = 100 μm, P = 5 μm (b) L = 100 μm, P = 50 μm (c) L = 1000 μm, P = 5 μm, (d) L = 1000 μm, P = 50 μm

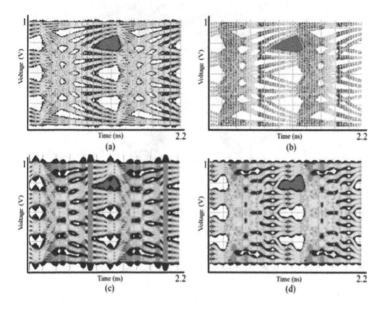

Fig. 17. PAM4 Eye for (a) L = 100 μm, P = 5 μm (b) L = 100 μm, P = 50 μm (c) L = 1000 μm, P = 5 μm, (d) L = 1000 μm, P = 50 μm

causing more ISI. The effect of termination resistance can be seen when trying to push the design operating frequency to a higher value. The Fig 18a shows the eye diagram for a relatively smaller length and very high pitch coplanar microstrip design at 10 GS/s for PAM4. There is no clear eye opening and the diagram looks completely distorted. The Fig 18b shows the eye diagram for the same design but with a 50 Ω termination resistance. We see that the eye has clear and well-defined openings making the received signal easily detectable.

Notice that amplitude of the eye diagram before the addition of the termination resistance is 1 V while that after addition is approximately 0.4 V. This is the signal attenuation mentioned above. Thus, adding a termination resistance will be a design choice to either embrace lower energy per bit at lower data rate

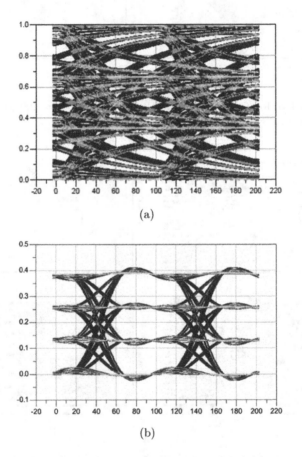

(a)

(b)

Fig. 18. 10 GS/s PAM4 receiver eye diagram (a) without and (b) with 50 Ω termination resistance.

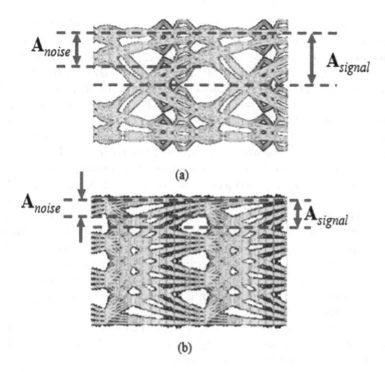

Fig. 19. Channel Operating Margin Definition based on Eye Diagram for (a) NRZ and (b) PAM4

or higher energy per bit at higher data rate. In this article, we chose to forgo the slight improvement in data rate for lower energy per bit transmitted.

5.4   Channel Operating Margin and Highest Signaling Rate

The channel operating margin (COM) is a measure of channel performance which was originally developed for IEEE 802.3bj and IEEE 802.3bs Gigabit Ethernet (GbE) standards. The concept of COM has been applied for the channels under consideration. The COM is defined w.r.t to eye-diagram in Fig. 19 as

$$COM = 20 log_{10} \frac{A_{Signal}}{A_{noise}} \tag{11}$$

The standard requirement for a communication channel transmitting NRZ data is that COM $\geq$ 3 dB. For PAM4 signaling, since the amplitude of the ideal signal is 1/3rd that of NRZ, the target COM $\geq$ 9.5 dB. In the limiting case, it will be 3 dB for NRZ and 9.5 dB for PAM4. For PAM4, the average of COM for all the three eyes is taken. Here in the simulation, we determine the highest data rate that can be achieved while meeting the COM requirement for every configuration of channel length and pitch. This is done by setting an optimization goal to meet the COM requirement and sweeping over a suitable frequency range. All the measurements are made for a BER of 1e-15.

The intensity plot versus the channel dimensions are depicted in Fig. 20 for NRZ system and Fig. 21 for PAM4 system [39]. The channel pitch is along the X axis and the channel length is along the Y axis. The highest data rate that can be achieved for the given pitch and length while meeting the Channel Operating Margin requirement is indicated by intensity of the color in each box.

The ideal scenario of data rate increasing with increasing channel pitch can be seen for channel length of 600 µm in case of NRZ. At 40 µm pitch in PAM4, the ideal trend of data rate decreasing with increasing channel length can be observed. That being said, we need to look at the general trend of the data rate as the channel dimensions are varied while considering that the maximum frequency of operation is controlled by the electromagnetics of the channel, effective dielectric constant of the substrate, characteristic impedance, resonant frequencies and so on. Traditionally channels are designed by fixing most of the physical channel parameters, but here we perform a design space exploration to identify the limits of parallel IO links.

Figure 22 show the shoreline BW density vs channel length for a sample of four pitch configurations for NRZ and PAM4 systems. The direct implication of the finer pitch is increased shoreline density.

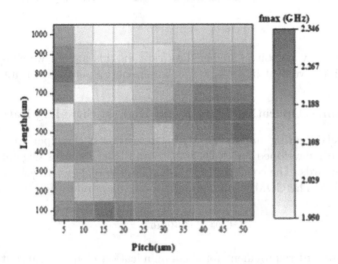

Fig. 20. Maximum Frequency of Operation for NRZ for iso-BER of 1e-15

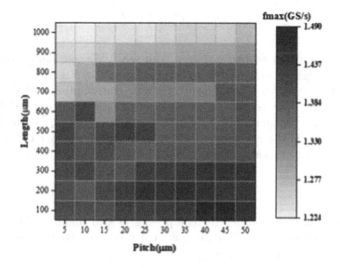

Fig. 21. Maximum Frequency of Operation for PAM4 for iso-BER of 1e-15

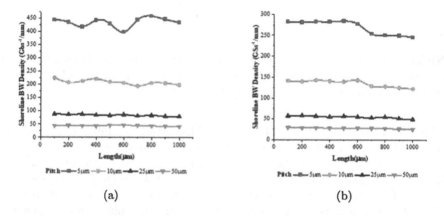

Fig. 22. Shoreline BW density versus Channel Length for (a) NRZ and (b) PAM4.

6   Power Estimations

6.1   Transmitter

NRZ: In our assumptions of single ended voltage mode transmission, the driver is a buffer circuit that needs to drive the wire and the pad capacitance. The magnitude of the wire capacitance is much smaller compared to that of the pad capacitance. If C_{pad} is the pad capacitance, f_{clk} is the frequency of operation at which the data bits are transmitted, V_{dd} is the supply voltage, then the power dissipation can be written as

$$P_{TX} = C_{pad} f_{clk} V_{dd}^2 \qquad (12)$$

PAM4: The transmitter for PAM4 is a 2-bit DAC. We consider a simple capacitive binary-weighted array DAC structure as show in Fig. 23. The capacitive switching will be the key component of power consumption in this structure. [40] provides a power estimation of such structures; when applied to a 2-bit DAC with equal probability of 0's and 1's gives Eq. (13). f_{clk} is the frequency of operation, C_0 is the capacitance of the unit capacitor, V_{ref} is the reference voltage for the conversion.

$$P_{DAC} = \frac{9}{32} f_{clk} C_0 V_{dd}^2 \qquad (13)$$

A simple current mode driver comprising of two binary weighted current sources with tail currents I_T and $2I_T$ can be utilized to drive the signal as shown in Fig. 24. The power is given be (14)

$$P_{CMD} = 3V_{dd}I_T \qquad (14)$$

6.2   Receiver

NRZ: The single ended receiver is a buffer that decodes the signal to a 0 or 1 level and has the same power expression as that of the transmit buffer given by (5) but with load capacitance just another buffer.

PAM4: The receiver for PAM4 is a 2-bit ADC. With the inherent advantages of high speed of operation and the low-resolution requirements for case under discussion, a flash ADC is the best candidate. A flash ADC consists of $2^N - 1$ comparators and an encoder. For a $N = 2$ bit flash ADC, we will need three comparators (Fig. 25). The power of a matching limited comparator [41] is given by (15), where C_{ox} is the oxide capacitance, A_{VT} is the threshold voltage mismatch coefficient, V_{inp-p} is the peak to peak input voltage, C_{Cmin} is the minimum required capacitance.

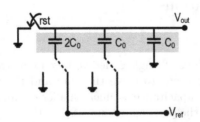

Fig. 23. Binary Weighted 2 bit Capacitive DAC

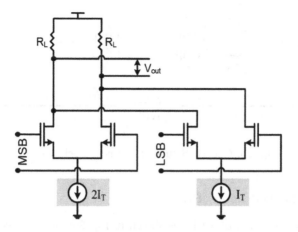

Fig. 24. 2 bit Current Mode Driver

$$P_{Comp} = (144 \cdot 2^{2N} C_{ox} A_{VT}^2 \frac{V_{dd}^2}{V_{inp-p}^2} + C_{Cmin} V_{dd}^2) \cdot (2^N - 1) f_{clk} \qquad (15)$$

The power of a Wallace Encoder [42] in terms of number of bits N, typical gate energy E_{gate} and operating frequency f_{clk} is given by

$$P_{enc} = 5 \cdot (2^N - N) \cdot E_{gate} \cdot f_{clk} \qquad (16)$$

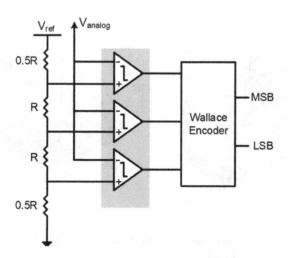

Fig. 25. Two bit Flash ADC with three comparators and Wallace Encoder

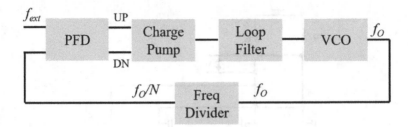

Fig. 26. Generic Structure of Phase Locked Loop

6.3 Phase Locked Loop (PLL)

A generic block diagram of a PLL is shown in Fig. 26. Here, we consider a non-differential 5 stage VCO along with the phase-frequency detector (PFD) from [43]. [44] provides with elaborate power estimations treating PLL as a second order continuous time system. Given the damping factor of 0.707 and a natural frequency of 9.375 MHz with a multiplier of N = 32, the power of the PLL can be written as (17), where C_{PFD}, C_{DIV}, C_{VCO} are the total capacitances of Phase-Frequency Detector, Frequency Divider and Voltage Controlled Oscillator respectively. The frequency divider circuit under consideration is a series of True Single Phase Clocked (TSPC) Flops [45] along with Transmission Gate (TG) multiplexers and inverters and P_{BIAS} is the power of the bias circuitry.

$$P_{PLL} = (C_{PFD} + C_{DIV} + C_{VCO}) \cdot V_{dd}^2 \cdot f_{clk} + P_{BIAS} \qquad (17)$$

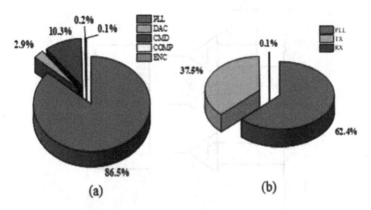

Fig. 27. Power consumption of various components of NRZ and PAM4 system for their highest frequency of Operation

Table 2. Parameters and Values used in Power Estimation

Process Parameters	Typical 28 nm Node Value
C_{ox}	45 fF/μm^2
A_{VT}	1.2 mV–μm
E_{gate}	1.2 fJ
C_{Cmin}	5 fF
C_0	1 pF
Other Parameters	**Value**
I_T	0.5 mA
V_{dd}	1 V
$V_{in\,p-p}$	1 V
P_{BIAS}	0.5 mW

The value of various parameters used in power estimation is shown in Table 2. The total power for a *2.345* Gb/s NRZ is *31.2* mW leading to an energy-efficiency of *13.323* pJ/b. For the *1.49* GS/s PAM system, the power is *14.53* mW producing an energy-efficiency of *4.876* pJ/bit.

Figure 27 show the breakdown of power consumption. As expected, the PLL is the major consumer with up to 62.4% in NRZ and 86.5% in PAM. The receiver in both cases is negligible, as we do not use any equalizer or CDR.

7   Conclusion and Future Scope

In this paper we develop a tool chain from channel modelling to channel simulation and power estimation. The different industry standard tools used in the process include HFSS, ADS and MATLAB. We explore the coplanar microstrip based channels as a model for die to die interconnects for 2.5D integration. We show that higher order modulation like PAM can be applied with more than 63% energy efficiency per bit. This is enabled by the simple transceiver structures for short channel lengths. At high channel densities of up to 5 μm pitch, we note that we can achieve 445 Gb/s/mm of shoreline-BW-density with NRZ and 565 Gb/s/mm with PAM4.

As an extension to the current work, we are also tuning the design to match the industry trends. Currently we propose to explore ultra-fine pitches of up to 1 μm and characterize the same. The choice of the substrate material is another important factor. We also need to quantify the energy per bit at various termination resistance and choose the one that yields the best results. The circuits discussed need to be simulated for more accurate power numbers. Thus, we think there is sufficient opportunity to enhance this design simulation framework.

References

1. Hennessy, J.: The End of Moore's Law & Faster General Purpose Computing, and a New Golden Age, DARPA ERI Summit, July 2018
2. Holt, B.: Advancing Moore's Law. Intel Investor Meeting, Santa Clara (2015)
3. LaPadeus, M.: Big Trouble At 3nm, Semiconductor Engineering, June 2018. https://semiengineering.com/big-trouble-at-3nm/
4. Zhang, X., Im, S.H., Huang, R., Ho, P.S.: Chip package interactions. In: Bakir, M., Meindl, J. (eds.) Integrated Interconnect Technologies for 3D Nanoelectronic Systems, Artech House, Norwood, MA, USA, Chapter 2 (2008)
5. Iyer, S.S.: Heterogeneous Integration for Performance and Scaling. IEEE Trans. Compon. Packag. Manuf. Technol. **6**, 973–982 (2016)
6. Mahajan, R., et al.: Embedded multidie interconnect bridge–a localized, high-density multichip packaging interconnect. IEEE Trans. Compon. Package. Manuf. Technol. **9**(10), 1952–1962 (2019). https://doi.org/10.1109/TCPMT.2019.2942708
7. Collaert, N.: 1.3 future scaling: where systems and technology meet. In: IEEE International Solid-State Circuits Conference (ISSCC), pp. 25–29 (2020). https://doi.org/10.1109/ISSCC19947.2020.9063033
8. Heterogeneous Integration Roadmap (HIR): Chapter 22: Interconnects for 2D and 3D Architectures. https://eps.ieee.org/images/files/HIR_2019/HIR1_ch22_2D-3D.pdf
9. Lee, H.J., Mahajan, R., Sheikh, F., Nagisetty, R., Deo, M.: Multi-die integration using advanced packaging technologies. In: IEEE Custom Integrated Circuits Conference (CICC), pp. 1–7 (2020). https://doi.org/10.1109/CICC48029.2020.9075901
10. Erdmann, C., et al.: A heterogeneous 3D-IC consisting of two 28 nm FPGA die and 32 reconfigurable high-performance data converters. IEEE J. Solid-State Circuits **50**(1), 258–269 (2015). https://doi.org/10.1109/JSSC.2014.2357432
11. Kim, D.H., et al.: Design and analysis of 3D-MAPS (3D massively parallel processor with stacked memory). IEEE Trans. Comput. **64**(1), 112–125 (2015). https://doi.org/10.1109/TC.2013.192
12. Lin, M.S., et al.: A 7nm 4GHz Arm®-core-based CoWoS® Chiplet design for high performance computing. In: Symposium on VLSI Circuits, Kyoto, Japan, pp. C28–C29 (2019). https://doi.org/10.23919/VLSIC.2019.8778161
13. Vivet, P., et al.: 2.3 a 220GOPS 96-core processor with 6 Chiplets 3D-stacked on an active interposer offering 0.6 ns/mm latency, 3Tb/s/mm2 Inter-Chiplet Interconnects and 156mW/mm2@ 82%-Peak-Efficiency DC-DC Converters. In: IEEE International Solid-State Circuits Conference (ISSCC), San Francisco, CA, USA, pp. 46–48 (2020). https://doi.org/10.1109/ISSCC19947.2020.9062927
14. Mahajan, R., et al.: Embedded multi-die interconnect bridge (EMIB) - a high density, high bandwidth packaging interconnect. In: IEEE Electronic Components and Technology Conference (ECTC), Las Vegas, NV, pp. 557–565 (2016). https://doi.org/10.1109/ECTC.2016.201
15. Jo, P.K., Rajan, S.K., Gonzalez, J.L., Bakir, M.S.: Embedded polylithic integration of 2.5-D and 3-d chiplets enabled by multi-height and fine-pitch CMIs. IEEE Trans. Comput. Packag. Manuf. Technol. **10**(9), 1474–1481 (2020). https://doi.org/10.1109/TCPMT.2020.3011325
16. England, L., Arsovski, I.: Advanced packaging saves the day! - How TSV technology will enable continued scaling. In: IEEE International Electron Devices Meeting (IEDM), San Francisco, CA, pp. 3.5.1–3.5.4 (2017). https://doi.org/10.1109/IEDM.2017.8268320

17. Wei, H., Shulaker, M., Wong, H.S.P., Mitra, S.: Monolithic three-dimensional integration of carbon nanotube FET complementary logic circuits. In: IEEE International Electron Devices Meeting (IEDM), Washington, DC, pp. 19.7.1–19.7.4 (2013). https://doi.org/10.1109/IEDM.2013.6724663

18. Liu, C., Lim, S.K.: A design tradeoff study with monolithic 3D integration. In: International Symposium on Quality Electronic Design (ISQED), Santa Clara, CA, pp. 529–536 (2013). https://doi.org/10.1109/ISQED.2012.6187545

19. Beyne, E.: Short course on: heterogeneous system partitioning and the 3D interconnect technology landscape. In: Symposia on VLSI Technology and Circuits (2020)

20. Kaul, A., Peng, X., Kochupurackal Rajan, S., Yu, S., Bakir, M.S.: Thermal modeling of 3D polylithic integration and implications on BEOL RRAM performance. In: IEEE International Electron Devices Meeting (IEDM), Virtual Conference (2020)

21. Zhang, Y., Zhang, X., Bakir, M.S.: Benchmarking digital die-to-die channels in 2.5-D and 3-D heterogeneous integration platforms. IEEE Trans. Electron. Devices **65**(12), 5460–5467 (2018). https://doi.org/10.1109/TED.2018.2876688

22. Sinha, S., et al.: A high-density logic-on-logic 3DIC design using face-to-face hybrid wafer-bonding on 12nm FinFET process. IEEE International Electron Devices Meeting (IEDM), Virtual Conference (2020)

23. Panth, S., Samadi, K., Du, Y., Lim, S.K.: High-density integration of functional modules using monolithic 3D-IC technology. In: Asia and South Pacific Design Automation Conference (ASP-DAC), Yokohama, pp. 681–686 (2013). https://doi.org/10.1109/ASPDAC.2013.6509679

24. Lee, C.C., et al.: An overview of the development of a GPU with integrated HBM on silicon interposer. In: Electronic Components and Technology Conference (ECTC), Las Vegas, NV, pp. 1439–1444 (2016). https://doi.org/10.1109/ECTC.2016.348

25. Tsugawa, H., et al.: Pixel/DRAM/logic 3-layer stacked CMOS image sensor technology. In: IEEE International Electron Devices Meeting (IEDM), San Francisco, CA, 2017, pp. 3.2.1–3.2.4 (2017). https://doi.org/10.1109/IEDM.2017.8268317

26. Srimani, T., Hills, G., Lau, C., Shulaker, M.: Monolithic three-dimensional imaging system: carbon nanotube computing circuitry integrated directly over silicon imager. In: IEEE International Electron Devices Meeting (IEDM), Symposium on VLSI Technology, Kyoto, Japan, 2019, pp. T24–T25 (2019). https://doi.org/10.23919/VLSIT.2019.8776514

27. Shulaker, M.M., et al.: Three-dimensional integration of nanotechnologies for computing and data storage on a single chip. Nature **547**, 74–78 (2017). https://doi.org/10.1038/nature22994

28. Lee, J.C.: High bandwidth memory(HBM) with TSV technique. In: International SoC Conference(ISOCC), Jeju, pp. 181–182 (2016). https://doi.org/10.1109/ISOCC.2016.7799847

29. Gomes, W., et al.: 8.1 Lakefield and mobility compute: A 3D stacked 10nm and 22FFL hybrid processor system in 1212mm2, 1mm package-on-package. In: IEEE International Solid-State Circuits Conference - (ISSCC), San Francisco, CA, USA, pp. 144–146 (2020). https://doi.org/10.1109/ISSCC19947.2020.9062957

30. Batude, P., et al.: 3D monolithic integration. In: IEEE International Symposium on Circuits and Systems (ISCAS), Rio de Janeiro, pp. 2233–2236 (2011). https://doi.org/10.1109/ISCAS.2011.5938045

31. Bishop, M.D., Wong, H.S.P., Mitra, S., Shulaker, M.M.: Monolithic 3-D integration. IEEE Micro **39**(6), 16–27 (2019). https://doi.org/10.1109/MM.2019.2942982

32. Kirschning, M., Jansen, R.H.: Accurate wide-range design equations for the frequency dependent characteristic of parallel coupled microstrip lines. MTT-32, January 1984. https://doi.org/10.1109/TMTT.1984.1132616

33. Veyres, C, Fouad Hanna, V. : Extension of the application of conformal mapping techniques to coplanar lines with finite dimensions. Int. J. Electron. **48**(1), 47–56 (1980)
34. Ghione, G., Naldi, C.U.: Parameters of coplanar waveguides with lower ground plane. Electron. Lett. **19**(18), 734–735 (1983)
35. Ghione, G., Naldi, C.U.: Coplanar waveguides for MMIC applications: effect of upper shielding, conductor backing, finite-extent ground planes, and line-to-line coupling. IEEE Trans. Microwave Theory Tech. **35**(3), 260–267 (1987)
36. Bedair, S., Wolff, I.: Fast and accurate analytic formulas for calculating the parameters of a general broadside-coupled coplanar waveguide for MMIC applications. IEEE Trans. Microwave Theory Tech. **37**(5), 843–850 (1989)
37. Wang, Y.C., Okoro, J.A.: Impedance calculations for modified coplanar waveguides. Int. J. Electron. **68**(5), 861–875 (1990)
38. Simons, R.N.: Coplanar Waveguide Circuits, Components, and Systems. Wiley (2001). ISBN 0-471-16121-7
39. Saligram, R, Kaul, A, Bakir, M. S, Raychowdhury, A: A model study of multilevel signaling for high-speed chiplet-to-chiplet communication in 2.5D integration. In: 28th IFIP/IEEE International Conference on Very Large Scale Integration (VLSI-SoC), October 2020
40. Saberi, M., Lotfi, R., Mafinezhad, K., Serdijn, W.A.: Analysis of power consumption and linearity in capacitive digital-to-analog converters used in successive approximation ADCs. IEEE Trans. Circuits Syst. I Regular Papers **58** (2011). https://doi.org/10.1109/TCSI.2011.2107214
41. O'Driscoll, S., Shenoy, K. V., Meng, T. H.: Adaptive resolution ADC array for an implantable neural sensor. IEEE Trans. Biomed. Circuits Syst. **5**(2), 120–130 (2011). https://doi.org/10.1109/TBCAS.2011.2145418
42. Murmann, B.: Energy Limits in A/D Converters, SSCS Talk (2012)
43. Jeong, D.K., Borriello, G., Hodges, D.A., Katz, R.H.: Design of PLL-based clock generation circuits. IEEE J. Solid-State Circuits **22**(2), pp. 255–261 (1987). https://doi.org/10.1109/JSSC.1987.1052710
44. Duarte, D., Vijaykrisnan, N., Irwin, M.J.: A complete phase-locked loop power consumption model. In: Proceedings 2002 Design, Automation and Test in Europe Conference and Exhibition, Paris, France, 2002, p. 1108. https://doi.org/10.1109/DATE.2002.998464
45. Rabaey, J.: Digital Integrated Circuits: A Design Perspective. Prentice-Hall International, NJ (2003)

From Informal Specifications to an ABV Framework for Industrial Firmware Verification

Samuele Germiniani, Moreno Bragaglio, and Graziano Pravadelli[✉]

Department of Computer Science, University of Verona, Verona, Italy
{samuele.germiniani,moreno.bragaglio,graziano.pravadelli}@univr.it

Abstract. Firmware verification for small and medium industries is a challenging task; as a matter of fact, they generally do not have personnel dedicated to such activity. In this context, verification is executed very late in the design flow, and it is usually carried on by the same engineers involved in coding and testing. The specifications initially discussed with the customers are generally not formalised, leading to ambiguity in the expected functionalities. The adoption of a more formal design flow would require the recruitment of people with expertise in formal and semi-formal verification, which is not often compatible with the budget resources of small and medium industries. The alternative is helping the existing engineers with tools and methodologies they can easily adopt without being experts in formal methods.

The paper follows this direction by presenting MIST, a framework for the automatic generation of an assertion-based verification environment and its integrated execution inside an off-the-shelf industrial design tool. In particular, MIST allows generating a complete environment to verify C/C++ firmware starting from informal specifications.

Given a set of specifications written in natural language, the tool guides the user in translating each specification into an XML formal description, capturing a temporal behaviour that must hold in the design. Our XML format guarantees the same expressiveness of linear temporal logic, but it is designed to be used by designers that are not familiar with formal methods. Once each behaviour is formalised, MIST automatically generates the corresponding testbench and checker to stimulate and verify the design. To guide the verification process, MIST employs a clustering procedure that classifies the internal states of the firmware. Such classification aims at finding an effective ordering to check the expected behaviours and to advise for possible specification holes.

MIST has been fully integrated into the IAR System EmbeddedWorkbench. Its effectiveness and efficiency have been evaluated to formalise and check a complex test plan for industrial firmware.

The research has been partially supported by the project "Dipartimenti di Eccellenza 2018–2022" funded by the Italian Ministry of Education, Universities and Research (MIUR); and with the collaboration of IDEA S.p.a.

A. Calimera et al. (Eds.): VLSI-SoC 2020, IFIP AICT 621, pp. 179–204, 2021.
https://doi.org/10.1007/978-3-030-81641-4_9

180   S. Germiniani et al.

Keywords: verification · testing · simulation · checker · PSL · LTL · specification

1   Introduction

In the last few decades, verification has become one of the most crucial aspects of developing embedded systems. Thoroughly verifying the correctness of a design often leads to identifying bugs and specification holes far earlier in the deployment process, exempting the developing company from wasting resources in costly maintenance.

Software bugs can become exceptionally expensive when they are intentionally used to exploit vulnerabilities [1] or when they cause accidental software failures [2]. The cost worsens depending on how late the bug is discovered in the developing process. The Systems Sciences Institute at IBM [3] reports that fixing a bug discovered during the implementation phase is roughly six times more costly than fixing a bug identified during requirements analysis; fixing an error discovered after release is up to 100 times more expensive than one identified during maintenance. To sum things up, the cost of bugs escalates exponentially after each step of the developing cycle. The National Institute of Standards and Technology (NIST) estimates that the US economy loses 60 billion annually in costs associated with developing and distributing patches that fix software faults and vulnerabilities [4].

However, our experience suggests that many companies have to cut down the verification process due to the lack of time, tools and specialized engineers. To make things worse, developing time is often hard to assess correctly [5], while managers usually tend to underestimate it. As a result, engineers and programmers are subject to very firm deadlines; hence they are mostly concerned about conjuring functionalities instead of carefully verifying the design [6].

That is even more critical in the case of firmware verification, which requires exceptional consideration to deal also with the underlying hardware. Complex industrial designs usually include various firmware instances executed on different target architectures, which need to be co-simulated. Furthermore, virtual platforms and simulators are not available for each target architecture or they are not equipped with the proper verification tools. Therefore, several companies postpone firmware verification at the end of the design process, when the real hardware is available, finally asking the verification engineers to manually check if the firmware meets the specifications.

Indeed, one of the main problems that prevent an effective and efficient firmware verification process is the incapability of formalizing the initial design specification, which is generally written in extremely long and ambiguous natural-language descriptions. Such descriptions risk being differently interpreted by designers and verification engineers, as well as by the project's customers themselves, thus leading to the misalignment between the initial specification and the final implementation [7]. Besides, the lack of formalisation prevents the engineer from exploiting automatic tools for verification, with the consequent adoption of ineffective and inefficient (semi-)manual approaches. In particular, without a well-defined specification, it becomes impractical to define any formal or semi-formal verification strategy. Generally, those strategies require describing the expected behaviours in terms of logic assertions unambiguously. In the case of semi-formal approaches, the verification engineer has to define a set of testbenches to stimulate the design under verification. To accomplish that, the verification engineer must identify and learn additional tools, further increasing the verification overhead.

To fill in the gap, we present MIST: an all-in-one tool capable of generating a complete environment to verify C/C++ firmware starting from informal specifications. The tool provides a user-friendly interface to allow designers and their customers, which are not familiar with temporal logic, to formalise the initial specifications into a set of non-ambiguous temporal behaviours. From those, MIST generates a verification environment composed of monitors (checkers) and testbenches to verify the correctness of the firmware implementation automatically. Then, in order to guide the verification process, MIST employs a clustering procedure that classifies the internal states of the firmware. Such classification aims at finding an effective ordering to check the expected behaviours and to advise for possible specification holes. The verification environment has been fully integrated with the popular IAR Embedded Workbench toolchain [8]. We evaluated the tool by verifying the correctness of an already released industrial firmware, allowing the discovery of bugs that were never detected previously.

The rest of the paper is organized as follows. Section 2 summarizes the state of the art. Section 3 overviews the methodology. Sections 4, 5, 6, 7 explain in detail the methodology implemented in MIST. Section 8 reports the experimental results. Finally, in Sect. 9 we draw our conclusions.

2 Background

Formalisation of specifications is the process of translating requirements of a design into logic properties that can be used to verify its correctness automatically. Usually, the procedure consists of two main steps. Firstly, the verification engineer has to disambiguate the informal specifications written in natural language. Secondly, a formal specification language must be adopted to formalise the specifications into logical formulas that will be used to verify the design.

During the past decades, numerous approaches have been developed to perform verification with the above paradigm.

Moketar et al. [9] introduce an automated collaborative requirements engineering tool, called TestMEReq, to promote effective communication and collaboration between client stakeholders and requirements engineers for better requirements validation. The proposed tool is augmented with real time communication and collaboration support to allow multiple stakeholders to collaboratively validate the same set of requirements.

In [10] the authors describe a method to formalise specifications in a domain specific language based on regular expressions. The approach mainly consists in using a set of parallel non-deterministic Finite state machines to map formal specifications into behavioural models.

Subramanyan et al. [11] propose an approach to verify firmware security properties using symbolic execution. The paper introduces a property specification language for information flow properties, which intuitively captures the requirements of confidentiality and integrity.

In [12], Buzhinsky presents a survey of the most popular existing approaches to formalise discrete-time temporal behaviours.

All the above works either use a standardised (such as PSL [13], SVA [14]) or a domain-specific formalisation language relying on temporal logic formalisms such as LTL (linear temporal logic) and CTL (computation tree logic). The LTL logic allows the formalisation of temporal behaviours unfolding on a single computational path; CTL is an extension of LTL which additionally allows branching time and quantifiers.

Once the informal specifications are thoroughly translated into logic formulas, automatic verification can be applied to the target design. The process of verifying a design using a set of formalised behaviours is called assertion-based verification (ABV); this technique aims at checking if the formalised behaviours hold in the design. ABV can be performed using model checking tools; although these procedures are capable either of proving that a property holds or generating a counterexample, they are not scalable, as they must explore the whole state-space of the design. To address the scalability problem, simulation-based approaches have been introduced to perform ABV. This techniques consist of simulating a design with a limited set of stimuli and memory configurations; therefore, they do not prove that properties hold for every possible computational path. To apply this verification model to a design, the verification engineer needs two additional elements aside from the assertions: a set of meaningful testbenches to stimulate and a virtual platform to simulate.

A set of significant testbenches is essential to thoroughly verify all functionalities of a design, to maximize its statement/branch coverage, and if possible, to discover hidden bugs.

Frattini et al. [15] address the topic of test-case generation by deepening into the possibility of generating a much more complete minimum set of stimuli for simulation-based verification.

In [16], the authors propose a self-tuning approach to guide the generation of constrained random testbenches using a sat solver. They employ a greedy search strategy to obtain a high-uniform distribution of stimuli.

Cadar et al. [17] present KLEE, a symbolic simulation tool capable of automatically generating tests that achieve high coverage for C/C++ programs.

In [18], the authors introduce a purely SAT-based semi-formal approach for generating multiple heterogeneous test-cases for a propositional formula.

"A Virtual Platform is a software based system that can fully mirror the functionality of a target System-on-Chip or board. These virtual platforms combine high-speed processor simulators and high-level, fully functional models of the hardware building blocks, to provide an abstract, executable representation of the hardware to software developers and to system architects" [19]. With a virtual platform, the DUV can be verified by injecting testbenches and by checking if the assertions hold during simulation. In this work, we generated a verification environment for the virtual platforms provided by IARSystem.

3   Methodology

As shown in Fig. 1, the proposed methodology is composed of four main steps
executed sequentially. The input of MIST is a set of temporal behaviours generated in the first step of the methodology starting from informal specifications
written in natural language. The output is a collection of files that need to be
added to a target simulator to perform the verification of the design.

   (1) Formalisation of specifications: The first step consists of translating
the informal requirements into logic formulas. Initially, the user has to reinterpret
the specifications into a set of cause/effect propositions, which naturally translate
to logic implications $a \rightarrow c$. The user must fill in an XML scheme containing
the implications, where each antecedent/consequent pair (a, c) is still written in
natural language. After that, (a, c) pairs are formalised into formulas predicating
on inputs/outputs and internal variables of the design under verification (DUV).
To do so, the user uses an intuitive language of our craft to easily model complex
temporal behaviours.

   (2) Checker synthesis: In the second step, the tool parses the formalised
specifications from the XML schema and generates a checker for each formula.
Firstly, each formula is translated into a Büchi automaton. Secondly, a C/C++
representation of a corresponding checker is obtained from the automaton.

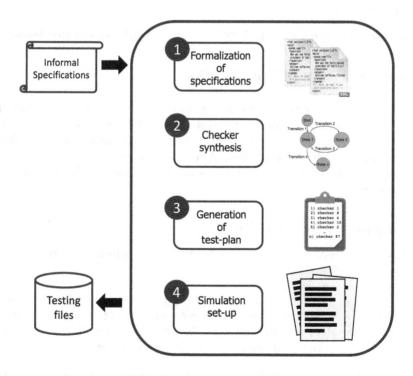

Fig. 1. Execution flow of MIST.

(3) Generation of test plan: The third step of the methodology aims at finding an effective verification order for the given specifications. Each behaviour must be verified when the firmware reaches a specific memory state that we call "precondition state", otherwise the verification would be vacuous. In this state, the behaviour can be verified by providing the proper stimuli. During the verification of a behaviour, the firmware changes to a new memory state that we call "postcondition state". Considering these assumptions, we identify a sorted list of behaviours that would connect each "postcondition state" to the "precondition state" of the following behaviour in the list to guarantee an effective verification process.

(4) Simulation set-up: In the last step, the tool generates all the files necessary to set-up the verification environment. This phase handles the architecture-dependent features of the employed simulator, such as time flow, interrupts and breakpoints. The output files can be described as follows:

- A set C/C++ source files implementing the checkers;
- A set of testbenches to stimulate the design;
- An orchestration file to verify each behaviour in the optimal "pre/postcondition" order;
- A set-up file to initialize the verification environment;
- A set of utility functions to handle the time flow and to manage the interrupts (if present).

Details related to the four steps implemented by MIST are reported hereafter.

4   Formalisation of Specifications

In this section, we describe in detail how to employ our approach to formalise the specifications and to generate the testbenches. The process of formalisation consists of two subsequent steps. Firstly, the specifications are partially disambiguated using a high-level formalism. After that, they are completely formalised using our newly created language. If necessary, testbenches can be defined during formalisation.

4.1   High-Level Formalisation

To clarify the whole procedure, we refer to the formalisation of the following example of specification:

"Firmware is in standard mode, boiler temperature is equal to 18°. Switches A and B are pressed or auto mode is active for at least 2000 ms, after that the boiler's temperature starts rising, then the firmware enters in comfort mode and sends an acknowledgment as output"

The user has to interpret the specification and translate it into a cause/effect behavior, which is represented by a high-level XML file as follows.

```
<assertion id=66>
  <precondition>
  Firmware is in standard mode, boiler temperature
    is equal to 18
  </precondition>
  <postcondition>
  Firmware is in comfort mode
  </postcondition>
  <antecedent>
  Switches A and B are pressed or auto mode is
    active for at least 2000 ms, after that the
    boiler's temperature starts rising
  </antecedent>
  <consequent>
  The firmware enters in comfort mode and sends an
    acknowledgement as output
  </consequent>
</assertion>
```

Listing 1.1. High-level specification

As depicted in the example, the high-level XML file consists of 5 tags:

- <assertion> contains the *id* attribute to uniquely identify the behavior;
- <antecedent> contains the antecedent part of the informal specification;
- <consequent> contains the consequent part of the informal specification;
- <precondition> contains the memory state the firmware must reach before checking the antecedent;
- <postcondition> contains the memory state reached by the firmware after the consequent has been successfully verified.

By performing this preliminary step, the user prepares the ground for the complete formalisation. Furthermore, the semi-formal specifications allow a better understanding of the quality of the informal specifications. Indeed, a specification that can not be formalised with the above pattern is either a non-functional specification or a poorly defined functional specification that must be clarified with the customer. This formalisation model could be even used directly during the initial interaction with the customer to guide the creation of a set of well-formed specifications from the beginning.

4.2   Low-Level Formalisation

When the high-level XML file is completed, the user fills in the low-level XML file by adding unambiguous details to formalise the behaviors. To help non-expert in formal logic and temporal methods during the formalisation process, we defined a new language whose grammar is showed below.

```
assertion :  antecedent -> consequent |  precondition
     | postcondition
precondition : proposition
postcondition : proposition
antecedent : next_fragment
consequent : next_fragment
next_fragment : fragment | fragment; next_fragment
fragment : proposition [min, max, times, delay,
     forced, man_forced,  until]
proposition : c_boolean_expression
```

Through this language, the user can formalise the specifications in forms of implications, where each antecedent/consequent is an ordered list of *fragments*. Each fragment contains a proposition p and a set of attributes specifying the temporal behavior of p. A proposition is a C/C++ boolean expression. From a temporal perspective, the verification of a consequent starts in the same instant in which the antecedent becomes true, and each fragment is evaluated one instant after the evaluation of the previous fragment completes. For example, in the implication $a \rightarrow c$, where a contains the sequence of fragments $[f_1; f_2; f_3]$ and c contains $[f_4; f_5]$: if f_1 holds in the interval $[t_0, t_n]$, f_2 evaluation starts at time t_{n+1}; on the contrary, if f_3 holds in the interval $[t_k, t_l]$, f_4 evaluation starts at t_l, since t_3 belongs to the antecedent while t_4 to the consequent. A fragment represents then a sequence of boolean events, similar to a PSL SERE [13]. Given a fragment f with a set of attributes $[min, max, times, delay, until]$ containing a proposition p, the semantics of the evaluation of f at time t_0 can be described as follows:

- **min** $= n$ with $n > 0$: f is true if p holds from t_0 to t_{n-1}. In other words, *min* attribute means that the proposition must remain true for a minimum of n instants.
- **max** $= n$ with $n > 0$: f is true if p becomes false before t_n. In other words, *max* attribute means that the proposition must remain true for a maximum of n instants.
- **times** $= m$ with $m > 0$ and **max** $= n$ with $n > 0$: f is true at time $t_k <= t_n$ if p holds for m (not necessarily consecutive) instants. If attribute *times* is set, then *max* must be set, while *min* and *until* are ignored.
- **delay** $= n$ with $n > 0$: f is true at time t_{n-1}.
- **until** $= q$ where q is a proposition, and **max** $= n$ with $n > 0$: f is true if q holds at time t_f with $t_0 \leq t_f \leq t_{n-1}$ and p holds from time t_0 to t_{f-1}. If attribute *until* is set then *max* must be set, while *min* and *times* are ignored.

To exemplify the use of the proposed language, we report hereafter the low-level XML resulting from the formalisation of the behavior previously used as a running example.

```
<assertion id=66>
  <precondition>
      mode == 0 && bTemp == 18.0
  </precondition>
  <postcondition>
      mode == 1
  </postcondition>
  <antecedent>
    <fragment min=2000 >
      (P0 == 0  && P4 == 16 && P12 == 4) || autoMode
    </fragment>
    <fragment until=bTmpRising max=9000>
        true
    </fragment>
  </antecedent>
  <consequent>
    <fragment min=1>
      mode == 1 && P16 == 1
    </fragment>
    <fragment min=1>
      (P16 >> 1) == 1
    </fragment>
  </consequent>
</assertion>
```

Listing 1.2. Low-level specification

The precondition (postcondition) is represented as a proposition identifying a concrete memory state that must be reached before (after) the verification of the behavior. In this example, the memory configuration identified by $mode == 0$ && $bTemp == 18.0$ is forced before checking the rest of the behaviour. The antecedent contains two fragments that, according to the described semantics, identify the following behavior: the first fragment is true if $P0 == 0$ && $P4 == 16$ && $P12 == 4 \parallel autoMode$ holds true for 2000 consecutive instants; after that, the second fragment is true if $bTmpRising$ becomes true within 9000 instants. The consequent also contains two fragments. In the first fragment the proposition $mode == 1$ && $P16 == 1$ must be true for one instant. In the following instant, the second fragment is evaluated, and the proposition $(P16 >> 1) == 1$ must be true. From a temporal perspective, the antecedent is evaluated from time t_0 to t_k with $2000 < k < 11000$ while the consequent is evaluated from t_k to t_{k+1}.

4.3   Type System

In addition to the features described above, the propositions used in each fragment completely supports a C-compliant type system. In particular, variables can be defined using the usual C-styled syntax to declare their type. Moreover, the propositions support the explicit and implicit C type casting. Since the DUV already contains the required declarations in the source code, the user needs only to spend few seconds to copy and paste them to the low-level XML file.

Furthermore, the user can declare debug variables to simplify the formalisation of complex behaviours. Debug variables are used during simulation but are held in memory outside the firmware under verification. This feature can be exceptionally useful to store intermediate values during the simulation of a behaviour. Listing 1.3 shows a possible declaration for the variables used in Listing 1.2.

```
<declaration>
    unsigned char P0;
    unsigned char P4;
    unsigned char P12;
    unsigned char P16;
</declaration>
<assertion id=66>
  <declaration>
      int mode;
      float bTemp;
      bool bTmpRising;
      bool autoMode;
  </declaration>
  ...
</assertion>
```

Listing 1.3. Variables declaration

Note that we provide support for both global and local declarations. Local declarations are valid only inside the assertion in which they are defined; global declarations extend to all defined assertions.

4.4   Testbench Generation

The formalisation language used in MIST provides three additional attributes: "**nTB**", "**forced**" and "**manual_forced**" to allow the generation of testbenches. The attribute **forced** can be specified for a fragment f to guide the testbench generator during the DUV simulation. If $forced = n$ with $n > 0$, MIST calls a SAT solver to generate a model for the proposition p that returns an assignment $var_i = val_i$ for each variable var_i included in p. If f is evaluated at time t_0, then each var_i is forced to value val_i in the interval $[t_0, t_{n-1}]$. The attribute nTB specifies how many testbenches must be generated for the current behaviour. If nTB is equal to p with $p > 1$, MIST generates p distinct test-vectors for the current fragment. If the number of available distinct test-vectors is less than p, MIST replicates the last generated test-vector to fill the empty spots.

```
<FRAGMENT forced="200" delay="200">
        x || y
</FRAGMENT>
```

Consider the example above, if $nTB = 4$ and $x||y$ is the proposition defined in the fragment, then there can exist only 3 distinct test-vector: (x = true, y = false), (x = false, y = true), (x = true, y = true). In this scenario, MIST replicates (x = true, y = true) to fill the fourth test-vector. Note that the attributes *forced* is completely independent of the evaluation of the fragment. If *forced* is the only attribute defined in the fragment, then the fragment is considered "empty"; nonetheless, a test-vector is generated anyway, but the evaluation of the empty fragment is skipped and the evaluation of the next fragment begins in the same instant (and not one instant later).

The attribute **manual_forced** follows the same semantic described for **forced**, except that the generated test-vector is manually provided by the user instead of being generated automatically. This is exceptionally useful in cases where the stimuli must vary in time or must follow a certain pattern. Moreover, the user could exploit this feature to integrate testbenches generated with specialised external tools, remarkably increasing the flexibility of MIST.

The syntax of manual_forced is slightly different: $manual\_forced = n$, where n is the id of a test-vector declared in the current assertion. Note that forced and manual_forced are mutually exclusive, only one of them can be used in a fragment at any time. A test-vector is defined with the following syntax:

```
<test_vector id="uInt">
     [var_1, var_2, ... , var_n] = {
                tv_tb_1;
                tv_tb_2;
                   ...
                tv_tb_m;
     }
</test_vector>
```

$[var_1, var_2, ... , var_n]$ is the list of variables on which to apply the stimulus. tv_tb_i is the ith test-vector to be injected in the fragment when the simulator is stimulating the design with the ith testbench. Each tv_tb_i follows the syntax showed below.

```
tv_tb_i   : =
(var_1_val_1,  var_2_val_1, ...,  var_n_val_1,  duration_1),
(var_1_val_2,  var_2_val_2, ...,  var_n_val_2,  duration_2),
                   ...
(var_1_val_k,  var_2_val_k, ...,  var_n_val_k,  duration_n)
```

Each tuple $(var_1\_val_j, var_2\_val_j, ... , var_n\_val_j, duration_j)$ identifies a piece of test-vector where the variables $var_1, var_2, ... , var_n$ are forced with the values $var_1\_val_j, var_2\_val_j, ... , var_n\_val_j$ for $duration_j$ instants. Once the values are injected for $duration_j$ instants, the following tuple $(j + 1)$ is used to inject the values.

In the example depicted in Listing 1.2, we assumed that pressing the bottom and rising the temperature were internal events of the firmware that did not require any external stimulus. However, in many cases this is not true; usually, the user has to provide as input a sequence of stimuli to test the correct behaviour. In the example below, we propose again the same formalised behaviour where the fragments of the antecedent are used to inject testbenches. Note that the consequent is the same of Listing 1.2.

```
<assertion id=66 nTB=2>
  <precondition>
      mode == 0 && bTemp == 18.0
  </precondition>
  <postcondition>
      mode == 1
  </postcondition>
  <antecedent>
    <fragment forced=2000 delay=2000>
      (P0 == 0  && P4 == 16 && P12 == 4) || autoMode
    </fragment>
    <fragment man_forced=7 delay=1200/>
  </antecedent>
  <test_vector id=7>
    [bTemp] ={
    (18.0,200),(18.2,200),(18.4,200),(18.6,200)
    ,(18.8,200),(19.0,200); }
  </test_vector>
</assertion>
```

Listing 1.4. Low-level specification with testbenches

In this example, there are both automatic and manual test-vectors.

Since nTB = 2, MIST generates two testbenches.

In the first fragment of the antecedent, the generated test-vector is (P0 = 0, P4 = 16, P12 = 4, autoMode = false) for the first testbench and (P0 = 0, P4 = 0, P12 = 0, autoMode = true) for the second testbench. The second fragment contains a manual test-vector with ID equal to 7. We also use the attribute "delay" to postpone the evaluation of the second fragment after injecting the test-vector of the first fragment. Likewise, we put off the evaluation of the consequent by delaying the second fragment. If we combine the automatic test-vector of the first fragment with the manual test-vector of the second fragment, MIST generates the following testbenches:

1. (P0 = 0, P4 = 16, P12 = 4, autoMode = false) for 2000 instants, (bTemp = 18.0) for 200 instants, (bTemp = 18.0) for 200 instants, (bTemp = 18.2) for 200 instants, (bTemp = 18.4) for 200 instants, (bTemp = 18.6) for 200 instants, (bTemp = 18.8) for 200 instants, (bTemp = 19.0) for 200 instants
2. (P0 = 0, P4 = 0, P12 = 0, autoMode = true) for 2000 instants, ... the rest is the same of the previous testbench.

Note that in the second testbench, the test-vector for the second fragment is the same used for the first. This happens because only one test-vector was defined for the second fragment while 2 were needed to generate the required testbenches.

From a temporal point of view, the two testbenches can be represented as in Fig. 2. Both testbenches are injected from time t_0 to time t_{3199}.

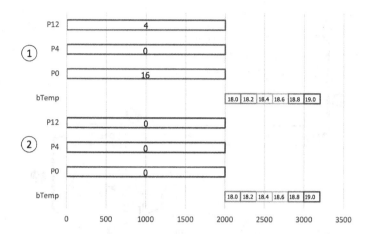

Fig. 2. Testbenches timeline

5   Checker Synthesis

In the second step of the methodology, MIST parses the formalised specifications in the low-level XML files and generates a C/C++ checker for each implication. The process works in three main sub-steps. Firstly, the tool translates each XML assertions to a PSL formula. Secondly, each PSL formulas is used to generate its equivalent Büchi automaton. Finally, the Büchi automaton is translated to C/C++.

We treat each implication as two independent formulas, one for the antecedent and one for the consequent. This separation is necessary to pinpoint scenarios where the implication is vacuously true. If we considered the implication as a whole, a true evaluation could either mean that the consequent was true or the antecedent was false, we want to distinguish both cases to better warn the user. To convert an XML assertion to PSL, each sequence of *fragments* is treated as a PSL SERE. For example, the consequent of the specification used in Sect. 4 translates to the following PSL formula $\{mode == 1$ && $P16 == 1; (P16 >> 1) == 1\}$.

Since the PSL syntax does not allow the use of many C operators such as the bit shift operator ($<<$), we execute an intermediate step to provide support to all C operators that can be used to form a boolean expression. In this step, the tool substitutes each fragment's proposition with a placeholder boolean variable representing the proposition. For example, the above formula would be translated to $\{ph1; ph2\}$ where $ph1$ is the placeholder for $mode == 1$ && $P16 == 1$ and $ph2$ is the placeholder for $(P16 >> 1) == 1$; Once the translations above are completed, we generate a Büchi automaton for each formula. To do so, we use spotLTL [20], an external library capable of generating automata from LTL/PSL formulas. Finally, the resulting automaton is visited to generate a C/C++ implementation of the corresponding checker.

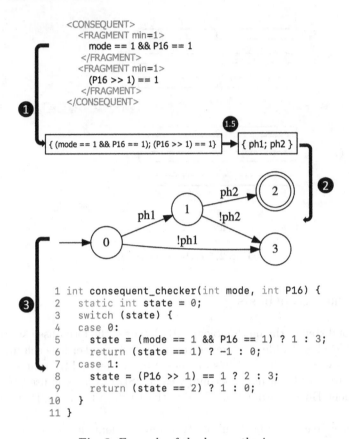

Fig. 3. Example of checker synthesis.

Figure 3 shows an example to clarify the process. In steps (1) and (1.5), the fragment is converted to PSL, and its proposition is substituted with placeholders according to the aforementioned procedure. In step (2), the LTL formula is given as input to spotLTL to generate the depicted Büchi automaton. Before synthesizing the C/C++ checker, each placeholder is substituted back to its original proposition. In Fig. 3, placeholder $ph1$ and $ph2$ are substituted back to $mode == 1 \&\& P16 == 1$ and $(P16 >> 1) == 1$. In step (3), the automaton is visited starting from the first state. For each state, the tool generates a *case* of a C *switch*, for each edge the tool generates the next-state function in each case. Note that the accepting (rejecting) state is optimized away. For example, the generated checker contains a *case* in which *state* is equal to 0. In this case, if the condition $mode == 1 \&\& P16 == 1$ is satisfied then *state* is changed to 1, otherwise it is changed to 3. In this scenario, states 2 and 3 are respectively the accepting and rejecting states where the checker returns 1 (true) and 0 (false). In all other states, the checker returns −1 (unknown).

6   Test Plan Generation

In the third step of the methodology, the low-level XML file is used to generate an effective testing order. Such an order is intended for generating testbenches that make the firmware evolve in the right memory state before the verification of a behaviour is performed. Otherwise, the checker may pass vacuously or fail due to a wrong precondition state reached by the firmware when the checker is executed.

MIST can generate a test plan following two different strategies: a guided and an unguided strategy. The unguided strategy does not leverage the information provided by the postconditions to generate an effective testing order; therefore it is more prone to errors. On the other hand, since it does not require the definition of postconditions, it is easier to use. Inexperienced users should become confident with this first strategy before exploring the more sophisticated second one. The guided strategy makes full use of the postconditions to reduce unexpected failures of checkers due to formalisation mistakes. Furthermore, it provides feedback on the quality of the formalised specifications.

6.1   Unguided Test Plan Generation

This procedure can be used to quickly generate a test plan without exploiting the relation between preconditions and postconditions. Although it is less secure, it might be more preferable for developers who do not want to put in the extra effort of applying the guided approach.

First, the user has to define a safe condition and a set of behaviours. After that, MIST automatically generates a test plan operating as follows. During the simulation, the verification process waits until the safe condition is satisfied. Then, the verification process stores the current firmware memory; this memory state is called "safe state". From there on, the following algorithm is executed:

1. Pick an untested behaviour (b_i); if all behaviours are tested, this process ends.
2. Load the safe state in the firmware's memory.
3. Force the precondition pr_i of b_i to be true in the current simulation, if pr_i does not hold after being forced, prompt an error and return to 1.
4. Test b_i using testbench tb_j^i and dump the result of the test in the verification report.
5. If j is the index of the last testbench of b_i, then go to 1, else, increment j and return to 2.

The safe condition is a non-temporal boolean expression following the same semantics of a fragment proposition. If it becomes true during simulation, it prompts the beginning of the verification process. Delaying the verification process until the safe condition is satisfied allows the simulation to perform a proper initialisation of the firmware; this step is mandatory for most implementations before testing any functional behaviour. A precondition is forced following a similar procedure to the one used to force a proposition inside a fragment. Once again, we use a sat solver to identify an assignment of variables that satisfies the proposition, this assignment is then forced during the simulation.

Dumping and loading safe states are inexpensive procedures both computationally and memory wise. This is true because only a small writable part of the firmware's memory is dumped, as it is the only portion of memory that could change during execution, the rest remains unchanged for all simulations. Furthermore, only one safe state needs to be stored to make this approach work.

6.2   Guided Test Plan Generation

The unguided test plan generation already provides a quick and simple approach to enable verification using MIST. However, to apply that procedure correctly without mistakes, the user would have to annotate each formalised behavior with the *exact* memory state to be forced before starting the test. This process can be extremely time-consuming and error-prone; as a matter of fact, to be sure of reaching the correct memory configuration, the user might have to address in the precondition the value of all variables used in the firmware, which could be thousands of variables in most industrial firmware. In many cases, errors in this procedure lead to a vacuous verification; the test is unable to fire the antecedent of the target assertion, as the testbench is injected in the wrong memory configuration. In this situation, the verification engineer would have to go through an excruciating process of trial and error to find the correct precondition.

To address this issue, we developed a guided test plan generation, to produce an effective testing order. This procedure relies on the assumption that the DUV was developed by following a coherent logic flow. The generated testing order tries to mimic the behavior of a human that manually tests the DUV. To check the correctness of a design, the human starts from the initial state and provides a sequence of stimuli to the DUV. Each sequence of stimuli moves the DUV from one configuration to the next in a coherent flow, such that the ending configuration represents the starting precondition for effectively checking the next behavior in a cause-effect cascade fashion. Through this approach, the specifications are verified in the order intended by the designer, thus reducing the necessity of forcing the memory state that represents the precondition of the target behavior, since the DUV gets naturally brought to the proper state. In other words, the verification engineer no longer has to regard the whole memory of the firmware in the precondition; the correct memory configuration is partially reached as a "side-effect" of the previously tested behaviours.

The guided test plan generation consists of two main procedures. Firstly, all assertions formalised in the low-level XML file are divided into subsets through a clustering procedure. Secondly, each subset is treated as a node of a multilevel graph, and a verification order is defined by generating a path that connects all nodes. Such a path is then traversed to generate an effective testing order.

In this procedure, we consider the precondition and postcondition tags of each assertion. Each precondition/postcondition consists of a propositional formula following the template $variable_1 == constant_1 \& variable_2 == constant_2 \& ... \& variable_n == constant_n$ that represents a concrete memory

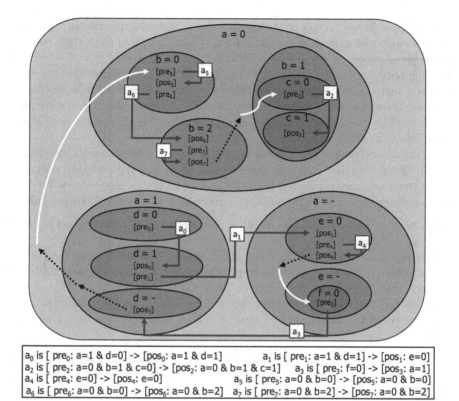

a_0 is [pre_0: a=1 & d=0] -> [pos_0: a=1 & d=1]	a_1 is [pre_1: a=1 & d=1] -> [pos_1: e=0]
a_2 is [pre_2: a=0 & b=1 & c=0] -> [pos_2: a=0 & b=1 & c=1]	a_3 is [pre_3: f=0] -> [pos_3: a=1]
a_4 is [pre_4: e=0] -> [pos_4: e=0]	a_5 is [pre_5: a=0 & b=0] -> [pos_5: a=0 & b=0]
a_6 is [pre_6: a=0 & b=0] -> [pos_6: a=0 & b=2]	a_7 is [pre_7: a=0 & b=2] -> [pos_7: a=0 & b=2]

Fig. 4. Example of test plan generation

configuration. To simplify the exposition, we will use the term "memory state" while referring to a precondition/postcondition.

In the clustering phase, the goal is to divide the set of all memory states into subsets. We will refer to the example depicted in Fig. 4 to clarify the procedure. At the bottom of Fig. 4 we report the list of assertions used in the example. For instance, the assertion described in Sect. 4 is represented in the example as "a_{66} is [pre_{66} : $mode = 0$] $->$ [pos_{66} : $mode = 1$]", where pre (pos) is the precondition (postcondition) of the assertion with id equal to 66. The clustering process starts by considering the whole set of memory states, and then it is recursively repeated for each generated sub-set until no set can be further divided. The process counts the occurrences of each variable in all memory states in the current set; the variable with the highest count is used to perform the split. In the example, the most frequent variable in the whole set is a. The current set is split into as many sub-sets as the number of different assignments of the most frequent variable. Also, we add an optional sub-set containing all memory states that do not include the most frequent variable (do not care sub-set). In the example, the whole set is divided into three clusters, two clusters for $a = 0$ and $a = 1$ and one don't care cluster $a = -$. The same process is repeated until all sub-sets contain only memory states with equivalent assignments. In the example, the cluster identified by $a = 0$ and $b = 0$ contains three equivalent memory states $[pre_5]$, $[pos_5]$, $[pre_6]$ that have the same assignments $[a = 0 \ \& \ b = 0]$. This heuristic approach is intuitively justified by the assumption that the most frequent variables represent better the whole state; therefore, it is reasonable to make them represent wider clusters than those represented by less frequent variables. The clustering procedure aims at making all similar memory states "close" to each other.

In the second part of the approach, each sub-state is used to infer an effective testing order. Starting from the precondition of an assertion chosen randomly (or by the user), the tool finds a path that covers all the memory states. To move from one memory state to the next, the procedure applies the following rules:

R1: Checking an assertion i in memory state $[pre_i]$ moves the process to $[pos_i]$ (solid red arrow);

R2: If the process can not find any other unused precondition in the current state cluster, it must jump to its upper cluster and continue the search (dotted black arrow);

R3: After a jump, the process searches for the first unused precondition $[pre_j]$ in the current cluster. If it finds one, it continues the process from that state (rounded white arrow).

To clarify the procedure, we explain the process by considering the example of Fig. 4. In this example, the user chooses to start with assertion a_0; therefore, the starting state is $[pre_0]$. By applying rule R1, assertion a_0 is added to the test plan, and the execution moves to state $[pos_0]$. In the destination cluster, we find an unused precondition $[pre_1]$. We apply again rule R1, assertion a_1 is added to the test plan, and the execution is moved to pos_1. We repeat the process for assertion a_4, and we reach the state pos_4. In this case, no more preconditions are available in the current cluster; therefore, the execution must apply rule R2 and jump to the upper cluster identified by $a = -$. By applying rule R3, the process finds an unused precondition pre_3 and continues from there. Again, we add assertion a_3 to the test plan, and we move the execution to pos_3. We apply rule R2 as no other preconditions can be found in the current cluster, and we reach cluster $a = 1$. We must apply rule R2 again for the same reason and jump to the upper cluster. The procedure continues as described above until all assertions are added to the test plan. The resulting test plan is $[a_0, a_1, a_4, a_3, a_5, a_6, a_7, a_2]$.

Note that the ideal case, where all behaviors described by the initial specification perfectly connect to form a coherent path, requires the user to completely formalise the specifications such that all assertions belong to a unique cluster. This requirement could be extremely tedious to achieve manually and could be unfeasible for most large-scale designs. For this reason, each time we identify a hole in the specification, such that the postcondition of an assertion does not connect with the precondition of any other assertion, our heuristic approach jumps to a similar close state and warn the verification engineer. To be clear, in the case of fully connected specifications, our approach uses only rule R1. Each time rules R2 and R3 are used, we are approximating.

Table 1. Completeness analysis for example in Fig. 4

max applications of rule R2	completeness
0 times	62.5%
1 times	87.5%
2 times	100%

After generating the test plan, MIST informs the user of the *completeness* of the given set of behaviors by comparing the total number of assertions with the number of times rule R2 was applied to continue the clustering process. The completeness index is calculated with the following formula:

$(1 - exceeded\_maxR2\_applications/tot\_assertions)$.

Where $exceeded\_maxR2\_applications$ represents the number of times the process has to violate the maximum number of consecutive applications of rule R2. Intuitively, the resulting completeness is an index describing how much the set of behaviors is likely to cover all functionalities of the DUV without holes. Each time a missing link is found, the completeness is reduced.

Table 1 shows the completeness for the running example. The first row of the table shows the completeness when no approximation is allowed, or in other words, when the process should not use rule R2 to continue. In the example, rule R2 is used 3 times non-consecutively; therefore, the resulting completeness is $(1 - 3/8) = 0.625$. In the example, the second (third) row shows the completeness reachable by allowing the consecutive application of rule R2 at most once (twice).

The user can exploit this information to improve the set of formalised behaviors such that rule R2 is applied as less as possible while achieving high completeness.

7 Simulation Setup

7.1 Setup

In the last step of the methodology, the verification environment is set up. This phase handles the architecture-dependent features of the target simulator. For now, MIST is capable of generating a verification environment for the IARsystem workbench, which is an industrial compiler and debugger toolchain for ARM-based platforms. In particular, we exploit the provided breakpoint system to evaluate the checkers and to handle the time flow.

Since our checkers provide support for temporal behaviors, we need a way to sample the time flow. To accomplish that, we provide a debugging variable *sim_time* that can be used by the user to simulate the advancement of time in the DUV. To capture this event in the debugger, we place a breakpoint on that variable to recognize *write* operations. Each time *sim_time* is incremented, the simulated time advances by one instant producing a re-evaluation of the active checker. Usually, the best way to use *sim_time* is to place it in a timed interrupt that keeps increasing it at a constant rate. Furthermore, we use breakpoints to inject stimuli in the ports and variables of the fragments using the *forced* and *manual_forced* attributes. Following the above mechanisms, MIST generates the files to perform the verification of the DUV using IARsystem. The generated files consist of an entry point to set up the verification environment, utility functions to handle the time events, the orchestration file that executes each checker using either a guided or unguided strategy and a set of files containing the checkers. To integrate the generated verification environment with IARSystem, the user only has to provide the MIST's entry point file to the simulator; after that, the verification process proceeds automatically until its completion.

7.2 Report

```
 1 [CHECKER #66_a]
 2 FRAGMENT FALSE in Antecedent, Fragment 2
 3 -> Testbench none
 4     - Proposition "true until bTmpRising, max = 9000" is false!
 5     - Reason: timer ran out!
 6
 7 [CHECKER #66_b]
 8 FRAGMENT FALSE in Consequent, Fragment 1
 9 -> Testbench 2
10     - Proposition "mode == 1 && P16 == 1" is false!
11     - Reason: mode = 1, P16 = 4 after 0 instants of <min,1>
12
13 ###############################
14 ########## SUMMARY ###########
15 ###############################
16 - Number of tests: 10
17 - Test plan order [checker id, nTB]: [1, 1] [1, 2] [66_a, none]
18 [66_b, 1] [66_b, 2] [2, 1] [3,1] [3,2] [3,3] [3,4]
19 - Verified : 8 [80%]
20 - Vacouse : 1 [10%]
21 - Failed : 1 [10%]
22
23
```

Fig. 5. Example of report

Once all behaviours are tested, the verification process provides a verification report containing the results of the simulation. The report includes information related to the coverage and failure of checkers, together with the applied test-benches. Checkers whose antecedent was false are reported as vacuously satisfied; otherwise, they are either reported as "verified" if the consequent was true, or as "failed" if the consequent was false.

Since our formalisation language has a well-structured and simplified syntax, failed checkers are also capable of reporting additional information about the failure. Not only they can report exactly the location of the failure in the behaviour, but they can also infer its cause. We show an example of a verification report in Fig. 5.

In this example, we show the result of two possible failures for the running examples depicted in Listing 1.2 (66_a) and 1.4 (66_b). In particular, 66_a is vacuously verified, as the failure makes the antecedent false; 66_b fails on testbench 2, as the failure occurred in the consequent. All other behaviours are correctly verified for all testbenches. The verification report is composed of two main parts, the first part contains the details of the failures, while the second part contains the summary of the whole simulation. For each failed test, the verification environment is capable of reporting the exact location of the failure. For behaviour 66_b, it is reported that the failure occurred in the first fragment of the consequent while injecting the second testbench. Thanks to the limited number of temporal operators and a well-defined structure of the propositions, we can provide a custom message for each failure, greatly simplifying the understanding of its cause. These messages usually contain the assignment of variables that made the proposition fail together with additional remarks on the applied temporal operator. By reading the message for behaviour 66_b, we can quickly understand the cause of the failure: the assignment of variables $mode = 1$, $P16 = 4$ clearly does not satisfy proposition $mode == 1$ && $P16 == 1$. In particular, variable $P16$ is the cause of the failure. Furthermore, the message "after 0 instants of $\langle min, 1 \rangle$" warns the user when the proposition became false, that is, in the first instant of evaluating a fragment annotated with the min attribute.

8   Experimental Results

The experimental results have been carried out on a 2.9 GHz Intel Core i7 processor equipped with 16 GB of RAM and running Windows 10.

8.1   Case Study

We evaluated the effectiveness of our tool to verify an industrial firmware composed of over 10000 lines of C code. The analyzed case study is represented by firmware implementing the controller of a boiler implant. The user can interact with the firmware through an HMI (Human machine interface) composed of LCD display and 4 alphanumeric digits, 7 keys, an RS485 connection and 1 TTL connection (possibility of a second modbus with the addition of the ITRF14 interface). Moreover, the firmware is connected to several external devices providing inputs/outputs such as thermostats, boilers, clocks and an internet gateway. The firmware runs on an RL78 microcontroller, allowing communications with the external devices through Modbus and I2C protocols. Finally, the internal time flow is handled using timed interrupts. The case study configuration is depicted in Fig. 6.

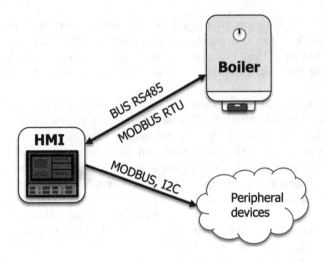

Fig. 6. Case study

8.2   Results

We put emphasis on the timing results of the complete verification process, from the formalisation of specifications to the simulation of the behaviours. Starting from the informal specification of the firmware, we formalised 100 behaviours. On average, each behaviour takes 30 s to be formalised into the high-level XML format. The formalisation of the low-level XML format depends significantly on the skill of the verification engineer and his/her knowledge of the underlying implementation details. After some practice, we were capable of formalizing a behaviour in less than three minutes. Overall, we formalised all 100 behaviours in less than 6 h. After that, MIST generated the testing files and produced an effective test plan in less than 10 s. We don't report numerical results proving the scalability of the tool in terms of time/memory as the complexity of the approach is linear with respect to the number of formalised behaviours; therefore, the tool might take minutes at most to formalise thousands of behaviours. Finally, we set-up the verification environment in the simulator (IAR System Workbench). The simulation took less than 40 min to verify non-vacuously each behaviour and to produce a report of the verification.

The employment of our methodology to an industrial legacy firmware discovered numerous bugs related to an inaccurate sampling of time. One notable example concerns the usage of switches in the HMI. Many specifications implied that some switches needed to be pressed for a certain amount of time to active a functionality. However, during simulation, the correct behaviour did not occur even when providing the correct stimuli. Using MIST for the verification of such a firmware was considerably helpful in identifying a temporal inconsistency of Modbus and I2C protocols that caused a delay in its execution.

Table 2. Completeness analysis for the considered case study.

max applications of rule R2	completeness
0	45.5%
1	72.73%
2	79.22%
3	81.82%
4	97.73%
5	100%

Table 3. Completeness analysis of the case study after the improvements.

max applications of rule 2	completeness
0	48.5%
1	75.73%
2	88.2%
3	100%

Furthermore, the generation of the test plan for 100 behaviours suggested a remarkable incompleteness in the firmware specifications. In Table 2 we can observe the completeness estimations produced for the case study by considering the approach proposed in Sect. 6. We used those statistics to improve the completeness of the specifications by adjusting the behaviours underlining the highest incompleteness and by adding 10 behaviours to cover some specifications holes. After completing this procedure, we achieved new completeness estimations reported in Table 3. To achieve 100% completeness with the new specifications, we needed to apply rule R2 only 3 times, while with the initial specifications, it was used 5 times.

To test the effectiveness of the new language developed for MIST, we arranged a 2-day workshop with the company that provided the industrial case study. In this short time, the developers have been capable of quickly grasping the fundamentals of the language, and before long, they have begun formalising specifications and using the tool on their own.

9   Conclusions and Future Works

In this paper, we presented MIST, an all-in-one tool capable of generating a complete environment to verify C/C++ firmwares starting from informal specifications. MIST reduces the verification effort by providing a user-friendly interface to formalise specifications into assertions and to generate the verification environment automatically. Furthermore, MIST employs a clustering procedure to generate an effective test plan that reduces potential mistakes while formalizing the specifications.

Collaborating with the industry gave us the opportunity to make the tool go through a long tuning process. Moreover, the feedback received by experienced developers allowed us to thoroughly assess the potentials and limitations of MIST. The majority of limitations were overcome during the tuning process; however, there are still few issues that need to be addressed in future works. Most drawbacks of the verification environment generated by MIST are related to unjustified constraints imposed by C-Spy, which is the debugger used in the IARSystem Workbench. Below, we report some of those constraints.

- No observability of non-static variables: we can not test the value or put breakpoints on automatic variables, therefore, we can not write assertions with those variables
- Macros declared with the "#define aliasName originalName" C statement are not visible during simulation: the user is forced to use the right side of the macro when writing propositions, as the debugger does not keep track of aliasing. This limitation deeply affect the readability of the formalised behaviours.
- Lack of strongly typed variables and complex C data structures in the C-Spy language: this major constraint strongly affected the development of MIST; furthermore, we believe that it will also heavily affect extensibility and maintainability.

To avoid being dependent on the constraints imposed by a specific simulator, we will modify the back-end of MIST to be easily extendable to other target simulators.

Hereafter, we report some limitations of MIST that we would like to overcome in future releases.

- No support to generate testbenches that affect only a portion of bits of a target variable: consider the variable *unsigned char P0*, for now, the user can not generate a testbench that, for instance, would modify the value of the first bit of P0 while keeping the other bits unchanged. We planned to introduce a custom operator to overcome the above limitation.
- All behaviours are linked to the same temporal event: we would like to have the user define what temporal event should produce the advancement of time inside each behaviour.

MIST is an open source project (GNU license) freely available at https://gitlab.com/SamueleGerminiani/mist.

References

1. Shamal, P.K., Rahamathulla, K., Akbar, A.: A study on software vulnerability prediction model. In: 2017 International Conference on Wireless Communications, Signal Processing and Networking (WiSPNET), pp. 703–706 (2017)

2. Nagappan, N., Ball, T.: Static analysis tools as early indicators of pre-release defect density, pp. 580–586, June 2005

3. Dawson, M., Burrell, D., Rahim, E., Brewster, S.: Integrating software assurance into the software development life cycle (SDLC). J. Inf. Syst. Technol. Plann. **3**, 49–53 (2010)

4. Zhivich, M., Cunningham, R.K.: The real cost of software errors. IEEE Secur. Priv. **7**(2), 87–90 (2009)

5. Jørgensen, M., Teigen, K., Moløkken-Østvold, K.: Better sure than safe? Overconfidence in judgement based software development effort prediction intervals. J. Syst. Softw. **70**, 79–93 (2004)

6. Oyetoyan, T.D., Milosheska, B., Grini, M., Soares Cruzes, D.: Myths and facts about static application security testing tools: an action research at Telenor digital. In: Garbajosa, J., Wang, X., Aguiar, A. (eds.) XP 2018. LNBIP, vol. 314, pp. 86–103. Springer, Cham (2018). https://doi.org/10.1007/978-3-319-91602-6_6

7. Osman, M.H., Zaharin, M.F.: Ambiguous software requirement specification detection: an automated approach. In: 2018 IEEE/ACM 5th International Workshop on Requirements Engineering and Testing (RET), pp. 33–40 (2018)

8. https://www.iar.com/iar-embedded-workbench

9. Moketar, N.A., Kamalrudin, M., Sidek, S., Robinson, M., Grundy, J.: An automated collaborative requirements engineering tool for better validation of requirements. In: 2016 31st IEEE/ACM International Conference on Automated Software Engineering (ASE), pp. 864–869 (2016)

10. Kakiuchi, Y., Kitajima, A., Hamaguchi, K., Kashiwabara, T.: Automatic monitor generation from regular expression based specifications for module interface verification. In: 2005 IEEE International Symposium on Circuits and Systems, vol. 4, pp. 3555–3558 (2005)

11. Subramanyan, P., Malik, S., Khattri, H., Maiti, A., Fung, J.: Architecture of a tool for automated testing the worst-case execution time of real-time embedded systems firmware. In: 2016 Design Automation & Test in Europe Conference & Exhibition (DATE), pp. 337–342 (2016)

12. Buzhinsky, I.: Formalization of natural language requirements into temporal logics: a survey. In: 2019 IEEE 17th International Conference on Industrial Informatics (INDIN), pp. 400–406 (2019)

13. IEEE standard for property specification language (PSL). IEEE Std. 1850-2010 (Revision of IEEE Std. 1850-2005), pp. 1–182 (2010)

14. IEEE standard for systemverilog-unified hardware design, specification, and verification language - redline. IEEE Std. 1800-2009 (Revision of IEEE Std. 1800-2005) - Redline, pp. 1–1346 (2009)

15. Yang, S., Wille, R., Drechsler, R.: Improving coverage of simulation-based verification by dedicated stimuli generation. In: Formal Methods in Computer Aided Design, pp. 599–606 (2014)

16. Zhao, Y., Bian, J., Deng, S., Kong, Z.: Random stimulus generation with self-tuning. In: 13th International Conference on Computer Supported Cooperative Work in Design, pp. 62–65 (2009)

17. Cadar, C., Dunbar, D., Engler, D.R., et al.: KLEE: unassisted and automatic generation of high-coverage tests for complex systems programs. In: OSDI, vol. 8, pp. 209–224 (2008)

18. Agbaria, S., Carmi, D., Cohen, O., Korchemny, D., Lifshits, M., Nadel, A.: SAT-based semiformal verification of hardware. In: Formal Methods in Computer Aided Design, pp. 25–32 (2010)

19. https://www.esa.int
20. Duret-Lutz, A., Lewkowicz, A., Fauchille, A., Michaud, T., Renault, É., Xu, L.:
    Spot 2.0—a framework for LTL and ω-automata manipulation. In: Artho, C.,
    Legay, A., Peled, D. (eds.) ATVA 2016. LNCS, vol. 9938, pp. 122–129. Springer,
    Cham (2016). https://doi.org/10.1007/978-3-319-46520-3_8

Modular Functional Testing: Targeting the Small Embedded Memories in GPUs

Josie Esteban Rodriguez Condia$^{(\boxtimes)}$ and Matteo Sonza Reorda

Dip. di Automatica e Informatica (DAUIN), Politecnico di Torino, Torino, Italy
{josie.rodriguez,matteo.sonzareorda}@polito.it
http://www.cad.polito.it

Abstract. Graphic Processing Units (GPUs) are promising solutions in safety-critical applications, e.g., in the automotive domain. In these applications, reliability and functional safety are relevant factors. Nowadays, many challenges are impacting the implementation of high-performance devices, including GPUs. Moreover, there is the need for effective fault detection solutions to guarantee the correct in-field operation. This work describes a modular approach to develop functional testing solutions based on the non-invasive Software-Based Self-Test (SBST) strategy. We propose a scalar and modular mechanism to develop test programs based on schematic organizations of functions allowing the exploration of different solutions using software functions. The Flex-GripPlus model was employed to evaluate experimentally the proposed strategies, targeting the embedded memories in the GPU. Results show that the proposed strategies are effective to test the target structures and detect from 98% up to 100% of permanent stuck-at faults.

Keywords: Graphics Processing Units (GPUs) Software-Based Self-Test (SBST) · Modular Test program · In-field Testing

1 Introduction

Graphics Processing Units (GPUs) are powerful devices devoted to processing high-demand data-intensive applications, such as multimedia, multi-signal analysis, and High-Performance Computing (HPC). Moreover, GPUs' flexibility and programming capabilities have boosted the operational scope of these technologies into new domains, so these devices are now also used for safety-critical applications with substantial requirements in terms of reliability and functional safety.

In the automotive field, safety-critical applications, such as Advanced Driver Assistance Systems (ADAS) [1] and sensor-fusion systems, usually require huge computational power and real-time capabilities. For this purpose, cutting-edge technologies are used to implement modern GPU platforms to maximize performance and reduce power consumption. Nevertheless, some studies [2,3] have

© IFIP International Federation for Information Processing 2021
Published by Springer Nature Switzerland AG 2021
A. Calimera et al. (Eds.): VLSI-SoC 2020, IFIP AICT 621, pp. 205–233, 2021.
https://doi.org/10.1007/978-3-030-81641-4_10

proven that devices with the latest transistor technologies are prone to be affected by faults during the device's operative life. One of the most critical challenges arises when permanent faults (for example, caused by wear-out or aging [4]) affect a module during the in-field operation, potentially altering the functionality and the reliability of a device. Thus, end-of-manufacturing testing is no longer sufficient. These recent challenges require additional testing procedures executed during the in-field operation of a device.

In practice, test engineers employ three main methods to perform testing during the operational phase of digital devices. These mechanisms are based on *i)* hardware, *ii)* software and *iii)* hybrid approaches and can be used to solve the new reliability and technology challenges in GPUs. The hardware mechanisms include solutions based on the addition of Design for testability (DfT) structures, such as *Logic* and *Memory Built-in Self-Test* [5], which can be activated at the Power-on or during idle times of the operation and stimulate/observe the internal modules of a device detecting possible faults [6]. Furthermore, 'Error Correcting Codes' (ECC) structures can detect errors and also provide mitigation features into memory modules or communications peripherals.

On the other hand, software solutions are based on designing special programs using appropriate combinations of instructions to test a target functionally. These non-invasive and flexible mechanisms are formally called *Software-Based Self-Test* (SBST) [7]. Finally, the last approach is based on hybrid mechanisms, combining hardware structures and software programs to detect [8] or mitigate [9] faults located in the different modules of a device. Both (hardware and hybrid) solutions are costly when targeting small modules in a GPU and should be developed and included in a design before the production phase. Moreover, both methods cannot be used in already existing hardware platforms.

The testing procedures of GPUs must consider that these special-purpose parallel architectures are particularly efficient when executing embarrassingly parallel programs, as a result of two main factors: the parallel operation of threads and the efficient procedures of loading and storing operands from/to memory. However, real applications are far from this behavior, and most of them are composed of non-easily-parallelizable algorithms. Thus, these applications usually include intra-warp divergence, which is produced when a group of threads (also known as *Warp*) follows different execution paths with different instructions. In [10], the authors analyzed the applications in the CUDA Software Development Kit (SDK) and concluded that approximately 33% of the total execution on them is devoted to process intra-warp divergence. Furthermore, in [11], the authors profile a divergence map of typical programs and workloads in GPUs. Results show that most applications might produce thousands or millions of divergence conditions during the operation of the applications.

The GPUs include several structures and features to manage issues related with the intra-warp divergence. A special structure called Convergence Management Unit (CMU) (also known as Branch Convergence/Divergence Controller, Branch Controller, or Divergence Controller) is employed to manage the intra-warp divergence. The CMU controls the operation of multiple paths in the same group of threads. Internally, the CMU evaluates control-flow instructions and uses a stack memory to store relevant information concerning the execution paths. Thus, the CMU is crucial for the correct operation of an application in the GPU, and a fault affecting this unit can propagate through the modules and collapse the entire operation of the device and the application.

On the other hand, the use of several levels of memory supports an efficient management of operands and reduces latencies generated by the inactive threads, allowing high-performance operation in GPUs [12]. In the GPU parallel architecture, several in-chip and out-chip memories cooperate on hiding stall conditions during the operation of programs that become more critical when a few threads access dispersed memory locations. Faults in these structures might compromise the operation of a thread. Some hardware solutions, such as ECC structures are now common. However, these solutions are not always acceptable and the best tradeoffs are adopted (i.e., in some cases the ECCs are limited to massive memory structures, such as the cache, the shared memory and the register file), leaving other structures unprotected.

Several works demonstrated that SBST solutions [7] could be successfully integrated into safety-critical applications, such as the automotive ones [13]. Most previous works on GPUs proposed SBST strategies targeting some data-path modules [14], including the execution units [15,16], the register file [17], the pipeline registers [18] and some embedded memories [19]. Moreover, other solutions targeted critical modules in the control-path (i.e., the warp scheduler [20], their internal memories [21,22], and parts of the convergence management unit [23]). Nevertheless, to the best of our knowledge, most of the proposed strategies were designed after relevant programming efforts and analyses, considering the specific micro-architectural details of the targeted structures, complicating portability and generalization. Thus, practical strategies to provide convenient procedures in developing SBST mechanisms are still missing in parallel architectures, including GPUs.

In the present work, we go beyond traditional approaches of developing test programs using assembly instructions only and we propose a modular approach to develop functional test procedures using the SBST strategy. The validation of this proposed approach employs as targets some relatively small but critical memory modules in the GPU.

The proposed modular approach exploits a key feature of most SBST strategies in which a test program corresponds to a combination of several routines, which are linked together and integrated into the test program. Thus, each routine's intended functionality can be seen as a 'modular' and independent block. This abstraction level (routines as blocks) can be used to explore alternative descriptions and observe the advantages and limitations of diverse topologies for a given target. Moreover, this method allows to port test routines between different targets, simplifying the development of functional test programs.

This manuscript is an extension of a previous work [23], which introduced a modular approach to develop parametric test programs. The procedures were experimentally validated using the memory in the convergence management module. The main novelties of this work with respect to [23] are: *i)* a detailed description of the proposed modular strategy to generate test programs, *ii)* the exploration of different test-program topologies for a given module, *iii)* the implementation of different test routines (in a test program), considering operational constraints, and *iv)* the validation through experiments using the small embedded memories in the GPU core.

The proposed modular approach, and the developed SBST strategies are implemented and evaluated resorting to the FlexGripPlus model, an open-source version of the NVIDIA GPU architecture. Results show that the flexibility of the proposed modular test programs do not compromise the fault detection capabilities (from 98% to 100%) for the evaluated modules.

This work is organized as follows. Section 2 introduces a basic overview of the GPU architecture, with special emphasis on the FlexGripPlus and the memory modules targeted to validate the proposed strategies. Section 3 describes the modular SBST strategies to test permanent faults. Sections 4, 5, and 6 describe the procedures to develop test programs in the stack memory, the Predicate register file, and in the address register and vector register files, respectively. Section 7 reports the main constraints and limitations during the development of the test programs. Section 8 reports the experimental results, and Section IX draws some conclusions and outlines future works.

2   Background

2.1   General Organization of GPUs

GPUs are special-purpose parallel processing devices composed of arrays of execution units (also called 'Streaming Multiprocessors', or SMs), implementing the Single-Instruction Multiple-Data (SIMD) paradigm [24] or variations, such as the Single-Instructions Multiple-Thread (SIMT). An SM is the main operative core inside a GPU and is organized as a few pipeline stages, including various execution units (also known as Stream/Scalar Processors, or SPs), some cache memories, a Register File (RF), one or more scheduler controllers, and one or more dispatchers. More in detail, the operation of an SM starts when the scheduler controller submits an available group of threads (also called Warp or Work-group) and one instruction is fetched, decoded and executed in the available SPs. Then, a new instruction is loaded and executed.

The SM also includes a CMU able to control different execution path in a warp, which are produced when conditional assessments are present in a parallel program. Modern SM implementations also include a memory hierarchy composed of several levels of memories, aiming at the reduction of latency and race conditions when load and store operations are performed.

2.2   FlexGripPlus

FlexGripPlus is a microarchitectural RT-level GPU model described in VHDL [25]. This model is a new version built on top of the original FlexGrip model [26].

FlexGripPlus implements the Nvidia G80 microarchitecture, supporting up to 52 assembly instructions, and is also compatible with the CUDA programming environment. The latest version of the GPU model has the flexibility to select among 8, 16, or 32 SPs and may be configured to include both Floating-Point Unit (FP32) and Special Function Unit cores.

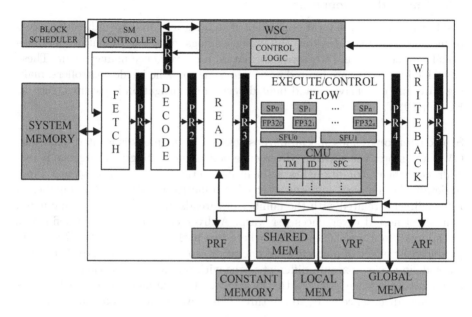

Fig. 1. A general scheme of the SM architecture in FlexGripPlus.

The FlexGripPlus architecture is based on the SIMT paradigm and exploits a SM core with five stages of pipeline (Fetch, Decode, Read/Issue, Execute/Control-flow and Write-back), as shown in Fig. 1. In the SIMT paradigm, the controller (WSC) submits a warp (32 threads) and one instruction is fetched, decoded, and distributed to be processed on an independent SP. The Read/Issue and Write-back stages load and store data operands from/to the Register File (RF), shared, global, local or constant memories. Moreover, the Address Register File (ARF) and a Predicate Register File (PRF) are used to perform the indirect addressing of memory resources and to store conditional flags, respectively.

The Execute/Control-flow stage is composed of the SPs, FP32s and other accelerators. Moreover, this stage contains one CMU used for intra-warp branching and also controls and traces the intra-warp divergence (caused when threads of a warp follow different execution paths, so executing different instructions). The CMU handle two paths in the same level of divergence by executing every path in a serial manner until both paths return to convergence (all threads in a warp execute the same instruction). The number of supported nesting divergence is proportional to the number of threads in a warp. Furthermore, the CMU also stores the information related to perform conditional branches with several execution paths.

The following subsection describes the purpose of the embedded memories in the GPU architecture and in the FlexGripPlus model.

2.3 Embedded Memories

Inside the SM core, several embedded memories are used to indirectly access to memory resources, to store the predicate flags, after the execution of conditional instructions, and to store information for divergence management. These embedded memories are limited in size, in some cases lie inside controllers, making hard and expensive to add fault detection or mitigation structures, such as ECC or BIST.

Stack Memory: This special-purpose embedded memory is located inside the CMU and stores the starting (divergence point) and ending (convergence point) addresses when a conditional assessment instruction is executed by a warp. More in detail, the memory contains a set of 32 Line Entries (LEs). The number of LEs is directly related with the number of threads in a warp and the maximum number of nested divergences per warp. A divergence point can be defined as the address, in a parallel program, where two paths (Taken and No-Taken) are produced by effect of a conditional operation, so causing intra-warp divergence (threads in a warp execute different paths with different instructions). Furthermore, a convergence point is the location in the parallel program where the intra-warp divergence ends, so the threads in a warp execute one path again.

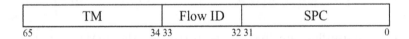

TM	Flow ID	SPC
65	34 33 32 31	0

Fig. 2. Organization of one LE in the stack memory of FlexGripPlus.

Each LE in the stack is composed of three fields, (see Fig. 2). These fields are the 'thread mask' (TM), the flow ID, and the 'program counter of a warp' (SPC). The TM stores the status of the active threads in a warp and an active logic state represents the number of active threads executing a path (Taken or No-Taken). The flow ID represents the execution state of the intra-warp divergence. This field can be '01' (for a branch condition) or '00' (for a convergence point or embarrassingly parallel condition). The SPC can store the starting address of the paths or the convergence point address after both paths are executed.

The CMU employs two LEs to manage the intra-warp divergence. The first LE stores the convergence point (also known as synchronization point) and the number of active threads at the moment of starting the divergence. The second LE stores the starting address for the No-taken path and the threads to execute this path. It is worth noting that the CMU uses a new set of LEs to store the status once nesting divergence is produced.

Predicate Register File (PRF): This module stores the predicate flags after the execution of conditional assessments, by each thread, in a warp. These conditional assessments are the product of logic-arithmetical operations or explicit setting operations. When the GPU model is configured with 8 SPs, 2,048 one-bit size locations are assigned per SP. These locations are divided in groups of 4-bits registers (C0, C1, C2 and C3) and distributed among the available threads. Each predicate register Cx stores the logical state of the zero (Z), the sign (S), the carry (C), and the overflow (O) flags for each thread. The flags remain constant in the subsequent clock cycles until the execution of a new instruction affects their state. Furthermore, these predicate flags are also used as conditions for the executions of instructions, so these are commonly read before the execution if required. Recent implementations of the PRF provide support for up to 8 predicate registers per thread.

Address Register File (ARF): This module is a structure of registers devoted to perform indirect indexing for external memories to the SM, including the shared and constant memories. These additional registers are mainly used in case of performance optimization for the several threads in a program and are mainly focused on the efficient access of memory sectors organized as arrays or matrices. Furthermore, the ARF reduces latency of accessing frequently used data by a kernel.

Each one of the eight SPs has an associated ARF module composed of 512 registers of 32 bit-size holding up to 128 threads. Each ARF module is distributed among the threads, so four registers (A0, A1, A2, and A3) can be employed per thread.

Vector Register File (VRF): This is a massive structure composed of 16KB general-purpose registers of 32 bit-size and located inside of an SM. This structure is the fastest element in the memory hierarchy of the SM and is one of the most critical units in the operation of a thread, since most instructions store or load operands from this structure. The VRF is divided among the eight cores and it is distributed among the threads in a program during the configuration phase.

Since recent GPU architectures protect the VRF against fault effects through ECC structures, this module is not considered as the main target for the development of SBST programs. However, we employ this module to validate and also explore different options of implementing test programs.

3   Modular Functional Testing Approach

The modular approach for testing is a generic strategy to develop functional test programs taking into account the microarchitectural composition of a target module, the interaction with the parallel architecture of the GPU, its functional operation, its constraints, and the fault model. This modular approach is based

on the development of a group of generic procedures, which are represented as
a set of interconnected blocks, that once translated, compose a test program.

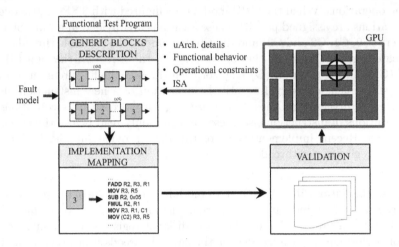

Fig. 3. A general scheme of the proposed modular approach to develop functional test
programs.

The approach for modular testing considers three steps: *i)* Generic blocks
description, *ii)* Implementation or mapping, and *iii)* validation, see Fig. 3.

In the beginning, the organization of the test program is initially defined as
a set of generic high-level blocks, which are then divided into a group of interconnected procedures to generate the intended test functionality. This modular
abstraction provides flexibility that can be used to explore and address different
approaches of functional test in any module.

The Generic blocks description is a strategy to represent the behavior of the
interconnected procedures aiming the test a given target module. This representation considers the operation of the module and its interaction with the system,
the operational constraints, and the features of the target fault model.

In this stage, the most relevant functionalities of each hardware module are
employed to define a sequence of generic procedures (blocks) that, once combined, allows the functional test of the module. Each procedure is intended to
aim one of this three functionalities: 1) *Fault Controllability*, 2) *Fault Observability* or 3) *Program Monitoring*. *Fault Controllability* procedures are directly
related to the ability to inject test patterns through the available instructions
and structural resources. *Fault Observability* procedures propagate the effect of
a fault in the module into one of the available outputs of the GPU, such as
control signals, buses, or external memories.

In principle, a *Fault Controllability* procedure injects test patterns in the
target module. However, the feasibility of applying those patterns must be evaluated for each target module. It is worth noting that SBST is a non-invasive

test strategy, so it is possible that some modules have not controllability support (i.e., instructions able to activate faults in the module) to apply a test pattern. On the other hand, *Fault Observability* procedures describe the feasible methods to propagate the fault effect to any visible output. This feature becomes important in modules that are operated by different threads. In a parallel architecture, such as the GPU, the observability of faults might implicitly include parallel fault propagation. The micro-architectural features of a module provide the composition and contribute to identifying the *Fault Controllability* and *Fault Observability* procedures for a module. Finally, *Program Monitoring* procedures introduce optional management, tracing, or check-pointing in the test program. They can be used to increase the observability of faults or other purposes, such as the test program's division into parts. In this stage, a general analysis of the module's observability and controllability allows the definition of the procedures to integrate the functional test program.

The operational constraints and the target fault model provide the relevant limitations regarding the controllability or the fault's observability. At this level, the constraints are used to propose alternative procedures aiming at the management or even removing these limitations. The features of the fault model are used as complementary information to verify that each procedure and the combination of them allow the test of faults.

For illustration purposes, the method is supported in a scheme describing the procedures (software functions) of the modular test program, see Fig. 4. This scheme is composed of *blocks* (1, 2 and 3), representing modular procedures, and a set of *interconnections* (Arrows), indicating the serial sequence of operations during the test. Finally, dotted modules in a scheme represent loop functions as the repetition of one or several blocks. It is worth noting that in parallel architectures, and depending on the structural location of the target module, several threads might execute the same test program in parallel.

The flexibility of the modular approach allows the exploration of test programs by composing different block interconnections and different routines, so potentially allowing test designers to explore different benefits or constraints in the development of a test program.

The second step (Implementation or mapping) builds a test program by translating the blocks in the modular scheme into equivalent software routines. In fact, the modular schemes only consider the main functional features of a test program and include all microarchitectural constraints. Thus, the implementation stage is based on the translation or mapping of each procedure (block or function) into the equivalent software routines using the available instructions of the GPU's microarchitecture. In this step, the interconnections and internal loop are also considered and included in the mapping process.

The identification of the specific set of instructions allows the operation of any intended functionality from the modular organization, so aiming the test of the targeted modules. More in detail, the implementation of the modular test program requires the use of an incremental approach. Initially, each block (procedure) is analyzed and translated individually. Then, a preliminary evaluation

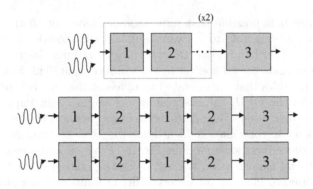

Fig. 4. An example of the modular organization of a test program. General organization and test program description (Top), Equivalent organization per thread (Bottom).

is performed to verify the functional test operation. This process is repeated for each procedure in the modular scheme. Then, the main interconnections among the blocks are mapped and checked. Finally, the internal loop is automated to provide portability according to the number of resources per thread and warps in the test program.

Each procedure (block) can be composed of a number of instructions ranging from simple instruction up to complex program procedures. Similarly, the internal loop requires the addition of several instructions at the beginning or at the end of the routines, which are commonly included to manage the control flow and the sequence of the program. In the end, the blocks of all proposed SBST strategies are described as a combination of a high-level programming language, such as CUDA (when possible), and instructions at the assembly-level (SASS for the used GPU). The main advantage is that minimal changes in a block (procedure) are required to change the functionality of a test program (i.e., the test can be focused on fault detection or diagnosis).

Finally, in the third step (validation), the self-test routines are verified using fault injection campaigns into the target modules. The output reports can be employed to improve the quality of a test program.

The following sections describe the development of the functional blocks and schemes used to develop SBST programs for the divergence stack memory, PRF, ARF, and the VRF in a GPU core.

4   Stack Memory

As introduced above, the stack memory is a particular module in a parallel architecture. This module is part of the control-flow management, so one warp may access this memory to push or pop information.

4.1   Controllability

The controllability (and the injection of test patterns) of this module is achieved by forcing the execution of controlled divergences for each thread in a warp. The generation of divergences forces the stack to store the information of the number of active threads in the TM field and the starting instruction address in the SPC field, so both fields are excited each time a divergence is produced. When more than one divergence is produce, two possible effects in the stack are observed. In the first case, a serial divergence only access the same LE in the stack and changes the values of TM and SPC. On the other hand, a nesting divergence changes the target LE and both values (TM and SPC) are stored in a new addressed LE.

The detection of permanent faults in the stack is reduced to generate and perform a sequence of divergence paths as a method to excite the TM field of each LE in the Stack memory.

Using the previous information, we propose two possible methods to control the address pointer of the LEs and inject test patterns in both fields (TM and SPC) of the LEs in the stack.

The first method (*Nesting*), see Fig. 5 (Top), generates test patterns by using a sequence of recursive intra-warp divergence routines, so nesting functions cause the movement of the address in the stack pointer into a deeper LE. The divergence is produced by successive conditional assessments between the thread identified of each thread in a warp and constant values, so generating an ordered number of comparisons (following a specific path, grey path in Fig. 3) and producing the required test pattern in the TM field of each LE.

On each comparison, one or a group of threads is disabled, so defining a pattern to be stored into the deeper LE and generating two execution paths. This method is useful in managing the addressing of the LEs and injecting patterns into the TM field. The routines on each path (Taken and No-taken) expose the presence of a permanent fault in the TM. The previous process is repeated for half the number of threads in a warp, hence two LEs are required during nesting divergence management. Once the Taken routine finishes, the DMU submits the No-taken path routine when a fault is present.

A fault-free divergence stack always executes the routine in the Taken path, which generates new divergence paths and forces the test of other levels of LEs. Moreover, once a divergence is generated, two LEs store the synchronization point and the address to start the not-taken path (which can be used as test patterns). Thus, a fault can be detected when retrieving the stored values, or when the number of threads executing a path is different from the expected one, so making the fault effects visible in the outputs.

The Nesting strategy can inject test patterns on the even LEs of the stack memory. However, the odd ones are missing. The generation of test patterns for these fields requires the explicit addition of one synchronization function (SSY) before start the comparisons causing the divergence. The effect of SSY is the movement of the address pointer to the next or deeper LE in the stack memory. Then, the same previous procedure can be applied again, so testing the odd LEs.

On the other hand, the main issue of this strategy is the procedure to manage disabled threads. When a thread is disabled, this cannot be turned active again until the divergence paths are executed, and a convergence point is reached. Thus, it is not possible to test or detect a permanent fault in a deeper LE location. This restriction implies that the comparisons should be performed multiple times, targeting different threads in the TM field. We anticipate that this strategy may suffer from considerable code length and excessive execution times.

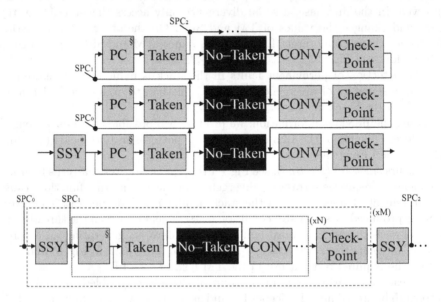

Fig. 5. A general scheme of the proposed modular SBST strategies Nesting (Top) and Sync-Trick (Bottom) to test the stack memory. (*) Optional function to test the odd LEs. (§) Optional functions to distribute the test functions in the system memory.

The second method (called *Sync-Trick*), see Fig. 5 (Bottom), exploits the functionality of synchronization functions (SSY) to deceive the CMU when testing the stack memory. This method allocates SSY functions in strategically selected locations in the test program to generate the movement in the stack pointer.

More in detail, one SSY is explicitly located before each sequence of controlled divergence functions to test the TM of a LE. Hence, this function forces the controller to allocate a new level of LE in the memory without the need to generate an intra-warp divergence explicitly. The advantage of this method is that each LE can be addressed without the need of disabling specific threads to create nesting addressing of the memory. Thus, this strategy replaces the generation of nesting divergence by the management of the stack pointer and the execution of sequential controlled divergences.

The sequences of intra-warp divergence operations, generating the Taken and No-taken paths, inject the test patterns into the target LE. This process can be repeated N times (number of threads in a warp) to use different active threads and memory addresses as test patterns. Then, a new SSY addresses a deeper LE and the test procedure is restarted. It is worth noting that this mechanism is effective to move across one direction and reach deeper LEs in the memory. However, the returning phase (to a previous LE) requires the achievement of the convergence point address, which is initially stored in the stack by the execution of the SSY instruction.

4.2 Observability

The fault effect propagation is achieved using the Signature per Thread (SpT) strategy [18, 21, 27]. This mechanism assigns one signature to each thread to map and to propagate the effect of a permanent fault into the global memory. Each SpT is updated, taking advantage of both paths (Taken and No-taken) produced during an intra-warp divergence. Thus, the same mechanism used to test faults is used to increase the observability of the structure under test. Each SpT computes and accumulates intermediate results for each verified LE. The SpTs are finally grouped and stored in global memory for later analyses.

4.3 Test Program Organization

The interconnections and the main architecture of each proposed test approach are defined knowing the stack memory's observability and controllability methods.

Figure 5 presents the basic schemes of the modular composition of the Nesting and Sync-Trick test mechanisms.

In the first case (Nesting), the test generation is based on nesting divergences, so the general test strategy starts with selecting the target LE in the stack (optional use of the SSY function). Then, one divergence (two paths) divides the number of active threads, followed by the execution of a taken routine. This routine is in charge of update the SPT in the active threads. Then, a new divergence is produced (two new paths). Similarly, the same procedure restarts again, and a new taken routine is operated. The previous procedure continues until all LEs in the stack are addressed. Finally, the No-Taken paths are operated before reach the routine of convergence (CONV).

In the second approach (Sync-Trick), the operation starts selecting a target LE in the stack (using the SSY function). Then, the divergence is generated, and the two paths are created. The taken (function) path updates the signature per thread, and, finally, the Not-Taken path is executed, and both paths reach the convergence function (CONV). The previous procedure is repeated as the number of threads in a warp (N). Then, a new target LE in the stack is addressed, and the procedure is restarted again until the total number of LEs in the stack (M) is tested.

In both schemes, the address pointers SPC0, SPC1, and SPC2 represent each block function's effect on the stack address pointer and the values stored in the SPC field of the stack memory.

As depicted in both schemes, the PC and Check-point procedures are also included in the test strategy. These complementary functions are introduced to increase observability or to allow the division into parts when possible.

A control-flow routine (PC) can be included before or in one of the divergence paths to test the high bits in the SPC field. In fact, a detailed overview of the SPC field revealed that this field is partially tested. This issue is mainly caused by the short length of the test program for both strategies. In order to complete the test of the SPC field, the test routines are redistributed across the system memory, so generating the missing test patterns and the PC routine is used to address those test routines distributed in the memory.

The check-point routines are included to verify the testing of the SPC field of the LEs in the stack. These routines are located after the convergence point. In this way, any permanent fault in the SPC is detected when the convergence point or the starting address of the No-Taken path are incorrectly read from the LEs by the effect of any permanent fault. A fault in the SPC field generates an unexpected addressing in the system memory. The permanent fault is detected by mismatches in time execution and through the signatures stored in the global memory.

The check-point routines verify, through a check-point signature, the correct flow execution of a program. Moreover, this function compares an expected check signature value with the actual accumulated value during the test program's execution. When the comparison matches, the accumulated signature is updated, otherwise the test program finishes propagating in memory the error in the SPC field of the evaluated LE. The same strategy can be applied to any of the two controllability methods (Nesting or Sync-Trick).

The use of these additional functions (Check-Point and PC) is optional, considering that these strategies are costly in memory overhead for an in-field execution. It is worth noting that the proposed technique takes into account the operational restrictions to develop the test programs using the Stuck-at fault model. Other fault models would require the adaptation of the Sync-trick mechanism. However, it would be hard or impossible to follow the Nesting strategy. The convergence function (CONV) synchronizes both paths' operation and restart (from that point) the embarrassingly parallel operation of all threads in a warp.

4.4 Implementation

The synch-trick strategy cannot be directly described in CUDA, and explicit assembly level descriptions are required. In contrast, the Nesting mechanism can be directly mapped into the CUDA without modifications. The implemented code for both test methods is composed of the following functions: *i)* Initialization function, *ii)* synchronization function (SSY), *iii)* flow control function (PC), *iv)* intra-warp divergence function and SpT update functions (Taken and No-Taken), and *v)* check-point function (Check-point).

Each function is described independently and can be attached depending on the target of a test program. The initialization function defines and initializes the registers for each thread. Moreover, this function initializes the addresses to store the SpTs and check-point signatures. The functionality of other functions was introduced in the previous section.

Two main operations can be employed to manage the addressing of LEs in the stack memory. Initially, the convergence function is implemented using one synchronization instruction (SSY), which affects the stack pointer in the memory, and moves it to the next LE. When the program reaches the convergence point, the pointer returns to the previously addressed LE. During the execution, the first LE is used only for storing purposes. In contrast, the second LE is employed during the management of the divergence, and control-flow instructions can affect this LE with writing or reading operations. Thus, when the operation of the first path ends, the information in the second LE is used to start the not-taken path until the convergence point is reached. The CONV function, which is interpreted as the return from an addressed LE to the previous one, is described using exit control-flow instructions, such as (NOP.S).

The PC functions are relocations in the memory of the intra-warp divergence routines. These PC functions require of some instructions (in the format of 32 and 64 bits) located before each relocated function. These instructions avoid hanging conditions by permanent faults in the SPC field. In this way, when the program counter is affected by a fault, and it jumps to any unexpected memory location, it is always possible to retake control of the program and finish the execution of the GPU. Nevertheless, it is expected degradation in performance by the effect of the permanent fault. On the other hand, the intra-warp divergence routines are generated by successive comparisons between the Thread.id values, of a warp, with a constant value. The constant value is loaded using immediate instructions. The check-point signatures are predefined before execution and also loaded through immediate instructions. Then, the two paths are executed.

The functions in both paths (Taken and No-taken) update the SpT, which is firstly loaded from memory and then increased as a counter according to the path. A similar procedure is applied in the check-point routines that update check-point signatures to verify the step-by-step execution of the program, so avoiding infinite loops or unexpected branches by faults in the SPC field.

The modular description of both SBST strategies allows the exploration of multiple options for the programs. In the Nesting method, the modular approach guides the addition of functions, such as the nesting divergence, and also provides support to add or to remove optional functions targeting the SPC field (PC and Check-point). In contrast, the modularity presents considerable advantages for the Sync-Trick method. The code description of this method is scalable and modular, so it is possible to append or remove block functions in the description of the program, targeting the individual test of LEs in the stack memory. This modularity gives us the possibility to address any or a group of LEs and to generate an independent test program. The division of the test contributes to reducing the execution time of the test program during the in-field operation of a GPU.

The Sync-Trick method can employ two approaches to evaluate LEs in memory. The first approach (Accumulative or Acc) aims the test of a consecutive group of LEs and accumulates the signatures in memory. This approach must always start from the first LE and can finish at any of the other 31 LEs in the stack.

On the other hand, the second approach (Individual or Ind) targets the testing of an individual LE and then the retrieving of signature results to the host. This approach only focuses on one of the LEs in the memory and is intended to have a reduced execution time. The performance cost (execution time (ST)) of both approaches (Acc and Ind) can be calculated using the Eqs. (1) and (2).

$$ST(Acc) = Ts \cdot n + Ch \cdot n + SSY \cdot (n-1) \tag{1}$$

$$ST(Ind) = Ts + Ch + SSY \cdot (n-1) \tag{2}$$

where n represents the target LE in the stack memory. SSY, Ts, and Ch represent the execution time of the synchronization, test pattern injection, and check-point functions, respectively. The initialization function was not included considering that it is constant for both cases, and it is negligible in terms of duration.

From Eqs. (1) and (2), it is clear that the cost of the Accumulative version (Acc) is higher than for the Ind version. The cost is mainly caused by the different approaches in each case. In the Acc version, the program is intended to test the number of selected LEs sequentially. In contrast, the Ind approach targets the test on one LE, so the test patterns and check-point functions are used once. The number of synchronization functions depends on the target level of LE in the stack memory.

On the other hand, the performance cost of the Nesting method is described by the expression in Eq. (3).

$$Ns = N \cdot Ch \cdot \sum_{i=0}^{m}(SSY + Ts) \tag{3}$$

where N represents the total number of threads in a warp, and m is the target LE to be tested. CH, SSY, and Ts have the same meaning than in Eqs. (1) and (2). As introduced previously, the target LE could be even or odd. Thus, the starting value of i in the summation could be 0 or 1.

5   Predicate Register File

This module is a parallel structure in the GPU and it is addressed in parallel by the active threads during the execution of a program, so the maximum number of threads per core are required to perform the test of the complete module.

Controllability. The PRF stores homogeneous information, so each active thread in a program have direct access to this memory, Thus, only one procedure is required to inject test patterns. The test of each register is based on the generation of load procedures (Ld), see Fig. 6. Initially, Ld targets one predicate register per thread (Cx) and assigns a value by using two possible methods: *i)* conditional assessments(PRF_T) or *ii)* direct assignments(PRF_T_R2C).

In the first case, a sequence of conditional assessments causes the activation of each predicate flag, injecting a test pattern, and propagates its effect for evaluation. On the other hand, in the direct assignment, the movement operation changes the content of the predicate register. It is worth noting that in both cases, one flag was targeted to clearly identify a fault.

5.1   Observability

A function (PROP) performs conditional evaluations to identify and classify a fault. This function propagates the effect of the target predicate register. The conditional evaluations produce two paths (Taken and No-taken). Both paths are used to update an SpT to identify if a fault was present in a given flag of a predicate register. As depicted in Fig. 6, the gray path describes the fault-free case of the test. When there are no detected faults, the test program remains convergent for all threads in a warp. In contrast, when a fault is detected, an intra-warp divergence is produced as effect of the fault and the SpT are updated indicating a detected fault. It is worth nothing that four serial procedures of conditional evaluations are required to test each register.

5.2   Test Program Organization

Two different approaches of modular test can be proposed for this module. In the first case (PRF_T), see Fig. 6 (Top), the organization of the test program is fully sequencial, so the Ld procedure injects a test pattern into a target register in the PRF. Then, the Prop routine propagates any fault and evaluates the previously register in search of faults. The taken and not-taken routines are used to update the SpT and propagate any fault effect into the available outputs. The Taken routine is intended to be operated when a faults are not present in the evaluated register of the PRF. Once, both paths reaches convergence, the previous sequence is repeated as the number of exclusive predicate registers per thread (M), the total number of flags (N) and the number of test patterns to inject per register (T).

In the second case (PRF_T_R2C), see Fig. 6 (Bottom), the organization of the test program varies and is divided as a sequence of individual operations. First, The injection is performed using the Ld procedure and propagated with the Prop routine. Then, it is repeated M times, as the number of registers, so injecting the same test pattern to each register.

The evaluation is performed using the one divergence and the Taken procedures. Again, these procedures are repeated as the number of registers per

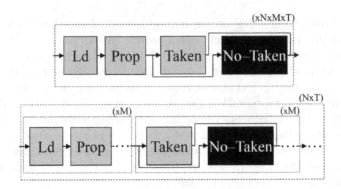

Fig. 6. General schemes of the modular approaches to test the PRF.

thread, so evaluating all previously addressed flags. Finally, the complete procedure of injection, propagation and evaluation is repeated as the number of flags
per register and the number of test patterns to inject. It is worth noting that
the main fault model target of the proposed strategy is stuck-at faults. However,
it is also possible to adapt the second case to evaluate other fault models in the
PRF.

5.3 Implementation

Three versions of the Ld function can be described; one based on logic-arithmetic
instructions (IOP.AND, IOP.XOR) and a second version using setting instructions (ISETP) to modify a flag in the predicate register. Furthermore, it is also
possible to modify a register using a direct assignment (R2C). Thus, the main
functionality (inject a test pattern) can be obtained through several descriptions.
The block functions in the SBST strategy for the PRF are parametrically developed, so it is possible to easily replace one function (such as Ld) by another in the
program. It is worth noting that the first two cases require several instructions
before the comparison or setting.

The Prop function also supports different implementation methods. One
method is based on a sequence of conditional operations, which are executed once
a specific flag is active. The other method is through intra-warp divergence, so
explicitly producing two execution paths corresponding to the faulty (No-Taken)
and fault-free (Taken) cases. In both versions, the parametric description allows
the selection of a predicate register and a target flag, so simplifying the procedures for the generation of the test program.

The routines on each path follow a similar description with respect to those
developed for the stack memory, so in principle, these functions are imported
into these SBST programs.

Equations 4 and 5 represent the performance cost of both strategies for testing the PRF. As you can observe, both equations are equivalent and the performance of both strategies remains the same. The main difference between the

two approaches is the order of executing the test on each register of the PRF module.

$$ST = ((Ld + Prop) \cdot M + T \cdot M) \cdot N \cdot T \tag{4}$$

$$ST = (Ld + Prop + T) \cdot N \cdot M \cdot T \tag{5}$$

The Ld implementation presents the same cost for the IOP (arithmetic and logical) and the ISETP (setting) descriptions of the functions. However, for the R2C alternative, the total description and memory footprint is reduced to a total of 36 instructions.

6   Address Register File and Vector Register File

These modules are parallel in the operation of a program in the GPU and can be accessed in parallel by the active threads.

6.1   Controllability

The ARF and the VRF modules stores homogeneous information on each register, so there are not internal field divisions. This feature allows the use of only one procedure (Ld) to perform the test pattern injection. The main idea of the Ld procedure is to perform direct assignation of test patterns on each register of both modules (General Purpose Registers Rx in the VRF and address registers Ax in the ARF). The addressing routine of the registers is mainly sequential. However, the direction and the limits are defined according to the number of threads in a program (T). It is worth noting that all active threads can access the ARF or VRF during the execution of the instructions.

6.2   Observability

The propagation of a fault is performed using a function (Comp). This procedure performs conditional assessments and compare the value in any register with several predefined masks. These masks are used to identify any fault in the evaluated registers and are the base for the comparison.

There are two possible selections of the mask: *i)* Fine-grain and *ii)* Coarse-grain. A fine-grain mask allows identifying the location of the fault affecting a register. However, several detection procedures are required. On the other hand, a coarse-grain mask allows the rapid detection of a fault, but it is not possible to identify its location.

After each comparison, a divergence is produced. This divergence is employed as mechanism to evaluate the propagation of a fault and also to update the SpT. The gray (see Fig. 7) path shows the embarrassingly parallel operations, when the test approach is used and there are not fault in the module. In contrast, the Not-taken path in black is used when a fault is detected.

6.3   Test Program Organization

The organization of the modular test programs can be defined in two methods and can be applied for both modules (ARF and VRF). It must be considered that the internal content of each routine is adapted according to the target module. In the representative schemes, we considered a test program configured with a defined number of register per thread in a warp (N), a defined number of warps (M), a predefined number of parallel threads (P) and a fixed number of test patterns to inject (T).

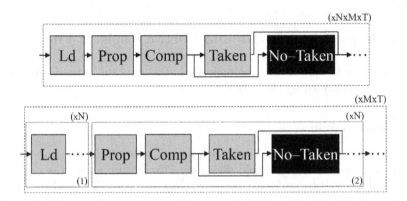

Fig. 7. General schemes of the modular approaches to test the ARF and VRF.

In the first case, see Fig. 7(Top), the procedure is performed targeting a sequential test detection. First, the Ld procedure injects test patterns in one register. Then, the Prop procedure propagates the faults effect (if present) and a comparison is performed using the Comp procedure. This comparison starts the divergence and the Taken path is evaluated to update the signature for each active thread. Finally, the previous procedure is repeated as the number of registers per thread in a warp, number of warps in the test program and the number of test patterns to inject.

The second approach, see Fig. 7(Bottom), is intended to divide the test program into small parts, so the sequential procedure of test is replaced by a two independent stages that combined provide the same test functionality of the previously explained approach. These two independent stages are: general test patterns injection (1) and general evaluation (2). In (1), a complete sequence of one test pattern injection is performed injecting in all registers assigned to any thread. Then, in the stage (2), all propagation and comparison operations are performed to identify faults in the registers. Finally, both stages (1 and 2) are repeated as the number of warp in the program and the number of test patterns to inject.

6.4   Implementation

In the case of the ARF and the VRF memories, both approaches employ similar methods to implement the Ld function. This is based on the direct assign instructions R2A and MOV, respectively. However, the ARF structure can use an equivalent instruction to perform the assignation using another address register as source A2A.

The Comp function compares and enables a flag when mismatches are found. In both cases this function is implemented using similar mechanisms through constant values (from immediate instructions or loaded from memory). Finally, the same intra-warp divergence functions are imported and adopted for these modules. It is worth noting that the development of the blocks allows different targets of the SBST program. On the one hand, it is possible to develop the functions to only perform fault detection. Furthermore, the functions can be replaced with special versions, which provide fault diagnosis features (VRF_T_dia), so allowing the identification of the location causing the fault effect. A detailed evaluation shows that both versions of the R2A and A2A routines to implement the Ld function have the same cost in terms of execution and resource overhead.

Equation 6 describes the performance costs for both approaches, which are equivalent from the performance point of view. Nevertheless, the test can be performed in parts (ld + comp) when the modules are free and the application can be stopped for a long interval. Otherwise, the complete evaluation of each register and the splitting into parts can be employed when short interval times can be employed. It is worth noting that the performance of each approach is affected when faults are detected on each module by the execution of the missing path in order to update the detection signatures.

$$ST = ((Ld + Pr + Co + Ts) \cdot N \cdot M \cdot P = ((Ld) \cdot N + (Pr + Co + Ts) \cdot N) \cdot M \cdot P \tag{6}$$

7   Limitations and Constraints

Although the proposed modular approach can be applied to any hardware module in a GPU, several programming constraints must be consider in the mapping or implementation step.

In the implementation of the SBST techniques, we explored different possible description styles for each program using high-level and middle-level abstraction languages for programming the GPU (CUDA and PTX, respectively). However, we observed some constraints related to the implementation of the SBST technique in CUDA or PTX, due to the fact that particular combinations of instructions are required to excite any of the target modules. Furthermore, the generation of specific instructions at the two levels in some cases was not possible (e.g., the SSY instruction cannot be used in CUDA or PTX levels). Thus, we adopted the assembly language (SASS) to describe most SBST techniques that cannot be directly described at other abstraction levels.

It should be noted that compilers in the programming environment of GPUs have as main target the performance optimization of a program, so removing or reorganizing the intended test program and causing a mismatch in the intended behavior of the SBST programs. The solution to overcome this issue is based on a combination of different levels of description, when possible. This solution is affordable only when the Instruction Set Architecture (ISA) of a GPU device is well known, which unfortunately is not always the case.

8   Experimental Results

The RTL FlexGripPlus model was used in the experiments. Initially, the performance parameters of the implemented test programs are determined. Then, fault injection campaign results are reported showing the effectiveness of the proposed modular approach on the target modules.

8.1   Performance of the Test Programs

Table 1 reports the results concerning the performance parameters for all implemented test programs. It is worth noting that results reported in Table 1 were obtained by simulations performed resorting to the *ModelSim* environment.

The reported results show the performance parameters for the two possible test methods of the stack memory (Nesting and Sync-Trick methods under the accumulative and individual approaches). All versions present an overhead in the global memory of 64 locations (256 bytes) devoted to saving the SpTs and the Check-point signatures.

Regarding the performance results of both versions, it can be noted that the Sync-Trick (Ind) approach maintains an average performance cost to test any LE in the stack memory. The only difference among these programs is the number of SSY instructions included to address a selected LE. Similarly, the Sync-Trick (Acc) version can test a group of LEs consecutively. However, it requires additional execution time and cannot be stopped once the test program starts.

On the other hand, Table 1 also reports the required execution time to test the first and the second LEs in the stack using the Sync-Trick Ind (rows 2 and 3, column 4) and Sync-Trick Acc (row 5, column 4) approaches. The Individual approach requires 76 additional clock cycles to test the LEs, but it has the advantage of being able to test each LE independently. In contrast, the Accumulative method must check both LEs consecutively. Thus, the Ind approach can be adapted for in-field operation by the limited number of clock cycles required during the execution.

The performance parameters show that for the Nesting approach, there is a proportional relation between the number of instructions and the number of LEs to test. Similarly, the relationship between the execution time and the number of LEs to test presents an increasing exponential ratio. In the end, the Nesting method requires more than twice the execution time to test the entire stack than

Table 1. Performance parameters of the SBST programs using the two approaches to detect permanent faults in the LEs

Approach	Module	Instructions	Execution time [Clock cycles]	System memory overhead [Bytes]
Sync-Trick Ind	LE #1 Stack	403	33,449	1,612
	LE #2 Stack	404	34,211	1,616
	LE #10 Stack	412	34,589	1,648
Sync-Trick Acc	LEs 1 – 2 Stack	794	66,637	3,176
	LEs 1-10 Stack	3,922	326,423	15,688
	All Stack	12,524	1,030,473	50,096
Nesting	LE 1 Stack	683	37,986	2,732
	LEs 1-2 Stack	1,323	83,569	5,292
	LEs 1-10 Stack	6,443	528,086	25,772
	All Stack	19,883	2,567,209	79,532
PRF_T	PRF	434	1,890,106	1,736
PRF_T_R2C	PRF	398	1,795,596	1,592
ARF_T	ARF	122	338,240	488
VRF_T_det	VRF	82	108,958	368
VRF_T_dia	VRF	350	1,503,254	2,800

Sync-Trick using the Acc approach. The execution time could be the relevant parameter to take into account when targeting the in-field operation.

As observed in Table 1, the implemented test programs, targeting the PRF and using two different *Fault controllability* procedures (PRF_T and PRT_T_R2C) require different execution times. Moreover, the number of instructions in both test programs is different. However, the intended test functionality of both versions is the same, so showing that the modular approach can produce different test programs for the same module and allowing the exploration of different test solutions.

Regarding the implemented test programs for the VRF, The fault diagnosis (VRF_T_dia) version requires up to 13 times the execution time of the test program targeting fault detection (VRF_T_det), only. The interesting of both test programs is that the modular program is the same, but the implemented functions produce the difference in time execution and intended functionality.

8.2   Fault Injection Results

The fault injection environment follows the methodology described in [18], and we injected permanent faults using the Stuck-at Fault model. On each target module, fault simulation campaigns were performed injecting faults in every location of each module, meaning 4,224, 32,768, 262,144 and 262,144 permanent faults in the stack memory, PRF, ARF and VRF, respectively. These fault simulation campaigns were performed using both representative benchmarks and the test programs implementing the proposed SBST strategies. Moreover, the SBST programs targeting the stack memory were evaluated with and without the optional PC functions.

The representative benchmarks have been carefully selected to compare the detection capabilities they can achieve with the ones provided by the proposed SBST programs. Descriptions and details regarding the chosen benchmarks can be found in [18]. For the sake of completeness and comparison, the different versions of the SBST strategy are reported in Table 2. The results are reported based on the output effect of the faults as: Faults corrupting the output results, or 'Corrupted Output Data' (Data)), faults corrupting the complete execution of the system, or 'Hang', and fault affecting the performance of a given benchmark, or 'Timeout'.

The last column of Table 2 reports the testable FC (TFC) of the benchmarks and the proposed SBST strategy. The TFC is defined as the ratio between the number of detected faults and the number of injected faults after removing the untestable faults. The untestable faults are those faults that due to structural or functional issues cannot be tested and cannot produce any failure. A detailed analysis of the stack memory revealed that a total of 192 faults are untestable. These are related to the lowest bits of the SPC field of each LE, which does not affect the execution of an instruction. Thus, these faults were removed when computing the TFC.

The Sync-Trick strategy provides a moderate FC for both cases (Ind and Acc). Moreover, the FC increases when adding the PC functions and the relocation of the test functions in the memory. These comprehensive approaches (Ind+SP and Acc+SP) obtain a high percentage of FC for the target structure.

An in-depth analysis of the results shows that the Individual approach allows detecting 100% of the faults in the TM of all LEs by looking at the results of the test procedure "Data" type faults. In contrast, the Acc version causes a small percentage (0.75%) of faults produced in the TM field and visible because they hang or crash the GPU. This behavior can be explained considering that in the Ind approach, each LE is evaluated individually, and so all detections can be labeled as Data. On the other hand, for the Acc method, a permanent fault in one LE affects the synchronization point, thus corrupting the convergence point and causing the Hang condition. More in detail, a Stuck-at-0 fault is a sensitive case during the run of the test program. A fault affecting one LE when used as synchronization causes the Hang condition.

The Nesting SBST program has a slightly lower FC than Sync-Trick with an increment of more than twice the percentage of faults causing hanging and timeout. This fault effect is equivalent to the effect shown by in the Acc version of Sync-Trick. In this case, the Nesting method generates intra-warp divergence to move the stack pointer among the LEs (in the stack memory), testing all LEs even when a fault is detected, so other LEs are also tested. The continuous evaluation generates issues when a fault affects the LE used for synchronization purposes (when testing the even LEs). Thus, the test program may confuse the convergence point and produce the Hang or Timeout condition. According to results, the Nesting strategy seems to be more susceptible to Hang and Timeout effects than the Sync-Trick using the Acc approach.

In both approaches, the addition of the relocation in memory and the SPC functions increase the testable coverage in the stack memory. However, as explained previously, these optional functions can be employed when it is possible to use the entire system memory to relocate the test functions in specific memory locations, or the application code allows this adaptation. Similarly, both SBST approaches can detect a considerable percentage of the permanent faults in the stack memory. However, a direct comparison involving the performance parameters from Table 1 shows that the Nesting approach consumes more than twice the execution time and 37% of additional instructions. In conclusion, the Sync-Trick strategy seems to be a feasible candidate for in-field operations. Moreover, the Ind strategy can be divided into parts and adapted with the application code.

Regarding the SBST program for the PRF module, the two implemented versions obtain the 100% of fault coverage. The main advantage of both versions is the fault propagation to the global memory, so enabling the detection as Data. In fact, all faults detected are identified using this classification. Thus, the main difference between SBST approaches is the performance and overhead cost, which are mainly caused by the internal description of one modular function (Ld). The previous fault coverage results allow us to validate the exploration of different methods to implement different modular functions. In both cases, the replacement of a modular function does not affect the final fault coverage. A similar situation is observed in the SBST programs for VRF. In both approaches (Detection (Dec) and Diagnosis (Dia)), the programs reach a full fault coverage (100%). However, the performance degradation rises up to 13.8 times when employing the diagnosis version of the test program. Nevertheless, this SBST version can be affordable with mild system time constraints, such as during the Switch-on of the system.

Although Table 2 reports one SBST program for the PRF, the two versions were evaluated changing each time the Ld function. The two versions achieved the same fault coverage (100%) and the Ld functions, in both versions, have the same performance cost, so both solutions can be used identically.

A comparison of the FC obtained by the proposed SBST strategies and the representative benchmarks shows that the FC using these specialized programs is higher for the targeted modules than the FC obtained with typical applications. Thus, the FC capabilities of a representative benchmark is mostly lower. This behavior can be explained considering that most applications only use parts of the modules (e.g., only the first levels of stack memory to handle the divergence or certain registers per thread in the ARF or VRF modules) to operate the instructions of each application.

Table 2. FC results for the representative benchmarks and the proposed SBST strategies

SBST strategy or benchmark		Module	(%)				
			Data	Hang	Timeout	FC	TFC
MxM		Stack	0.00	0.38	-	0.38	0.40
		PRF	0.00	0.38	-	0.38	0.38
		ARF	25.07	0.0	-	25.07	25.07
		VRF	18.26	8.24	-	26.5	26.5
Sort		Stack	0.15	0.04	-	0.19	0.19
		PRF	0.16	0.04	-	0.20	0.20
		ARF	0.00	0.00	-	0.00	0.00
		VRF	0.18	0.07	-	0.25	0.25
FFT		Stack	0.14	0.19	-	0.33	0.35
		PRF	0.15	0.19	-	0.34	0.34
		ARF	0.0	0.0	-	0.00	0.00
		VRF	0.19	0.21	-	0.4	0.4
Edge		Stack	0.15	0.28	-	0.43	0.47
		PRF	0.00	7.05	-	7.05	7.05
		ARF	0.00	0.00	-	0.00	0.00
		VRF	12.25	5.6	-	17.85	17.85
Sync-Trick	*Ind*	Stack	65.64	2.08	1.01	68.75	72.02
	Acc		64.89	2.84	1.01	68.75	72.02
	Ind + PC		83.00	8.49	2.44	93.93	98.41
	Acc + PC		82.24	9.25	2.44	93.93	98.41
Nesting		Stack	54.12	11.81	1.23	67.16	70.04
	+ PC		76.94	13.16	2.81	92.91	97.34
PRF_T		PRF	100.0	-	-	100.0	100.0
	R2C		100.0	-	-	100.0	100.0
VRF_T	*Det*	VRF	100.0	-	-	100.0	100.0
	Dia		100.0	-	-	100.0	100.0
ARF_T		ARF	100.0	-	-	100.0	100.0

The matrix multiplication application generates one level of divergence. Thus, other levels inside the Stack memory are not employed, and the fault effect in not detected or propagated into the application. On the other hand, the VRF and the ARF modules are excited in almost 25% and 20%, which helps to explain the fault coverage obtained for both modules (26.5% and 25.07%, respectively). In contrast, the Sort application can generate intra-warp divergence, depending on the input data operands, but it remains limited to the first LE in the stack memory. However, the percentage of detection (0.33% and 0.19%) is negligible in comparison with the proposed test strategies. A similar behavior is observed for the ARF, PRF and VRF when executing this application.

The FFT benchmark produces two levels of intra-warp divergence, so using up to four LEs during the operation. This behavior slightly increases the percentage of faults detected. Nevertheless, the achieved percentage remains small. Finally, the Edge application causes two levels of intra-warp divergence and can detect some faults as Data and hangs. However, the total coverage of all representative kernels is minimal.

The previous scenario supports the idea that executing applications and checking their results (as it is often done when using a functional test approach) is definitely not enough to verify the functionality of crucial hardware modules in the GPU. Thus, special test programs, as those proposed in this work using the modular approach, are required to guarantee the correct operation of a module inside a device used in a safety-critical application.

The main advantage of the proposed method lies in its modularity and scalability. Scalability allows the configuration and the selection of the number of LEs to be tested in the SBST programs for the stack memory. Moreover, the test programs for the ARF, PRF and VRF can also be reduced to target only specific registers in the target modules. Finally, the scalability of their structure allows splitting the overall program in several parts, as presented for the Sync-Trick SBST program.

As introduced previously, the implementation of the test programs required the combination of high-level descriptions (about 15% of the total code in all SBST strategies), and the addition of assembly functions (about 85%). For both proposed SBST strategies targeting the memory stack, the synchronization functions (SSY) were implemented in assembly language. In this way, we could also avoid that the compiler removes or changes important parts of the test code. Similarly, in the PRF test program, the Comp modular function used specific procedures that required assembly language support. Thus, these parts and others are written at the assembly level. These limitations show that the development of test programs for these complex structures in GPUs requires access to the assembly formats to provide feasible and efficient solutions. The implementation effort could be reduced by the design of an automatic tool to include the subroutines at the assembly or binary level. Moreover, such a tool could also be employed to develop modular approaches, targeting other modules, such as functional units in the GPU.

Although the proposed SBST strategies targeted the test of unprotected memories in a GPU model with the G80 micro-architecture, we still claim that the proposed methodology can be adapted and used for the most recent GPU architectures, such as Maxwell and Pascal that include similar structures. Moreover, other parallel architectures can also use the proposed method.

9   Conclusions

We introduced a modular and scalable method to design functional programs for testing in the field the small embedded memories in GPU cores. For this purpose, each target embedded memory was analyzed and based on controllability, observability and composition features, a set of parametric functions were developed and then combined to test each target structure in the GPU. Results show that the modular solution allows the exploration of the advantages and limitations of different routines employed in a test program. Moreover, this technique also allows the split of a test program into several parts, while still achieving the same FC, so allowing to adjust the test program to potential requirements of in-field operations.

As future works, we plan to extend the proposed method to test other functional units and critical modules in parallel architectures. Moreover, we plan to use the modular approach to target other fault models.

Acknowledgments. This work has been partially supported by the European Commission through the Horizon 2020 RESCUE-ETN project under grant 722325.

References

1. Shi, W., Alawieh, M.B., Li, X., Yu, H.: Algorithm and hardware implementation for visual perception system in autonomous vehicle: a survey. Integration **59**, 148–156 (2017)
2. Hamdioui, S., Gizopoulos, D., Guido, G., Nicolaidis, M., Grasset, A., Bonnot, P., Reliability challenges of real-time systems in forthcoming technology nodes. In: 2013 Design, Automation Test in Europe Conference Exhibition (DATE), pp. 129–134 (2013)
3. Agbo, I., Taouil, M., Hamdioui, S., Weckx, P., Cosemans, S., Catthoor, F., Dehaene, W.: Read path degradation analysis in SRAM. In: 2016 21th IEEE European Test Symposium (ETS), pp. 1–2 (2016)
4. Chen, X., Wang, Y., Liang, Y., Xie, Y., Yang, H.: Run-time technique for simultaneous aging and power optimization in GPGPUs. In: 2014 51st ACM/EDAC/IEEE Design Automation Conference (DAC), pp. 1–6 (2014)
5. Becker, A.J., Pathirane, C.A.S., Aitken R.C.: Memory built-in self-test for a data processing apparatus, US Patent 9,449,717, 20 September 2016
6. Gulati, R., et al.: Self-test during idle cycles for shader core of GPU, US Patent 10,628,274, 21 April 2020
7. Psarakis, M., Gizopoulos, D., Sanchez, E., Sonza Reorda M.: Microprocessor software-based self-testing. IEEE Design Test Comput. **27**(3), 4–19 (2010)
8. Condia, J.E.R., Narducci, P., Sonza Reorda, M., Sterpone, L.: A dynamic hardware redundancy mechanism for the in-field fault detection in cores of GPGPUs. In: 2020 23rd International Symposium on Design and Diagnostics of Electronic Circuits Systems (DDECS), pp. 1–6 (2020)
9. Condia, J.E.R., Narducci, P., Sonza Reorda, M., Sterpone, L.: A dynamic reconfiguration mechanism to increase the reliability of GPGPUs. In: 2020 IEEE 38th VLSI Test Symposium (VTS), pp. 1–6 (2020)
10. Baghsorkhi, S.S., Delahaye, M., Patel, S.J., Gropp, W.D., Hwu, W.-M.W.: An adaptive performance modeling tool for GPU architectures. SIGPLAN Not. **45**(5), 105–114 (2010)
11. Coutinho, B., Sampaio, D., Pereira, F.M.Q., Meira Jr., W.: Profiling divergences in GPU applications. Concurr. Comput. Pract. Exp. **25**(6), 775–789 (2013)
12. Mei, X., Chu, X.: Dissecting GPU memory hierarchy through microbenchmarking. IEEE Trans. Parallel Distrib. Syst. **28**(1), 72–86 (2017)
13. Bernardi, P., Grosso, M., Sanchez, E., Ballan, O.: Fault grading of software-based self-test procedures for dependable automotive applications. In: 2011 Design, Automation Test in Europe, pp. 1–2 (2011)
14. Abdel-Majeed, M., Dweik, W.: Low overhead online periodic testing for GPGPUs. Integration **62**, 362–370 (2018)
15. Di Carlo, S., et al.: A software-based self test of CUDA fermi GPUs. In: 2013 18th IEEE European Test Symposium (ETS), pp. 1–6 (2013)

16. Defour, D., Petit, E.: A software scheduling solution to avoid corrupted units on GPUs. J. Parallel Distrib. Comput. **90–91**, 1–8 (2016)
17. Sabena, D., Sonza Reorda, M., Sterpone, L., Rech, P., Carro, L.: On the evaluation of soft-errors detection techniques for GPGPUs. In: 2013 8th IEEE Design and Test Symposium, pp. 1–6 (2013)
18. Condia, J.E.R., Sonza Reorda, M.: Testing permanent faults in pipeline registers of GPGPUs: a multi-kernel approach. In: 2019 IEEE 25th International Symposium on On-Line Testing and Robust System Design (IOLTS), pp. 97–102 (2019)
19. Condia, J.E.R., Sonza Reorda, M.: On the testing of special memories in GPGPUs. In: 2020 IEEE 26th International Symposium on On-Line Testing and Robust System Design (IOLTS), pp. 1–6 (2020)
20. Di Carlo, S., Condia, J.E.R., Sonza Reorda, M.: An on-line testing technique for the scheduler memory of a GPGPU. IEEE Access, vol. 8, pp. 16 893–16 912 (2020)
21. Du, B., Condia, J.E.R., Sonza Reorda, M., Sterpone, L.: About the functional test of the GPGPU scheduler. In: 2018 IEEE 24th International Symposium on On-Line Testing And Robust System Design (IOLTS), pp. 85–90 (2018)
22. Di Carlo, S., Condia, J.E.R., Sonza Reorda M.: On the in-field test of the GPGPU scheduler memory. In: 2019 IEEE 22nd International Symposium on Design and Diagnostics of Electronic Circuits Systems (DDECS), pp. 1–6 (2019)
23. Condia, J.E.R., Sonza Reorda, M.: Testing the divergence stack memory on GPGPUs: a modular in-field test strategy. In: 28th IFIP/IEEE International Conference on Very Large Scale Integration (VLSI-SoC 2020), pp. 1–6 (2020)
24. Flynn, M.J.: Some computer organizations and their effectiveness. IEEE Trans. Comput. **C-21**(9), 948–960 (1972)
25. Condia, J.E.R., Du, B., Sonza Reorda, M., Sterpone, L.: FlexGripPlus: an improved GPGPU model to support reliability analysis. Microelectr. Reliab. **109**, 113660 (2020)
26. Andryc, K., Merchant, M., Tessier, R.: FlexGrip: a soft GPGPU for FPGAs. In: International Conference on Field-Programmable Technology (FPT) 2013, pp. 230–237 (2013)
27. Apostolakis, A., Psarakis, M., Gizopoulos, D., Paschalis, A., Parulkar, I.: Exploiting thread-level parallelism in functional self-testing of CMT processors. In: 2009 14th IEEE European Test Symposium, pp. 33–38

RAT: A Lightweight Architecture Independent System-Level Soft Error Mitigation Technique

Jonas Gava[1]([✉]), Ricardo Reis[1]([✉]), and Luciano Ost[2]([✉])

[1] Instituto de Informática, PGMicro,
Universidade Federal do Rio Grande do Sul - UFRGS, CP. 15064, Av. Bento
Gonçalves, 9500., Porto Alegre 91501-970, Brazil
{jfgava,reis}@inf.ufrgs.br
[2] Wolfson School, Loughborough University, Loughborough, UK
l.ost@lboro.ac.uk

Abstract. To achieve a substantial reliability and safety level, it is imperative to provide electronic computing systems with appropriate mechanisms to tackle soft errors. This paper proposes a low-cost system-level soft error mitigation technique, which allocates the critical application function to a pool of specific general-purpose processor registers. Both the critical function and the register pool are automatically selected by a developed profiling tool. The proposed technique was validated through more than 400K fault injections considering a Linux kernel, different benchmarks, and two multicore Arm processor architectures (ARMv7-A and ARMv8-A). Results show that our technique significantly reduces the code size and performance overheads while providing soft error reliability improvement compared with the Triple Modular Redundancy (TMR) technique.

Keywords: Multicore · Soft error reliability · Mitigation technique · Fault tolerance

1 Introduction

Multicore architectures are being adopted in many industrial segments such as automotive, medical, consumer electronics, and high-performance computing (HPC). Applications running on such architectures differ in terms of security, reliability, performance, and power requirements. To achieve a substantial reliability and safety level, it is imperative to provide electronic computing systems with appropriate mechanisms to tackle systematic or transient faults, also known as soft errors or Single Event Upset (SEU). While the former originates from hardware and software design defects, soft errors are those caused by alpha particles or atmospheric neutrons [24]. The occurrence of soft errors can either corrupt the memory data, the output of a program, or even crash the entire system, which depending on its criticality level can lead to life-threatening failures.

© IFIP International Federation for Information Processing 2021
Published by Springer Nature Switzerland AG 2021
A. Calimera et al. (Eds.): VLSI-SoC 2020, IFIP AICT 621, pp. 235–253, 2021.
https://doi.org/10.1007/978-3-030-81641-4_11

The soft error mitigation problem can be tackled both in hardware and software [23]. While hardware approaches lead to the area and power overhead, software techniques are generally implemented on a per-application basis that usually incurs in performance penalties due to the redundant computation. Such additional overhead might restrict the use of costly mitigation techniques under resource-constrained devices. Furthermore, the adoption of soft error mitigation techniques also adds development complexity, which has a direct impact on the time-to-market. Examples of soft error mitigation techniques include, among others, Error Detection and Correction Code (EDAC) and Triple Module Redundancy (TMR).

This paper addresses the above challenges by proposing a novel lightweight system-level soft error mitigation technique, called Register Allocation Technique (RAT) [13]. The proposed technique along with the developed profiling toolset enables software engineers to isolate and allocate the most critical application function to a pool of least used general-purpose processor registers. RAT was compared against a selective TMR technique [11], considering a Linux kernel, 13 applications, a dual-core and a quad-core ARM processor. Results demonstrated that RAT reduces the code size and performance overheads while providing reliability improvement.

The rest of this paper is organized as follows. Section 2 presents basic concepts and related works in software soft error mitigation techniques. Section 3 describes the proposed mitigation technique. In Sect. 4, the experimental setup and adopted evaluation metrics are presented. In Sect. 5, the efficiency of RAT is evaluated, and a specific case study analyzing the registers criticality is presented. Section 6 evaluates the impact of instruction set architectures (ISAs) on the RAT efficiency (i.e., ARMv7-A 32 and ARMv8-A 64 bits). Finally, Sect. 7 presents final remarks and future works.

2   Fundamental Concepts and Related Works

2.1   Fault Tolerance Taxonomy

The soft error assessment and mitigation literature is abundant, requiring a taxonomy to classify the different approaches. This work considers the definitions from [3,17] for fault, error, and failure. A fault is an event that may cause the internal state of the system to change, e.g., a radiation particle strike. When a fault affects the system's internal state, it becomes an error. If the error causes a deviation of at least one of the system's external states, then it is considered as a failure.

The most commonplace classification for soft error assessment considers three classes: Silent Data Corruption (SDC) occurs when the system does not detect a fault and the outcome of the application is affected; In Detected Unrecoverable Error (DUE) on the other hand, the fault is detected and it is not possible to continue the execution (e.g., segmentation fault); and Masked, when the application outcome and the system state are the same as a faultless execution.

As mentioned before, soft error mitigation techniques can be implemented in hardware, software, or a combination of both. The next Section reviews only the software-based approaches.

2.2 Software-Based Soft Error Mitigation Techniques

A processor-based system can be affected by two main types of soft errors: control-flow and data-flow. A control-flow error occurs when the error causes deviation from the correct program flow (e.g., incorrect branch). The data-flow error refers to the soft error caused by a bit-flip in a storage component, such as a register or memory element. They can, for instance, affect the output of a program generating an SDC, or leading to a DUE when computing a wrong memory address.

Aiming to mitigate both types of soft error effects, the following works have promoted some software system-level techniques, i.e., techniques that can be applied at the software architectural level (e.g., application, operating system (OS)). In [6] and [18] tools that apply fault tolerance techniques in C/C++ applications are proposed. Supported transformations are architecture-independent, but the language is fixed, and the compiler may remove redundant code during the compiler optimization phases. The focus of [18] is on low-cost safety-critical applications, where the high memory and speed overheads (about 3–4 times) are not important metrics. Another similar tool is the REliable Code COmpiler (RECCO) [6], which relies on code reordering and selective variable duplication. In [22], authors use genetic algorithms to find a combination of optimization parameters (i.e., compilation flags) that increase the reliability of the final binary and present a reasonable trade-off in terms of performance, and memory size. The proposed technique was evaluated considering an FPGA implementation that was exposed to a proton irradiation test. In [21], the authors implemented in C code two mitigation techniques: the TMR and the Conditional Modular Redundancy (CMR). Their results have shown that both techniques do not provide a reasonable protection to a complex system executing Linux kernel. According to the authors, the OS itself is an enormous source of errors and need to be protected if employed on safety-critical systems.

The downside of aforementioned approaches is the fact that during the compiler optimization phase, parts of the protected code (e.g., redundant functions) may be wrongly removed. One solution to overcome such restriction relies on modifying the assembly code after the compilation. A popular instruction-level mitigation technique introduced by [19] is the Swift-R, which implements TMR to recover from soft errors in the register file. Instead of duplicating instructions, it triplicates, and changes the checking points to a voter mechanism. In [16], they apply the SWIFT-R to protect specific registers and find the best trade-off. They developed a generic intermediate language and their own compilation infrastructure. Although the idea is interesting, a considerable effort is necessary to support new processor architecture, limiting its usability. Authors in [10] proposed the Configurable Fault Tolerance Tool (CFT-tool) that modifies the assembly code by applying different data-flow and control-flow protection techniques. Although this approach does not suffer from compiler optimization, it is architecture-dependent. The CFT-tool uses a configuration file to minimize this limitation. However, this file needs to be hand-made for each new ISA. Shirvani et al. [23] propose a software implementation of EDAC, i.e., an independent task that is executed periodically. Results show their approach provides protection for code segments and can enhance the system reliability with a lower check-bit overhead with relation to other techniques (e.g., Hamming, Parity).

Different from the reviewed works, RAT does not involve code redundancy, and it is an architecture-independent approach. Furthermore, RAT is a fully automated approach that is developed on the basis of LLVM backend, enabling its extension and combination with other soft error mitigation techniques, as shown in Sect. 5.

3   Register Allocation Technique (RAT)

Rather than implementing a toolset from scratch, we have adopted a flexible virtual platform (VP) that provides us with the necessary means (i.e., simulator with processor and component models, full software behavior observability) to implement the proposed technique. RAT was implemented on the basis of OVP-sim framework [14] to enable a fast design space exploration, but other VPs with similar support could also be used (e.g., gem5 [7]). The main steps of the RAT (Fig. 1) are as follows:

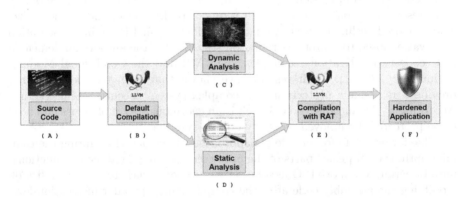

Fig. 1. Main steps of proposed register allocation technique (RAT).

A. Software stack (i.e., application, operating system, drivers) source code selection.
B. Target processor architecture selection and source code compilation using Clang/LLVM 6.0.1.

C. In this step, the application is executed, and essential information are extracted (i.e., processor register file utilization and critical function). Note that the software engineer can either determine the most critical application function or use the default option of our toolset, which selects the most executed one.

D. Here, our tool extracts, from the object code, the type (i.e., 32 or 64-bit) and the number of registers needed to be reserved to the function defined as critical in the previous step. In this stage, the register pool is set following the strategy of allocating least-used general-purpose registers for the critical function.

E. In this step, a new compilation is performed, taking into account the critical function and the register pool previously set. The underlying compilation uses a modified version of the LLVM Fast Register Allocator, which considers arguments (i.e., restrictions) that are passed to LLVM Static Compiler (LLC) through a command line (Fig. 2). Note that we do not control the use of the registers available in the pool, the compiler decides which ones to prioritize.

F. Finally, the resulting hardened binary is generated by the LLVM linker (LLD).

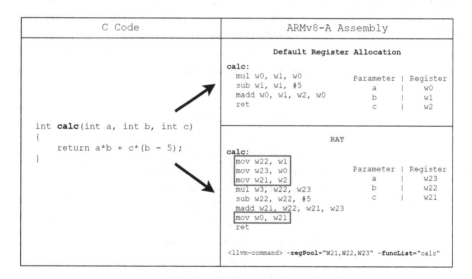

Fig. 2. Example of C code conversion to ARMv8-A assembly without and with RAT flags compilation.

The left-side of Fig. 2 shows an example of a C language function that takes three integer parameters as input, performs arithmetic operations, and returns an integer value. The resulting 64-bit ARM (Aarch64) assembly code is shown in the right-side of Fig. 2, where at the top the default register allocation is shown.

In turn, at the bottom right of Fig. 2 the RAT technique is applied, limiting the function register pool to "W21, W22, W23". By the calling convention, the ARMv8-A general-purpose registers with indexes from 0 to 7 are used for inputs and result. When restricting registers outside this range, the compiler only needs to insert some MOV instructions at the beginning and end of the function. As mentioned before, RAT is a compiler-based mitigating technique, thus it can be associate with other techniques as well. Such capacity is explored in Sect. 5.

4 Experimental Setup and Evaluation Metrics

In order to demonstrate the effectiveness of RAT, we adopted the fault injection simulator proposed in [5], which is also implemented on the basis of OVPsim. Fault analyzes are obtained by injecting faults (i.e., bit-flips) in the general-purpose registers (i.e., X0-X30) of a dual-core and a quad-core ARM Cortex-A72, in a random order. Conducted experiments include 320K fault injections in a realistic software stack including unmodified Linux kernel, a standard parallelization library (OpenMP), and considering 13 applications taken from the Rodinia Benchmark Suite [9] as shown in Table 1. One of the main concerns when assessing the reliability of a system is to develop a precise, well-covered and realistic approach. In this sense, this work sought to ensure that the number of fault injections has a statistical significance by applying the equations developed by [15]. This work injects 3100 faults per campaign, thus generating a 1.75% error margin with 95% confidence level.

Table 1. Rodinia Benchmarks

#	Benchmark	Domain
A	Backprop	Pattern Recognition
B	BFS	Graph Algorithms
C	HeartWall	Medical Imaging
D	HotSpot	Physics Simulation
E	HotSpot3D	Physics Simulation
F	Kmeans	Data Mining
G	LUD	Linear Algebra
H	Myocyte	Biological Simulation
I	NN	Data Mining
J	particle-filter	Medical Imaging
K	PathFinder	Grid Traversal
L	SradV1	Image Processing
M	SradV2	Image Processing

Depending on the application's nature, the three categories classification described in Sect. 2. A may be inadequate to express all the possible misbehaviors. With this in mind, the results are classified according to Cho [12], which defines five possible behaviors for a system in the presence of a fault: **Vanish:** no fault traces are left in both memory and architectural state; **Output not Affected (ONA):** the resulting memory is not modified, however, one or more remaining bits of the architectural state is incorrect; **Output Memory Mismatch (OMM):** the application terminates without any error indication, and the resulting memory is affected; **Unexpected Termination (UT):** the application terminates abnormally with an error indication; **Hang:** the application does not finish requiring a preemptive removal.

Software engineers might categorize the criticality of application functions entirely differently depending on their criteria and/or system domains. For the sake of simplicity, this work assumes that most executed functions are the critical ones. Although not ideal, such an approach is adequate to evaluate the benefits and drawback of the proposed mitigation technique. RAT reliability, code and performance overheads are compared against the selective TMR implementation (i.e., VAR3+) [4].

4.1 Reference Mitigation Technique - Selective TMR

In [11], the authors describe a set of rules for data-flow techniques that aim to detect faults affecting values stored in registers bank and memory devices. In this work, we use a triplication instead of duplication since the target is to mitigate the occurrence of soft error. The selective TMR technique implementation was based on [8] inside the Clang/LLVM 6.0.1. The VAR3+ technique was chosen due to its capability of increasing reliability while maintaining a low code and performance overhead compared with previous TMR-based techniques. In this technique, each register has a replica (rule G1), and all instructions, except for branches and stores, are replicated (D2). The replicas are checked before every load, store, or branch instruction (C3, C4, C5, C6). Some acronyms used in the following sections are RAT: reference application + register allocation technique, TMR: selective TMR technique (VAR3+), and TMR+RAT: TMR + register allocation technique.

4.2 Evaluation Metrics

To adequately assess the soft error mitigation technique reliability, [20] introduced a metric called Mean Work To Failure (MWTF), which is calculated by the average amount of work that an application can perform for each error. A unit of work is a general concept whose specific definition depends on the application. The unit work is defined here as a correct program execution (i.e., Vanished fault), while the number of errors is defined as the sum of ONA, OMM, UT, and Hang results as shown in (1).

$$MWTF = \frac{Vanished}{ONA + OMM + UT + Hang} \tag{1}$$

This work also employs the *Fault Coverage* metric, which describes the percentage of faults that are either detected or masked. It is represented as the ratio of detected and masked faults (i.e., Vanished) to the total number of faults that occurred, as shown in (2).

$$F_{coverage} = \frac{UT + Vanished}{ONA + OMM + Hang} \tag{2}$$

Finally, we use the Fault Coverage Increase (FCI) to describe the gain in the percentage of fault coverage when comparing the mitigation techniques.

5   RAT Efficiency Analysis

5.1   RAT Code and Performance Overhead

To provide relevant overhead measures, the **code size** information was extracted from the application object files, while the **performance** figures were obtained from the gem5 full system simulator [7].

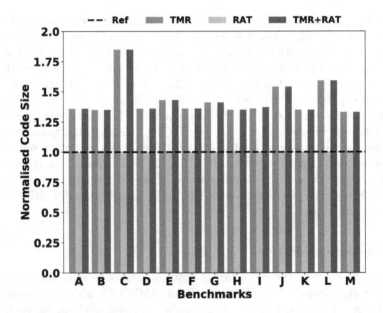

Fig. 3. Code size overhead for ARM Cortex-A72 processor when comparing the impact of the mitigation techniques with the original reference benchmark (Ref).

Figure 3 shows a substantial code size overhead (e.g., up to 84.86% - benchmark C) when the TMR technique is used. In turn, the cost of the proposed technique is negligible, 0.15% in the worst case (benchmark K). Such low overhead is due to the RAT approach, which only adds MOV instructions at the beginning and end of the critical functions. As a consequence, the performance of applications is not jeopardized when RAT is used (i.e., less than 1% for all scenarios).

Results in Fig. 4a and b show that the use of the TMR can lead to up to 38.5% and 50% of performance penalty (benchmark C) when running on dual and quad-core ARM Cortex A72 processors. The reason why there is an increase in the execution time in the quad-core when compared to the dual-core is due to the increasing execution of OS thread synchronization routines that is not linear with the number of cores. Note that the additional execution time of TMR is small for a technique that triples instructions and inserts voters into the code. This behavior is justified by the fact that only instructions inside the application's scope are replicated, and the majority of Rodinia applications rely on external library calls. One possible solution to this problem implies replicating function calls; however, there are possible collateral damages inherent to this approach (e.g., modifying the same data structure multiple times).

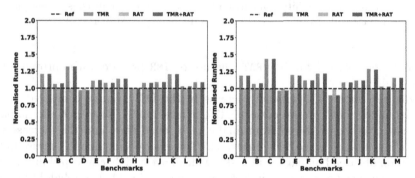

(a) Dual-core performance overhead (b) Quad-core performance overhead

Fig. 4. Performance overhead for dual (b) and quad-core (c) ARM Cortex-A72 processor when comparing the impact of the mitigation techniques with the original reference benchmark (Ref).

5.2   RAT Soft Error Reliability Evaluation

Techniques Comparison. Figure 5 and 6 show the reliability comparison between the three mitigation techniques. In terms of MWTF on Fig. 5, the TMR implementation provides higher reliability in 5 out of 13 cases (C, D, F, I, K), while the RAT in 4 cases (A, E, J, L), and the TMR+RAT in the other 4 cases (B, G, H, M). Results show that RAT can also provide reliability improvements of up to 40% in some cases compared to TMR. Results also show that, depending on the application nature, TMR+RAT is an appropriated combination to improve system reliability. For instance, taking the benchmarks B and K as examples, it is possible to identify a considerable difference in the MWTF gain when comparing the two TMR implementations. While benchmark B showed a reliability

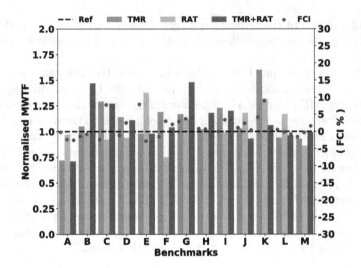

Fig. 5. Normalized reliability comparison between each technique considering the original benchmark code as reference (Ref) for a dual-core ARM Cortex-A72.

improvement of 40% for TMR+RAT, the use of TMR provides an improvement of 51% for K.

Figure 6 shows a significant increase in the FCI average compared to the results in the dual-core processor, 5.47% versus 1.48%. Note that all reliability metrics have been reduced from dual-core to quad-core, and the increase was only about the reference benchmark. This behavior occurs due to the rise in the execution of thread management tasks, which have a higher susceptibility to soft errors, as mentioned earlier. The TMR technique obtained better reliability results in 6 of the 13 benchmarks (C, E, F, J, K, L), RAT was better in 2 cases (D, H), and TMR+RAT was better in 5 cases (A, B, G, I, M). Note that the applications' reliability varies from one mitigation technique to another. For that reason, we claim that engineers can use our toolset to analyze the impact of different mitigation techniques at the system-level, so they might be able to identify the most suitable one considering their application's/system's constraints. Further, a more in-depth analysis is carried out, verifying the results of the fault injections in each register for a specific case study.

Registers Criticality Analysis. Figur 7 shows how the 64-bit ARM (AArch64) calling convention works. The X0–X7 registers are used for input parameters and return functions; the X8 is used to hold an indirect return location address; the X9–X15 are used to hold local variables (caller saved); the X16 and the X17 are the Intra-Procedure-call scratch registers; the X18 can be used for some OS-specific purpose; the X19–X28 are callee-saved registers; the X29 is the frame pointer; while the X30 is the link register, used to return from subrou-

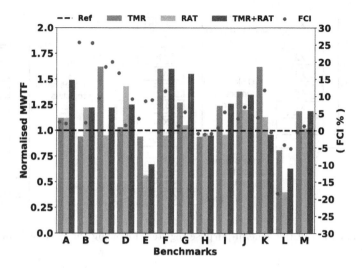

Fig. 6. Normalized reliability comparison between each technique considering the original benchmark code as reference (Ref) for a quad-core ARM Cortex-A72.

tines. To better explain the RAT benefits, we chose the particle-filter benchmark (J) as a case study.

The results show that half of the registers (X0–X16) do not suffer significantly from soft errors (Fig. 8), when the particle-filter benchmark (J) is executed on a dual-core ARM Cortex-A72 processor. In contrast, the rest of the registers suffers strongly from the injected faults. Especially the callee-saved category that is used to hold long-lived values that must be preserved across calls and are used by the Linux kernel. Theoretically, there are registers that take a longer time to get written, but they are continuously read. However, as shown in Fig. 9, the fault masking increases when we apply the RAT technique and limit the number of registers that will be used to execute the most performed function. In general, this effect occurs because when entering the critical function, the callee-saved registers are saved in memory and return to their original values at the end of the execution. In practice, this behavior ends up reducing the lifetime of these registers, making them more resilient to soft errors. The best examples are from the X17 and X19 registers. For the X17 register, we have a fault-masking rate of 70% in the reference application, and 98% when using the RAT mitigation technique. For the X19 register, we have a fault-masking rate of 37% in the reference application, and 58% when using the RAT technique.

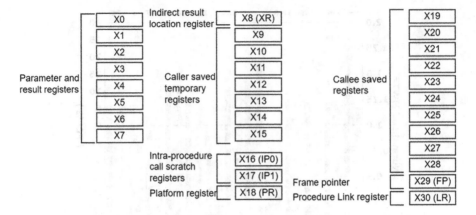

Fig. 7. Allocation of the general-purpose registers following the AArch64 calling convention [2].

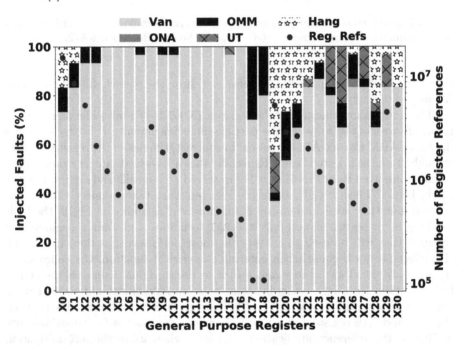

Fig. 8. Registers criticality for the Reference particle-filter benchmark running on a dual-core ARM Cortex-A72.

Results demonstrated that RAT reduces the code size and performance overheads while providing reliability improvement when considering a state-of-the-art 64-bits processor, which has a large register pool (i.e., 32 general-purpose registers). Researchers and industrial leaders are also developing optimized machine-learning algorithms [1], aiming to enable their execution in resource-constrained

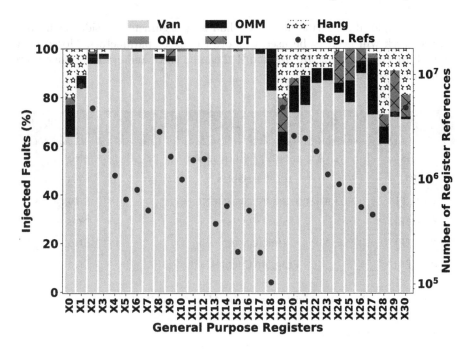

Fig. 9. Registers criticality for the RAT version of particle-filter benchmark running on a dual-core ARM Cortex-A72.

devices. The resulting scenario calls for lightweight soft error mitigation techniques such as the one proposed here. The next Section investigates the RAT efficiency when applied to a more resource-constrained architecture.

6   RAT Efficiency in Distinct Processor Architectures

To assess the impact of the processor architecture on RAT efficiency, this Section considers the ARMv7-A 32-bit and the ARMv8-A 64-bit instruction set architectures.

6.1   ARMv7-A General-Purpose Registers

The ARMv7-A has 16 registers (R0–R15) with 32 data bits each. Removing the special use registers (IP, SP, LR, PC), there are only 12 extra registers that RAT can use to allocate the application critical function. As explained in the Sect. 5.2, there is also a particular ARMv7-A calling convention. As shown in Fig. 10, the initial registers (R0-R3) are used to pass input and function return parameters, the R4–R11 are used for local variables, and the R12–R15 are special registers responsible for managing stack, function return address, and jumps during the application execution.

For example, if a routine has more than four arguments, besides using R0–R3, the stack will need to be used to store the extra parameters. Moreover, if R4–R11 are not sufficient, R0–R3 and R12 can be used, and even LR when there are no other subroutine calls.

Registers	Function	Value preserved during call
R0-R3	Arguments / Return values	No
R4-R11	Local variables	Yes
R12 (IP)	Intra-procedure-call scratch reg.	No
R13 (SP)	Stack Pointer	Yes
R14 (LR)	Link register	No
R15 (PC)	Program Counter	No

Fig. 10. Register usage for ARMv7 architecture.

6.2 Soft Error Reliability Assessment for the ARMv7-A Considering Different Mitigation Techniques

In order to understand how limiting the number of available registers affects the soft error reliability results, the experiments consider a subset of seven applications of the Rodinia Benchmark Suite executing in dual-core and quad-core Arm Cortex-A9 processors. For each scenario, 1600 SEU fault injections were performed targeting the 16 general-purpose registers. Based on the equation defined in [15], our results have a margin of error of 2.45% with a 95% confidence level.

Figure 11 shows the MWTF results normalized by the reference application version indicated on the left y-axis. Each bar in the graph indicates a mitigation technique, and each group of three bars refers to a different application. The right y-axis shows the increase/decrease in the fault coverage for each case, which are indicated by the red dots. Following the same format adopted in the previous Section, results consider dual-core and quad-core processor architectures and the three soft error mitigating techniques (i.e., TMR, TMR-RAT, and RAT). For the dual-core results (Fig. 11a), it is possible to observe a low soft error reliability improvement when applying the mitigation techniques (see MWTF and FC values). While TMR presents the higher MWTF factor for the kmeans application (19%), RAT shows the best FCI factor for the same application (9%).

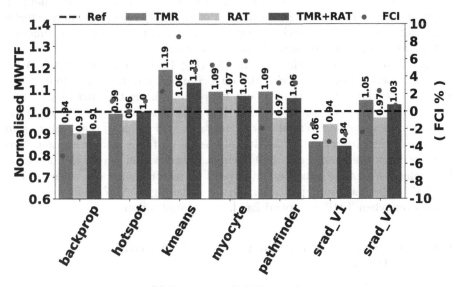

(a) Dual-core reliability results

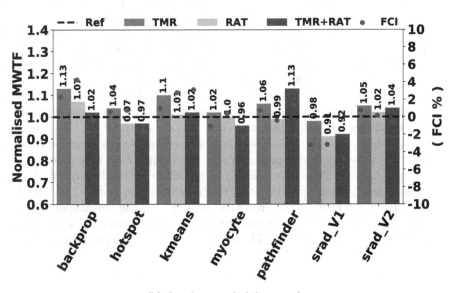

(b) Quad-core reliability results

Fig. 11. Reliability improvement for dual (a) and quad-core (b) Arm Cortex-A9 processor when comparing the impact of the mitigation techniques with the original reference benchmark (Ref).

The application of RAT leads to a low reliability improvement (MWTF factor equal to 7% - best case) at a low extra code overhead. The low reliability improvement is expected; since the number of available registers is low, the registers' allocation can be precisely the same as the reference version if the function defined as critical already uses all possible registers.

Quad-core soft error reliability results (Fig. 11b) provide a lower MWTF and FCI average compared with the dual-core configuration. The more cores the higher is the probability of a fault happening during the operating system execution. In this case, the operating system puts more pressure on the registers, leading to more spilling to temporary values stored in memory, thus requiring an increase in the proportional time slice of the application's total execution. This effect reduces the chance of a fault being masked within one of the hardened functions. For instance, the best achieved FCI factor is only 4% when RAT is applied to the backprop application. In turn, the higher MWTF factor of 13% is achieved when TMR is applied for the same application.

6.3 RAT Soft Error Efficiency Comparison: ARMv7-A *vs* ARMv8-A

The purpose of this section is to make a more detailed comparison of the reliability results when applying TMR, TMR-RAT, and RAT techniques to seven Rodinia applications running on different processor architectures.

Figure 12 shows the normalized MWTF of each application (i.e., unprotected and protected versions) obtained from the fault injection campaigns considering the Arm Cortex-A72 and the Arm Cortex-A9. Each bar in the 4-bar structure of the graph indicates a different version of each application.

Analyzing Fig. 12a, we see that the ARM Cortex-A72 dual-core provides a significant MWTF improvement in all applications. The minimum increase is 1.93× (pathfinder - R), and the maximum 4.33× (backprop - TMR). Results show RAT can benefit from processors with a larger number of registers. Results obtained from the quad-core processor scenarios (Fig. 12b), show a reasonable reduction in the MWTF improvement. The minimum reliability improvement of 0.92× is achieved when applying RAT to the hotspot application. In turn, the use of TMR+RAT incurs an improvement of 3.11× for the kmeans application. Therefore, the increase of system resource utilization leads to a decrease of more than 70% in the normalized MWTF in some cases (i.e., hotspot and myocyte).

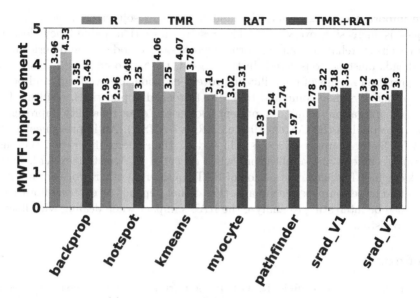

(a) Dual-core reliability mismatch results

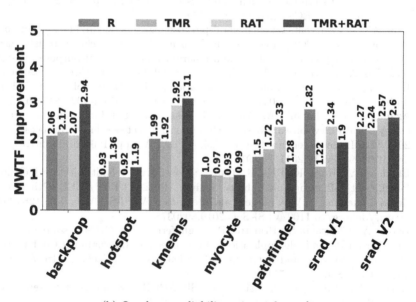

(b) Quad-core reliability mismatch results

Fig. 12. Reliability mismatch for dual (a) and quad-core (b) Arm Cortex-A72 processor when comparing with Arm Cortex-A9.

7   Conclusion and Future Works

The importance of using selective and lightweight soft error mitigation techniques is increasing every year. The results show that redundancy does not always ensure reliability, and the other factors such as code size and performance overheads must be considered. In this regard, the proposed RAT offers a good compromise in terms of reliability improvement, code size overhead, and performance penalty when compared to TMR. Hardened applications, resulting from adopted mitigation techniques, present a lower soft error reliability improvement when executed in the Cortex-A9 (i.e., ARMv7-A ISA). An improvement in the MWTF factor of up to 4.33 × is achieved for the same configuration (i.e., mitigation technique and application) when executed in Arm Cortex-A72. Future works include further investigation of RAT considering other processor architectures and more complex benchmarks that do not depends on external libraries. It may also be interesting to analyze the RAT's impact when dealing with floating point registers.

References

1. Abich, G., Gava, J., Reis, R., Ost, L.: Soft error reliability assessment of neural networks on resource-constrained IoT devices. In: 2020 27th IEEE International Conference on Electronics, Circuits and Systems (ICECS), pp. 1–4 (2020). https://doi.org/10.1109/ICECS49266.2020.9294951
2. Arm: ARMv8-A parameters in general-purpose registers (2020). https://developer.arm.com/docs/den0024/latest/the-abi-for-arm-64-bit-architecture/register-use-in-the-aarch64-procedure-call-standard/parameters-in-general-purpose-registers
3. Avižienis, A., Laprie, J.-C., Randell, B.: Dependability and its threats: a taxonomy. In: Jacquart, R. (ed.) Building the Information Society. IIFIP, vol. 156, pp. 91–120. Springer, Boston, MA (2004). https://doi.org/10.1007/978-1-4020-8157-6_13
4. Azambuja, J.R., Lapolli, A., Altieri, M., Kastensmidt, F.L.: Evaluating the efficiency of data-flow software-based techniques to detect sees in microprocessors. In: 2011 12th Latin American Test Workshop (LATW), pp. 1–6 (2011). https://doi.org/10.1109/LATW.2011.5985914
5. Bandeira, V., Rosa, F., Reis, R., Ost, L.: Non-intrusive fault injection techniques for efficient soft error vulnerability analysis. In: 2019 IFIP/IEEE 27th International Conference on Very Large Scale Integration (VLSI-SoC), pp. 123–128 (2019). https://doi.org/10.1109/VLSI-SoC.2019.8920378
6. Benso, A., Chiusano, S., Prinetto, P., Tagliaferri, L.: A C/C++ source-to-source compiler for dependable applications. In: Proceeding International Conference on Dependable Systems and Networks, DSN 2000, pp. 71–78 (2000). https://doi.org/10.1109/ICDSN.2000.857517
7. Binkert, N., et al.: The gem5 simulator. SIGARCH Comput. Archit. News **39**(2), 1–7 (2011). https://doi.org/10.1145/2024716.2024718
8. Bohman, M., James, B., Wirthlin, M.J., Quinn, H., Goeders, J.: Microcontroller compiler-assisted software fault tolerance. IEEE Trans. Nucl. Sci. **66**(1), 223–232 (2019). https://doi.org/10.1109/TNS.2018.2886094
9. Che, S., et al.: Rodinia: a benchmark suite for heterogeneous computing. In: 2009 IEEE International Symposium on Workload Characterization (IISWC), pp. 44–54 (2009). https://doi.org/10.1109/IISWC.2009.5306797

10. Chielle, E., Barth, R.S., Lapolli, A.C., Kastensmidt, F.L.: Configurable tool to protect processors against SEE by software-based detection techniques. In: 2012 13th Latin American Test Workshop (LATW), pp. 1–6 (2012). https://doi.org/10. 1109/LATW.2012.6261259

11. Chielle, E., Kastensmidt, F.L., Cuenca-Asensi, S.: Overhead reduction in data-flow software-based fault tolerance techniques. In: Kastensmidt, F., Rech, P. (eds.) FPGAs and Parallel Architectures for Aerospace Applications, pp. 279–291. Springer, Cham (2016). https://doi.org/10.1007/978-3-319-14352-1_18

12. Cho, H., Mirkhani, S., Cher, C.Y., Abraham, J.A., Mitra, S.: Quantitative evaluation of soft error injection techniques for robust system design. In: Proceedings of the 50th Annual Design Automation Conference, DAC 2013. Association for Computing Machinery, New York (2013). https://doi.org/10.1145/2463209.2488859

13. Gava, J., Reis, R., Ost, L.: RAT: a lightweight system-level soft error mitigation technique. In: 2020 IFIP/IEEE 28th International Conference on Very Large Scale Integration (VLSI-SOC), pp. 165–170 (2020). https://doi.org/10.1109/VLSI-SOC46417.2020.9344080

14. Imperas: OVPsim Simulator (2020). http://www.ovpworld.org

15. Leveugle, R., Calvez, A., Maistri, P., Vanhauwaert, P.: Statistical fault injection: quantified error and confidence. In: 2009 Design, Automation Test in Europe Conference Exhibition, pp. 502–506 (2009). https://doi.org/10.1109/DATE.2009. 5090716

16. Martinez-Alvarez, A.: Compiler-directed soft error mitigation for embedded systems. IEEE Trans. Dependable Secure Comput. **9**(2), 159–172 (2012). https://doi. org/10.1109/TDSC.2011.54

17. Mukherjee, S.S., Emer, J., Reinhardt, S.K.: The soft error problem: an architectural perspective. In: 11th International Symposium on High-Performance Computer Architecture, pp. 243–247 (2005). https://doi.org/10.1109/HPCA.2005.37

18. Nicolescu, B., Velazco, R.: Detecting Soft Errors by a Purely Software Approach: Method, Tools and Experimental Results, pp. 39–51. Springer, Boston (2003). https://doi.org/10.1007/0-306-48709-8_4

19. Reis, G.A., Chang, J., August, D.I.: Automatic instruction-level software-only recovery. IEEE Micro **27**(1), 36–47 (2007). https://doi.org/10.1109/MM.2007.4

20. Reis, G.A., Chang, J., Vachharajani, N., Rangan, R., August, D.I., Mukherjee, S.S.: Software-controlled fault tolerance. ACM Trans. Archit. Code Optim. **2**(4), 366–396 (2005). https://doi.org/10.1145/1113841.1113843

21. Rodrigues, G.S., Kastensmidt, F.L., Reis, R., Rosa, F., Ost, L.: Analyzing the impact of using pthreads versus OpenMP under fault injection in ARM Cortex-A9 dual-core, pp. 1–6 (2016). https://doi.org/10.1109/RADECS.2016.8093180

22. Serrano-Cases, A., Morilla, Y., Martín-Holgado, P., Cuenca-Asensi, S., Martínez-Álvarez, A.: Nonintrusive automatic compiler-guided reliability improvement of embedded applications under proton irradiation. IEEE Trans. Nucl. Sci. **66**(7), 1500–1509 (2019). https://doi.org/10.1109/TNS.2019.2912323

23. Shirvani, P.P., Saxena, N.R., McCluskey, E.J.: Software-implemented EDAC protection against SEUs. IEEE Trans. Reliab. **49**(3), 273–284 (2000). https://doi.org/ 10.1109/24.914544

24. Snir, M., et al.: Addressing failures in exascale computing. Int. J. High Perform. Comput. Appl. **28**(2), 129–173 (2014). https://doi.org/10.1177/1094342014522573

SANSCrypt: Sporadic-Authentication-Based Sequential Logic Encryption

Yinghua Hu$^{(\boxtimes)}$, Kaixin Yang, Shahin Nazarian, and Pierluigi Nuzzo

University of Southern California, Los Angeles, CA 90089, USA
{yinghuah,kaixinya,shahin.nazarian,nuzzo}@usc.edu

Abstract. Sequential logic encryption is a countermeasure against reverse engineering of sequential circuits based on modifying the original finite state machine of the circuit such that the circuit enters a wrong state upon being reset. A user must apply a certain sequence of input patterns, i.e., a key sequence, for the circuit to transition to the correct state. The circuit then remains functional unless it is powered off or reset again. Most sequential encryption methods require the correct key to be applied only once. In this paper, we propose a novel Sporadic-Authentication-Based Sequential Logic Encryption method (SANSCrypt) that circumvents the potential vulnerability associated with a single-authentication mechanism. SANSCrypt adopts a new temporal dimension to logic encryption, by requiring the user to sporadically perform multiple authentications according to a protocol based on pseudo-random number generation. We provide implementation details of SANSCrypt and present a design that is amenable to time-sensitive applications. In SANSCrypt, the authentication task does not significantly disrupt the normal circuit operation, as it can be interrupted or postponed upon request from a high-priority task with minimal impact on the overall performance. Analysis and validation results on a set of benchmark circuits show that SANSCrypt offers a substantial output corruptibility if the key sequences are applied incorrectly. Moreover, it exhibits exponential resilience to existing attacks, including SAT-based attacks, while maintaining a reasonably low overhead.

Keywords: Hardware Security · Sequential Encryption · Sporadic Authentication

1 Introduction

The ever-increasing costs for the design and manufacturing of modern VLSI systems have led to a global supply chain, where several important steps, such as verification, fabrication, testing, and packaging, are outsourced to third-party companies. As proprietary design information and intellectual property (IP) blocks inevitably get to the supply chain, an untrusted third party may gain access to a sufficient amount of critical design information to potentially reverse

© IFIP International Federation for Information Processing 2021
Published by Springer Nature Switzerland AG 2021
A. Calimera et al. (Eds.): VLSI-SoC 2020, IFIP AICT 621, pp. 255–278, 2021.
https://doi.org/10.1007/978-3-030-81641-4_12

engineer the design and massively reproduce it for illegal profit. Another possible consequence of reverse engineering is Hardware Trojan (HT) insertion, which can either disrupt the normal circuit operation [1] or provide the attacker with access to critical data or software running on the chip [2]. Both types of HTs can be destructive for safety-critical applications, such as autonomous driving cars and implantable medical devices.

Countermeasures for reverse engineering, such as logic encryption [3–6], integrated circuit (IC) camouflaging [7], split manufacturing [8], and watermarking [9] have been developed over the past decades to either increase the hardness of IC reverse engineering or embed unique proprietary signatures on the IC. Among these, logic encryption has received significant attention as a promising, low-overhead countermeasure. Logic encryption achieves IC protection by properly modifying the original circuit such that a user can only access the correct function after configuring the circuit with a correct key pattern. Otherwise, the circuit function remains hidden, and the output different from the correct one.

Various logic encryption techniques [3–6] and potential attacks [10–12] have appeared in the literature, as well as methods to systematically evaluate them [13, 14]. A category of techniques [3–5], referred to as *combinational encryption*, is designed to modify and protect combinational circuits or the combinational logic portions of sequential circuits. When the circuit scan chains are accessible to the attackers, one of the most successful attacks against combinational encryption is the Boolean satisfiability (SAT)-based attack [10]. Even if the scan chains are not accessible, e.g., due to scan chain encryption and obfuscation [15–17], a variant of SAT-based attacks [18,19] can still succeed, at a higher cost, by leveraging methods from bounded model checking to unroll the sequential circuit. Another possible vulnerability of combinational encryption methods stems from the correlation between the circuit structure and the correct key, as recently exposed by an increasing number of attacks [20,21] and theoretical analyses [22]. On the other hand, *sequential logic encryption* [6,23,24] targets the state transitions of the original finite state machine (FSM). Sequential encryption methods typically introduce additional states and transitions in the original FSM, such that the circuit enters the *encrypted mode* upon being reset, exhibiting an incorrect function. A user must apply a certain sequence of input patterns, i.e., a key sequence, for the circuit to transition to the correct initial state and enter the *functional mode*. Then, the circuit remains functional unless it is powered off or reset again.

Recently, a set of attacks have been reported against sequential encryption schemes, aiming to retrieve the correct key sequence or the correct circuit function. Similarly to the aforementioned SAT-based attacks [18,19] to combinational encryption, sequential encryption can also be attacked via an approach based on circuit unrolling and bounded model checking [25]. Another attack based on automatic test pattern generation (ATPG) [26] uses concepts from excitation and propagation of stuck-at faults to search the key sequence among the test patterns generated by ATPG. The ATPG-based attack assumes that most stuck-at faults can only be triggered and detected in the functional mode. Therefore, the correct authentication key sequence must appear in most of the test patterns generated by ATPG tools. Furthermore, when the attackers have some knowledge of the topology of the encrypted FSM, then they can extract and analyze the state transition graph and bypass the encrypted mode [25]. Overall, the continuous advances in FSM extraction and analysis tools tend to challenge any of the existing sequential encryption schemes and call for approaches that can significantly increase their robustness.

This paper presents a novel Sporadic-Authentication-based Sequential Logic Encryption scheme (SANSCrypt), which raises the attack difficulty via a *multi-authentication protocol*, whose decryption relies on *retrieving a set of correct key sequences as well as the time at which each sequence should be applied*. Our contributions can be summarized as follows:

- A robust, multi-authentication-based sequential logic encryption method that for the first time, to the best of our knowledge, systematically incorporates the robustness of multi-factor authentication (MFA) [27] in the context of hardware encryption.
- An architecture for sporadic re-authentication where key sequences must be applied at multiple times, determined by a random number generator, to access the correct circuit functionality.
- A design of the multi-authentication protocol that is suitable for time-sensitive applications, as it ensures that the real-time execution of time-critical and safety-critical tasks is not disrupted.
- Security analysis and empirical validation of SANSCrypt on a set of ISCAS'89 benchmark circuits [28], showing exponential resilience against existing attacks, including SAT-based attacks, and reasonably low overhead.

Analysis and validation results show that SANSCrypt can significantly enhance the resilience of sequential logic encryption under different attack assumptions. A preliminary version of the results of this paper appeared in our previous publication [29], where we first introduced SANSCrypt. In this paper, we present an improved architecture and protocol design that are specifically amenable to time-sensitive applications, by allowing the authentication task to be interrupted or postponed upon request from higher-priority tasks. Moreover, we extend our analysis of the brute-force attack resilience to account for the attack difficulty brought by the timing uncertainty about when to apply the correct key sequences. Finally, we offer an extensive validation of the proposed construction, showing its ability to protect time-sensitive applications without affecting the execution of time-critical tasks.

The rest of the paper is organized as follows. We provide an overview of existing sequential logic encryption methods and related attacks in Sect. 2. In Sect. 3, we present a multi-authentication protocol applicable to sequential logic encryption and introduce the basic design and implementation details of SANSCrypt. We then describe an enhanced design that is compatible with time-sensitive applications. The security level of SANSCrypt is analyzed in Sect. 4, while Sect. 5 reports the results from functional testing and the overhead after synthesis. Conclusions are drawn in Sect. 6.

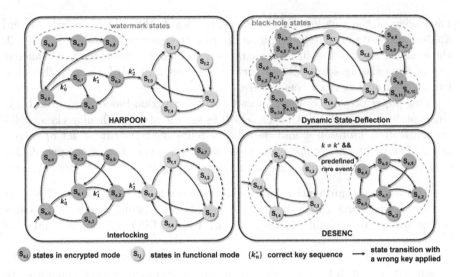

Fig. 1. State transition diagrams for different sequential encryption techniques.

2 Overview of Sequential Logic Encryption

A first sequential logic encryption method based on encrypting the finite state machine (FSM) of a circuit is *HARPOON* [6]. After encryption with HAR-POON, the resulting FSM exhibits two main modes of operation, namely, an encrypted mode and a functional mode, as shown in Fig. 1 (top left). When powered on, the circuit starts in the encrypted mode and exhibits incorrect functionality. The user must apply an appropriate sequence of input patterns during the first few clock cycles to enter the functional mode, in which the correct functionality is recovered. To claim ownership of the circuit, HARPOON also creates a set of watermark states in the encrypted mode that can be entered only when another unique sequence of input patterns, known to the circuit designer, is applied. However, due to the simple mechanism of HARPOON, there is only one transition connecting the encrypted mode portion to the functional mode portion of the state transition diagram (STG) of the FSM. This distinguishable feature may help attackers locate and bypass the encrypted mode by FSM extraction and analysis methods [25].

Several tools [30–32] have been recently developed to facilitate FSM extraction by identifying the state registers from the circuit netlist. The increasing accuracy and efficiency of these methods call for encryption techniques that are more robust in the way they manipulate and obfuscate the STG of the circuit.

Interlocking [23] improves HARPOON by modifying the circuit FSM such that multiple transitions are available between the states of the encrypted mode FSM and the ones of the functional mode FSM, as shown in Fig. 1 (bottom left), making it harder for the attacker to detect the boundary between the two modes. However, in both HARPOON and Interlocking, once the circuit enters the func-

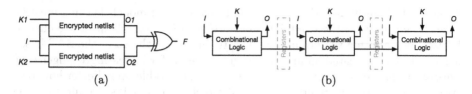

Fig. 2. (a) A miter circuit and (b) an unrolled circuit that represents the behavior of the sequential circuit for the first 3 cycles.

tional mode, it remains there unless it is powered off or reset. Moreover, because the correct circuit function can only be accessed when the correct key sequence is applied, attacks based on Automatic Test Pattern Generation (ATPG) [26] can be successfully mounted most of the times. ATPG-based attacks are based on the assumption that many stuck-at faults can only be triggered and detected when the circuit is in the functional mode. Therefore, the correct key sequence can be efficiently retrieved by analyzing common sub-sequences in the test patterns generated by ATPG tools.

Dynamic State Deflection [33] adds another level of protection by requiring an additional key input verification step in the functional mode. If the additional key input is incorrect, the FSM transitions to a black-hole state cluster which can no longer be left, as shown in Fig. 1 (top right). However, since the correct value for the extra key input is fixed over time, the scheme becomes more vulnerable to SAT-based attacks [18,19].

The original SAT-based attack [10] has proven to be powerful on combinational logic encryption [3–5] when the circuit scan chains are accessible to attackers. The attack can efficiently prune out wrong keys by iteratively solving a set of SAT problems. At the first iteration, a miter circuit, consisting of two copies of the encrypted circuit, is assembled as shown in Fig. 2(a). The miter circuit is used to generate a SAT instance that is solved to search for a *distinguishing input pattern* (DIP). A DIP is an input pattern i, such that there exist at least two different key patterns, k_1 and k_2, leading to different outputs for the encrypted circuits, i.e., $F = 1$ in Fig. 2(a). Once a DIP is found, the attack queries an oracle, i.e., a functional circuit that is assumed to be available, to find the correct output for this DIP. The DIP and the correct output provide additional constraints for the SAT instance at the next iteration, which contributes to eliminating a group of wrong keys that do not result in the correct output when applying the DIP to the encrypted circuit. When no new DIPs are found, the SAT-based attack terminates, indicating that the remaining keys can all be used as correct keys.

When the scan chains are not available, a combinational miter circuit cannot be directly formed and SAT-based attacks [18,19] leverage methods from bounded model checking [34] to "unroll" the logic loops in the sequential circuit and obtain a combinational circuit that represents the behavior of the original circuit over a time horizon, as pictorially shown in Fig. 2(b). The miter circuit is then built out of the unrolled circuit to execute the SAT-based attack. However, to successfully terminate the attack, additional steps of model checking must be taken to ensure that the candidate keys are not only correct up to the current horizon but also for the original circuit. If this is not the case, the SAT-based attack must be repeated on unrolled circuit versions for increasingly longer time horizons to prune out wrong keys that were not detectable over shorter horizons. As suggested in the literature [25], a similar technique based on circuit unrolling can be used to attack sequential logic encryption methods. However, a detailed evaluation of these attacks on sequential encryption has been elusive.

While most of the encryption techniques mentioned above corrupt the circuit function immediately after reset unless the correct key sequence is applied, *DES-ENC* [24], shown in Fig. 1 (bottom right), determines the cycle for transitioning to the encrypted mode by counting the number of occurrences of a user-defined rare event in the circuit, unless the correct key sequence is applied. After the number of occurrences reaches a given threshold, the circuit enters the encrypted mode. This scheme is more resilient to sequential SAT-based attacks [35] because it requires unrolling the circuit FSM a large number of times to find the key. However, the initial transparency window may still expose critical portions of the circuit functionality.

3   Multi-authentication-Based Sequential Encryption

We introduce the design and implementation details for SANSCrypt, starting with the underlying threat model.

3.1   Threat Model

SANSCrypt assumes a threat model that is consistent with the previous literature on sequential logic encryption [6,19,25]. The goal of the attack is to access the correct circuit functionality, by either finding the correct key sequence or reconstructing the correct circuit function. To achieve this goal, the attacker can leverage one or more of the following resources: (i) the encrypted netlist; (ii) a working circuit providing correct input-output pairs; (iii) knowledge of the encryption technique. In addition, we assume that the attacker has no access to the scan chain and cannot directly observe or change the state of the circuit.

3.2   Authentication Protocol

As shown in Fig. 3(a), existing sequential logic encryption techniques are mostly based on a single-authentication protocol, requiring users to be authenticated only once before accessing the correct circuit function. After the authentication, the circuit remains functional unless it is powered off or reset. To attack the circuit, therefore, it is sufficient to discover the correct key sequence that must be applied to the encrypted circuit upon reset.

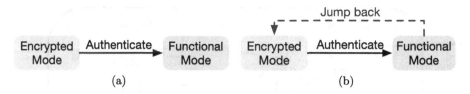

Fig. 3. Conventional (a) and proposed (b) authentication protocols for logic encryption.

We adopt, instead, the authentication protocol in Fig. 3(b), where the circuit can "jump" back to the encrypted mode from the functional mode. Once the back-jumping occurs, another round of authentication is required to resume the normal operation. The back-jumping can be triggered multiple times and involves a different key sequence for each round of re-authentication. The hardness of attacking this protocol stems from both the increased number of the key sequences to be applied and the uncertainty on the time at which each sequence should be applied. A new temporal dimension adds to the difficulty of the decryption procedure, which poses a significantly higher threshold to the attackers.

3.3   Overview of the Encryption Scheme

SANSCrypt is a sequential logic encryption scheme which supports random back-jumping, as represented in Fig. 4. When the circuit is powered or reset, the circuit falls into the reset state $E0$ of the encrypted mode. Like other sequential logic encryption schemes, the user must apply at startup the correct key sequence at the primary input ports for the circuit to transition to the initial (or reset) state $N0$ of the functional mode.

Once the circuit enters the functional mode, it can deliberately, but randomly, jump back, as denoted by the blue edges in Fig. 4, to a state s_{bj} in the encrypted mode, called *back-jumping state*, after a designated number of clock cycles t_{bj}, called *back-jumping period*. The user then needs to apply another key sequence to return to the state right before the back-jumping operation and resume normal operations, as shown by the red arrows in Fig. 4. Both the back-jumping state s_{bj} and the back-jumping period t_{bj} are determined by a pseudo-random number generator (PRNG) embedded in the circuit. Therefore, when and where the back-jumping operation happens is unpredictable unless the attacker is able to break the PRNG given the resources described in Sect. 3.1. An in-package key management circuit will be in charge of automatically applying the key sequences from a tamper-proof memory at the right time, as computed from a hard-coded replica of the PRNG. The schematic of SANSCrypt is shown in Fig. 5 and consists of two additional blocks, that is, a back-jumping module and an encryption finite state machine (ENC-FSM), besides the original circuit. We discuss each of these blocks in the following subsections.

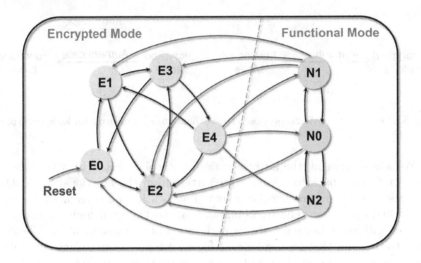

Fig. 4. State transition diagram of SANSCrypt.

3.4 Back-Jumping Module

The back-jumping module consists of an n-bit *PRNG*, an n-bit *Counter*, and a *Back-Jumping Finite State Machine* (BJ-FSM). BJ-FSM continually checks the output from the PRNG and the counter, and determines the back-jumping operations, as summarized by the flowchart in Fig. 6. Upon circuit reset, BJ-FSM keeps checking the authentication status. Once the authentication is successful and the circuit enters the functional mode, BJ-FSM samples the current PRNG output and stores this value as the back-jumping period t_{bj}. At the same time, the counter is set to zero.

The counter increments its output at each clock cycle until it reaches t_{bj}, when BJ-FSM samples again the PRNG output r. By taking the PRNG outputs at different clock cycles, r and t_{bj} are generally not the same. The BJ-FSM then implements a function of r to determine the back-jumping state, i.e.,

$$s_{bj} = f(r).$$

For example, if s_{bj} is an l-bit binary number, BJ-FSM can arbitrarily select l bits from r and assign the value to s_{bj}. If the first l bits of r are selected, we have

$$f(r) = r[0 : l - 1].$$

Meanwhile, BJ-FSM sends a back-jumping request to the other blocks of the circuit, such that the circuit back-jumps to s_{bj} in the encrypted mode, where it keeps checking the authentication status of the circuit. SANSCrypt does not set any specific requirement on the PRNG. Any PRNG architecture can be used based on the design budget and the desired security level. For example, linear PRNGs, such as Linear Feedback Shift Registers (LFSRs), provide higher

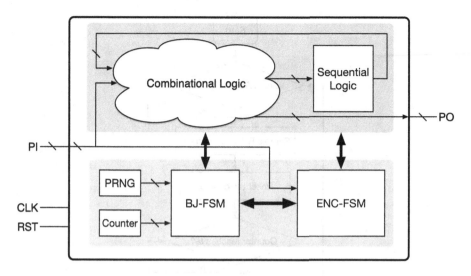

Fig. 5. Schematic view of SANSCrypt.

speed and lower area overhead but tend to be more vulnerable than cipher-based PRNGs, such as AES, which are, however, more expensive.

3.5   Encryption Finite State Machine (ENC-FSM)

The Encryption Finite State Machine (ENC-FSM) determines whether the user's key sequence is correct and, if it is not correct, takes actions to corrupt the functionality of the original circuit. Without creating extra input ports for the authentication, the input of the ENC-FSM is provided via the primary input ports. The output enc_out of ENC-FSM is an n-bit-long array, which can be used, together with a set of XOR gates, to corrupt the circuit function [3]. For example, in Fig. 7, a 3-bit array enc_out is connected to six nodes in the original circuit via XOR gates. In this paper, XOR gates are inserted at randomly selected nodes. However, any other combinational logic encryption technique is also applicable. As a design parameter, we denote by *node coverage* the ratio between the number of inserted XOR gates and the total number of combinational logic gates in the circuit.

Only one state of ENC-FSM, termed *auth*, is used in the functional mode. In *auth*, all bits in enc_out are set to zero and the original circuit functionality is not corrupted. In the other states, the value of enc_out changes based on the state, but at least one bit is set to one to guarantee that the circuit output is incorrect. A sample truth table for a 3-bit enc_out array is shown in Table 1. When the circuit is not in *auth*, i.e., in the encrypted mode, enc_out changes its value based on the state of the encryption FSM. Such an approach makes it difficult for signal analysis attacks, aiming to locate signals with low switching activity in the encrypted mode, to find enc_out and bypass ENC-FSM. After a

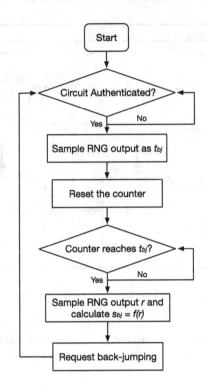

Fig. 6. Flowchart of BJ-FSM.

successful authentication, the circuit resumes its normal operation. Additional
registers are, therefore, required in the ENC-FSM to store the circuit state before
back-jumping so that it can be resumed after authentication.

3.6   Guaranteeing Real-Time Operation

Unlike previous sequential logic encryption methods, SANSCrypt requires the
user to sporadically be re-authenticated amid the circuit's normal operation.
As discussed in Sect. 4, this feature can significantly raise the attack difficulty.
However, it can also cause timing overhead and impact the performance in time-
sensitive applications that require prompt, real-time response, or guarantees that
a time-critical or safety-critical task meets a pre-defined deadline. For example,
upon detection of a vehicle collision, authentication tasks should be preempted
by the airbag control in the attempt to protect passengers. In this Section, we
present an enhanced back-jumping FSM (EBJ-FSM) design that delivers precise,
guaranteed, and predictable timing for real-time operation.

We denote by V_I and V_S the set of all possible primary input patterns and
states of a circuit, respectively. We then assume without loss of generality that
any input pattern in a set

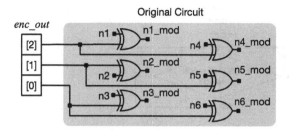

Fig. 7. *enc_out* controls the original circuit via XOR gates.

Table 1. Truth Table for a 3-Bit *enc_out* Array

State	E0	E1	E2	E3	E4	Auth
enc_out[0]	0	1	1	1	1	0
enc_out[1]	1	0	1	1	0	0
enc_out[2]	1	1	1	0	0	0

$$I_p = \{i_1, i_2, ..., i_n\},$$

where $I_p \subseteq V_I$, can trigger a time-critical task whose execution should immediately start or be queued after the ongoing time-critical task. Such tasks should be completed, without interruption, within a number of clock cycles given by a function *deadline*. We assume that a task deadline depends, in general, on the triggering input and the current state of the circuit, i.e.,

$$deadline : V_I \times V_S \rightarrow \mathbb{N}.$$

When a time-critical task is requested by an input pattern in I_p, the deadline function returns the remaining number of clock cycles required without interruption to finish this task and the ongoing time-critical tasks, if any, based on the current state s. When the circuit is in an idle state, i.e., no time-critical task is being executed, and the current input pattern i satisfies $i \notin I_p$, the *deadline* function returns zero. The *deadline* function models the scheduling algorithm determining the priority among tasks and can be customized based on the desired application. Figure 8 shows the flowchart of EBJ-FSM for time-sensitive applications. On top of the basic back-jumping feature, two locations in the flow chart handle task prioritization in the encrypted mode (①) and the functional mode (②), respectively.

High-Priority Task Triggered in the Encrypted Mode (Case ①). The enhanced BJ-FSM (EBJ-FSM) allows the circuit to enter the functional mode in two scenarios: (1) upon a successful authentication, and (2) when a high-priority

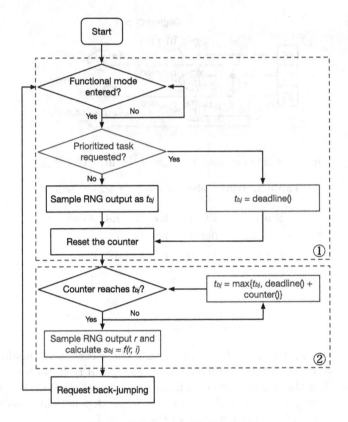

Fig. 8. Flowchart of EBJ-FSM.

task is triggered. EBJ-FSM monitors these two events at each clock cycle. Once the functional mode is entered, EBJ-FSM checks whether the second scenario occurred, i.e., a high-priority task was triggered. If this is the case, meaning that the authentication process was interrupted, EBJ-FSM sets the back-jumping time t_{bj} to the time required to complete the task execution as computed by the *deadline* function. When the high-priority task terminates and there are no new task requests with high priority, the circuit back-jumps to the encrypted mode and the authentication procedure is resumed.

High-Priority Task Triggered in the Functional Mode (Case ②). In the functional mode, EBJ-FSM continually checks whether the counter output has reached the threshold t_{bj}. If so, it will request back-jumping as is the case for the BJ-FSM design in Fig. 6. However, in this case, the back-jumping time t_{bj} is updated at each clock cycle via the following formula,

$$t_{bj,k} := \max\{t_{bj,k-1}, deadline() + counter()\},$$

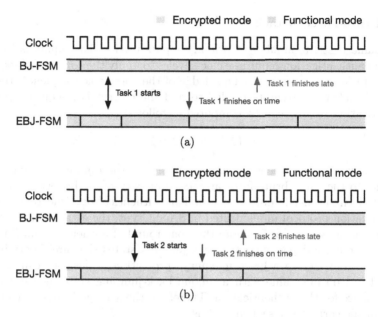

Fig. 9. Examples of high-priority tasks triggered in (a) the encrypted mode and (b) the functional mode. Both tasks require 5 clock cycles to finish with BJ-FSM and EBJ-FSM.

where $counter()$ returns the current counter output and $t_{bj,k}$ refers to the stored back-jumping time at time k. Effectively, the back-jumping time t_{bj} is prolonged if a high-priority task cannot be completed before the next designated back-jumping operation.

Figure 9 shows the timing diagrams for two high-priority tasks triggered in two different modes. While the basic SANSCrypt protocol causes delays to the task execution, the EBJ-FSM guarantees that there is no delay in the execution of the critical tasks and no impact on the real-time performance of the circuit.

As a further enhancement, we observe that the function that determines the back-jumping state s_{bj} can also be modified by adding the current input value i as an argument. We propose this modification to mitigate a potential vulnerability associated with FSM structural analysis of the basic SANSCrypt architecture, as further illustrated in Sect. 4.

4   Security and Performance Analysis

We analyze SANSCrypt's resilience against existing attacks and estimate its timing overhead due to the multi-authentication protocol.

4.1   Brute-Force Attack

We assume that the number of primary inputs used as key inputs is $|i|$ and a round of authentication requires c clock cycles to apply the correct key sequence. If the attacker has no *a priori* knowledge of the correct key sequence, then the average number of attempts needed to find the correct key sequence for each authentication step, $\overline{\tau}$, can be computed as follows:

$$\overline{\tau} = (2^{|i| \cdot c} + 1)/2 \approx 2^{|i| \cdot c - 1},$$

where we use $\overline{\tau}$ to represent the expected value of the random variable τ. This amounts to the same brute-force attack complexity of HARPOON, where the encrypted circuit needs only one round of authentication. Due to the multi-authentication protocol implemented in SANSCrypt, the attacker needs to find the correct key sequences for more than one round of authentication. Each correct key sequence depends on the back-jumping states that are determined by the PRNG output. To achieve maximum protection, a designer can associate each PRNG output value with a unique back-jumping state, hence a unique key sequence for the authentication. Therefore, the average brute-force effort to guess all the correct key sequences $\overline{T}$ is

$$\overline{T} = N_r \cdot \overline{\tau} = N_r \cdot 2^{|i| \cdot c - 1},$$

where N_r is the number of possible values of the PRNG output. For a 10-bit PRNG, if $|i| = 32$ and $c = 8$, this average attack effort reaches 5.8×10^{79}.

Even if all the key sequences are known, it still remains challenging to infer when each key sequence should be applied, as the attacker should find the back-jumping time associated with the sequence, and this is independent of the sequence itself. To account for the time uncertainty, we first estimate the effort for guessing the back-jumping time for one authentication round. The back-jumping time ranges from one to N_r cycles following a uniform distribution. Therefore, the average brute-force effort to correctly guess the time is

$$\overline{t}_{bj} = \frac{N_r}{2},$$

while the average effort to correctly find both the key sequence and the time at which to apply it becomes

$$\overline{t}_{bf} = E[\tau t_{bj}] = \overline{\tau} \overline{t}_{bj} = \frac{N_r}{2} \cdot 2^{|i| \cdot c - 1}.$$

Suppose the attacker needs to perform at least m rounds of authentication, where $m \geq N_r$ and all N_r key sequences are used for the authentication at least once. The expected value for m can be calculated as follows, using a result from the coupon collector's problem [36]:

$$\overline{m} = N_r \cdot \left(\frac{1}{1} + \frac{1}{2} + \cdots + \frac{1}{N_r - 1} + \frac{1}{N_r} \right).$$

In our previous example, where $N_r = 1024$, we have $\overline{m} = 7689$. The average brute-force attack effort to find the back-jumping times and the key sequences for m authentication steps would then be

$$\overline{T}_{bf} = E\left[(t_{bj}\tau)^m\right] = E_m\left[E[(t_{bj}\tau)^m \mid m]\right] = E_m\left[\left(\frac{N_r}{2}2^{|i|\cdot c-1}\right)^m \Big| m\right].$$

For simplicity, we provide a lower bound for the expectation above. Since $m \geq N_r$ and $\frac{N_r}{2} \cdot 2^{|i|\cdot c-1} > 1$, we have the following lower bound for $\overline{T}_{bf}$:

$$\overline{T}_{bf} \geq \left(\frac{N_r}{2} \cdot 2^{|i|\cdot c-1}\right)^{N_r}.$$

In our example, the average brute-force effort will be lower bounded by 1.8×10^{81379}, which makes a brute-force attack infeasible and exponentially harder than in previous sequential obfuscation methods.

4.2 Sequential SAT-Based Attack

A SAT-based attack can be carried out on existing sequential logic encryption methods by unrolling the sequential circuit [25]. In this paper, we implement such an attack to validate the resilience of methods such as HARPOON and SANSCrypt by adapting previously proposed attack strategies [18,19] to a setting in which a dynamic key, i.e., a sequence of keys applied at different clock cycles, is presented via the primary input ports of the circuit.

Figure 10 shows the schematic of an unrolled circuit under the assumption that the number of clock cycles, n, required by the encrypted circuit to enter the functional mode after reset is known. The primary input ports of the first n replicas of the encrypted circuit, marked in red, act as the key ports K of the unrolled circuit. Starting with the $(n+1)^{th}$ circuit replica, the primary input and output ports of the encrypted circuit, marked in blue and magenta, act, instead, as the primary input ports I and the primary output ports O of the unrolled circuit, respectively. A combinational miter circuit can then be assembled using this unrolled circuit to mount a combinational SAT-based attack and find the correct key. If the SAT-based attack fails to find the correct key with $(n+1)$ circuit replicas, the circuit will be unrolled once more to repeat the attack.

The attack described above would still be ineffective on SANSCrypt, since it can retrieve the first key sequence but would fail to discover when the next back-jumping occurs and what would be the next key sequence. Even if the attacker knows when the next back-jumping occurs, the attack will fail due to the large number of circuit replicas needed to find all the key sequences, as empirically observed in Sect. 5.

4.3 FSM Extraction and Structural Analysis

As discussed in Sect. 2, a common shortcoming of previous sequential encryption schemes is the easy separation of states between the encrypted mode and the

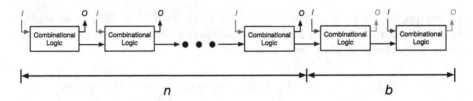

Fig. 10. An unrolled version of the encrypted circuit which requires n clock cycles to find the key sequence.

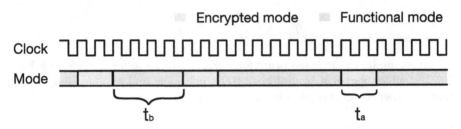

Fig. 11. Circuit mode switching for an authenticated user.

functional mode due to the fact that only one transition goes though the two modes. SANSCrypt addresses this issue by designing more than one transition between the two modes, as shown in Fig. 4. In a basic BJ-FSM design, shown in Fig. 6, the back-jumping state is solely determined by the PRNG. Because transitions in FSM are typically determined also by the primary input, attackers can potentially identify all the back-jumping transitions by analyzing the transition conditions. The enhanced BJ-FSM design (EBJ-FSM), shown in Fig. 8, circumvents this vulnerability by also using the primary inputs to determine the back-jumping state.

Without extracting the FSM, an attacker may also try to locate and isolate the output of ENC-FSM by looking for low signal switching activities when the circuit is in the encrypted mode. SANSCrypt addresses this risk by expanding the output of ENC-FSM from one bit to an array. The value of each bit changes frequently with state changing in the encrypted mode, which makes it difficult for attackers to find them based only on signal switching activities.

4.4 Cycle Delay Analysis

Due to multiple back-jumping and authentication operations in SANSCrypt, additional clock cycles will be required. Suppose that each authentication requires t_a clock cycles and the circuit stays in the functional mode for t_b clock cycles before the next back-jumping occurs, as shown in Fig. 11. Assuming that no higher-priority tasks are triggered, the cycle delay overhead can be computed as the ratio $O_{cd} = t_a/t_b$.

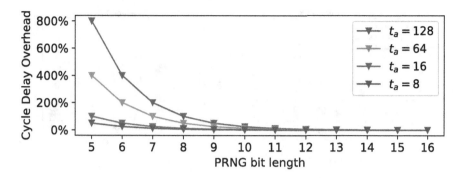

Fig. 12. Average cycle delay as a function of PRNG bit length when the key sequence cycle length t_a is 8, 16, 64, and 128.

Table 2. Overview of the Selected Benchmark Circuits

Circuit	s27	s298	s1238	s9234	s15850	s35932	s38584
Input	4	3	14	36	77	35	38
Output	1	6	14	39	150	320	304
DFF	3	14	18	211	534	1728	1426
Gate	10	119	508	5597	9772	16065	19253

Specifically, for an n-bit PRNG, the average t_b is equal to the average output value, i.e., 2^{n-1}. To illustrate how the cycle delay overhead is influenced by this encryption, Fig. 12 shows the relation between average cycle delay overhead and PRNG bit length. The clock cycles (t_a) required for each authentication are set to 8, 16, 64, and 128. When the PRNG bit length is small, the average cycle delay increases significantly as t_a increases. However, the cycle delay can be reduced by increasing the PRNG bit length. For example, the average cycle delay overhead becomes negligible ($\leq 1\%$) for all the four cases when the PRNG bit length is 14 or larger.

5   Simulation Results

We first evaluate the effectiveness of SANSCrypt on seven ISCAS'89 sequential benchmark circuits of different sizes, as summarized in Table 2. All the experiments are executed on a Linux server with 48 2.1-GHz processor cores and 500-GB memory. We implement our technique on the selected circuits with different configurations and use a 45-nm Nangate Open Cell Library [37] to synthesize the encrypted netlists for area optimization under a critical-path delay constraint that targets the same performance as for the original netlists. For the purpose of illustration, we realize the PRNG using Linear Feedback Shift Registers (LFSRs) with different sizes, ranging from 5 to 15 bits. An LFSR provides an area-efficient implementation and has often been used in other logic

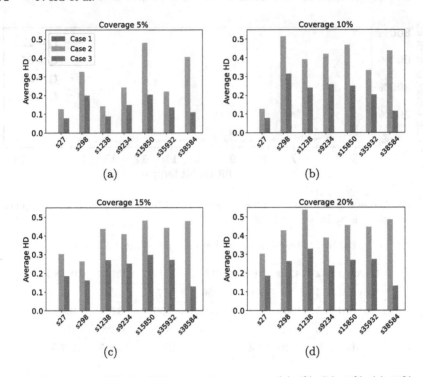

Fig. 13. The average HD for different node coverage: (a) 5%, (b) 10%, (c) 15%, and (d) 20%.

encryption schemes in the literature [8,38]. We choose a random 8-cycle-long key sequence as the correct key, and select 5%, 10%, 15%, and 20% as node coverage levels. Finally, we use the Hamming distance (HD) between the correct and the corrupted output values as a metric for the output corruptibility. If the HD is 0.5, the effort spent to identify the incorrect bits is maximum.

Functional Verification. First, we simulate all the encrypted circuits with (case 1) and without (case 2) the correct key sequences, by applying a randomly generated input vector that is 1000-cycle long. We then compare the circuit output with the golden output from the original netlist and calculate the HD between the two. Each simulation is repeated for 1000 times to obtain the average HD. Moreover, we demonstrate the additional robustness of SANSCrypt by simulating a scenario (case 3) in which the attacker assumes that the encryption is based on a single-authentication protocol and, thus, provides only the first correct key sequence upon reset. Figure 13 shows the average HD in these three cases. For all the circuits, the average HD is zero only in case 1, when all the correct key sequences are applied at the right clock cycles. Otherwise, in case 2 (orange) and case 3 (green), we observe a significant increase in the average HD. The average HD in case 3 is always smaller than that of case 2 because, in case

Table 3. SAT-based attack runtime for finding the first 7 key sequences

Key Seq. Index	1 (HARPOON)	2	3	4	5	6	7
Runtime [s]	4	123	229	1941	1301	2202	25571

Table 4. ADP Overhead Results for Full Encryption

Circuit	s27				s298				s1238				s9234			
Node Coverage	5%	10%	15%	20%	5%	10%	15%	20%	5%	10%	15%	20%	5%	10%	15%	20%
Area [%]	1418.5	1418.5	1403.2	1403.2	413.0	427.3	425.2	453.8	144.8	165.7	176.0	189.2	114.6	131.7	144.5	160.1
Power [%]	1627.7	1627.7	1627.5	1627.5	385.7	390.6	389.9	402.8	217.8	232.1	235.0	249.8	197.8	197.5	188.0	190.6
Delay [%]	0.0	0.0	1.4	1.4	0.0	0.0	0.0	0.5	0.0	0.0	0.0	5.8	0.0	0.0	0.9	3.6
Circuit	s15850				s35932				s38584				Average*			
Node Coverage	5%	10%	15%	20%	5%	10%	15%	20%	5%	10%	15%	20%	5%	10%	15%	20%
Area [%]	92.9	112.1	120.1	133.9	116.3	129.5	139.4	151.6	133.5	140.9	158.7	165.6	120.4	136.0	147.8	160.1
Power [%]	127.4	142.3	153.2	163.0	98.4	101.9	101.2	103.0	123.9	128.8	142.0	140.3	149.5	160.5	163.9	169.4
Delay [%]	−0.3	0.0	0.1	0.6	−0.4	0.0	4.3	5.3	0.6	2.0	0.4	4.9	0.0	0.4	1.1	4.0

*Excluding s27 and s298.

3, the correct functionality is recovered for a short period of time, after which the circuit jumps back to the encrypted mode. The longer the overall runtime, the smaller will be the impact of this transparency window in which the circuit exhibits the correct functionality.

Sequential SAT-Based Attacks. We apply the sequential SAT-based attack in Sect. 4 to circuit *s1238* with a 5-bit LFSR and 20% node coverage, under a stronger attack model, in which the attacker knows when to apply the key sequences. Table 3 shows the runtime to find the first set of 7 key sequences. The runtime remains exponential in the number of key sequences, which makes sequential SAT-based attacks impractical for large designs.

Impact of High-Priority Tasks. We further characterize the behavior of SANSCrypt in the presence of high-priority tasks. We consider the largest ISCAS benchmark *s38584* and assume, without loss of generality, that all the high-priority tasks to be executed on the encrypted circuit have the same deadline t_d. For a sequence of input patterns, we define the high-priority task load L as the ratio between the number of high-priority task requests in the sequence and the sequence length. Figure 14(a) and Fig. 14(b) show simulation results under different task loads and deadlines for 10,000 clock cycles, when the PRNG length is 5 and 10, respectively. L ranges from 0 to 0.3, while the task deadline takes four different values within 5 and 20. When $L = 0$, no high-priority tasks are requested and the numbers of authentications within 10,000 clock cycles are 480 and 25 for the two different PRNG lengths, respectively. When L or t_d increases, it is more likely for a high-priority task to either interrupt or postpone the authentication step, leading to a decreasing number of authentications, as shown in Fig. 14(a). However, in a scenario in which the number of authentications is already as low as 25 without execution of high-priority tasks, as in Fig. 14(b),

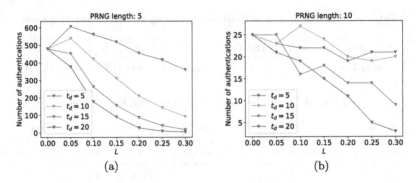

Fig. 14. Number of authentications required within 10,000 clock cycles on *s38584* for different priority task loads L. The PRNG length is (a) 5 and (b) 20.

the likelihood that a task needs to interrupt or postpone the authentication process decreases. As a result, increasing L or t_d does not significantly affect the number of authentications as in the scenario of Fig. 14(a). When $L = 0.05$ and $t_d = 5$ or 10, the number of authentications becomes larger than in the absence of high-priority tasks in Fig. 14(a), an artifact due to the non-ideality of the LFSR used in the design, which disappears when using a higher-quality PRNG. On the other hand, when many time-consuming high-priority tasks need to be executed, i.e., when the task load L is 0.3 and the deadline t_d is 20, we observe that 5 and 3 authentications are still required per 10,000 clock cycles in Fig. 14(a) and (b), respectively, which keeps the multi-authentication protocol effective. Overall, SANSCrypt is capable of delivering security as well as precise, guaranteed, and predictable timing in the execution of time-critical tasks.

Implementation Overhead. Finally, Table 4 reports the synthesized area, power, and delay (ADP) overhead due to the implementation of our technique. In more than 70% of the circuits, the delay overhead is less than 1%, and exceeds the required clock cycle by at most 5.8%. Except for *s27* and *s298*, characterized by a small gate count, all the other circuits show average area and power overhead of 141.1% and 160.8%, respectively, which is expected due to the additional number of registers required in ENC-FSM to guarantee that the correct state is entered upon re-authentication. However, because critical modules in large SoCs may only account for a small portion of the area, this overhead becomes affordable under partial obfuscation. For example, we encrypted a portion of state registers in *s38584*, the largest ISCAS'89 benchmark, using SANSCrypt. We then randomly inserted additional XOR gates to achieve the same HD as in the case of full encryption. Table 5 reports the overhead results after synthesis, when the ratio between the encrypted state registers and the total number of state registers decreases from 100% to 1%. Encrypting 10% of the registers will only cost 33.4% of the area while incurring negative power overhead and 4.2% delay overhead. On the other hand, implementing the enhanced design based on

Table 5. ADP Overhead Results for Partial Encryption

Encrypted registers/Total registers	100%	50%	25%	10%	5%	2.5%	1%
Area [%]	133.5	71.6	49.1	33.4	27.8	23.5	22.4
Power [%]	123.9	40.2	9.6	−12.8	−20.5	−22.1	−25.0
Delay [%]	0.6	1.8	2.1	4.2	5.4	3.9	4.6

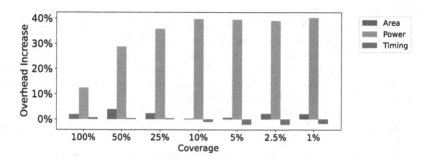

Fig. 15. Area, timing, power overhead increase, compared with the original SAN-SCrypt scheme, after the implementation of EBJ-FSM under different coverage ratios on *s38584*.

the EBJ-FSM on *s38584*, while using the same settings as in Table 5, causes an increase in the ADP overhead with respect to the basic SANSCrypt architecture, as shown in Fig. 15. Yet, the increase in both the area and timing overhead is below 4%, with the timing overhead often being lower than in the baseline. The increase in power overhead is substantial, but it is partially compensated by the negative power overhead of the baseline design in Table 5, and therefore still acceptable.

6   Conclusion

We proposed SANSCrypt, a robust sequential logic encryption technique relying on a sporadic authentication protocol, in which re-authentications are carried out at pseudo-randomly selected time slots to significantly increase the attack effort. By allowing flexible interruption and postponement of authentication tasks upon requests from high-priority tasks, SANSCrypt is capable of guaranteeing reliable timing and seamless operation in real-time and time-sensitive applications. Future work includes optimizing the implementation to further reduce the overhead, and investigating key manager architectures to guarantee reliable key delivery in large systems on chip.

Acknowledgments. This work was supported in part by the Air Force Research Laboratory (AFRL) and the Defense Advanced Research Projects Agency (DARPA) under agreement number FA8650-18-1-7817.

References

1. Karri, R., Rajendran, J., Rosenfeld, K., Tehranipoor, M.: Trustworthy hardware: identifying and classifying hardware trojans. Computer **43**(10), 39–46 (2010)
2. Tehranipoor, M., Koushanfar, F.: A survey of hardware trojan taxonomy and detection. IEEE Des. Test Comput. **27**(1), 10–25 (2010)
3. Rajendran, J., et al.: Fault analysis-based logic encryption. IEEE Trans. Comput. **64**(2), 410–424 (2013)
4. M. Yasin, Sengupta, A., Nabeel, M.T., Ashraf, M., Rajendran, J.J., Sinanoglu, O.: Provably-secure logic locking: from theory to practice. In: Proceedings of SIGSAC Conference Computer and Communications Security, pp. 1601–1618 (2017)
5. Yasin, M., Mazumdar, B., Rajendran, J.J., Sinanoglu, O.: SARLock: SAT attack resistant logic locking. In: IEEE International Symposium on Hardware Oriented Security and Trust (HOST), pp. 236–241 (2016)
6. Chakraborty, R.S., Bhunia, S.: HARPOON: an obfuscation-based SoC design methodology for hardware protection. IEEE Trans. Comput. Aid. Des. Integr. Circ. Syst. **28**(10), 1493–1502 (2009)
7. Yasin, M., Mazumdar, B., Sinanoglu, O., Rajendran J.: CamoPerturb: secure IC camouflaging for minterm protection. In: 2016 IEEE/ACM International Conference on Computer-Aided Design (ICCAD), pp. 1–8 (2016)
8. Xiao, K., Forte, D., Tehranipoor, M.: Efficient and secure split manufacturing via obfuscated built-in self-authentication. In: IEEE International Symposium on Hardware Oriented Security and Trust (HOST), pp. 14–19 (2015)
9. Charbon, E.: Hierarchical watermarking in IC design. In: IEEE Proceedings of Custom Integrated Circuits Conference, pp. 295–298 (1998)
10. Subramanyan, P., Ray, S., Malik, S.: Evaluating the security of logic encryption algorithms. In: IEEE International Symposium on Hardware Oriented Security and Trust (HOST), pp. 137–143 (2015)
11. Chakraborty, P., Cruz, J., Bhunia, S.: SURF: joint structural functional attack on logic locking. In: IEEE International Symposium on Hardware Oriented Security and Trust (HOST), pp. 181–190 (2019)
12. Shen, Y., Li, Y., Kong, S., Rezaei, A., Zhou, H.: SigAttack: new high-level sat-based attack on logic encryptions. In: Design, Automation and Test in Europe Conference and Exhibition (DATE), pp. 940–943 (2019)
13. Menon, V.V., et al.: System-level framework for logic obfuscation with quantified metrics for evaluation. In: Secure Development Conference (SecDev), pp. 89–100 (2019)
14. Hu, Y., Menon, V.V., Schmidt, A., Monson, J., French, M., Nuzzo, P.: Security-driven metrics and models for efficient evaluation of logic encryption schemes. In: ACM-IEEE International Confernce on Formal Methods and Models for System Design (MEMOCODE), pp. 1–5 (2019)
15. Sengar, G., Mukhopadhyay, D., Chowdhury, D.R.: Secured flipped scan-chain model for crypto-architecture. IEEE Trans. Comput. Aid. Des. Integr. Circ. Syst. **26**(11), 2080–2084 (2007)
16. Paul, S., Chakraborty, R.S., Bhunia, S.: VIm-scan: a low overhead scan design approach for protection of secret key in scan-based secure chips. In: IEEE VLSI Test Symposium (VTS), pp. 455–460 (2007)
17. Wang, X., Zhang, D., He, M., Su, D., Tehranipoor, M.: Secure scan and test using obfuscation throughout supply chain. IEEE Trans. Comput. Aid. Des. Integr. Circ. Syst. **37**(9), 1867–1880 (2017)

18. El Massad, M., Garg, S., Tripunitara, M.: Reverse engineering camouflaged sequential circuits without scan access. In: 2017 IEEE/ACM International Conference on Computer-Aided Design (ICCAD), pp. 33–40. IEEE (2017)
19. Shamsi, K., Li, M., Pan, D.Z., Jin, Y.: KC2: key-condition crunching for fast sequential circuit deobfuscation. In: Design, Automation and Test in Europe Conference and Exhibition (DATE), pp. 534–539 (2019)
20. Chakraborty, P., Cruz, J., Bhunia, S.: SAIL: machine learning guided structural analysis attack on hardware obfuscation. In: IEEE Asian Hardware Oriented Security and Trust Symposium (AsianHOST), pp. 56–61 (2018)
21. Sisejkovic, D., Merchant, F., Reimann, L.M., Srivastava, H., Hallawa, A., Leupers, R.: Challenging the security of logic locking schemes in the era of deep learning: a neuroevolutionary approach. arXiv preprint arXiv:2011.10389 (2020)
22. Hu, Y., Yang, K., Dutta Chowdhury, S., Nuzzo, P.: Risk-aware cost-effective design methodology for integrated circuit locking. In: Design, Automation and Test in Europe Conference and Exhibition (DATE), pp. 1182–1185. IEEE (2021)
23. Desai, A.R., Hsiao, M.S., Wang, C., Nazhandali, L., Hall, S.: Interlocking obfuscation for anti-tamper hardware. In: Proceedings of Cyber Security and Information Intelligence Research Workshop, pp. 1–4 (2013)
24. Kasarabada, Y., Raman, S.R.T., Vemuri, R.: Deep state encryption for sequential logic circuits. In: IEEE Computer Society Annual Symposium VLSI (ISVLSI), pp. 338–343 (2019)
25. Meade, T., Zhao, Z., Zhang, S., Pan, D., Jin, Y.: Revisit sequential logic obfuscation: attacks and defenses. In: IEEE International Symposium on Circuits and Systems (ISCAS), pp. 1–4 (2017)
26. Duvalsaint, D., Liu, Z., Ravikumar, A., Blanton, R.: Characterization of locked sequential circuits via ATPG. In: IEEE International Test Conference in Asia (ITC-Asia), pp. 97–102 (2019)
27. Bhargav-Spantzel, A., Squicciarini, A.C., Modi, S., Young, M., Bertino, E., Elliott, S.J.: Privacy preserving multi-factor authentication with biometrics. J. Comput. Secur. **15**(5), 529–560 (2007)
28. Brglez, F., Bryan, D., Kozminski, K.: Combinational profiles of sequential benchmark circuits. In: IEEE International Symposium on Circuits and Systems (ISCAS), pp. 1929–1934 (1989)
29. Hu, Y., Yang, K., Nazarian, S., Nuzzo, P.: SANSCrypt: a sporadic-authentication-based sequential logic encryption scheme. In: IFIP/IEEE International Confefrence on Very Large Scale Integration (VLSI-SoC), pp. 129–134 (2020)
30. Meade, T., Jin, Y., Tehranipoor, M., Zhang, S.: Gate-level netlist reverse engineering for hardware security: control logic register identification. In: IEEE International Symposium on Circuits and Systems (ISCAS), pp. 1334–1337 (2016)
31. Brunner, M., Baehr, J., Sigl, G.: Improving on state register identification in sequential hardware reverse engineering. In: IEEE International Symposium on Hardware Oriented Security and Trust (HOST) (2019)
32. Geist, J., et al.: RELIC-FUN: logic identification through functional signal comparisons. In: Proceedings of Design Automation Conference (DAC) (2020)
33. Dofe, J., Yu, Q.: Novel dynamic state-deflection method for gate-level design obfuscation. IEEE Trans. Comput. Aid. Des. Integr. Circ. Syst. **37**, 273–285 (2018)
34. Biere, A., Cimatti, A., Clarke, E.M., Strichman, O., Zhu, Y.: Bounded model checking (2003)
35. Kasarabada, Y., Chen, S., Vemuri, R.: On SAT-based attacks on encrypted sequential logic circuits. In: International Symposium on Quality Electronic Design (ISQED), pp. 204–211 (2019)

36. Flajolet, P., Gardy, D., Thimonier, L.: Birthday paradox, coupon collectors, caching algorithms and self-organizing search. Discret. Appl. Math. **39**(3), 207–229 (1992)
37. Silvaco: 45nm open cell library (2019)
38. Rahman, M.S., et al.: Dynamically obfuscated scan chain to resist oracle-guided attacks on logic locked design. IACR Cryptol. ePrint Arch., vol. 2019, p. 946 (2019)

3D Nanofabric: Layout Challenges and Solutions for Ultra-scaled Logic Designs

Edouard Giacomin[1]([✉]), Juergen Boemmels[2], Julien Ryckaert[2],
Francky Catthoor[2,3], and Pierre-Emmanuel Gaillardon[1]

[1] University of Utah, Salt Lake City, UT, USA
{edouard.giacomin,pierre-emmanuel.gaillardon}@utah.edu
[2] IMEC, Leuven, Belgium
[3] KU Leuven, Leuven, Belgium

Abstract. In the past few years, novel fabrication schemes such as parallel and monolithic 3D integration have been proposed to keep sustaining the need for more cost-efficient integrated circuits. By stacking several devices, wafers, or dies, the footprint, delay, and power can be decreased compared to traditional 2D implementations. While parallel 3D does not enable very fine-grained vertical connections, monolithic 3D currently only offers a limited number of transistor tiers due to the high cost of the additional masks and processing steps, limiting the benefits of using the third dimension. This book chapter introduces an innovative planar circuit netlist and layout approach, enabling a new 3D integration flow called *3D Nanofabric*. The flow, consisting of N identical vertical tiers, is aimed at single instruction multiple data processor *Arithmetic Logic Units* (ALUs). By using a single metal routing layer for each vertical tier, the process flow is significantly simplified since multiple vertical layers can potentially be patterned at once, similar to the 3D NAND flash process. In our study, we thoroughly investigate the layout constraints arising from the *Nanofabric* flow and the non-crossing planar graph constraint and propose several techniques to overcome them. We then show that by stacking 32 layers to build a 32-bit ALU, the footprint is reduced by 8.7× compared to a conventional 7 nm FinFET implementation.

Keywords: 3D Logic Integration · Nanotechnologies · Emerging Technologies · Layout

1 Introduction

For many years, the semiconductor industry has continued to scale down the *Metal-Oxide-Semiconductor Field-Effect Transistor* (MOSFET) to increase the number of devices per area unit, thus enhancing the performances of *Integrated Circuits* (ICs). Novel transistor topologies have emerged in the past few years as an alternative to planar transistors, such as FinFETs [1]. They allow better electrostatic control, decreased leakage, and reduced short-channel effects, improving electrical performances. However, FinFETs still suffer from the short-channel

© IFIP International Federation for Information Processing 2021
Published by Springer Nature Switzerland AG 2021
A. Calimera et al. (Eds.): VLSI-SoC 2020, IFIP AICT 621, pp. 279–300, 2021.
https://doi.org/10.1007/978-3-030-81641-4_13

effect and other physical limitations, such as quantum effects [2], and can not
be scaled indefinitely. Therefore, alternative routes are being investigated to: (i)
first, keep pushing the cost scaling for a given performance and (ii) then pack
more performance for the same cost to enable more functionality per area.

In particular, in recent years, three-dimensional integrated circuits (3D ICs)
have been proposed [3–19]. A 3D IC is an integrated circuit manufactured by
stacking silicon wafers, dies, or transistors. They are then interconnected vertically to achieve performance improvements at reduced power due to shorter
interconnects than conventional 2D approaches. Furthermore, stacked device layers increase the number of transistors per unit footprint without requiring costly
feature size reduction. In the past few years, two 3D integration schemes have
emerged: parallel 3D [3–9], where wafers or dies are stacked and interconnected
using *Through Silicon Vias* (TSVs) and bonding techniques, and monolithic
3D [10–19], where multiple layers of transistors and/or memory are deposited
sequentially on top of one another on the same starting substrate.

While the large size of the TSVs limits the interconnection density of parallel 3D integration, monolithic 3D allows a finer interconnection granularity. However, state-of-the-art monolithic 3D works [10–19] are currently constrained by
the number of active tiers (2–4), limiting the potential offered by 3D integration.
In this book chapter, we extend our previous work [20] that introduces a new 3D
integration scheme, called *3D Nanofabric*. The *Nanofabric* consists of N identical
vertical tiers, each realizing the same logic function. As such, it can be used in *Single Instruction Multiple Data* (SIMD) processor *Arithmetic Logic Units* (ALUs),
where each vertical tier is one ALU bit. We propose here to use a single metal routing layer at each vertical tier to greatly simplify the process flow, as multiple vertical layers can potentially be patterned at once. Note that the only practical way to
process multiple vertical layers at once in a one-shot fashion, both for deposition
and etching of materials, is to restrict the process flow to a single layer. This leads
to a non-crossing planar graph requirement, which will be formulated a bit further. While we are aware of the challenges 3D technologies bring, such as thermal
aspects including cooling, power distribution, yield, and reliability, those are out
of the scope of this book chapter and are part of ongoing and future work. Instead,
this book chapter focuses on the layout constraints and proves that conventional
designs can be integrated into the *3D Nanofabric* flow, given the constraints of a
planar graph without crossing wires within a vertical tier.

The contributions of this book chapter are:

- We introduce a novel 3D design style using a very simplified set of masks
  and describe a possible process flow that could enable a sufficiently high yield
  across all layers.
- We investigate the physical design constraints arising from our proposed *3D
  Nanofabric* flow.
- We propose several solutions at the gate and netlist levels to design complex
  logic gates under the different non-crossing planar graph layout constraints.
- We provide a footprint comparison of different conventional logic
  gates between our proposed *3D Nanofabric* and a 2D 7 nm FinFET
  implementation.

– At the circuit level, we show that by stacking up to 32 layers to build a larger 32-bit ALU, the footprint is reduced by 8.7× compared to a 2D planar 7 nm FinFET implementation.

The rest of this book chapter is organized as follows: Sect. 2, presents related work. Section 3 briefly presents the proposed *3D Nanofabric* concept and describes a possible technology process flow. Section 4 discusses the different physical design constraints of the *3D Nanofabric*. Section 5 proposes several solutions. Section 6 provides experimental footprint comparisons with a conventional 2D technology. Section 7 concludes this book chapter.

2   Background and Related Work

Our proposed *3D Nanofabric* aims at a similar objective as the 3D NAND, namely, to exploit repetitive vertical layers to decrease the footprint, but is targeted at logic applications. However, this can only be achieved by proposing a circuit netlist topology and layout that relies solely on a single layer where the device channel, poly, and metal wires are all embedded without any other crossing than the gate on top of the device channel. To the best of our knowledge, that is a crucial challenge that has not been enabled by any other proposed netlist approach in literature.

2.1   Parallel 3D

Parallel 3D integration [3–9], also called stacked 3D integration, refers to a 3D integration scheme in which devices on separate wafers are fabricated in parallel prior to a bonding or stacking step, as shown in Fig. 1(a). In this process, wafers, dies, or packages are vertically interconnected, allowing several partitioning schemes, such as subsystem, block or die. Parallel 3D can be realized by employing several techniques, like TSV [5–7] or bonding [8]. Bonding is used to join the surface of two wafers or chips using various chemical and physical processes [9], while TSVs are vertical connections that pass completely through a silicon wafer or a die. While TSVs allow a fine-grained integration of several dies into a single 3D stack, they also consume a significant area, which otherwise could be used for logic gates. As a result, the 3D interconnection density is considerably limited by the large size of the TSVs (μm range), and the maximum TSV density achievable today is around 10^5 vias/mm^2 [16].

2.2   Monolithic 3D

Monolithic 3D [10–19] refers to multiple transistor tiers and/or memory cells vertically stacked sequentially on the same starting substrate, as shown in Fig. 1(b). More particularly, the bottom transistor tier is first processed with or without interconnects, called *Intermediate Back-End-Of-Line* (iBEOL). The top tier is then processed, followed by a contact processing step. This 3D integration

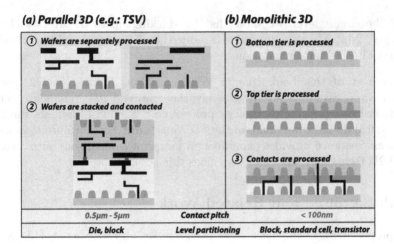

Fig. 1. 3D integration schemes: (a) Parallel integration (e.g.: TSV); (b) Monolithic integration.

scheme can achieve a very low 3D contact pitch, similar to a standard contact (<100 nm), since the devices can be stacked using the lithography precision aliment. Compared to the parallel integration scheme, monolithic 3D achieves a larger interconnection density (up to 2×10^7 vias/mm^2), using conservative 65 nm design rules [11]. However, monolithic 3D is challenging as processing the top tier can damage the bottom tier [13], so low thermal budget devices, such as junction-less devices [14], are required for the top tier. Moreover, it is difficult to obtain a stable iBEOL between the two tiers as copper metallization can contaminate the bottom tiers [13]. Monolithic 3D opens several opportunities, such as stacking 2 nodes $N-1$ instead of a node N [17], in a Logic-on-Logic or Memory-on-Logic way [10], or more disruptive approaches where emerging technologies can be stacked on top of CMOS [18,19]. However, only four active tiers have been demonstrated up to this date [19], limiting the benefits of using the third dimension. Besides, for pure homogeneous logic stacking, the potential cost benefits of these approaches to extend to more than 2 layers appears to be even more limited [10,12].

2.3   Other Logic 3D Technologies

Recent works proposed to use gate-all-around devices in an array fashion [21,22] to further decrease the footprint compared to parallel or monolithic 3D. In Skybridge 3D [22], a junctionless vertical nanowire template structure is employed to design static logic gates. As the template is pre-doped with p and n-type horizontal stripes, any static CMOS gate can be designed by forming the pull-up and pull-down networks through series and parallel devices. For instance, series networks are built with series devices implemented on a single nanowire, while parallel connections are achieved using devices on different nanowires. Similarly to [22] a *Stacked Horizontal Nanowire based 3-D IC* (SN3D) was introduced [21], where junctionless horizontal nanowires are employed. Each static CMOS gate can be designed by stacking several nanowires on top of each other. Common contact and horizontal insulation features are used to connect or isolate the different source and drain regions to realize series and parallel connections. While these works showed a significant footprint reduction (5.5–40× s) compared to conventional 2D and monolithic 3D implementations, the number of masks and processing costs remain high as they have to be accumulated for every sequential layer that is added. This implies that no real cost scaling is feasible in this way. Hence, that is not compatible with our objectives, as introduced in the introduction.

2.4   3D NAND Memory

3D NAND memory has been proposed [23–25] to sustain the continuous demand for data storage. This 3D technology consists of many same vertical layers, stacked on top of each other and processed in a single shot. Since it has a highly repetitive mask set, 3D NAND technology is very cost-effective. Recently, up to 128 vertical layers have been demonstrated for the 3D NAND [24], resulting in a minimal footprint per stored bit. As a result, 3D NAND is currently replacing 2D NAND in the SSD market. While our proposed *3D Nanofabric* is aimed at logic applications and not memory, it uses a similar concept to 3D NAND as it consists of repetitive vertical layers stacked on top of each other, where multiple layers can be patterned at once. However, the complexity and challenges for this logic extension are highly non-trivial, as we will show in the rest of this book chapter. Hence, several disruptive novel aspects have to be employed to enable this.

3   Proposed *3D Nanofabric* Concept

In this section, we briefly summarize the proposed *3D Nanofabric* concept and then present a possible fabrication flow.

3.1   General Overview

The goal of our proposed 3D Nanofabric is to substantially decrease the manufacturing costs so that scaling many layers becomes truly attractive. This is achieved by: (i) considerably reducing the area by stacking many layers vertically; (ii) using a simplified process flow where all vertical layers can be patterned at once, similarly to what 3D NAND has achieved. While inspired by the 3D NAND process flow, our proposed 3D Nanofabric is aimed at logic applications. The proposed *3D Nanofabric* consists of N identical stacked vertical tiers, depicted in Fig. 2(a). In other words, the *3D Nanofabric* is a 3D ALU where each tier is an ALU bit. Hence, it is aimed at realizing SIMD processor datapaths,

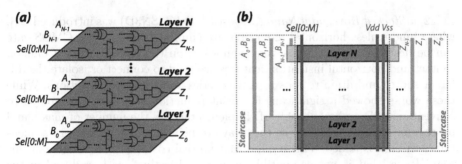

Fig. 2. *3D Nanofabric* concept: (a) Identical transistor tiers; (b) Cross-section general organization.

where the datapath is composed of an array of 3D ALUs. The way the *Nanofabric* communicates with the other parts of the processor (control, memory, *etc.*) is out of the scope of this book chapter and will be investigated in future work. To stack many vertical layers, we propose here to use a very restricted set of masks (i.e., only a single metal routing track), which allows multiple layers to be patterned at once during fabrication, as will be explained in Sect. 3.2. As shown in Fig. 2(b), the global signals which are shared among all the vertical layers, such as the select signals $Sel[0 : M]$ (M depending on the number of operations the ALU can realize) or V_{dd} and V_{ss}, are provided through vertical pillars. The other signals (inputs and outputs of each ALU slice) are fed independently to each vertical layer from the side, using staircase-like structures similar to 3D NAND [26] chips. To stack many layers, we propose here to use a very restricted set of masks (i.e., only a single metal routing track) on top of using physically identical vertical tiers. This small set of masks and layout regularity enables a low-cost manufacturing process flow, in which multiple layers can be patterned at once, as will be explained in the next subsection.

3.2 Potential *3D Nanofabric* Process Flow

In this section, we briefly describe a possible technological solution for manufacturing the proposed *3D Nanofabric*. Based on the Coventor® modeling software, the process flow has been used to derive the design and layout rules presented in this section and employed to obtain the results of Sect. 6. Note that a more complete and thorough process flow study is out of the scope of this book chapter. While a simple solution would be to create the structure sequentially layer-by-layer, this would not be cost-effective at all as most steps would have to be repeated for each layer. Instead, we propose a solution that only uses a single metal routing layer and patterns multiple vertical layers at once.

The gate-forming processing flow steps are illustrated in Fig. 3(a)–(h). As shown in Fig. 3(a), the flow starts by depositing the layer-stack: for each vertical tier, we deposit an active layer (blue), a sacrificial layer (green), which will become the gate (dummy-gate, referred to as *GATE_INTEND*), and an

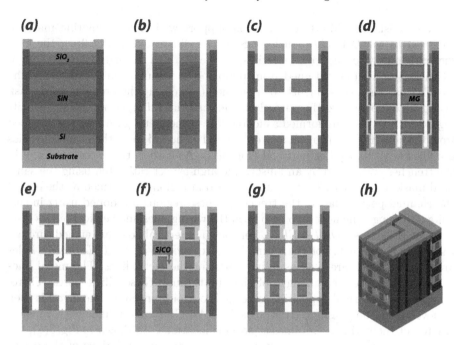

Fig. 3. *3D Nanofabric* gate forming process flow steps: (a) Layer-stack deposition; (b) Trenches creation, where source and drain regions will be formed; (c) Dummy-gate removal; (d) Gate-oxide and metal-gate filling; (e) Metal recess; (f) Spacer fill and etch-back; (g) Metal lines formation; (h) Resulting 3D structure. (Color figure online)

inter-dielectric layer (grey). Note that for the sake of the readability of the figure, only 3 active layers are depicted, but the described process is extendable to N tiers. While there are multiple possible options for creating active layers, we propose here to use a layer transfer of crystalline silicon, as it is done for *Silicon On Insulator* (SOI) processes. Those SOI-like silicon devices are well understood and have good electrical characteristics. The sacrificial layer may be a nitride layer, such as S_iN or some other material that can be etched with a sufficient selectivity with respect to the active and the inter-dielectric layers. The process relies on an indirect fabrication of the gates, which are formed in a collateral fashion. As depicted in Fig. 3(b), the layer-stack is patterned through an etching process by forming trenches through where source and drain regions will be formed. As such, a high-aspect-ratio etch is employed, such as reactive-ion etch or any suitable dry etching process. As a result, the layer-stack is then partitioned by a number of sub-stacks separated by trenches, referred to as channel-islands. The dummy-gate material is then removed by using a selective isotropic etch process, as shown in Fig. 3(c). As a considerable amount of material is removed from the layer-stack, a mechanical support is required for the active layer and inter-dielectric layer. This is achieved by the design rule that every gate-island is abutting a vertical support wall of an insulating material (referred to as *OXWALL*), such as S_iO_2. As illustrated in Fig. 3(d), the gate dielectric and gate electrode materials are then formed through conformal deposition in the cavities obtained from removing the dummy-gate. Note that the trenches can then subsequently be re-etched (by reusing the previous hard mask of Fig. 3(b)) to remove the gate electrode material filling them. Then, insulating sidewall spacers are formed as follows: first, the metal gate lines are recessed from the side (Fig. 3(e)) by an isotropic metal etch, and then, the formed cavities are filled with the spacer material (Fig. 3(f)). As earlier, the excess material in the trenches is removed by an anisotropic high-aspect-ratio etch using the same hard mask of Fig. 3(b). Then, source and drain regions are formed at the end of the channel portion facing the trenches. These regions are doped using in-situ epitaxy doping. The next step is to form the wiring lines and vertical pillars (i.e., vias, referred to as *CONT_VERT*). For the vias, vertical holes are etched through the whole layer-stack. For the wiring lines (referred to as *METAL_LINE*), holes are formed, which are used as filling ports for the metal lines. The metal lines are filled over the whole length of the line through these filling ports. Therefore, a very conformal deposition is needed to avoid pinch-off. The metal is then removed from the plugs (referred to as *METAL_CUT*) and refilled with a dielectric to cut the wiring metal lines at specific locations. As shown in Fig. 3(g), the wiring lines extend across and over the source and drain regions of the active semiconductor.

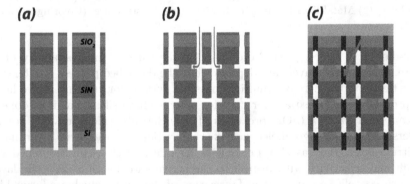

Fig. 4. *3D Nanofabric* active patterning process flow steps: (a) Cut a narrow gap; (b) Silicon isotropic etch; (c) Oxide selective deposit to recreate the vertical gating.

Figure 3(h) shows the resulting 3D structure. Gate lines extend across and over the channel region portions of the horizontal channel transistors. The gate lines and wiring lines are arranged side-by-side and their separation is ensured by the spacers. The single layer of the gate lines and wiring lines of each logic cell of each device tier is readily visible in the figure, indicating a common geometric horizontal plane intersected by all gate lines and wiring lines of each logic cell.

Similar to the gate patterning, the *ACTIVE* layer employs sideways processing. After the active patterning, we need to "repair" the inter-dielectric layer, as the gate is crossing over the edge of the active. "Repairing" can only be done over small distances, so the initial patterning does not use final dimensions. The active design will be upsized until only a small gap is left. As illustrated in Fig. 4(a), this gap is etched into the layer-stack with another high-aspect-ratio etch, which exposes the active on the sidewall. As shown in Fig. 4(b), a high selective silicon etch is then used to trim the active silicon to the target size. This way of patterning will impact some design restrictions on the *ACTIVE* layer: the distance between two *ACTIVE*-polygons should either be the nominal value or be big enough to fit a double-gap into it. Once the active is patterned, the inter-dielectric layer gap is closed by selective deposition of oxide on oxide, as depicted in Fig. 4(c).

3.3 *3D Nanofabric* Layout Examples

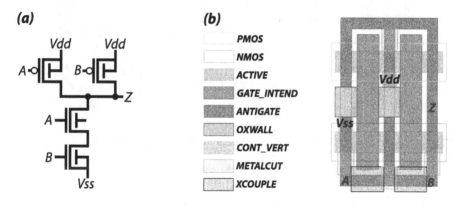

Fig. 5. NAND2: (a) Schematic; (b) Layout with layer legend.

The layout of a conventional NAND2 gate is depicted in Fig. 5(b) to illustrate our proposed flow. As discussed, each gate (*GATE_INTEND*) is surrounded by a *METAL_LINE* layer. As such, some metal breakers are required (*METAL_CUT*) to achieve all the different connections. The *XCOUPLE* layer is used to connect the gate and the routing layer (*METAL_LINE*). Two *OXWALL* squares in direct contact with the gate can be observed and are used to mechanically support the vertical structure. They also act as metal routing breakers. Besides, the V_{dd} and V_{ss} supply lines are fed through vertical pillars (brown *CONT_VERT* squares) to the logic gate. Note that, as explained earlier, the *GATE_INTEND* layer is not a physical mask as the gates are formed indirectly throughout the flow. This layer is only shown here for layout purposes to ease the design step. Also, the

XCOUPLE layer is used to form a connection between the *GATE_INTEND* and *METAL_LINE* layers.

Figure 6(a)–(c) depicts the layouts of an INV, NAND3, and SRAM6T cells, respectively. As can be observed, such simple gates can be efficiently designed with the proposed *3D Nanofabric* as their internal organization is straightforward, resulting in compact gates. This is because gates such as AND, OR, NAND, or NOR simply require a stack of series transistors and a stack of parallel transistors, so most of the source and drain regions can be shared. However, as will be described in the next sections, more complex logic gates require specific techniques to be designed and will result in an area overhead compared to traditional 2D layouts. Note that the SRAM 6T uses both vertical and horizontal gate patterns to result in a more compact gate.

(a)   **(b)**   **(c)**

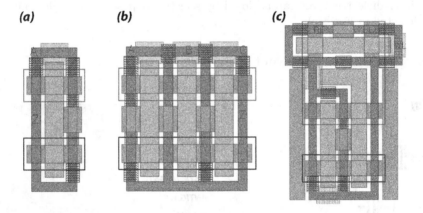

Fig. 6. Layout of various cells using the proposed *Nanofabric* rules: (a) INV; (b) NAND3; (c) SRAM6T.

4   Layout Challenges

In this section, we describe the different layout challenges arising from the technology assumptions and the *Nanofabric* manufacturing flow. It will be shown that these challenges are very different from the ones that have to be dealt with in the 3D NAND case.

4.1   Gate Layer Forming

In conventional 2D technologies (planar or FinFET), the metal routing layers often span across unrelated gate and active layers, as they are distinct from a processing point of view, as shown in Fig. 7, depicting a conventional planar layout of an AOI211 gate. In the proposed *Nanofabric* flow, this is not possible due to the fabrication process: as explained in Sect. 3.2, the $GATE\_INTEND$ layer is derived from a boolean operation on the $ANTIGATE$ layer. As such, it is strictly impossible to have the $ANTIGATE$ layer spanning on the $GATE\_INTEND$ layer, as it is the case in traditional 2D designs, which limits the freedom in terms of physical layout. Also, as depicted in Fig. 5(b), the $GATE\_INTEND$ layer has to be surrounded on all sides by the $ANTIGATE$. As a result, some breakers have to be employed to achieve distinct connections on the different source and drain sides. While it is not an issue for a simple gate like the NAND2, it brings some challenges for more complex gates like the XOR2 or AO22.

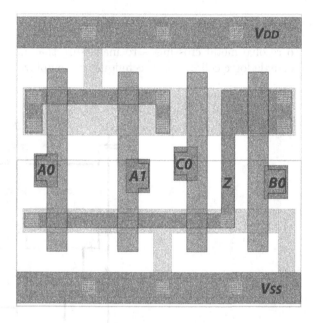

Fig. 7. Conventional planar layout of a AOI211 gate.

4.2 Single Metal Level Routing

As discussed earlier, the main layout limitation is that only a single metal routing track can be used within the *Nanofabric*, which considerably restricts the physical design. This means that when designing, no upper metal level layers can be used in case of metal crossing in high congestion areas. Without any crossing possibility, it means that complex gates, such as XOR2 or the FA are challenging to design. However, it is still possible to design such kinds of gates, and some solutions are proposed in the next section. Another requirement arising from the single metal rule is that the standard cell input and output pins have to be located on the border to be accessed externally, as illustrated in Fig. 5(b). Since the flow only uses a single routing metal layer, there is no way to access the pins located in the center of the cell through higher levels of metals, as is the case in conventional 2D designs. As an example, the inputs *A1* and *C0* in Fig. 7 would make the cell non-routable using the proposed *Nanofabric* flow.

5   Layout Solutions

In this section, we present the algorithm, consisting of several steps, used in the *Nanofabric* to overcome the planar non-crossing layout restrictions. We first describe each step with examples and then provide the complete algorithm.

5.1   Step 1: Resolving Loops at the Cell Level

The first step to resolve metal crossing is to make sure that no metal loop is present within a single logic cell. Several techniques are employed:

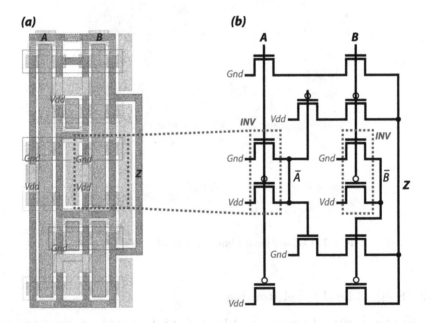

Fig. 8. XOR2 logic gate: (a) Layout using the proposed *Nanofabric* rules; (b) Transistor-level schematic. Note that the schematic is identical to a traditional static CMOS XOR2 gate.

Transistor Placement and Stacking: Due to the non-conventional way of designing logic cells, there is more freedom to move the transistors vertically and horizontally, instead of having fixed top *p-well* and bottom *n-well* zones as in traditional 2D designs. While this is not the case for simple gates like the NAND2, more complex gates will require such arrangement, as depicted in Fig. 8 for a XOR2. Due to the complexity of the XOR2 cell and the non-crossing planar graph constraints, the transistor sharing the same gate signals (mainly A and B) are all stacked on each other to relieve congestion within the cell. In particular, the internal inverters are also stacked as they share the same inputs as the XOR2 gate. Note that unlike conventional design styles, there is no fixed height for the different logic cells, as complex gates such as the XOR2 will require a larger height due to the transistor stacking. Therefore, more different design styles are possible for a given cell, depending on its desired shape and internal structure.

Vertical Signals: Global signals, including V_{dd}, V_{ss}, or the ALU control signals shared among all the vertical layers to perform the same logic function, are provided to the *Nanofabric* through vertical pillars. In particular, unlike conventional 2D designs, the standard cell power supply grid lines are removed. This relieves metal routability since those signals will not block the metal routing layer. Note that for an ALU, the primary inputs and outputs are independent for each vertical tiers. Hence, they cannot be provided through vertical pillars spanning among all tiers. Instead, similarly to the 3D NAND process [26], staircase-like structures are employed to convey all the signals to the appropriate tier independently.

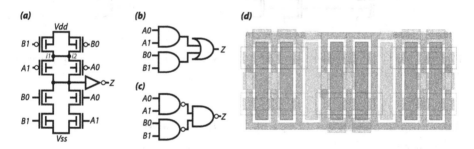

Fig. 9. AO22: (a) Transistor-level based schematic; (c) Gate-level based schematic using AND/OR gates; (d) Gate-level based schematic using NAND gates; (d) Layout using NAND gates with the proposed *Nanofabric* rules.

Gate-Based Logic Cells: A solution to design complex gates is to use gate-level based designs instead of transistor-level based designs. For the AO22 gate, which transistor level-based design is depicted in Fig. 9(a), the different connections, notably *i1* and *i2*, make it impossible to be designed using the proposed *Nanofabric* flow. Since each gate has to be surrounded by the metal layer, and there is only a single metal layer, these kinds of connections where 4 transistors share the same drain or source are particularly challenging. However, using the gate-level based design shown in Fig. 9(b) greatly simplifies the routing and makes it possible by merely cascading basic gates (NAND2, NOR2, *etc.*). While the gate-level based design uses more transistors (18 instead of 10), it can be rearranged using De Morgan's equation, as shown in Fig. 9(c), and only uses 2 more transistors than the transistor-level based implementation. The layout of AOI22 gate based on NAND2 gates is depicted in Fig. 9(d).

Propagate an Internal Signal Using Inverters: Another way of resolving specific metal crossing is to propagate the signal within the logic gate. As depicted in Fig. 10, transistor $N1$ and $P1$ are driven by input A, while transistor $N2$ is driven by $\bar{A}$. One way to achieve this without crossing is to use a first inverter to generate $\bar{A}$ to drive transistor $N2$. Then, another inverter is used to invert signal $\bar{A}$ back to A to drive transistor $P1$. That way, signal A is propagated internally within the logic gate.

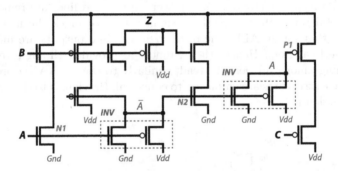

Fig. 10. Signal propagation using internal inverters. Here, signal A is propagated within the logic cell.

5.2   Step 2: Resolving Loops at the Netlist Level

Once all logic gates do not contain any internal metal loop, they can be used to build more complex blocks, such as a complete ALU. Duplicated gates can be used to resolve any additional metal loop in the netlist when connecting the different gates. As illustrated in Fig. 11(a), the input arrangement of the AO22 gate is causing a metal crossing, and there is no way to move the gates to overcome this issue. This metal crossing can be resolved by duplicating the OR2 gate (in blue) on the side. As depicted in Fig. 11(b), its output can now be connected to the AO22 gate without being confined, as it was the case before. Note that while it brings an area overhead, duplicating logic gates will always resolve any crossing issue as the gates can be duplicated up to the netlist primary inputs.

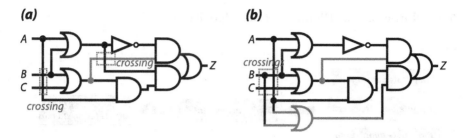

Fig. 11. Logic circuit schematic: (a) Containing 2 metal crossings; (b) Alleviating 1 metal crossing through duplicated inputs from the staircase. (Color figure online)

5.3 Step 3: Duplicating Signals Through Staircases and Vertical Signals

As explained in Sect. 3.1, each 2D layer will receive its primary inputs from its sides. However, the first logic level of the ALU may require some inputs to be fed to several parallel gates, implying possible metal crossing, as shown in Fig. 12(a). In this example, input B is driving three parallel gates. However, since there is no way to place them next to each other, the B metal wire has to cross inputs A and C. Since the primary inputs of each 2D layer are provided through a vertical staircase, they can be duplicated to be fed to more gates in the ALU. As depicted in Fig. 12(b), both metal crossings can be resolved by duplicating the primary inputs A and B. Besides, as using step 2 might also result in several duplicated primary inputs, the staircase will be able to feed them to the ALU while avoiding metal crossing. As the control signals are provided through vertical pillars, those can also be easily duplicated if they need to control several logic gates.

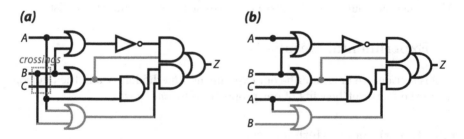

Fig. 12. Logic circuit schematic: (a) Containing 1 metal crossings; (b) Alleviating the metal crossing by using duplicated inputs from the staircase.

5.4 Non-crossing Planar Graph Algorithm

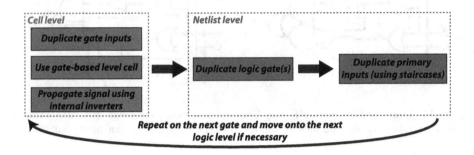

Fig. 13. Non-crossing planar graph algorithm illustration.

In this sub-section, we present the complete algorithm, illustrated on Fig. 13, to produce the layout for an ALU netlist while only using a single metal layer. The algorithm, described with more details in Algorithm 1, consists of all the previous layout solutions presented in Sect. 5 combined. The algorithm starts from one of the last logic gate (producing an output) and propagates backward through the netlist. It first solves the internal gate crossings for each gate, before solving the metal loops at the netlist level (between several gates). Once all the gates of a given logic level have been treated, it moves to the previous logic level until it reaches the primary inputs. If necessary, those primary inputs are duplicated through the staircases or the vertical signals. Here, we assume that the netlist does not contain feedback loops. While feedback loops are generally present in sequential circuits, the goal here is to design combinational ALUs for SIMD processors, so it is unlikely to happen. Besides, a proper synthesis of the ALU function would also eliminate the feedback loops within the netlist.

6 Experimental Results

In this section, we first describe our experimental methodology and then demonstrate the footprint benefits of our proposed *3D Nanofabric*.

6.1 Experimental Methodology

We developed an in-house PDK for the *3D Nanofabric* flow for the footprint evaluations, following the technological assumptions presented in Sect. 3.2. For the 2D baseline, we considered 2 cases: (a) the ASAP 7 nm FinFET design kit from ASU [27] and (b) an in-house FinFET IN7 node. For a fair area comparison, transistors are minimum sized in all cases. For *both 2D* cases, the ALU area values were obtained after synthesis by using the complete available logic libraries. For the 3D case, an extra step is performed to draw the layout by hand, following the novel approach described above.

Algorithm 1: *3D Nanofabric* non-crossing planar graph algorithm.

Starts at the output node (last level of logic depth);
Logic_level = *Get_Total_Nb_Logic_Levels*();
while *(Logic_level != 1)* **do**
    Number_gates = *Get_Current_Logic_Level_Nb_Gates*();
    while *(Number_gates != 1)* **do**
        if *Current_gate has internal crossings* **then**
            Duplicate_Gate_Inputs();
            Use_Gate_Based_Logic_Cell();
            Propagate_Signal_Using_Inverters();
        else
            Use_Transistor_Based_Logic_Cell();
        end
        Number_gates = *Number_gates* − 1;
    end
    if *Crossing between gates* **then**
        Duplicate_Gate();
    end
    Logic_level = *Logic_level* − 1;
end
if *Crossing between primary inputs* **then**
    Duplicate_Signals();
end

6.2 Logic Gate Area Comparison

Table 1 shows the area of a few conventional logic gates, using the proposed *3D Nanofabric* flow compared to other technologies.

Table 1. Logic gates area (in μm^2) using ASAP7, IN7 and the proposed *3D Nanofabric* process.

Gate	ASAP7	IN7	*3D Nanofabric*
INVD1	0.044	0.016	0.029
NOR2D1	0.058	0.024	0.041
AO22D1	0.092	0.040	0.127
XOR2D1	0.117	0.072	0.083
NOR3D1	0.073	0.032	0.052
Average	0.077 (−17%)[*]	0.037 (+1.8×)[*]	0.066

[*] *3D Nanofabric* area overhead/reduction, when compared to ASAP7 and IN7 respectively.

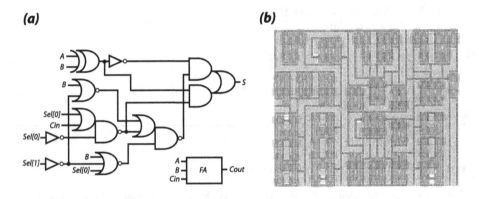

296   E. Giacomin et al.

As expected, compared to a highly and aggressively optimized IN7 library, using the *3D Nanofabric* process brings an area overhead (1.8× on average) due to the non-crossing rule, which requires extra transistors or spacing for complex gates. In particular, the area overhead is even more significant for gate-level based cell such as the AO22 gate due to the additional transistors. Note that the logic gate area is reduced (17% on average) compared to ASAP7 since the proposed *Nanofabric* allows us to design compact gates, as the *nmos* and *pmos* transistors can be placed closer to each other. Besides, the significant difference between ASAP7 and IN7 is from the fact that IN7 is equivalent to a commercial foundry 5 nm technology node due to its aggressive dimensions and multiple design boosters enabling a 6-track library, while ASAP7 can only achieve 7.5 tracks.

6.3   ALU Footprint Comparison

(a)   **(b)**

Fig. 14. 1-bit basic ALU: (a) Schematic; (b) Layout view using the proposed *3D Nanofabric* rules and process flow.

In this section, we consider a basic 1-bit ALU, whose schematic is depicted in Fig. 14(a). This 1-bit ALU is capable of performing the following operations:

- $A + B + C_{in}$
- $A\&B$
- $A|B$
- $A\char94 B$

We study the area of the 1-bit ALU for all 3 cases using ASAP7, IN7, and the proposed *3D Nanofabric*. For both ASAP7 and IN7, we only considered gates using minimum sized transistors, as we made the same assumption for the proposed *3D Nanofabric*. The layout of the 1-bit ALU using the *3D Nanofabric* is shown in Fig. 14(b). Note the presence of several *OXWALL* regions, which fill the extra empty spaces required to route the single metal level layer. Here, there is no need for dummy-poly as in a FinFET technology where the gate is needed to define the Source-Drain. Instead, the empty spaces are filled with the *OXWALL* dielectric layer. Also, the gate to gate distance is always enforced (36 nm) to ensure that all the gate are aligned, so the layout is fully regular. As shown in Table 2, ASAP7 and IN7 have a 1.6× and 3.7× smaller area than the proposed *3D Nanofabric*, respectively, for the 1-bit ALU as some gates have to be duplicated to avoid crossing. Besides, some extra space is required for routing where 2D processes use higher metal layers.

Table 2. *3D Nanofabric* ALU footprint compared to ASAP7 and IN7 for an *N*-bit ALU.

Number of bits N	Footprint (in μm^2)*		
	ASAP7	IN7	3D
1	0.787 (+1.6×)	0.338 (+3.7×)	1.257
2	1.822 (−1.4×)	0.758 (+1.7×)	1.257
3	2.186 (−1.7×)	1.193 (+1.05×)	1.257
4	2.668 (−2.1×)	1.516 (−1.2×)	1.257
8	4.765 (−3.8×)	2.991 (−2.4×)	1.257
16	11.033 (−8.8×)	5.539 (−4.4×)	1.257
24	16.169 (−12.9×)	8.265 (−6.6×)	1.257
32	21.257 (−16.9×)	10.999 (−8.7×)	1.257

* Also shows the *3D Nanofabric* footprint overhead/reduction, when compared to ASAP7 and IN7 respectively.

Note that while a single layer brings some area overhead due to the layout constraints, the main goal of the proposed flow is to stack many vertical layers, to achieve a footprint reduction. By going to 3D to build larger ALUs, we can observe considerable footprint gains. This is because stacking 4 vertical layers in 3D has the same footprint as a single layer, while the area of the 2D implementation increases for each additional bit. In particular, when going to 2 and 4 layers, we can already remark some footprint reduction when using the proposed *Nanofabric* flow when compared to ASAP7 (45%) and IN7 (20%), respectively. More importantly, using 32 vertical layers to build a 32-bit ALU reduces the footprint even further by a factor of 16.9× and 8.7× when compared to ASAP7 and IN7, respectively. We believe that stacking 32 vertical layers is a fair assumption, as current 3D NAND processes have demonstrated up to 128 stacked layers [24]. Hence, we can expect that a higher number of vertical layers could be considered once the technology is more mature in the long term. Note that while the results presented in this section are for the specific ALU depicted in Fig. 14(a), similar results are expected when considering different ALU designs.

7   Conclusion

In this book chapter, we introduced a novel 3D design flow called *3D Nanofabric*. The flow consists of several identical stacked logic layers, making it well suited for SIMD processor applications where many basic regular ALUs are repeated. We first proposed a possible fabrication flow and described how multiple vertical layers could be patterned at once to define the transistor structures. We then thoroughly investigated the layout constraints of the *Nanofabric* flow and proposed several solutions to overcome them so that basic ALUs can be designed. We showed the 32-bit ALU footprint is reduced by a factor of 8.7× compared to a traditional 2D approach using a 7 nm FinFET technology, when using 32 vertical layers. We believe that this novel 3D approach enables cost-effective 3D scaling as it enables more performant circuits at a smaller footprint with reduced production cost.

References

1. Natarajan, S., et al.: A 14nm logic technology featuring 2nd-generation FinFET, air-gapped interconnects, self-aligned double patterning and a 0.0588 μm^2 SRAM cell size. In: 2014 IEEE International Electron Devices Meeting, San Francisco, CA, pp. 3.7.1–3.7.3 (2014). https://doi.org/10.1109/IEDM.2014.7046976
2. Colinge, J.P.: FinFETs and Other Multi-Gate Transistors, 1st edn. Springer, Boston (2007). https://doi.org/10.1007/978-0-387-71752-4
3. Yoon, S.W., Yang, D.W., Koo, J.H., Padmanathan, M., Carson, F.: 3D TSV processes and its assembly/packaging technology. In: 2009 IEEE International Conference on 3D System Integration, San Francisco, CA, pp. 1–5 (2009). https://doi.org/10.1109/3DIC.2009.5306535
4. Chua, T.T., et al.: 3D interconnection process development and integration with low stress TSV. In: 2010 Proceedings 60th Electronic Components and Technology Conference (ECTC), Las Vegas, NV, pp. 798–802 (2010). https://doi.org/10.1109/ECTC.2010.5490728
5. Van Olmen, J., et al.: 3D stacked IC demonstration using a through silicon via first approach. In: 2008 IEEE International Electron Devices Meeting, San Francisco, CA, pp. 1–4 (2008). https://doi.org/10.1109/IEDM.2008.4796763
6. Beyne, E., et al.: Through-silicon via and die stacking technologies for microsystems-integration. In: 2008 IEEE International Electron Devices Meeting, San Francisco, CA, pp. 1–4 (2008). https://doi.org/10.1109/IEDM.2008.4796734
7. Chaabouni, H., et al.: Investigation on TSV impact on 65nm CMOS devices and circuits. In: 2010 International Electron Devices Meeting, San Francisco, CA, pp. 35.1.1–35.1.4 (2010). https://doi.org/10.1109/IEDM.2010.5703479
8. Ruythooren, W., Beltran, A., Labie, R.: Cu-Cu bonding alternative to solder based micro-bumping. In: 2007 9th Electronics Packaging Technology Conference, Singapore, pp. 315–318 (2007). https://doi.org/10.1109/EPTC.2007.4469706
9. Zheng, Z., et al.: Demonstration of ultra-thin buried oxide germanium-on-insulator MOSFETs by direct wafer bonding and polishing techniques. Appl. Phys. Lett. **109**(2), 023503 (2016). https://doi.org/10.1063/1.4955486
10. Batude, P., et al.: Advances, challenges and opportunities in 3D CMOS sequential integration. In: 2011 International Electron Devices Meeting, Washington, DC, pp. 7.3.1–7.3.4 (2011). https://doi.org/10.1109/IEDM.2011.6131506
11. Brunet, L., et al.: First demonstration of a CMOS over CMOS 3D VLSI CoolCube™ integration on 300mm wafers. In: 2016 IEEE Symposium on VLSI Technology, Honolulu, HI, pp. 1–2 (2016). https://doi.org/10.1109/VLSIT.2016.7573428

12. Mallik, A., et al.: The impact of sequential-3D integration on semiconductor scaling roadmap. In: 2017 IEEE International Electron Devices Meeting (IEDM), San Francisco, CA, pp. 32.1.1–31.1.4 (2017). https://doi.org/10.1109/IEDM.2017. 8268483
13. Brunet, L., et al.: Breakthroughs in 3D Sequential technology. In: 2018 IEEE International Electron Devices Meeting (IEDM), San Francisco, CA, pp. 7.2.1–7.2.4 (2018). https://doi.org/10.1109/IEDM.2018.8614653
14. Vandooren, A., et al.: 3D sequential stacked planar devices on 300 mm wafers featuring replacement metal gate junction-less top devices processed at 525°C with improved reliability. In: 2018 IEEE Symposium on VLSI Technology, Honolulu, HI, pp. 69–70 (2018). https://doi.org/10.1109/VLSIT.2018.8510705
15. Liu, C., Lim, S.K.: A design tradeoff study with monolithic 3D integration. In: Thirteenth International Symposium on Quality Electronic Design (ISQED), Santa Clara, CA, pp. 529–536 (2012). https://doi.org/10.1109/ISQED.2012.6187545
16. Andrieu, F., et al.: A review on opportunities brought by 3D-monolithic integration for CMOS device and digital circuit. In: 2018 International Conference on IC Design & Technology (ICICDT), Otranto, pp. 141–144 (2018). https://doi.org/10. 1109/ICICDT.2018.8399776
17. Gitlin, D., Vinet, M., Clermidy, F.: Cost model for monolithic 3D integrated circuits. In: 2016 IEEE SOI-3D-Subthreshold Microelectronics Technology Unified Conference (S3S), Burlingame, CA, pp. 1–2 (2016). https://doi.org/10.1109/S3S. 2016.7804408
18. Sabry Aly, M., et al.: Energy-efficient abundant-data computing: the N3XT 1,000 x. Computer **48**(12), 24–33 (2015). https://doi.org/10.1109/MC.2015.376
19. Shulaker, M., et al.: Three-dimensional integration of nanotechnologies for computing and data storage on a single chip. Nature **547**(7661), 74–78 (2017). https:// doi.org/10.1038/nature22994
20. Giacomin, E., Boemmels, J., Ryckaert, J., Catthoor, F., Gaillardon, P.: Layout considerations of logic designs using an N-layer 3D Nanofabric process flow. In: 28th IFIP/IEEE International Conference on Very Large Scale Integration (VLSI-SoC), Salt Lake City, UT, USA, 5–7 October 2020
21. Macha, N.K., Iqbal, M.A., Rahman, M.: Fine-grained 3-D CMOS concept using stacked horizontal nanowire. In: 2016 IEEE/ACM International Symposium on Nanoscale Architectures (NANOARCH), Beijing, pp. 151–152 (2016). https://doi. org/10.1145/2950067.2950079
22. Li, M., Shi, J., Rahman, M., Khasanvis, S., Bhat, S., Moritz, C.A.: Skybridge-3D-CMOS: a vertically-composed fine-grained 3D CMOS integrated circuit technology. In: 2016 IEEE Computer Society Annual Symposium on VLSI (ISVLSI), Pittsburgh, PA, pp. 403–408 (2016). https://doi.org/10.1109/ISVLSI.2016.56
23. Kang, D., et al.: 13.4 a 512Gb 3-bit/cell 3D 6th-generation V-NAND flash memory with 82MB/s write throughput and 1.2Gb/s interface. In: 2019 IEEE International Solid- State Circuits Conference - ISSCC, San Francisco, CA, USA, pp. 216–218 (2019). https://doi.org/10.1109/ISSCC.2019.8662493
24. Siau, C., et al.: 13.5 a 512Gb 3-bit/cell 3D flash memory on 128-wordline-layer with 132MB/s write performance featuring circuit-under-array technology. In: 2019 IEEE International Solid-State Circuits Conference - ISSCC, San Francisco, CA, USA, pp. 218–220 (2019). https://doi.org/10.1109/ISSCC.2019.8662445
25. Shibata, N., et al.: 13.1 a 1.33Tb 4-bit/cell 3D-flash memory on a 96-word-line-layer technology. In: 2019 IEEE International Solid-State Circuits Conference - ISSCC, San Francisco, CA, USA, pp. 210–212 (2019). https://doi.org/10.1109/ ISSCC.2019.8662443

26. Jang, J., et al.: Vertical cell array using TCAT (Terabit Cell Array Transistor) technology for ultra high density NAND flash memory. In: 2009 Symposium on VLSI Technology, Honolulu, HI, pp. 192–193 (2009)

27. Clark, L.T., et al.: ASAP7: a 7-nm finFET predictive process design kit. Microelectron. J. **53**, 105–115 (2016). https://doi.org/10.1016/j.mejo.2016.04.006. ISSN: 0026-2692

3D Logic Cells Design and Results Based on Vertical NWFET Technology Including Tied Compact Model

Arnaud Poittevin[1]([✉]), Chhandak Mukherjee[2], Ian O'Connor[1],
Cristell Maneux[2], Guilhem Larrieu[3,4], Marina Deng[2], Sebastien Le Beux[1],
François Marc[2], Aurélie Lecestre[3], Cedric Marchand[1], and Abhishek Kumar[3]

[1] Lyon Institute of Nanotechnology,
University of Lyon, CNRS UMR 5270, Ecole Centrale de Lyon, Ecully, France
{arnaud.poittevin,ian.oconnor,sebastien.le-beux,
cedric.marchand}@ec-lyon.fr
[2] University of Bordeaux, CNRS UMR 5218, Bordeaux INP Talence, Bordeaux,
France
{chhandak.mukherjee,cristell.maneux,marina.deng,
francois.marc}@u-bordeaux.fr
[3] Université de Toulouse, LAAS, CNRS, INP Toulouse, Toulouse, France
{guilhem.larrieu,aurelie.lecestre,abhishek.kumar}@laas.fr
[4] Institute of Industrial Science, LIMMS-CNRS/IIS, The University of Tokyo,
Tokyo, Japan
http://inl.cnrs.fr/
https://www.ims-bordeaux.fr/
https://www.laas.fr/

Abstract. Gate-all-around Vertical Nanowire Field Effect Transistors (VNWFET) are emerging devices, which are well suited to pursue scaling beyond lateral scaling limitations around 7 nm. This work explores the relative merits and drawbacks of the technology in the context of logic cell design. We describe a junctionless nanowire technology and associated compact model, which accurately describes fabricated device behavior in all regions of operations for transistors based on between 16 and 625 parallel nanowires of diameters between 22 and 50 nm. We used this model to simulate the projected performance of inverter logic gates based on passive load, active load and complementary topologies and to carry out a performance exploration for the number of nanowires in transistors. In terms of compactness, through a dedicated full 3D layout design, we also demonstrate a 48% reduction in lateral dimensions for the complementary structure with respect to 7 nm FinFET-based inverters.

Keywords: Vertical NWFET technology · compact model · VNWFET DC measurements · 3D logic circuit cell · circuit simulation results

© IFIP International Federation for Information Processing 2021
Published by Springer Nature Switzerland AG 2021
A. Calimera et al. (Eds.): VLSI-SoC 2020, IFIP AICT 621, pp. 301–321, 2021.
https://doi.org/10.1007/978-3-030-81641-4_14

1   Introduction

Data size and functionality requirements for computing are increasing, according to the expectation that hardware performance will continue to improve, irrespective of the actual implementation. This is particularly true for emerging computing paradigms such as Edge Computing, which is placing extraordinarily stringent constraints on computing hardware performances. However, the end of roadmapped technological scaling is anticipated around the 7 nm FinFET gate length node, mainly for cost reasons. In this context, vertical integration is an attractive approach to fully take advantage of 3D integration and scale pitch between contacts. Huge gains in silicon area are expected through the combination of extremely small elementary device footprint and minimal device usage with MIG (Majority Inverter Graph logic) and PTL (Pass Transistor Logic) design styles, for instance. This paper is the first attempt to quantify the gains in terms of compactness and energy efficiency of 3D logic blocks based on actual fabricated p-type VNWFET devices.

This chapter is organized as follows: Sect. 2 recalls the main features of the VNWFET technology while detailing its associated scalable compact model. In particular, the unified charge-based control model has been modified self-consistently in order to take into account depletion and accumulation regimes, electrostatic control, short-channel effects (SCE), drain-induced barrier lowering (DIBL) and band-to-band tunneling (BTBT) contributions through gate-induced drain leakage (GIBL). Simulated results are compared to measurements to illustrate the versatility of the p-type VNWFET model in terms of dimensions. An n-type VNWFET model has also been delivered using the electron mobility value from the literature. These scalable compact models have been implemented in Verilog-A, and subsequently implemented in a dedicated circuit design workspace. In Sect. 3, we demonstrate the efficiency of this design workspace to simulate and quantify the 3D logic blocks. 3D layouts implement inverter functions with various topologies: (i) passive load, (ii) active load and (iii) complementary. Their static and dynamic energy consumption and delays are given. In Sect. 4, we propose a layout footprint comparison between the 7 nm FinFET and the VNWFET through conventional rules. Going beyond this approach, Sect. 5 deals with large-scale integration considerations suitable for a fully 3D logic block architecture.

2   VNWFET Devices

2.1   Technology Description

The VNWFET technology has a junction-less architecture composed of a homogenous highly doped nanowire channel, patterned into boron doped

$(2 \times 10^{19} \mathrm{cm}^{-3})$ Si substrate. The current flows between silicided source/drain contacts and is controlled by a gate-all-around structure with a physical channel length of 14 nm (Fig. 1). As illustrated in the 3D schematic of a 1-bit adder logic cell consisting of vertically stacked VNWFETs, vertical integration allows higher flexibility over lateral devices in terms of gate, spacer and channel lengths without compromising on cell area, thus paving the way for scalable and innovative logic designs. More details on the fabrication steps can be found in [2]. Process parameters for the VNWFET under study are summarized in Table 1.

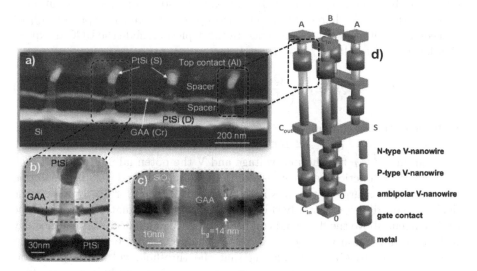

Fig. 1. The VNWFET: STEM image (*reproduced with authorization from* [1]) showing (a) the cross section of vertical transistor nanowire arrays, (b) single nanowire and (c) gate formation, (d) 3D schematic of a vertically stacked 3D integrated 1-bit adder logic cell

Table 1. Process parameters for the VNWFET under study

Process Parameter	Value
Physical gate length	14 nm
NW diameter	22 nm
NW in parallel	16
T_{ox}	5 nm
N_{ch}	$1.1 \times 10^{19} \mathrm{cm}^{-3}$
Gate work function	4.5 eV

2.2 Compact Model

Drain Current Formulation. The model formulation is based on the unified charge-based control model (UCCM) elaborated in [3] for long-channel devices, which furthers the physical basis of the junctionless nanowire transistor (JLNT) model presented in [4] and adapted in [5] for the JLNT technology under test [2]. The limitations of the model in [4] is mainly the piece-wise continuous drain-current model which requires additional smoothing functions and fitting parameters to smooth the transition between depletion and accumulation modes of operation. In order to overcome this, the explicit and non-piece-wise solution in [3] treats the mobile charge (Qm) to be decoupled between the depletion (Q_{DP}) and complementary (Q_C) components. In the depletion mode the UCCM expression has been formulated as [3] in Eq. 1.

$$Q_{DP} = Q_{eff} LW \left\{ \frac{Qsc}{Q_{eff}} exp \left(\frac{V_g - V_{th} - \eta V}{\eta \phi_T} + \frac{Q_{dep}}{Q_{sc}} \right) \right\} \qquad (1)$$

with the depletion charge, $Q_{dep} = \frac{qN_D R}{2}$, the effective charge during depletion, $Q_{eff} = \frac{Q_{sc}\eta C_{ox}\phi_T}{Q_{sc}+\eta C_{ox}\phi_T}$, $Q_{sc} = \frac{2\epsilon_{Si}\phi_T}{R}$, R being the nanowire diameter, η an interface trap parameter, ϕ_T the thermal voltage and V the potential along the channel. A Lambert W function has been used in both [3] and [4] to develop the solution of total mobile charge in the JLNT. While the expression for Q_{DP} predicts the depletion contribution correctly (for $V_g < V_{th}$), it underestimates the value of the drain current above the flat-band condition. So in accumulation mode, especially in high accumulation with $Q_C \leq Q_{dep}$, the charge Q_C has been derived to act complementary to Q_{DP}, considering that the threshold voltage is pinned at V_{FB} in the accumulation region, in order to avoid using additional smoothing functions and improve simulation time. Under high accumulation $Q_C \leq Q_{dep}$ and QC is simplified using another Lambert function (Eq. 2 [3]):

$$Qc = \eta C_c \phi_T LW \times \left\{ \frac{Q_{sc}}{\eta C_c \phi_T} \times e^{\frac{V_g - V_{FB} - \eta V}{\eta \phi_T}} \right\} \qquad (2)$$

with corrected electrostatic control through $C_c = C_{ox} - C_{eff}$, $C_{eff} = 1/C_{ox} + R/2\epsilon_{Si}$. Having evaluated both the depletion and complementary parts of the mobile charge, one can formulate the non-piece-wise continuous model of the total drain current in terms of Q_{DP} and Q_{DC} at the source and the drain end, Q_{DP0}, Q_{C0} and Q_{DPL}, Q_{CL}, respectively (Eq. 3).

$$I_{DS,0} = \mu_{eff} \frac{2\pi R}{L_{eff}} \phi_T \left[\frac{Q_{DP}^2}{2\eta\, C_{ox}\phi_T} + Q_{DP} + \frac{Q_c^2}{2\eta C_c \phi_T} + 2Q_c \right]_{\substack{Q_{DPL} \\ Q_{CL}}}^{\substack{Q_{DP0} \\ Q_{C0}}} \qquad (3)$$

The drain current expression is free of any fitting parameters and can be evaluated based on the physical device parameters such as that of geometry and doping. Additionally, short channel effects were taken into account considering velocity saturation, an effective mobility, μ_{eff}, and incorporating an effective gate length, $L_{eff} = L - \Delta L$, where L is the physical device gate length and ΔL is calculated following the expression in [6]. Considering that the source and drain access region resistances degrade the drain current above threshold, the final expression of the drain current can be written as a function of the long channel current ($I_{DS,0}$), using Eq. 3, taking into account the corrections due to short-channel effects [5], as in Eq. 4 [6].

$$\frac{I_{DS,0}NF}{1 + 2\pi \frac{R}{L_{eff}} NF\mu_{eff}(R_S + R_D)[(Q_{DP0} + Q_{C0}) - \eta_1(Q_{DP0} + Q_{C0} - (Q_{DP,VDeff} + Q_{C,VDeff}))]} \tag{4}$$

Here, R_S and R_D are the source and drain series access resistances, respectively; NF is the number of nanowires in parallel, η_1 is a fine tuning parameter to take into account the drain-voltage dependence of the series access resistances and $Q_{DP},V_{deff} + Q_C,V_{deff}$ is the total mobile charge at the drain end (pinch-off) of the channel. Additionally, considering formation of Schottky contacts at the source and drain access regions, the subthreshold leakage currents are also taken into account. Consequently, thermionic (I_{th}), tunneling (I_{tun}) and band-to-band tunneling (BTBT) contributions through gate-induced drain leakage (GIDL) are added as separate branch currents [7] to the total drain current, in order to model the subthreshold behavior of the drain current. Equation 5 gives the expression used in the compact model for the BTBT current at the drain end [7].

$$I_{GIDL} = 2\pi R L_{Access} NF \times A_{GIDL} V_{DS} \times E_{segd}^2 \times e^{-\frac{B_{GIDL}}{E_{segd}}} \tag{5}$$

where L_{Access} represents the lengths of the source and drain access regions outside the channel, B_{GIDL} is a physics-based parameter with a theoretical value of 21.3 MV/cm [7] and E_{segd} is the electric field in the drain overlap region, given in Eq. 6.

$$E_{segd} = \frac{C_{ox} \times \sqrt{V_{segd}^2 + (C_{GIDL} V_{DS})^2}}{\epsilon_0 \epsilon_{Si}} \tag{6}$$

Here, V_{segd} is the gate-drain voltage across the oxide and A_{GIDL}, C_{GIDL} are two GIDL fitting parameters. Lastly, additional model improvement has been achieved compared to the model reported in [5], in the subthreshold regime. In order to improve model accuracy, the accurate extraction of the parameter η is ensured in order to correctly adjust the subthreshold slope. Moreover, the effect of drain-induced barrier lowering (DIBL) is also taken into account in the compact model by a modification of the threshold voltage through the Eq. 7

$$V_{th} = V_{FB} - \frac{Q_{dep}}{C_{ox}} - DIBL(V_{DSmax} - V_{DSmin}) \tag{7}$$

with DIBL being the drain-induced barrier lowering in mV/V.

Gate Capacitance Calculation. To extract the gate capacitances, the total gate charge, Q_g, can be written in terms of the channel charge Q_{ch}, as [3],

$$Q_g = -Q_{ch} = 2\pi R \int_0^{L_{eff}} (Q_{DP} + Q_C)dy \tag{8}$$

The solution to the integral in Eq. 8 can be obtained by substituting the effective gate length as a function of the drain current in the depletion and the complementary region of operations. The channel charge can thus be represented as a function of the Q_{DP} and Q_C at the drain and source ends (Eq. 9) following Eqs. 1 and 2 [3].

$$Q_{ch} = \mu_{eff}(2\pi R)^2 \phi_T \left[\frac{Q_{DP}^3}{3I_{DP}\eta C_{ox}\phi_T} + \frac{Q_{DP}^2}{2I_{DP}} + \frac{Q_C^3}{3I_C\eta C_C\phi_T} + \frac{Q_C^2}{I_C} \right]_{Q_{CL}^{Q_{DPL}}}^{Q_{DP0}^{Q_{C0}}} \quad (9)$$

Here, I_{DP} and I_C are the depletion and complementary contributions of the drain current. Finally, the intrinsic gate-source and gate-drain capacitances are calculated using the expression in Eqs. 10 and 11, given the transconductance, output conductance and the terminal voltages [3] for a single nanowire,

$$C_{gs} = \frac{L_{eff}^2(g_{ds} + g_m)^2}{\mu_{eff}I_{DS}} - \frac{Q_g(g_{ds} + g_m)}{I_{DS}} \quad (10)$$

$$C_{gd} = \frac{-L_{eff}^2 g_{ds}^2}{\mu_{eff}I_{DS}} + \frac{Q_g g_{ds}}{I_{DS}} \quad (11)$$

The total gate capacitance of the nanowire arrays can thus be obtained with the expression in Eq. 12.

$$C_{gg} = NF \times (C_{gs} + C_{gd}) \quad (12)$$

2.3   Measured and Simulated Results

DC Validation. For the validation of the compact model against measurement results, we chose a wide range of geometries where test structures had diameters (D) ranging between 22–50 with 16–625 nanowires in parallel (NF). Figure 2 show the transfer characteristics, $I_D - V_{GS}$, of the JLNTs with D = 22 nm/NF = 16 (2a) and D = 50 nm/NF = 36 (2b), respectively. The model simulation results show very good agreement with the measurements over the entire bias range, indicating accuracy of individual modules of the compact model. Particularly, the improvement of the model accuracy in the subthreshold region is observable compared to the results reported in [5], leveraging Eqs. 5 and 7 as well as the parameter η. The improvement in drive current and subthreshold leakage with a higher number of nanowires in parallel is obvious from Fig. 2b, which however suffers from a more pronounced DIBL induced V_T-shift. This is most likely due to quantum confinement effects in smaller nanowire diameters [8]. Nevertheless, the compact model captures these effects with sufficient accuracy. A second order validation is performed in Figs. 3 depicting the output characteristics, $I_D - V_{DS}$, of the JLNTs, further affirming model accuracy.

Scalability. Model scalability is crucial for compact models to support predictive design at circuit level. Moreover, a scalable model parameter set is evidently

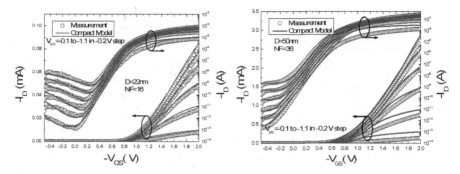

(a) 22nm diameter & 16 nanowires in par-   (b) 50nm diameter & 36 nanowires in parallel   allel

Fig. 2. $I_D - V_{GS}$ of JLNTs of a given diameter and channel multiplicity

more reliable for innovative 3D logic circuit design. Figure 4 depicts the normalized (with the effective NW width, $\pi D \times NF$) gate capacitance and drain current for all available geometries. The intrinsic gate capacitance shows better scalability, especially for smaller number of nanowires in parallel, compared to the drain current. It is also interesting to note that current scalability can be observed for mainly devices with diameters of 22 nm (the representative set from this technology), which have particularly reduced contributions from drain leakage currents that do not scale across devices, as depicted in Fig. 4b. Even though the present model formulation is inherently scalable, given the maturity of the technology, the measured drain current does not scale well across all devices under test as well as different technology generations owing to process variation. The deviation from linearity in larger nanowire diameters could also possibly be attributed to quantum confinement in smaller nanowire diameters [8].

Perspectives. Detailed formulation for the formation of Schottky barriers at the drain/source ends were not taken into account in the present model formulation in order to avoid model convergence issues due to increased computational complexity and only thermionic/tunneling subthreshold leakage currents as well as access region lumped resistances have been considered. This would be, however, an important aspect for further refinement of the model and improvement of its accuracy. Moreover, further model enhancement will also rely on improvement of process scalability in subsequent generations as well as design of dedicated test-fixtures in order to correctly extract the parasitic contributions within the device's 3D architecture.

3   Logic Performance Assessment

In this section, we leverage the developed compact model to assess the performance metrics of various topologies of an elementary logic gate in the VNWFET

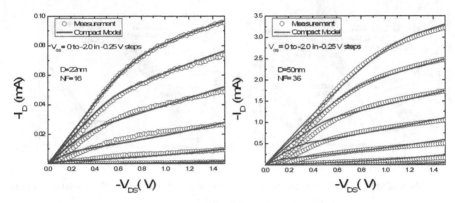

(a) 22nm diameter & 16 nanowires in par- (b) 50nm diameter & 36 nanowires in parallel   allel

Fig. 3. $I_D - V_{DS}$ of JLNTs of a given diameter and channel multiplicity

technology. While it is possible to simulate logic gates implementing multiple
Boolean operations, we focus in this paper on the comparison between several
topologies implementing a single inverter operation. This is partly due to the lack
of experimental devices and consequently measurements with which the compact
model parameters can be defined; but it also targets a full understanding of the relative merits and drawbacks of the device itself, minimizing design-specific issues.
In a first exploration we assess the simulated performance of p-type only inverters,
while in a second exploration, using a literature survey, we extrapolate the model
to n-type VNWFETs in order to explore a simple complementary inverter structure. Finally, we establish a comparison with the 7 nm FinFET technology node
using typical values, in preparation for further analysis in Sect. 4.

3.1   Simulated Structures

This work focuses on inverter structures implemented with passive- and active-
load topologies, as well as with complementary topologies.

P-type only Inverters. P-type only structures use a p-type device as conventional pull-up, and implement the pull-down branch as a resistance, with either
a passive (Fig. 5a) or an active (Fig. 5b) load. For the latter, we use a p-type
device configured as current source. In both cases, the pull-down load is responsible for the low logic state output. This type of structure is known to be less
efficient than their complementary counterparts, but firstly enables validation of
the use of experimental data for designing logic, and secondly gives first insights
into the use of such devices.

Complementary Inverter. For the complementary circuit, based on [9,10]
and shown in Fig. 5c, we conjecture a value for the carrier mobility in the n-type

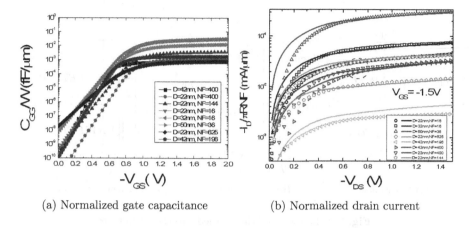

(a) Normalized gate capacitance   (b) Normalized drain current

Fig. 4. Normalized parameters for different VNWFET geometries

VNWFET channel and consequently its drive current. This value is 3x that of the p-type VNWFET. Hence to balance the circuit for a switching input voltage value halfway between the supply rails and for roughly equivalent noise margins, we target identical currents in both devices. To achieve this, we set the NF (number of nanowires) per device in the P-type equal to 3x that of the n-type.

3.2   Results

The goal of the following simulation-based exploration is to study the impact of using a large range of nanowires per transistor on typical static and dynamic logic performance metrics. In the simulation protocol, we assume that the gate capacitance behaves in the same way for both p- and n-type VNWFETs, and that the capacitive load on the output of each structure is equivalent to its own theoretical input capacitance (i.e. fanout of 1). Since the p-type VNWFET gate capacitance with NF = 16 is experimentally determined to be 50aF, and assuming that its evolution with NF is linear, we deduce a capacitance contribution per nanowire of 3.25aF. Measurements were performed using the model described in Sect. 2 as implemented in Verilog-A and simulated using the Spectre[TM] commercial simulator.

Static Performance. DC simulation points enable the extraction of typical static characteristics of the p-type VNWFET transistor.

- I_{on}/I_{off} **ratio**

In this analysis, we characterize the p-type VNWFET characteristics in terms of Ion/Ioff ratio for values of NF ranging from 3–300. To measure Ion (resp. Ioff), we set input A = 0 (resp. A = 1) such that the pull-up device is on (resp. off) in all structures. We observe a linear increase in the leakage current with NF at a rate of 61pA per nanowire. Given the 16 nm nanowire diameter, this translates to 0.3 $\mu A/\mu m^2$ leakage current density in the p-type VNWFET. However, device

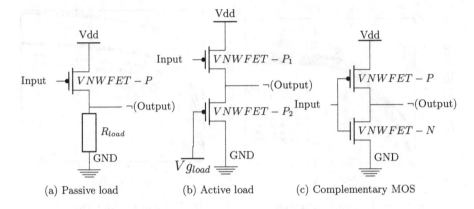

Fig. 5. Schematics of the studied inverter structures

Ion does not increase linearly with NF – in fact, the rate of increase slows down when using large values of NF. As a result, device Ion/Ioff ratio decreases with increasing NF, from 15 03 NF = 10 to 6.5 03 F = 300.

- **Logic level Degradation**

The load in the pull-down branch of both passive- and active-load inverters is a major factor both for logic '1' level degradation and for high-low propagation delay. Its value is a tradeoff: increasing the load decreases logic level degradation but increases propagation delay. For the studied structures the best compromise, as shown in Fig. 6, gives a 15% logic '1' level degradation and a 15% logic '0' level overshoot during high-low transitions at the output for a 1 GHz input signal.

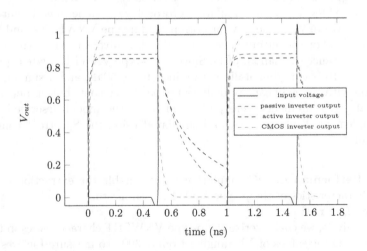

Fig. 6. Voltage across the load capacitor for the studied structures

Dynamic Performance. As shown in Fig. 6, we carried out transient simulations to extract relevant dynamic performance metrics, using a 1 GHz data input with rise and fall times equal to 10 ps. As previously indicated, each inverter shown in Fig. 5 was simulated with a fan-out of 1.

- **Propagation Delay**

For small values of NF, we observe a delay (measured as t Vout = 50%Vdd - t in = 50%Vdd) ranging from 5–10 according to the type of inverter (the lowest delay is achieved by the passive load inverter). When increasing NF, the gate delay increases. This result can be linked principally to the sublinear increase in Ion with NF, and the linear increase in gate capacitance with NF.

- **Dynamic Energy Consumption**

We also measure the energy required to transit through the transistor channel when changing state. We calculate the amount of charge for a low-high transition at the output for the self-loaded complementary inverter. This value varies linearly with NF and works out to 11aC per nanowire. With a 1 V supply voltage this gives us an energy consumption of 11aJ per nanowire for a low-high transition at the output.

Fanout Analysis. Due to the sublinear variation of Ion with NF, self-loaded logic cells with high values of NF cannot charge completely in the available time (Fig. 7). At 1 GHz and for $NF \geq 300$, an inverter cannot cascade with an identical logic cell. Similarly, when increasing the fan-out (number of cells controlled by the inverter), this boundary reduces until fan-out = 5, where a single nanowire transistor cannot drive 5 identical cells simultaneously. This information is crucial regarding power and delay management when designing larger cells.

3.3 Comparison with FinFET and Conclusion

Based on the previous results, there is a clear advantage for using logic cells with low NF, both for power consumption concerns and for fan-out. The values obtained are compared in Table 2 to FinFET values from the literature, both for static values [11] and for propagation delay [12]. Note that while being an academic non-optimized technology, the VNWFET shows similar order of magnitude compared with the industrial mature process 7 nm FinFET.

Table 2. VNWFET/FinFET comparison

Metric	VNWFET	7nm FinFET
Static leakage current density (μA/μm^2)	0.3	1
I_{on}/I_{off} ratio ($\times 10^4$)	[1.5–0.65]	≈ 8
Propagation delay (ps)	[5–10]	2.2

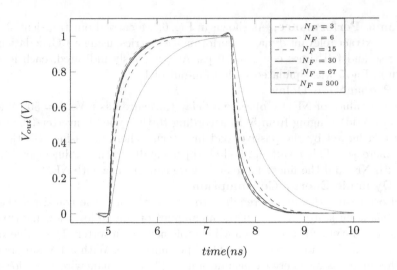

Fig. 7. Voltage across the load capacitance of the self-loaded complementary inverter according to NF (number of nanowires in the p-type VNWFET)

4   3D Logic Cells

4.1   Going Vertical: Implications on Physical Circuit Design

Paradigm Change. Vertical transistor channels lead to a paradigm change in the design of logic cells. Source and drain contacts, separated by the vertical channel, can occupy the same lateral space. Stacked series transistors further improve the gain in circuit density. Further, the additional dimension enables numerous spatial configurations for the same logic functionality [13]. However, careful evaluation of gate contacts and routing is necessary to ensure the best tradeoff between density and performance. In this section, we identify critical dimensional constraints, formulate λ rules for the VNWFET technology and leverage them to compare footprint to lateral FinFET technology. Although this article does not aim to explore complex logic structures using this technology, it lays the foundations for carrying out a complete and exhaustive study with this objective. For this reason, in order to deal with the significant differences between planar FinFET technology and vertical nanowire technology, initial designs must share as much common ground as possible with a tried-and-tested yet cutting-edge technology. Based on the comparison results we extrapolate the comparison metrics to projected figures considering using the potential of the VNWFET technology to its full extent.

Comparison Basis. A planar FinFET channel is composed of a number of fins, according to the desired transistor characteristics (Fig. 8). Similarly, a VNWFET channel is composed of several vertical nanowires. In this work, we aim to compare the footprint of VNWFET-based logic cells with respect to FinFET-based logic cells. We take as baseline reference λ rules for elementary standard cells based on the 7 nm FinFET technology [14] established in the context of exhaustive layout and performance benchmarking. λ rules constitute a simple tool that allows first order scaling by linearizing the resolution of the complete wafer implementation. While modern processes rarely shrink uniformly, λ rules remain useful to make first-order cross-technology spatial comparisons. The principle of λ-rules is to decorrelate characteristic sizes from absolute dimensions by expressing them as a function of some reference length unit (λ). The λ value used for the FinFET represents twice the fin thickness (Tsi – as shown in Fig. 8), which represents the smallest mask dimension (oxide thickness, established through epitaxial growth, is not correlated to lithography or mask limitations) . Correspondingly, the smallest dimension in the VNWFET transistor is the nanowire diameter D (see Fig. 9) and is accordingly used to define λ for the VNWFET technology . An important observation in both technologies is that dimensions in the transistor zone are comparable to λ, while dimensions comparable to $3 \times \lambda$ are used in the routing and contacting of the transistor. In the baseline reference, FinFET planar transistors are at the 7 nm node, such that $\lambda = 3.5$ nm, while the current state of VNWFET technology allows a minimal nanowire diameter such that $\lambda = 16$ nm. It should be stressed that this is representative of an emerging research technology under development rather than an inherent limitation to the technology. Table 3 shows the λ-rules as established in [14] for 7 nm FinFETs as well as those chosen in this paper for VNWFETs.

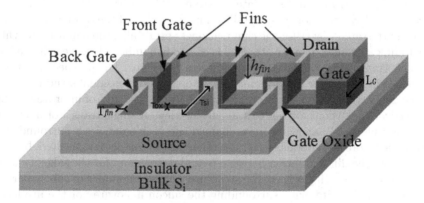

Fig. 8. Perspective view of a 7 nm node FinFET transistor [14]

Table 3. λ-Rule metric comparison between FinFET and VNWFET

Parameter	Value in 7nm FinFET (nm)	Value in projected VNWFET (nm)	Comment
T_{fin}/D	$3.5 = \lambda_{fin}$	$11 = \lambda_{NW}$	Fin thickness / nanowire diameter
T_{si}	$2 \times \lambda_{fin}$		Fin length
H_{fin}/H_{NW}	$4 \times \lambda_{fin}$	30	Height
T_{ox}	1.55	5	Oxide thickness
P_{fin}/P_{NW}	$2 \times \lambda_{fin} + T_{fin}$	$2 \times \lambda_{NW} + D$	Pitch
W_C	$3 \times \lambda_{fin}$	$3 \times \lambda_{NW}$	Contact size
W_{M2M}	$2 \times \lambda_{fin}$	$2 \times \lambda_{NW}$	Gate to contact space

4.2 The 3D Architecture of the VNWFET Technology

There are 3 metallic contacts along the transistor's vertical channel. This structure is shown in Fig. 9 [2]:

- The bottom PtSi contact surrounds the bottom of the nanowire and establishes a first access to the transistor channel. This contact is ultimately used as drain or source.
- A top Al contact covers the top of the nanowire and establishes a second access to the transistor channel. This contact is similarly used as a drain or source.
- A Cr layer in the middle surrounds the center of the nanowires and is separated from the silicon by a gate oxide. This metal contact acts as the gate.

It is worth noticing that the gate structure surrounds the channel, thus categorizing this type of transistor as a Gate-all-around (GAA) FET. Moreover, as compared to FinFET technologies, the silicon in the region of the drain and source is doped in the same way as for the channel zone. Specifically, the nanowire to which the drain, gate and source are attached is etched in a uniformly doped silicon bulk [1]. This transistor is thus also a junction-less transistor. The perspective view of the nanowire transistor provides insights into the tridimensional structure of the device. Since we focus on the lateral footprint and for the sake of improved visibility, vertical dimensions are not to scale in this view. A single transistor may comprise multiple (NF) nanowires in its channel and each nanowire is surrounded by gate oxide before any contacts other than the bottom contact is deposited. In order to facilitate the differentiation between p- and n-type, and for the sake of clarity, the figures representing VNWFET structures in the remainder of this paper will show neither the gate oxide surrounding the silicon nanowire nor the insulating spacers for each metallic layer. Spacers made of oxide are represented between top contact and gate and between gate and bottom contact to isolate those metals. In order to facilitate the differentiation between p- and n-type, and for the sake of clarity, the figures representing VNWFET structures in the remainder of this paper will show neither the gate oxide surrounding the silicon nanowire nor the insulating spacers for each metallic layer.

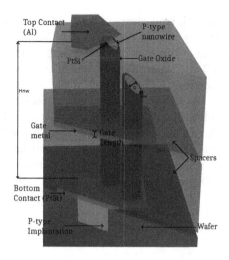

Fig. 9. Perspective and cut view of a projected VNWFET transistor

4.3   Footprint Estimation

As indicated previously, we focus on the footprint (lateral area) in order to keep common grounds with the FinFET technology. The vertical height of the logic cell is considered unimportant in this comparison and unrelated to any FinFET dimension. The same is true for gate length and contact thickness. In the standard cell approach, the lateral "height" of the cell (i.e. the distance between supply voltage and ground) is constant for all standard cells in a technology. Data inputs and outputs are typically located in the middle of the cell. Their position is not constrained and their access is not taken into account in the cell design. This type of layout allows the designer to assemble each logic gate on the same level with only inputs and outputs to route properly, usually through a dedicated routing channel. Several important points mentioned in Sect. 3 are taken into account in order to implement logic cells in the context of standard cell design. The current technology is used for characterization and trials on vertical nanowires. It is thus unable to sustain the requirements of the λ-rule constraints we introduced in Table 3. Indeed, the 16 nm diameter value is not the main concern, since the dimensions of the metallic layers are much larger for electrical characterization purposes and manufacturing process limitations. The lithography equipment used in the process is not intended for this scale of precision. These manufacturing changes, as compared to [1], remain credible in a foreseeable future. In a nutshell, the main assumption is that contact and gate dimensions are in the same range as the nanowire dimensions.

4.4   Layout Footprint Comparison Example

The comparison method explained above is applied to a CMOS inverter structure with balanced switching corresponding to nanowire mobility [9]. The difference between the mobility of both transistor channels suggests that the n-type and p-type transistors respectively possess one fin or one nanowire and one fin or three nanowires. In Fig. 10, the layout is composed of large voltage supply extensions for both VDD and GND and an active zone where the transistors are connected together. The layout footprint is the product of the width and length given in λ values. In both Figures. 10a and 10b, we notice a similar inverter structure, where the position of the supply voltages and input/output are indicated. The FinFET inverter footprint is 48λ long and 18λ wide while the VNWFET inverter footprint is 31λ long and 15λ wide. This represents a 48% footprint area reduction. If we choose a less restrictive comparison criterion and consider the active part alone (removing the 12λ supply contacts for both layouts), we observe an 84% footprint area reduction.

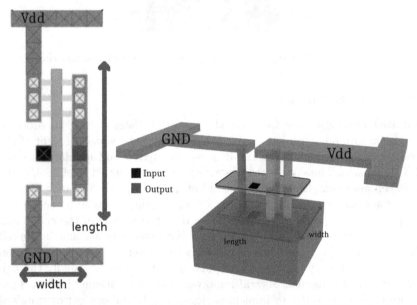

(a) Top view for the 7nm finFET technology [14]

(b) Perspective view for the VNWFET technology

Fig. 10. Representation of an inverter gate in both VNWFET and finFET technologies

5   A Custom EDA Tool

5.1   Specifications

EDA (Electronic Design Automation) tools are common and accessible nowadays. However, considering the technology under analysis, there are some specific aspects such as the vertical channel and routing rules resulting from it. These aspects are not easy to feed into EDA software. Indeed, usual supported circuits are a succession of 2D layers interconnected by vias. For this reason, we decided to develop a specific tool for interconnecting the VNWFET devices that will ease a few aspects of the work:

- Rendering the logic cell in 3D
- Creating masks suited for very specific manufacturing constraints
- Giving a computing basis for 3D parasitic extraction

5.2 Realisation

The tool under development is written in Python3 and requires 3D modeling software (Blender) as well as a mask editing and viewing software (Klayout). Its input is a Python file describing the structure of the logic cell. Ultimately, it will to be able to read a netlist.

5.3 Example of Studied Structure

Since we studied the inverter under different aspects, we can showcase the tool we have been using on this particular case. First, Fig. 11 shows a realistic (manufacturing wise) representation of the inverter cell with labels in blue for the signal to send to the logic cell, in comparison with the logic cell in Fig. 10b studied earlier, which was also generated with this tool but with a different manufacturing library. Last but not least Fig. 12 is the GDS file used for manufacturing the mask of this particular structure

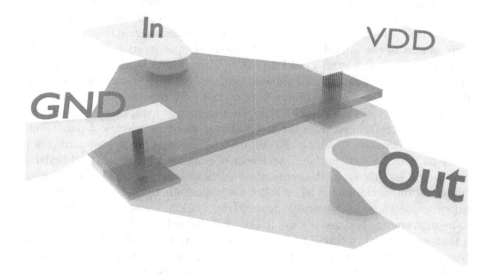

Fig. 11. Realistic view of the VNWFET CMOS inverter with manufacturing constraints taken into account (Color figure online)

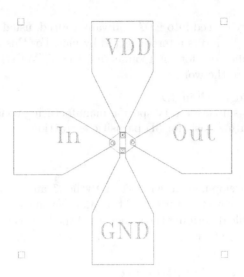

Fig. 12. Generated mask for a realistic VNWFET CMOS inverter design

6 Insights for Large Scale Integration

6.1 Promising Results for Further Designs

While devices based on vertical nanowires have been compared to lateral GAA devices in the past [15], this work used apparent mobility differences between both device channels to justify the difference in gate lengths. In order to achieve similar drive strength for both devices, the vertical device gate length is around 2 times that of the lateral device. Such electrical considerations help to set the vertical dimensions for the VNWFET. Gate length values in the referenced article are in the 10–20 range. This value fits our designs without any impact on the device footprint area and its impact on overall performance will be studied in the future. The fact that VNWFET dimensions such as gate, spacer and channel lengths are decorrelated from the lateral footprint allows electrical parameters to be tuned without touching the cell design. This favors the standardization of simple cells, as well as the achievement of complex logic design and scalable electronics. In this work, the comparison method separated electrical behavior concerns from device layout to establish a workflow and to enable the future consideration of stacked-gate vertical devices [16]. Stacking gates requires device Ion to be high enough to drive the whole common channel. We demonstrate in Sect. 3 that with current technology, the fan-out limit is 4 for a very low number of transistors. Thus, we can expect at least a functional 4-stacked gates transistor, which already enables significant opportunity for disruptive logic designs.

6.2   The Future of the VNWFET Technology

It was shown from the analysis in the last chapter that we would be able to stack up to 4 gates on a nanowire channel. This aspect of the VNWFET technology is crucial for its future success.

Making Stacking Possible. Considering the current state of the art, VNWFETs can be connected together on the top, gate or bottom level. Each of those levels can be accessed considering a single gate technology. What would happen if we stack multiple gate levels on the same nanowire channel is what we need to measure and plan for. Figure 13 shows how this transformation affects the structure.

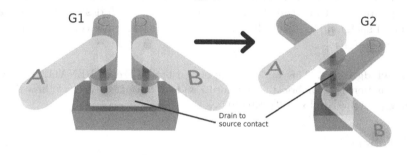

Fig. 13. Transition from 1 gate to 2 stacked-gates: structural changes visualisation for two transistor connected in a source-drain fashion

Reasons for Stacking Gates. When looking at a large scale circuit, we notice that around half of the metal paths are used by interconnections which consume a significant part of effective power and is also responsible for important delays. There are numerous ways to reduce interconnection length and complexity such as modifying the way logic cells are designed or going for regular and optimized structures. What we propose depends on the scale of the interconnects leveraging the properties of the VNWFETs:

- For an interconnect between 2 transistors, we hope to remove some of it by considering stacked gates as transistors in a drain-source connected configurations
- For an interconnect between 2 logic cells, owing to the vertical channel, outputs, inputs or power supplies can be connected through design on the chosen interconnect layers. No vias are therefore necessary.

Some previous works have focused on the theoretical advantages of 2 stacked gates 3D structures similar to the VNWFET technology [17] while [18] explores a manufacturing process for stacked gates applied for Tunnel FETs. In light of these articles, enhancement and optimization of this VNWFET technology and designing technology specific logic cells appears quite promising.

7 Conclusion

This work considers the use of VNWFETs as a means to implement 3D logic blocks. We have built a technology scalable physics-based compact model and implemented it in Verilog-A as incorporated in a dedicated circuit design workspace. This environment has been used to simulate innovative 3D layouts of inverter cells. The layout of the complementary inverter has been compared with projected 7 nm FinFET technology through the use of λ rules. We showed that the VNWFET-based approach achieves 48% footprint reduction and can reach 84% if only the active part is considered. Beyond λ rule comparisons, we presented another physical layout implementation that leverages the unique features of VNWFETs, where dimensions such as gate, spacer and channel lengths are de-correlated from the transistor footprint. This important property allows electrical parameters to be tuned without any impact on cell design. The standardization of such simple logic cells will pave the way for more complex VNWFET logic cell designs.

Acknowledgments. This work was supported by the French RENATECH network (French national nanofabrication platform) and by the LEGO project through ANR funding (Grant ANR-18-CE24-0005-01).

References

1. Larrieu, G., Han, X.-L.: Vertical nanowire array-based field effect transistors for ultimate scaling. Nanoscale **5**, 2437 (2013). https://doi.org/10.1039/c3nr33738c
2. Guerfi, Y., Larrieu, G.: Vertical silicon nanowire field effect transistors with nanoscale gate-all-around. Nanoscale Res. Lett. **11**, 210 (2016). https://doi.org/10.1186/s11671-016-1396-7
3. Hamza, A., Imail, R., Alias, N.E., Peng Tan, M.L., Poorasl, A.: Explicit continuous models of drain current, terminal charges and intrinsic capacitance for a long-channel junctionless nanowire transistor. Phys. Scr. **94**, 105813 (2019)
4. Lime, F., Moldovan, O., Iniguez, B.: A compact explicit model for long-channel gate-all-around junctionless MOSFETs. Part I: DC characteristics. IEEE Trans. Electron Devices **61**, 3036–3041 (2014). https://doi.org/10.1109/TED.2014.2340441
5. Mukherjee, C., Larrieu, G., Maneux, C.: Compact modeling of 3D vertical junctionless gate-all-around silicon nanowire transistors. In: EUROSOI ULIS (2020)
6. Lim, F., Àvila-Herrera, F., Cerdeira, A., Iñiguez, B.: A compact explicit DC model for short channel Gate-All-Around junctionless MOSFETs. Solid State Electron **131**, 24–29 (2017). https://doi.org/10.1109/TED.2014.2340441
7. Zhu, G., et al.: Subcircuit compact model for dopant-segregated Schottky gate-all-around Si-nanowire MOSFETs. IEEE Trans. Electron device **57**(4), 24–29 (2017). https://doi.org/10.1109/TED.2010.2041513
8. Sahay, S., Kumar, M.J.: Junctionless Field-Effect Transistors: Design, Modeling and Simulation. IEEE Press Series on Microelectronic Systems, Wiley, Hoboken (2019) https://b-ok.cc/book/4976757/3a8e5e
9. Gunawan, O., et al.: Measurement of carrier mobility in silicon nanowires. Nano Lett. **8**, 1566–1571 (2008). https://doi.org/10.1021/nl072646w

10. Colinge, J.-P., et al.: Nanowire transistors without junctions. Nat. Nanotechnol. **5**, 225–229 (2010). https://doi.org/10.1038/nnano.2010.15

11. Clark, L.T., et al.: ASAP7: a 7-nm finFET predictive process design kit. Microelectron. J. **53**, 105–115 (2016). https://doi.org/10.1016/j.mejo.2016.04.006

12. Raghavan, P., et al.: Holistic device exploration for 7 nm node. In: IEEE Custom Integrated Circuits Conference (CICC), pp. 1–5 (2015). https://doi.org/10.1109/IEDM.2016.7838497

13. Moroz, V., et al.: Power-performance-area engineering of 5nm nanowire library cells. In: International Conference on Simulation of Semiconductor Processes and Devices (SISPAD), pp. 433–436 (2015). https://doi.org/10.1109/SISPAD.2015.7292353

14. Cui, T., Xie, Q., Wang, Y., Nazarian, S., Pedram, M.: 7nm FinFET standard cell layout characterization and power density prediction in near- and super-threshold voltage regimes. In: International Green Computing Conference, pp. 1–7 (2014). https://doi.org/10.1109/IGCC.2014.7039170

15. Yakimets, D., et al.: Vertical GAAFETs for the ultimate CMOS scaling. IEEE Trans. Electron Devices **62**, 1433–1439 (2015). https://doi.org/10.1109/TED.2015.2414924

16. Shi, J., Li, M., Rahman, M., Khasanvis, S., Moritz, C.A.: NP-Dynamic Skybridge: A Fine-Grained 3D IC technology with NP-dynamic logic. IEEE Trans. Emerging Top. Comput. **5**, 286–299 (2017). https://doi.org/10.1109/TETC.2017.2684781

17. Veloso, A., et al.: Challenges and opportunities of vertical FET devices using 3D circuit design layouts. In: IEEE SOI 3D Subthreshold Microelectronics Technology Unified Conference (S3S), pp. 1–3 (2016). https://doi.org/10.1109/S3S.2016.7804409

18. Li, X., et al.: Vertically stacked and independently controlled twin-gate MOSFETs on a single Si nanowire. IEEE Electron Device Lett. **32**, 1492–1494 (2011). https://doi.org/10.1109/LED.2011.2165693

19. Chhandak, M., et al.: 3D logic cells design and results based on vertical NWFET technology including tied compact model. In: 2020 IFIP/IEEE 28th International Conference on Very Large Scale Integration (VLSI-SOC), pp. 76–81 (2020) https://doi.org/10.1109/VLSI-SOC46417.2020.9344094

Statistical Array Allocation and Partitioning for Compute In-Memory Fabrics

Brian Crafton$^{(\boxtimes)}$, Samuel Spetalnick, Gauthaman Murali, Tushar Krishna, Sung-Kyu Lim, and Arijit Raychowdhury

Georgia Institute of Technology, Atlanta, GA 30332, USA
brian.crafton@gatech.edu, arijit.raychowdhury@ece.gatech.edu

Abstract. Compute in-memory (CIM) is a promising technique that minimizes data transport, the primary performance bottleneck and energy cost of most data intensive applications. This has found widespread adoption in accelerating neural networks for machine learning applications. Utilizing a crossbar architecture with emerging non-volatile memories (eNVM) such as dense resistive random access memory (RRAM) or phase change random access memory (PCRAM), various forms of neural networks can be implemented to greatly reduce power and increase on chip memory capacity. However, compute in-memory faces its own limitations at both the circuit and the device levels. Although compute in-memory using the crossbar architecture can greatly reduce data transport, the rigid nature of these large fixed weight matrices forfeits the flexibility of traditional CMOS and SRAM based designs. In this work, we explore the different synchronization barriers that occur from the CIM constraints. Furthermore, we propose a new allocation algorithm and data flow based on input data distributions to maximize utilization and performance for compute-in memory based designs. We demonstrate a 7.47× performance improvement over a naive allocation method for CIM accelerators on ResNet18.

Keywords: Compute In-Memory · RRAM · PCRAM

1 Introduction

Modern computing systems are heavily dependent on the capacity and access time of expensive memory banks due to the ever increasing performance gap between main memory and logic. Furthermore, the cost of moving data has become more expensive than operating on it [1], and thus not only has the memory become the fundamental bottleneck of computing, but both reading and transporting the data has become more expensive than the operation we seek to perform. Popularization of data intensive applications like machine learning and artificial intelligence have further exacerbated this problem. To address

© IFIP International Federation for Information Processing 2021
Published by Springer Nature Switzerland AG 2021
A. Calimera et al. (Eds.): VLSI-SoC 2020, IFIP AICT 621, pp. 323–341, 2021.
https://doi.org/10.1007/978-3-030-81641-4_15

these issues, new architectures based on traditional CMOS attempt to minimize the transport of data by optimizing for data reuse [1] and adopting constraints inspired by the brain [2]. While these techniques yield strong results, they still face the fundamental technological limitations of CMOS.

Fortunately a new class of embedded non-volatile memory (eNVM) is positioned to minimize data transport by performing compute in-memory. In-memory computing seeks to perform matrix multiplication ($\mathbf{y} = W\mathbf{x}$) in a crossbar structure using Ohm's law and the non-volatile conductance state provided by the non-volatile memory. Using this technique, each weight of the matrix (W_{ij}) is programmed as a conductance to a cell and each value of the vector ($\mathbf{x_i}$) is converted to voltage and applied to the rows of the memory crossbar. By Ohm's law, the current through each cell is proportional to the product of the programmed conductance (W_{ij}) and applied voltage ($\mathbf{x}_i$). By Kirchhoff's current law (KCL), the resulting currents summed along the columns of the crossbar are proportional to the product of the matrix and vector, ($\mathbf{y}$). Under this procedure, the only data transport required for matrix multiplication is the feature vector ($\mathbf{x}$) from memory and result ($\mathbf{y}$) to memory. Therefore, in-memory computing eliminates the majority of data transfer and thus energy cost of data intensive operations.

Although compute in-memory using the crossbar architecture can greatly reduce data transport, the rigid nature of these large fixed weight matrices forfeits the flexibility of traditional CMOS and SRAM based designs. Given that eNVM has high density and unfortunately high write energy compared to traditional SRAM, CIM-based inference-only designs avoid writing to the eNVM cells once programmed. While this is advantageous for data transport and energy efficiency, it means each CIM processing element (PE) can only perform operations it has the weights for. This implies that if there is an unbalanced workload where some PEs operations take longer than others, we cannot simply re-allocate these operations to other PEs. Therefore, we must use synchronization barriers for all PEs so distributed matrix multiplication completes before another is started. In contrast, every CMOS and SRAM based PE are computationally identical and can perform any operation in the DNN graph.

Therefore a fundamental problem in CIM based designs is array utilization, the percent of time an array is in use. Recent large scale CIM designs [3], use weight duplication and layer pipelining techniques to maximize performance. We describe these techniques in detail in Sect. 2. While impressive performance is achieved, these techniques only perform well when the workloads are deterministic. Circuit level techniques like zero-skipping greatly increase performance, but create non-deterministic workloads that compromise array utilization. In this work [4] we identify and profile these new challenges using a simple simulator framework. We then propose a novel algorithm, which makes use of input statistics to find optimal array allocation policies to maximize utilization and *break* synchronization *barriers*. Furthermore, we introduce a new data flow that generalizes CIM arrays to maximize their utilization. We run our experiments on ImageNet [5] using ResNet18 [6] and CIFAR10 [7] using VGG11 [8]. Although we apply our techniques to deep learning, we claim that the techniques we propose can be extended to any compute in-memory application. We note that a combination of these strategies yield 7.47× improvement in performance over a baseline naive array allocation.

2 Background and Motivation

Compute in-memory systems use binary or multi-level cells as weights to perform matrix multiplication in memory. In this work we will focus our attention to binary cells given the current state of the art in eNVM [9–11] already struggles with variance thus making multi-level cells even more difficult to utilize. However, the same techniques demonstrated in this work can easily be applied to multi-level cells as well. Given binary cells, we must use 8 adjacent cells to form a single 8-bit weight, like those shown in the columns of Fig. 1. The 8-bit vector inputs to this array are shifted in 1 bit at a time, and the resulting binary product collected at the ADCs is shifted left by the same amount the inputs are shifted right. In this way, each array is able to perform an 8-bit matrix multiplication.

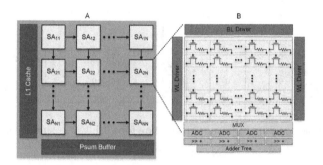

Fig. 1. Typical compute in-memory PE (processing engine) and sub-array (SA) architecture. (A) NxN sub-array PE with L1 cache and psum buffer. In this work N is 8. (B) Typical sub-array design with dual word line drivers, ADCs, shift and add units, and an adder tree.

2.1 Array Operation

In Fig. 2, we illustrate this process using a 4-bit, 2×2 matrix multiplication. In the top inset of the figure, we provide the example problem and solution of the matrix multiplication, along with how it is mapped to the crossbar array. The values of the matrix are mapped to the memory cells (RRAM) of the crossbar, and the input vectors are encoded as binary values to be shifted in one bit at a time. In the second inset of Fig. 2 we walk through the four cycles associated

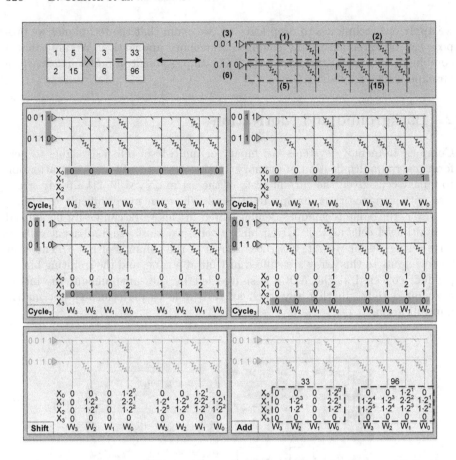

Fig. 2. Example compute in-memory procedure for a 4-bit, 2 × 2 matrix multiplication.

with the 4-bit matrix multiplication. In cycle 1 the select the first bit in each of the input values, and read the corresponding rows of RRAM cells, performing binary matrix multiplication. We continue this procedure through cycles 2 to 4, collecting all partial sums. In the third and final inset we perform post processing to combine the binary matrix multiplications into a 4-bit matrix multiplication using shift and add operations in CMOS. In Fig. 2F, we observe how shift is performed for each cycle. We multiply (shift) each output value by the cumulative magnitude of the corresponding input (X) and weight (W) bits. Lastly, in Fig. 2G, we sum all results together to get our solution vector. Although, in this example we performed 4-bit matrix multiplication, this technique generalizes to all input and weight precisions by combining matrix multiplication using shift and add post processing.

There are two constraints we face at the array level that limit performance: the number of columns that share an ADC and the precision of the ADC.

The number of columns that share an ADC is a function of the area of the ADC and the distance between bitlines. For every column that shares a single ADC, the number of cycles to perform a dot product multiplies. The precision of an ADC determines how many rows we can turn on at once, for if we read more rows than states we can successfully read, we overflow the column ADCs and incur errors.

There are two common techniques for performing compute in memory. The first technique, we call *baseline*, is simply reading as many rows as the ADC precision allows (e.g. for a 3-bit ADC, we read 8 rows simultaneously). The next technique is commonly called zero skipping [12], where only rows with '1's are read. This technique exploits sparsity in the input features or activations (for neural networks). Zero skipping performs faster than the baseline technique because for most cases it will process more total rows per cycle. In Fig. 3, we provide an example case for zero-skipping where 8 total rows are read using a 2-bit ADC. Baseline (Fig. 3A) requires 2 cycles since it targets four consecutive rows at a time. Zero-skipping (Fig. 3B) is able to finish all 8 rows in a single cycle because we only consider the '1's in the input vector. There are few reasons not to perform zero skipping, unless there is limited input data bandwidth or the eNVM has high variance and accumulated too many errors.

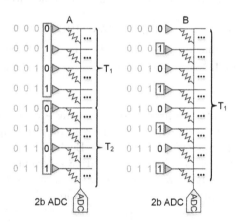

Fig. 3. Simplified breakdown of ADC reads in baseline and zero-skipping with 2-bit ADC precision. (A) Baseline targets four consecutive rows at a time since the 2-bit ADCs are capable of distinguishing 4 states. (B) Zero skipping targets the next 4 rows where the word line is enabled. This way we can read more rows and not overflow our ADC.

2.2 Array Allocation

By encapsulating the array, ADCs, and shift and add logic, a matrix multiplication engine can be created. Using these arrays as building blocks, prior work has implemented CNNs (Convolutional Neural Networks) where a group of arrays implement a larger matrix multiplication. Despite performing more complex operations, the core operations of CNNs are converted into matrix multiplication. In Fig. 1 we illustrate this idea, showing how a group of arrays is tiled together to form a PE. In Fig. 5 we further depict how these arrays can be pieced together to form a larger matrix. In this example, both input feature maps and filters are vectorized with the filters forming the columns of a matrix. The vectorized feature maps are input to the crossbar to perform matrix multiplication, where the results are output feature maps for this layer in a CNN.

Given the high density of these PEs, hundreds or thousands of them can be tiled in the same area used by modern ICs. Although similar in concept, CIM-based DNN accelerators have numerous differences from traditional CMOS based designs that introduce challenges in maximizing performance. First off, a CIM-based PE has fixed weights that cannot be reprogrammed due to the high energy cost of writing eNVM. Traditional CMOS based PEs are generalized compute units that can operate on any input data, since they do not contain fixed weights. Thus, while flexible CMOS PEs are challenged by data movement, the challenge with CIM-based PEs is weight allocation and placement.

Table 1. Energy and latency comparison for CMOS memories and eNVM [13].

Device	SRAM	DRAM	RRAM	PCRAM
Write Energy	1 fJ	10 fJ	10 pJ	10 pJ
Write Latency	1 ns	10 ns	10 ns	50 ns

In Fig. 4, we illustrate the process of allocating and mapping a matrix to a distributed group of memory arrays. In this example, we map a 256 × 128 8-bit matrix multiplication to a group of 16 arrays. Each array is a 128 × 128 RRAM array, where each cell is 1-bit. Since we require 8 adjacent cells to form a single weight, each 128 × 128 RRAM array can function as a 128 × 16 8-bit matrix multiplication engine. Next, we divide up the 256 × 128 matrix into an 8 × 2 grid of 128 × 16 arrays. From here the mapping process is simple, where we assign each point in the grid to a corresponding array in our design.

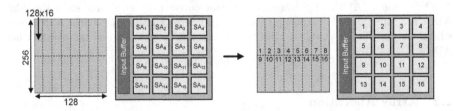

Fig. 4. Example weight allocation procedure for a 256 × 128 matrix multiplication.

2.3   Maximizing Utilization

So far we have discussed how CIM-based PEs contain fixed weights due to energy constraints, and thus weights must remain fixed. While this greatly simplifies both our dataflow and reduces traffic and thus power, it means compute units can only perform a subset of the matrix multiplications in the network. This implies that if a PE finishes its workload before another, we cannot simply redistribute the workload to keep both PEs utilized. Thus a fundamental issue in CIM-based accelerators is array utilization. Several works have addressed this issue introducing ideas such as weight duplication and layer pipelining.

Weight duplication [3] is used to maximize throughput in large scale CIM accelerators where the amount of on-chip memory exceeds the number of weights in the model. In [14], 24,960 arrays are used for a total on-chip memory capacity of nearly 104 MB (2b cells), while only using an area of 250 mm². Using this enormous on-chip memory capacity, they not only fit ResNet [6] but duplicate shallow layers up to 32×. When weights are duplicated, the input data is divided equally amongst each duplicate array so they can process in parallel. We illustrate this idea for a convolutional layer in Fig. 5. The input patches from the input feature maps (IFMs) are divided into groups based on the number of duplicates, and then mapped to each duplicate.

Layer pipelining [3] is used to maximize throughput in eNVM CIM accelerator, where arrays are not re-programmed due to large amounts of on-chip memory and high write energy. At the same time, most modern neural networks contain 20 or more layers that must be processed sequentially. Given that most designs use 128 × 128 arrays, it becomes infeasible to partition arrays such that they can be used for each layer without being re-programmed. This implies that the majority of PEs would sit idle waiting for their layer to be processed. To solve this problem, images are pipelined through the network to keep all arrays

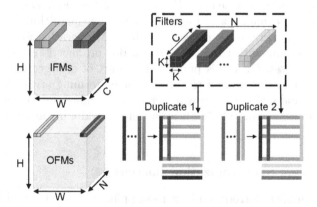

Fig. 5. Convolutional layer mapped to a CIM array. Both input features maps (IFM) and filters are vectorized with the filters forming the columns of a matrix. The vectorized feature maps applied to the crossbar to perform matrix multiplication, where the results are output feature maps (OFMs).

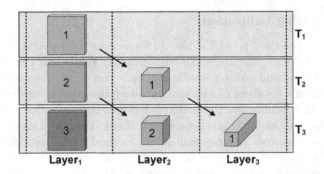

Fig. 6. Layer pipelining

utilized. Although this compromises single example latency, it maintains maximum throughput. We provide visualization in Fig. 6, where 3 feature maps from 3 different input examples are processed together.

3 Block-Wise Array Allocation

In the previous section, we discussed several techniques that are used in CIM accelerators to increase throughput, but each introduces it's own synchronization barrier that limits array level utilization. In this work, we identify two of these barriers and propose our solution to mitigate this problem. The two techniques that create these barriers are weight duplication and layer pipelining. In previous work these barriers were not a problem because array performance was deterministic. When zero-skipping is introduced, it instigates these barriers because it introduces non-deterministic computation time for each array. Zero skipping will only improve the performance of a CIM accelerator because it simply means each array will perform equal to or faster than the baseline algorithm. However, since the number of ones in the input vector of the CIM operation follows a random distribution, the amount of time to finish a dot product is non-deterministic. This means that several arrays performing a part of a larger matrix multiplication need to be synchronized to the slowest preforming array. As the size of the operation (and number of arrays) increases, the more stalls occur. In the following section, we explore the implications of zero skipping at the architectural level.

3.1 Identifying Synchronization Barriers

The non-determinism introduced by zero-skipping induces the need for synchronization barriers. A synchronization barrier is required when a group arrays are processing a distributed workload and finish at different times, but must be synchronized before starting another task. The first barrier occurs at the layer level and is a result of using layer pipelining. When the arrays are distributed to each layer, we attempt to divide them evenly so that all layers finish at the same time. If any layer is consistently performing faster than other layers, it will have to stall because layers downstream will not be able to buffer its outputs. Previous work [14] have allocated arrays to layers based on the number of duplicates required such that all layers in the pipeline complete their workload at the same time, and thus sustain full utilization. This allocation policy can be written as:

$$\textbf{Minimize:} \quad \max_{\forall L \in N} \frac{\# \ \text{MAC}_L}{\# \ \text{Array}_L}$$

This allocation method works under the assumption that all arrays perform at the same rate and we can choose the number of arrays on chip. However, as [12] points out neither of these assumptions will hold in a realistic design. Prior works [3,14] assume 128 cells can be read at once using 5 and 8 bit ADCs. Although feasible in theory, we note that such a design will yield very high error given that the state of the art devices have 5% device-to-device variance [9,15], and thus at most 8 rows (3-bit) can be read at once. Such a design also yields very poor memory density since large (5–8 bit) ADCs occupy over 10× the area of eNVM. Instead columns must be processed in batches using zero-skipping, where current summation is used for 8 rows and then intermediate results are stored and accumulated using existing digital logic in the array.

When zero skipping is used, each array performs at a non-deterministic speed that follows the distribution of input data it receives. In Fig. 7, we plot the average time for an array to perform a 128×16 matrix multiplication versus the percentage of '1's in all the 8-bit input features for the 20 convolutional layers in ResNet18. To compute the percentage of '1's for a layer, we average the 8 bits in all 8-bit input features together. For example, a 1000-entry 8-bit input vector contains 8000 bits and to determine the percentage of '1's, we average over 8000 bits to compute this percentage. From Fig. 7, we infer a linear relationship

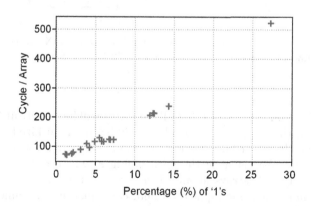

Fig. 7. Cycles per array versus the percentage of '1's in all 8-bit input features. Each point represents the average percentage for one of the 20 layers in ResNet18.

between the percentage of '1's in the input features to a layer, and the expected number of cycles to perform the matrix multiplication.

Naturally, we can use this information to better allocate duplicates to each layer in our design. We approach this problem by quantifying the total number of multiply-and-accumulate (MAC) operations in each layer, and the average number of MAC operations per cycle an array can perform. This new allocation policy can be written as:

$$\textbf{Minimize:} \quad \max_{\forall L \in N} \frac{\# \text{ MAC}_L}{\# \text{ Array}_L \cdot \text{Perf}_L}$$

where Perf_L is added in the denominator to take into account the performance of each array in the layer. In prior works, performance per array is constant since each array takes the same number of cycles to perform a matrix multiplication. Therefore, arrays are allocated to each layer based only on the total MACs per layer. When zero-skipping is introduced and performance per array is not constant, this allocation method fails to allocate evenly. To achieve equal utilization, we can instead allocate arrays to each layer based on the expected number of cycles it will take to finish without any duplicate arrays. We can compute the expected number of cycles it will take a layer to finish by dividing the total MACs in a layer by the average performance of each array in the layer. We call this allocation method *performance-based* allocation, whereas allocation that assumes all arrays perform evenly is *weight-based* allocation.

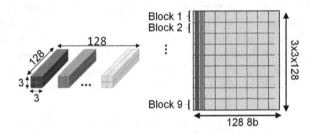

Fig. 8. The $3 \times 3 \times 128 \times 128$ filter used in layer 10 from ResNet18 converted into a matrix with annotated blocks. This filter requires 72 128×128 arrays to store in a 9×8 grid.

While this technique ensures that all our layers will be equally utilized, it does not ensure that the arrays inside each layer will be equally utilized. Each layer in our DNN (convolution or fully connected) is implemented as a matrix consisting of eNVM arrays. We visualize this idea in Fig. 8, where a $3 \times 3 \times 128 \times 128$ filter is mapped to 72 arrays arranged in a 9×8 grid. In each of the 9 rows, all 8 arrays share the same input data and, consequently, the same word lines. This implies that all 8 arrays will operate at the same speed and form our minimal deterministic compute unit that we call a *block*. Because the 9 different rows do not share the same input vectors, they will operate at different speeds.

If some arrays receive fewer '1's than other arrays, they will sit idle waiting for arrays that receive more '1's to finish. In Fig. 9, we plot the average cycle time of the arrays in each block of layers 10 and 15 (ResNet18) versus the percent of '1's they receive. Layer 10 is a $3 \times 3 \times 128 \times 128$ filter (Fig. 8) that contains 9 different blocks, and Layer 15 is a $3 \times 3 \times 256 \times 256$ filter that contains 18 different blocks. Just as before, we observe a linear relationship between cycle time and the percentage of '1's. Since layer 15 contains more blocks, it is more susceptible to longer delays because the expected slowest block's cycle time increases with the number of arrays. In this figure, we observe a 12% and 27% difference in cycle time for layers 10 and 15, which motivates a better allocation technique to prevent significant idle time.

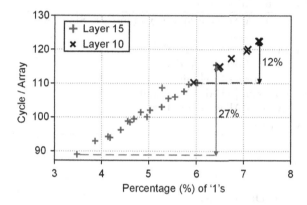

Fig. 9. Cycles per array versus the percentage of '1's in all 8-bit input features. The blue crosses represent the average percentage for 1 of the 18 blocks in layer 15 of ResNet18. The black ×s represent 1 of the 9 blocks in layer 10.

3.2 Optimizing Array Allocation

Finding the optimal allocation policy for blocks is more difficult. We cannot add redundant blocks to the same layer, because each layer only uses each weight once per operation. Instead, we adopt a new grouping strategy for arrays: rather than duplicating layers of arrays, we duplicate blocks of arrays. To find the optimal array allocation policy, we propose a linear time $(O(N)$ complexity) solution discussed below. This is especially important for larger networks like ResNet18, where there are 247 blocks and finding an optimal solution could be quite difficult.

With this new grouping strategy, we can allocate using the same technique as before. First we gather an approximation of the average MAC per cycle for each block of arrays. We can do this two ways. The first option, is running a cycle accurate simulator on some example data to get a very accurate approximation. The second option is to profile the distribution of '1's in the activations gathered from a large set of examples run on a GPU. Once we have an approximation for the MAC per cycle of each block, we can compute the expected number of cycles each block will take to perform it's partial dot product. Once we have cycle approximations for each block, we begin allocating arrays to each block. While we have free (not allocated) arrays, we loop through and allocate arrays to the block with the highest expected latency. We provide pseudo-code for this technique in Algorithm 1. Once we run out of arrays or the number of arrays left over is not enough to allocate to the slowest block we have found the optimal allocation. We call this allocation method *block-wise*, whereas allocation based on the layer is *layer-wise*.

Algorithm 1. Array Allocation

1: **procedure** ARRAY ALLOCATION(**Arrays** : integer, **Size** : Array, **Perf** : Array)
2:     Allocation = [0, 0, ... 0]
3:     min = Argmin(Allocation ⊙ Perf)
4:     **while** Arrays > Cost[min] **do**
5:         Arrays = Arrays - Size[min]
6:         Allocation[min] = Allocation[min] + 1
7:         min = Argmin(Allocation ⊙ Perf)
8:     return Allocation

3.3   Block-Wise Data Flow

To make use of our new allocation policy, a new data flow strategy is required. Since arrays from the same layer are not grouped together, we treat these blocks as generalized compute units rather than being bound to a specific duplicate. Therefore, we no longer stall for the slowest block in a layer, but rather just send work to the next available block. This means that the same blocks will no longer be working together on the same input data, and thus will not be part of the same gather and accumulate procedure. As a result, a new routing and scheduling policy is required because blocks will not always send their partial sums to the same accumulator for every input feature map. To implement this idea, we include output feature destination addresses in the packet containing data when sending input features to each block. Upon completing a partial dot product, a block sends their computed partial sums to the designated accumulator and requests additional work from the memory controller.

4   CIM-Based Architecture

Although our allocation policy will work for any general CIM based accelerator, we adopted a similar architecture to previous work [3,14]. Our basic processing element (PE) contains 64 128 × 128 arrays. We choose 64 arrays because it provides each block with sufficient network bandwidth and SRAM capacity, while maintaining good SRAM density and low interconnect overhead. Our input data, weights, and activations are all 8 bits. Each array has 1 3-bit ADC for every 8 columns where a single column is pitch-matched with a comparator. We choose 3-bit because state of the art devices [9] have 5% variance and 3-bits is the maximum precision that can be read with no error. We shift one bit from each of the 128 inputs in one at a time which takes 8 cycles. In the best case scenario, we perform all 128 rows at the same time. In the worst case scenario, it takes 16 cycles since we enable every single row. Therefore, each array takes anywhere from 64 to 1024 cycles and performs a 128×16 dot product. In all designs we consider, we use use the same 64 array PE and simply increase the count per design.

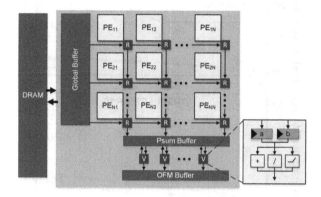

Fig. 10. Block-wise network architecture with 1 router (R) per PE. All input features are routed from the global buffer to PEs. All partial sums are routed from PE to vector unit (V), and vector unit to output feature buffer.

The activation inputs to the RRAM sub-arrays are stored in on-chip SRAM, while the input images are read in from external DRAM. Matrix multiplication is performed by the PEs, while custom vector units are used to perform vector-wise accumulation, bias addition, quantization, and relu. We use a $N \times N$ mesh network for communication between PEs, memory, and vector units shown in Fig. 10. Since blocks vary in size and no block contains 64 sub-arrays, we have to partition the PE to contain several blocks. This configuration implies that the different blocks share the same virtualized input and output ports. As discussed in Sect. 3, input and output vectors are packetized to include destination information. Each block in the PE is given an id that is used to route packets to and from. Upon completing a partial dot product, a block sends its partial sum to vector units where they are accumulated and activation functions and quantization is applied.

5 Results

To benchmark block-wise allocation, we compare with several other techniques: weight-based allocation, performance-based layer-wise allocation, and the baseline algorithm which does not use zero-skipping. We empirically evaluate performance and array utilization for the three techniques on ImageNet using ResNet18 and CIFAR10 using VGG11. We run these techniques in a custom simulation framework designed to evaluate performance and power of compute in-memory using standard CMOS and RRAM models from [16].

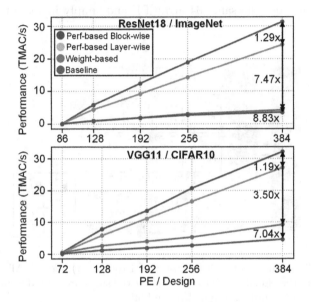

Fig. 11. Inference performance for ResNet18 and VGG11 by algorithm and design size assuming 100 MHz clock. For ResNet18, block-wise allocation sustains a 8.83×, 7.47×, and 1.29× speedup over baseline (no zero-skipping), weight-based, and performance-based layer-wise allocation. For VGG11, block-wise allocation sustains a 7.04×, 3.50×, and 1.19× speedup.

Our simulator performs cycle-accurate implementations of convolutional and fully connected layers. It is based in Python, but runs array level operations in C for faster evaluation. We model components in the design in object oriented fashion, iterating through all components in all PEs each cycle. We embed performance counters in our ADC and sub-array objects to track metrics like stalls so we can calculate utilization. As input, the simulator takes the network weights, input images, PE level configuration, and chip-level configuration. The PE-level configuration includes details like the precision of each ADC and size of the sub-array. The chip-level configuration contains the number of PEs and details about array allocation and mapping. As output, the simulator produces a table with all desired performance counters and all intermediate layer activations that are verified against a TensorFlow [17] implementation for correctness.

To show how our algorithm scales by the size of the design, we have evaluated the different allocation algorithms on several different designs with increasing numbers of PEs. In Fig. 11, we plot performance versus the number of PEs in the design for both ResNet18 and VGG11. For ResNet18, we begin at 86 PEs since this contains the minimum number of arrays (5472) required to store ResNet18. At 86 PEs, all algorithms yield the same result since no duplication can be done and weights are simply allocated to store ResNet18. From there, we begin increasing the design size by $\frac{1}{2}$ powers of 2. Block-wise allocation performs the best achieving 29% improvement over layerwise-allocation and 7.47× improvement over both weight-based and baseline (not zero-skipping) algorithms. We follow the same procedure for VGG11, however we observe that block-wise allocation yields less performance advantage. This is because VGG11 has roughly half the layers that ResNet18 has. It is more difficult to allocate evenly amongst a deeper network and therefore, block-wise allocation yields better results on deeper networks.

To better understand why we get these large performance improvements, it is useful to analyze array utilization. We define array utilization as the average utilization of all the arrays in the design, where utilization for a single array can be defined as:

$$\text{Utilization} = \text{Cycle}_{\text{Active}}/(\text{Cycle}_{\text{Active}} + \text{Cycle}_{\text{Stall}})$$

In Fig. 13, we visualize layer-wise utilization of the 20 convolutional layers from ResNet18 using the different techniques. It is clear that block-wise allocation sustains the highest array utilization across nearly all layers in the network, easily outperforming the other techniques. Weight-based allocation performs very poorly because of the very different speeds of each layer and block we showed in Figs. 7 and 9. It should be noted that we do not plot the baseline algorithm because it has different array level performance given that zero skipping is not used.

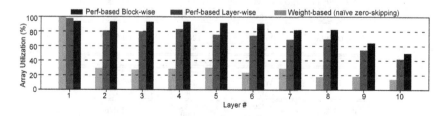

Fig. 12. Array utilization by layer for VGG11 on CIFAR10. Baseline not shown because zero skipping is not used.

In Fig. 13, we visualize layer-wise utilization of the 10 convolutional layers from VGG11 using the different techniques. We observe a similar pattern to

338   B. Crafton et al.

ResNet18, with a couple differences. First, the disparity in utilization between
the methods is not as significant since there is not as many layers, and thus the
pipeline is easier to balance. Second, the first layer's utilization is higher for the
layer-wise methods. This indicates it is a significant bottleneck in the pipeline
and that it is severely under-allocated.

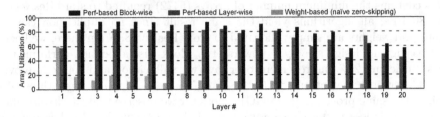

Fig. 13. Array utilization by layer for ResNet18 on ImageNet. Baseline not shown
because zero skipping is not used.

5.1 Power Evaluation

In this work we focus on performance evaluations, however higher array utilization results in less leakage power and improved energy efficiency. To compare
the power consumption of the various allocation methods and dataflows, we use
Neurosim [16] which has been developed to evaluate the performance of DNN
accelerators using eNVM technology. Like prior work for CMOS based memory
[18] and non-volatile memory [19], Neurosim models power throughout the system using a hierarchical model computing CV^2 for each component. Using the
models for these components, we can approximate the system level power for a
large scale CIM accelerator. In Fig. 14, we provide select parameters used by our
tool to approximate total power.

Component	Parameter	Specification	Energy
Processing Element (PE)			
Input Buffer	Type	SRAM	64 fJ/bit
	Width	128 bit	
	Size	4KB	
Sub-Array (SA)			
DFF	Type	Register	85 fJ/bit
	Width	256	
	Size	256b	
RRAM Array	Size	256 × 256	1.1 fJ/bit
	Cell Precision	1 bit	
ADC	Number	32	45 fJ/bit
	Precision	3 bit	
Shift, Add	Number	32	100fJ/op
	Precision	24 bit	

Fig. 14. Simulation parameters used for hardware components at both the sub-array
and processing element level.

Given that the computation being done by each method is identical, the differences in power occur from leakage current in the ADCs, SRAM, and logic as well as interconnect utilization. In Fig. 15, we plot TOP/W for the various allocation methods for both ResNet18 and VGG11. Power efficiency changes negligibly versus design size, and thus we only show results for the 256 PE design (16384 arrays). Overall, VGG11 has higher efficiency because it the feature maps (activations) are more sparse. For ResNet18, block-wise allocation yields the highest efficiency, achieving 1.07×, 1.75×, and 4.01× improvement over layer-wise, weight-based, and baseline, respectively. For VGG11, we see a similar result, where block-wise achieves 1.03×, 1.31×, and 4.48× improvement over layer-wise, weight-based, and baseline, respectively. The efficiency advantage for block-wise versus layer-wise and weight-based can be attributed to the lower latency, and thus less total leakage power. However, the massive improvement over baseline is due to zero-skipping.

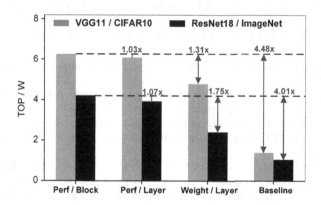

Fig. 15. Inference efficiency (TOP/W) for ResNet18 and VGG11 by algorithm.

6   Conclusion

In this paper we demonstrate the efficacy of a new technique and data flow to improve array utilization in CIM accelerators. Given that the write energy of eNVM is high, CIM arrays contain fixed weights unlike CMOS PEs which can perform any operation in a DNN. Thus array utilization becomes a key challenge since only some arrays can perform particular operations. By profiling input statistics and relaxing our data flow, we can allocate arrays to maximize utilization and as a result, performance. The proposed allocation algorithm and data flow performs 7.47× better than naive allocation and a layer-wise dataflow.

Acknowledgement. This work was funded by the U.S. Department of Defense's Multidisciplinary University Research Initiatives (MURI) Program under grant number FOA: N00014-16-R-FO05 and the Semiconductor Research Corporation under the Center for Brain Inspired Computing (C-BRIC) and Qualcomm.

References

1. Chen, Y.-H., Krishna, T., Emer, J.S., Sze, V.: Eyeriss: an energy-efficient reconfigurable accelerator for deep convolutional neural networks. IEEE J. Solid-State Circuits **52**(1), 127–138 (2017)
2. Davies, M., et al.: Loihi: a neuromorphic manycore processor with on-chip learning. IEEE Micro **38**(1), 82–99 (2018)
3. Shafiee, A., et al.: Isaac: a convolutional neural network accelerator with in-situ analog arithmetic in crossbars. ACM SIGARCH Comput. Architect. News **44**(3), 14–26 (2016)
4. Crafton, B., Spetalnick, S., Murali, G., Krishna, T., Lim, S.K., Raychowdhury, A.: Breaking barriers: maximizing array utilization for compute in-memory fabrics. In: 2020 IFIP/IEEE 28th International Conference on Very Large Scale Integration (VLSI-SoC), IEEE (2020)
5. Deng, J., Dong, W., Socher, R., Li, L.-J., Li, K., Fei-Fei, L.: Imagenet: a large-scale hierarchical image database. In: IEEE Conference on Computer Vision and Pattern Recognition, 2009 (CVPR 2009). pp. 248–255, IEEE (2009)
6. He, K., Zhang, X., Ren, S., Sun, J.: Deep residual learning for image recognition. In: Proceedings of the IEEE Conference on Computer Vision and Pattern Recognition, pp. 770–778 (2016)
7. Krizhevsky, A., Hinton, G., et al.: Learning multiple layers of features from tiny images (2009)
8. Simonyan, K., Zisserman, A.: Very deep convolutional networks for large-scale image recognition. arXiv preprint arXiv:1409.1556 (2014)
9. Wu, J., et al.: A 40nm low-power logic compatible phase change memory technology. In: 2018 IEEE International Electron Devices Meeting (IEDM), pp. 27–36, IEEE (2018)
10. Yoon, J.-H., Chang, M., Khwa, W.-S., Chih, Y.-D., Chang, M.-F., Raychowdhury, A.: Ternary-weight compute-in-memory RRAM macro with voltage-sensing read and write verification for reliable multi-bit rram operation. In: 2021 IEEE Custom Integrated Circuits Conference (CICC), pp. 1–4, IEEE (2021)
11. Yoon, J.-H., Chang, M., Khwa, W.-S., Chih, Y.-D., Chang, M.-F., Raychowdhury, A.: 29.1 a 40nm 64kb 56.67 tops/w read-disturb-tolerant compute-in-memory/digital RRAM macro with active-feedback-based read and in-situ write verification. In: 2021 IEEE International Solid-State Circuits Conference (ISSCC), vol. 64, pp. 404–406, IEEE (2021)
12. Yang, T.-H., et al.: Sparse RERAM engine: joint exploration of activation and weight sparsity in compressed neural networks. In: Proceedings of the 46th International Symposium on Computer Architecture, pp. 236–249 (2019)
13. Yu, S., Chen, P.-Y.: Emerging memory technologies: recent trends and prospects. IEEE Solid-State Circuits Mag. **8**(2), 43–56 (2016)
14. Peng, X., Liu, R., Yu, S.: Optimizing weight mapping and data flow for convolutional neural networks on processing-in-memory architectures. Regular Papers. IEEE Trans. Circuits Syst. (2019)
15. Crafton, B., Spetalnick, S., Raychowdhury, A.: Counting cards: exploiting weight and variance distributions for robust compute in-memory. arXiv preprint arXiv:2006.03117. (2020)
16. Chen, P.-Y., Peng, X., Yu, S.: Neurosim: a circuit-level macro model for benchmarking neuro-inspired architectures in online learning. IEEE Trans. Comput Aided Design Integr. Circuits Syst. **37**(12), 3067–3080 (2018)

17. Abadi, M., et al.: Tensorflow: a system for large-scale machine learning. In: 12th {USENIX} Symposium on Operating Systems Design and Implementation ({OSDI} 16), pp. 265–283 (2016)
18. Wilton, S.J., Jouppi, N.P.: Cacti: an enhanced cache access and cycle time model. IEEE J. Solid-State Circuits **31**(5), 677–688 (1996)
19. Dong, X., Xu, C., Xie, Y., Jouppi, N.P.: NVSim: A circuit-level performance, energy, and area model for emerging nonvolatile memory. IEEE Trans. Comput. Aided Design Integr. Circuits Syst. **31**(7), 994–1007 (2012)

abstractPIM: A Technology Backward-Compatible Compilation Flow for Processing-In-Memory

Adi Eliahu$^{(\boxtimes)}$, Rotem Ben-Hur, Ronny Ronen, and Shahar Kvatinsky

Technion - Israel Institute of Technology, 3200003 Haifa, Israel
{adieliahu,rotembenhur}@campus.technion.ac.il
ronny.ronen@technion.ac.il, shahar@ee.technion.ac.il

Abstract. The von Neumann architecture, in which the memory and the computation units are separated, demands massive data traffic between the memory and the CPU. To reduce data movement, new technologies and computer architectures have been explored. The use of memristors, which are devices with both memory and computation capabilities, has been considered for different processing-in-memory (PIM) solutions, including using memristive stateful logic for a programmable digital PIM system. Nevertheless, all previous work has focused on a specific stateful logic family, and on optimizing the execution for a certain target machine. These solutions require new compiler and compilation when changing the target machine, and provide no backward compatibility with other target machines. In this chapter, we present abstractPIM, a new compilation concept and flow which enables executing any function within the memory, using different stateful logic families and different instruction set architectures (ISAs). By separating the code generation into two independent components, intermediate representation of the code using target independent ISA and then microcode generation for a specific target machine, we provide a flexible flow with backward compatibility and lay foundations for a PIM compiler. Using abstractPIM, we explore various logic technologies and ISAs and how they impact each other, and discuss the challenges associated with it, such as the increase in execution time.

Keywords: Memristor · processing-in-memory · RRAM · stateful logic · ISA

1 Introduction

In recent years, the trend of data-intensive applications has become popular. Data-intensive applications process large volumes of data and also exhibit compute-intensive properties, and therefore, they require massive data transfer between the memory and the central processing unit (CPU). Since there is a large performance gap between the CPU and the memory [1], this massive data

© IFIP International Federation for Information Processing 2021
Published by Springer Nature Switzerland AG 2021
A. Calimera et al. (Eds.): VLSI-SoC 2020, IFIP AICT 621, pp. 343–361, 2021.
https://doi.org/10.1007/978-3-030-81641-4_16

transfer has become a bottleneck in execution of data-intensive applications. This bottleneck is often called the *memory wall*. As a result of the memory wall challenge, processing-in-memory (PIM) has become attractive [2,3]. Due to the recent advances in memory technologies, *e.g.*, resistive random access memory (RRAM) [4] and PCM [5], PIM has gained interest and has become an integral part of many computer architectures. The memristor, which functions as both a memory element and a computation unit, can help reducing data transfer between the CPU and the memory and thus addresses the memory wall problem. By applying voltage across the device, the memristor performs switching between two resistance values, high resistance value (R_{OFF}) and low resistance value (R_{ON}), therefore it can function as a binary memory element. To increase the memristor density, it can be programmed to have intermediate resistance between R_{OFF} and R_{ON}, thus achieving multi-level cell (MLC) storage capability.

In addition to their storage capabilities, memristors can also be used for computation. There are two approaches to use memristors as computation units. The first approach is using the memristor in application-specific architectures. Memristors can be used for the purpose of a specific computation. For example, in [6], an efficient vector-matrix multiplication using memristor analog computation is demonstrated. In this manner, the dual-function memristor can perform efficient computing and reduce data transfer requirements between the CPU and the memory. Numerous accelerators integrating analog memristor-based computations have recently been developed, mostly for artificial intelligence applications [7].

The second approach of using memristor as a computation unit, on which we focus in this chapter, is called 'stateful logic'. Using stateful logic, memristive logic gates are constructed within the memory array for general-purpose computation. Stateful logic enables programmable general-purpose architectures since every memristive cell can be used as a storage element, as well as an input, output or a register. Several memristor logic gate families have been designed, including MAGIC [8], IMPLY [9], and resistive majority [10].

Some stateful logic families can be easily integrated within a memristive crossbar array with minor modifications. Designing a functionally complete logic gate set using such a family, *e.g.*, a MAGIC NOR gate, enables in-memory execution of any function. Various logic gate families have been explored in the literature, each of them has different advantages. Previous efforts to execute a function within the memory concentrated on utilizing a specific PIM family and optimizing the latency, area, or throughput using this technology, *e.g.*, SAID [11] and SIMPLE [12] for optimizing latency in MAGIC technology [8], SIMPLER [13] for optimizing throughput in MAGIC technology [8] and K-map based synthesis [14] for optimizing latency and area in IMPLY [9].

While these previous works have considerably improved the logic function execution in terms of latency, area, or throughput, they are strongly dependent on the PIM family and its basic operations, and therefore are limited to a specific target machine. However, each PIM technology has different advantages, and therefore, flexibility in the used PIM technology has many motivations. For example, the MAGIC family provides memristive crossbar compatibility and high parallelism by executing MAGIC logic gates on aligned elements in different rows of the memristive crossbar. A different PIM technology, called CRS [15], provides flexibility by executing 16 Boolean functions in a single operation.

In this chapter, we propose a new hierarchical compilation method for PIM, which provides flexibility and is not restricted to a certain PIM technology. Our flow separates the code generation into two components. The first component is intermediate code generation using target independent instruction set architecture (ISA). The second component is microcode generation for a specific target machine and PIM technology. The third component, runtime execution, executes the code. The first component, which is run by the programmer, is independent of the PIM technology. In this component, a compiled program that consists of target-independent instructions is generated. In the second component, which is target-dependent, these instructions are translated into an execution sequence of micro-operations supported by the target machine. The second component is performed by the PIM technology provider. In the third component, at runtime, the compiled code instructions are sent from the CPU to the memory controller, which contains the instruction execution sequences from the second component. The controller translates the instructions into micro-operations and sends them to the memory. This third component is similar to an instruction-level opcode being executed using micro-operations in the x86 processors [16].

Figure 1 demonstrates the first and third flow components of a half adder logic for different ISAs and target machines. The first two implementations, shown in Fig. 1(a) and 1(b), demonstrate the use of the same target machine while using different ISAs. The code is compiled for a machine that its PIM technology supports only MAGIC NOR logic gates. However, the first example targets a controller which supports only NOR ISA commands, whereas the second example supports all the 2-input and 1-output logic functions as its ISA. In the first component, a netlist and compiled program composed of the ISA commands, dubbed *instructions*, are generated. In Fig. 1(a), the netlist is composed of five logic gates that implement the half adder logic, and in Fig. 1(b) it is composed of two gates (AND and XOR). The number of gates in the netlist is a representative of both the code size (or number of commands sent from the CPU to the PIM machine), and the control load between the CPU and the memory controller. We will refer to it for the rest of the chapter as *code size*. The code size is also a means of estimation of the code abstraction achieved by our flow. In these examples, the code sizes are five and two, respectively. The second component is the microcode generation, where each command is translated to a sequence of MAGIC NOR operations and is embedded in the controller. In the third component, the code is executed. The commands are sent from the CPU to the controller, and then from the controller to the memory; hence, the code size is reduced with minimal changes to the in-memory implementation, namely, adding a few states to the memory controller to support other operations.

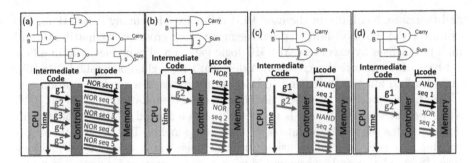

Fig. 1. Compilation example for a half adder using various ISAs and target machines. (a) A NOR ISA and MAGIC NOR target machine. (b) All 2-input and single-output ISA and MAGIC NOR target machine. (c) All 2-input and single-output ISA and MAGIC NAND target machine. (d) All 2-input and single-output ISA and 2-input and single-output MAGIC target machine.

Figures 1(b), 1(c) and 1(d) demonstrate the use of the same ISA while using different target machines. These three examples use all 2-input logic functions as their ISA, but the first machine uses MAGIC NOR technology, the second uses MAGIC NAND technology and the third uses all MAGIC 2-input logic functions. This example demonstrates the ISA definition flexibility and command hierarchy enabled by our method, and the possible reduction in code size and reduction in the control load between the CPU and the memory controller. It also demonstrates the backward compatibility feature; in Figs. 1(c)–(d), machines with technologies which enable lower execution time are used, and yet the generated intermediate code is backward compatible with other PIM technologies. The separation into two independent code generation components also enables the exploration of the impact of the ISA on the used target machine and vice versa.

This chapter makes the following contributions:

1. Development of technology-independent and ISA-flexible flow (first presented in [17]) for executing any logic function to a memristive crossbar array. Our technique, called abstractPIM, presents a hierarchical view and includes three components. It is a solid foundation for implementation of compilers for general-purpose memristive PIM architectures. This chapter also extends the work in [17] and discusses future work of the abstractPIM flow.
2. Examining the impact of the ISA and the target machine on each other using abstractPIM, in terms of flexibility, performance and code size.
3. A 56% reduction in the control load between the CPU and the memory controller as compared to state-of-the-art solutions [13], demonstrated for different benchmarks.

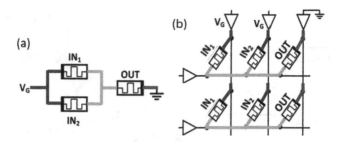

Fig. 2. MAGIC NOR gates. (a) MAGIC NOR gate schematic. (b) Two MAGIC NOR gates in a crossbar configuration, executed in parallel.

2 Background and Related Work

2.1 Stateful Logic

In stateful logic families [18], the logic gate inputs and outputs are represented by memristor resistance. We demonstrate the stateful logic operation using MAGIC [8] gates, which are used as a baseline in this chapter. Figure 2(a) depicts a MAGIC NOR logic gate; the gate inputs and output are represented as memristor resistance. The two input memristors are connected to an operating voltage, V_g, and the output memristor is connected to the ground. The output memristor is initialized at R_{ON} and the input memristors are set with the input values. During the execution, the resistance of the output memristor changes according to the ratio between the input values and the initialized value at the output. For example, when one or two inputs of the gate are logical '1', according to the voltage divider rule, the voltage across the output memristor is higher than $\frac{V_g}{2}$. This causes the output memristor to switch from R_{ON} to R_{OFF}, matching the NOR function truth table. The MAGIC NOR gate can be integrated in a memristive crossbar array row, as shown in Fig. 2(b). Integration within the crossbar array enables executing logic gates in different rows in the same clock cycle, thus providing massive parallelism.

2.2 Logic Execution Within a Memristive Crossbar Array

In CMOS logic, execution of an arbitrary logic function is performed by signals propagating from the inputs towards the outputs. However, in stateful logic, the execution is performed by a sequence of operations, each operation operates in a single clock cycle. In each clock cycle, one operation can be performed either on a single row, or on multiple rows concurrently. Overall, the execution takes several clock cycles. A valid logic execution is defined by mapping of every logic gate in the desired function to several cells in the crossbar array, and operating it in a specific clock cycle.

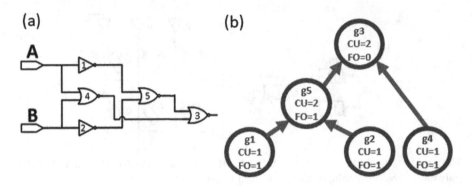

Fig. 3. SIMPLER CU and FO node values example. (a) An example netlist. (b) The SIMPLER DAG generated from the example netlist, including the CU and FO values.

Many tools to generate the sequence of operations and map them into the memristive crossbar array cells have been discussed in the literature, *e.g.*, SIMPLE [12], SAID [11], the tool suggested by Yadav *et al.* [19] and the tool suggested by Thangkhiew *et al.* [20]. These tools map the logic to several rows in the memristive crossbar. Recently, a new method, called SIMPLER [13], which maps the logic to a single row, has been presented. This method tries to minimize the number of initialization cycles in the execution sequence to reduce the overall number of execution cycles. The input logic function of SIMPLER is synthesized using the ABC synthesis tool [21], which generates a netlist implementing the function with NOT and NOR gates only. Then, an in-house mapping tool builds a directed acyclic graph (DAG), in which every node represents a gate in the netlist. Each node is given two values: fanout (FO) and cell usage (CU). The former indicates how many parents the node has (*i.e.*, how many gates are directly connected to its output), and the latter estimates the cell usage of the sub-graph starting from the node (*i.e.*, the number of cells necessary for the execution of the sub-graph). An example of the CU and FO node values is demonstrated in Fig. 3. Figure 3(a) shows a netlist, and Fig. 3(b) shows its corresponding SIMPLER DAG with the CU and FO node values.

The CU of a node V is calculated by:

– If V is a leaf then:
$$CU(V) = 1 \qquad (1)$$

– Else, sort all N children of V by descending order of their CU values. Then:
$$CU(V) = max\{CU(V_{child,i})\} + i - 1\}, \forall i = (1 \; to \; N) \qquad (2)$$

Based on the CU and FO values, the mapping tool determines the order in which the gates operate. Additionally, the mapping tool traces the number of available cells, and when they are all occupied, it adds an initialization cycle in which cells are initialized and then reused. The gate execution ordering is determined such that the number of initialization cycles, and consequently overall execution time, will be minimized.

The gap between target machine constraints and architectural design choices, *e.g.*, ISA, has not been addressed in the aforementioned mapping tools. Attempts have been made in existing mapping tools to support complex operations in the in-memory execution, *e.g.*, 4-input LUT function [11]. However, their flexibility is limited and they do not completely separate the intermediate code generation and microcode generation, therefore they impose target machine and ISA dependency and do not provide backward compatibility with other target machines.

3 abstractPIM: Three-Component Code Execution Flow for PIM

The abstractPIM flow includes two code generation components and one execution component. In the first component, *intermediate representation generation*, the program is compiled into a sequence of target independent instructions based on a defined ISA. In the second component, *microcode generation*, each instruction is translated into micro-operations that are supported by the target machine. The translation is performed once per instruction, and is embedded in the controller design. We adopt an existing mapping flow and modify it to support different ISAs and PIM technologies. In the third component, *runtime execution*, the instructions in the compiled code are sent from the CPU to the controller, which translates them into micro-operations and sends them to the memory.

Existing logic execution methods use a set of basic logic operations to implement a logic function. They rely on a memory controller which is configured to perform these operations by applying voltages on the rows and columns of the memory array. In this chapter, we assume that the memory controller is configured to perform several logic operations, dubbed *instructions*. Their execution sequence is determined according to a specific target machine and the PIM technology it supports. For example, if the ISA includes an AND instruction and the used technology is MAGIC NOR, 3 computation operations and 1 initialization cycle will be executed one after the other to run the AND instruction, as demonstrated in Fig. 1(b), gate 1. An alternative PIM technology that consists of NAND gates will perform the same AND instruction using two NAND computations and one initialization cycle (Fig. 1(c)). The instruction execution using different PIM technologies may differ in the execution time and cell usage. Our approach raises the system abstraction level and reduces the flow dependency of the specific PIM technology. It also moves one step closer towards defining a general instruction set to a memristor-based PIM architecture and designing its compiler.

The controller support of complex instructions also reduces the code size and hence the amount of code transfer between the CPU and the memory controller. However, there is a code size and execution time trade-off; the reduction in the code size may cause an execution time penalty. In a machine which supports NOR operations, the execution time, measured by the number of clock cycles in the execution sequence, is lowest when the ISA includes only NOR instructions since using basic instructions allows finer granularity. However, when using other instructions, they will be eventually executed using a NOR execution sequence. Any use of other instructions, which are, in fact, implemented using NOR micro-operations, might increase the number of NOR operations, hence the execution time.

For example, in Fig. 1, the first NOR-based implementation takes $5T_{NOR}$ clock cycles to operate, where T_{op} is the number of clock cycles required for execution of an *op* operation. The second implementation, however, takes a total of $T_{AND} + T_{XOR}$ clock cycles. In a machine which supports MAGIC NOR operations, the first implementation takes 10 clock cycles (2 cycles per NOR), and the second implementation takes 11 clock cycles (4 for the AND2 gate and 7 for the XOR2 gate, according to Table 1). Some execution cycles are computation cycles and some are initialization cycles, as further elaborated is Sect. 5.

The instruction hierarchy in abstractPIM improves the flexibility of the compilation flow, as demonstrated in Figs. 1(b)–(d). This is similar to high-level programming compared to assembly coding, which can improve flexibility at the cost of execution time penalty. While we demonstrate it using MAGIC-based logic families, the flow can be easily used for other target machines and stateful logic families. In our study, we choose different groups of ISAs, and different target machines that support different logic families. We demonstrate how they can be used to execute different benchmarks, and analyze the code size and execution time of the configurations.

4   Case Study: Vector-Matrix Multiplication

We showcase our flow with a vector-matrix multiplication (VMM) benchmark (a 5 element vector and a 5×5 matrix with 8-bit elements), which is useful in many applications, *e.g.*, neural networks. The benchmark is tested over a target machine with 1024-sized memristive memory row that supports the MAGIC NOR logic family. The supported set of operations (NOT, NOR2) by the target machine is called *TS0*. Other logic families are discussed in Sect. 6. We first compile the benchmark for a basic case, where the ISA is also the technology set, *i.e.*, *TS0*. The selection of this ISA enabled a fair comparison between abstractPIM and existing logic execution methods, such as SIMPLER [13], which do not use a two-component code generation process. The used technology sets supported by the target machines we use and their instruction parameters are listed in Table 1. Each instruction has three parameters: the number of inputs (I), the number of outputs (O) and the number of execution cycles (T). The first two parameters are technology independent, whereas the last parameter is technology dependent. The parameter corresponding to technology set N is T_N. For example, the OR instruction has two inputs and a single output ($I = 2$, $O = 1$), and requires, when using a target machine that supports *TS0*, three clock cycles for execution ($T_0 = 3$, two computation cycles and one initialization cycle). Using ISA=*TS0* for the VMM benchmark, there are 25470 execution cycles, out of which, half are initialization cycles and half are computation cycles. Therefore, the code size is 12735 instructions.

Table 1. Instruction Execution Characteristics for MAGIC Families

Instruction	I	O	T_0	T_1	$TS0$	$TS1$	$IS2$	$IS3$
NOT	1	1	$1+1$	$1+1$	✓	✓	✓	✓
NOR2	2	1	$1+1$	$2+1$	✓	✓	✓	✓
NOR3	3	1	$3+1$	$3+1$	-	-	-	✓
NOR4	4	1	$5+1$	$4+1$	-	-	-	✓
OR2	2	1	$2+1$	$1+1$	-	✓	✓	✓
OR3	3	1	$4+1$	$2+1$	-	-	-	✓
OR4	4	1	$6+1$	$3+1$	-	-	-	✓
AND2	2	1	$3+1$	$1+1$	-	✓	✓	✓
AND3	3	1	$6+1$	$2+1$	-	-	-	✓
AND4	4	1	$9+1$	$3+1$	-	-	-	✓
NAND2	2	1	$4+1$	$2+1$	-	-	✓	✓
NAND3	3	1	$7+1$	$3+1$	-	-	-	✓
NAND4	4	1	$10+1$	$4+1$	-	-	-	✓
XOR2	2	1	$6+1$	$5+1$	-	-	✓	✓
XOR3	3	1	$11+1$	$9+1$	-	-	-	✓
XOR4	4	1	$16+1$	$15+1$	-	-	-	✓
XNOR2	2	1	$5+1$	$5+1$	-	-	✓	✓
XNOR3	3	1	$11+1$	$6+1$	-	-	-	✓
XNOR4	4	1	$16+1$	$8+1$	-	-	-	✓
IMPLIES	2	1	$2+1$	$2+1$	-	-	✓	✓
!IMPLIES	2	1	$2+1$	$2+1$	-	-	✓	✓
MUX	3	1	$7+1$	$4+1$	-	-	✓	✓
HA	2	2	$7+1$	$6+1$	-	-	✓	✓
HS	2	2	$6+1$	$5+1$	-	-	✓	✓

The execution time format is $T_c + T_i$, where T_c is the number of computation cycles and T_i is the number of initialization cycles.

In attempt to reduce the code size, we used *IS2*, which contains all the functions with 1 or 2 inputs and 1 output, excluding trivial functions, *e.g.*, constant '0' and identity functions[1]. The set also includes common combinational functions with more than 2 inputs or more than 1 output. Since the number of such functions is large, even for a small number of inputs, we chose three functions which, according to experiments we conducted, were useful in certain benchmarks: half adder [HA], multiplexer [MUX] and half subtractor [HS]. These instructions demonstrate the ability of our system to support blocks with

---

[1] Identity functions, which are in fact copy operations, can be useful in other mapping methods [11,12], but not in our row-based flow.

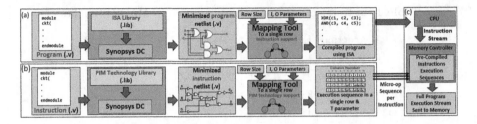

Fig. 4. abstractPIM general flow is composed of three components, two components are for code generation (differences between them are marked with purple.), and the last component is for execution. (a) Intermediate representation generation. (b) Microcode generation. (c) Runtime execution. (Color figure online)

more than two inputs or more than a single output. Because of the circular dependency limitation of our flow, which is further elaborated in Sect. 7, some useful instructions, *e.g.*, 4-bit adder, could not be used. Using *IS2*, code size is reduced by 52%, but execution time is increased by 16%.

To demonstrate the benefit of a larger number of instruction inputs and reduce the execution time, *IS3* was defined. It contains the *IS2* instructions, and the 2-input and single output symmetric functions from *IS2* extended to 3 and 4 inputs. Using *IS3*, lower execution time and code size, as compared to *IS2*, are achieved. The execution time is increased by only 8%, and the code size is reduced by 57%, as compared to *TS0*.

5 abstractPIM Flow and Methodology

The flow of abstractPIM is composed of three components, as shown in Fig. 4. In the first component, the *intermediate representation generation*, the input is a Verilog program. The program is synthesized using the Synopsys DC synthesis tool [22], where the synthesis standard cell library includes the ISA in .lib format. The Synopsys DC synthesis tool was chosen since it supports multi-output cell synthesis. Furthermore, whereas other tools, such ABC [21], support only structural Verilog, Synopsys DC supports behavioral SystemVerilog as well, therefore eases the burden of programming. Then, a compiled program is generated using a modified and extended version of the SIMPLER mapping tool [13]. This tool builds a directed acyclic graph (DAG). In its original form, every node represents a NOR gate in the netlist, since SIMPLER was designed specifically for the MAGIC NOR family [8]. In the modified mapping tool, each node represents a wider variety of instructions based on the ISA. Using the DAG, the inputs and outputs of the instructions are mapped to row cells in the memristive array, and a compiled program is generated. The I and O parameters are used to build the DAG and are technology-independent. The T parameters (see Table 1), which are technology-dependent and determined in the second component, are not used for compilation. Therefore, a complete separation between the code generation components and backward compatibility with other target machines is achieved.

The second component of the abstractPIM flow is *microcode generation*. For each instruction, a microcode is generated by synthesizing the instruction to a micro-operation netlist and then to an execution sequence, which includes mapping to the memristive crossbar array and intermediate computation cell allocation based on specific PIM technology. The second component input is the instruction implemented in Verilog. The instruction is synthesized using the Synopsys DC synthesis tool for a specific PIM technology, described in the synthesis standard cell library. In this chapter, we demonstrate the flow with the MAGIC [8] family, and therefore we extended the SIMPLER [13] mapping tool to support different MAGIC operations instead of only MAGIC NOR. The execution times, listed in Table 1, were calculated using this flow. The second component of abstractPIM can be replaced by handcrafted execution sequences or other mapping tools, depending on the PIM technology in use, which may produce even faster execution sequences. One such example is discussed in Sect. 7.4.

The general SIMPLER flow was adopted in our system for the two first components. Several modifications have been made to support different features in our tool:

1. **Modifications to the synthesis tool and library.** As stated above, the ABC synthesis tool [21] is replaced with Synopsys Design Compiler [22] to support synthesis with multi-output cells. The cell library format was changed to the Liberty library format, which is supported by the new synthesis tool.
2. **Modifications to the mapping tool.** While in SIMPLER each node represents a NOT or NOR operation, in abstractPIM, each node can represent a wider variety of instructions (in the first component) or micro-instructions (in the second component). Other minor changes to the SIMPLER algorithm were also performed, *e.g.*, determining the FO value of each node to include all the connected gates of each gate output and traversing the DAG accordingly, setting the CU values according to the number of outputs of the logic gates, and parsing the new synthesis tool output.

In the third component, *runtime execution*, the two components outputs are used for full program execution. Instructions are sent from the CPU to the controller, and micro-operations are sent from the controller to the memory.

The SIMPLER mapping tool [13] traces the number of available cells, and when they are all occupied, adds a cycle which initializes several unused cells in parallel. However, not all stateful logic families use initialization, therefore initialization cycles should not be part of the first component of the flow so we remove them. In the second component, since the flow is demonstrated using the MAGIC [8] family, we perform initialization. As opposed to SIMPLER, the second component is not aware of the full program and instruction dependencies, therefore optimized parallel initialization cannot be performed. Instead, output and intermediate computation cell initialization is performed at the first cycle of each instruction execution (if needed, additional initialization cycles can be added to the instruction execution sequence). Overall, the component separation enables flexibility and backward compatibility at the cost of execution time penalty.

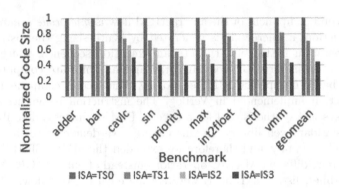

Fig. 5. Normalized code size with respect to TS0 for different ISAs.

In both code generation components, each standard library cell includes several parameters, *e.g.*, propagation delays and area. Since existing commercial synthesis tools are CMOS-oriented, we set these parameters differently and according to our memristor synthesis flow. Propagation delays, which are relevant for propagating signals in CMOS logic, are irrelevant in the context of memristor logic, where the execution time of each logic operation is a single clock cycle, and are set to 0. The area parameter is set equal for all the library cells, thus the synthesis does not prefer any particular cell, and minimizes the number of cells in the netlist, *i.e.*, minimizes the code size.

After developing abstractPIM and composing the ISAs, the code size and execution time were explored. We show the two metrics separately, due to the absence of a natural metric that combines both of them[2]. It is assumed that the clock cycle time was the same for all the technology sets, so that the execution time can be measured in clock cycle units.

We used the EPFL benchmark suite [23]. These benchmarks are native combinational circuits designed to challenge modern logic optimization tools. The benchmark suite is divided into arithmetic and random/control parts. Each benchmark was tested with different technology sets and ISAs, listed in Table 1, within a 512-sized row. One benchmark, *max*, could not be mapped to a 512-sized row and was therefore tested with a 1024-sized row.

6 Results

In this section we evaluate the abstractPIM code size reduction capabilities and execution time penalty, and discuss its abstraction, flexibility and backward compatibility advantages.

The abstraction achieved by our flow using different ISAs enables backward compatibility, and reduces the code size as compared to an implementation based on a specific PIM technology. In the absence of a metric that measures

---

[2] Weighted product of code-size and execution-time was found misleading.

the abstraction level achieved by our flow, we use the code size as a metric of abstraction. Figure 5 shows the code size needed for the execution of each benchmark using different ISAs: $TS0$, $TS1$ (used as ISAs and not as technology sets), $IS2$ and $IS3$. The code size is determined only by the ISA, and is independent of any target machine. Since the chosen sets are subsets of each other, i.e., $TS0 \subset TS1 \subset IS2 \subset IS3$, then $CS_{TS0} > CS_{TS1} > CS_{IS2} > CS_{IS3}$, where CS_{set} is the code size of set. Using $TS1$, $IS2$ and $IS3$ reduced the code size by 30%, 40% and 56% compared to $TS0$, respectively.

For execution time evaluation, we compiled the benchmarks with the different ISAs and for the different target machines to demonstrate the flexibility and PIM technology independence achieved by our flow. We used two "native" configurations: $TS0/TS0$, $TS1/TS1$, and four "abstract" configurations: $TS0/IS2$, $TS0/IS3$, $TS1/IS2$, and $TS1/IS3$, where the notation is target-machine/ISA. We also compare the results to a single-component target-specific flow, SIMPLER [13].

The results are shown in Fig. 6. When comparing $TS0/TS0$ with SIMPLER, the execution time is approximately doubled, since in our flow, every NOR or NOT operation takes an additional cycle for initialization. In SIMPLER, which operates at full program context and not at single instruction context, multiple initialization cycles can be combined and therefore the number of initialization cycles is negligible.

When comparing target machines that use native configurations ($TS0/TS0$ vs. $TS1/TS1$) we observe that the target machine which is more capable ($TS1$) runs faster (30%). When comparing target machines that use the same abstract configuration ($TS0/IS2$ vs. $TS1/IS2$ and $TS0/IS3$ vs. $TS1/IS3$) we also observe that the target machine which is more capable runs faster (32% and 33%, respectively). When comparing the execution time of a native configuration ($TS0/TS0$ and $TS1/TS1$) with that of an abstract configuration using the same target machine, we see that the abstract configuration is slower. $TS0/IS2$ and $TS0/IS3$ are 24% and 8% slower than $TS0/TS0$, respectively. Comparing the native $TS1/TS1$ configuration with the relevant abstract configurations exhibits similar results.

The above observations are quite expected. An important but less obvious benefit of abstractPIM is shown when changing a target machine. For example, when the target machine is upgraded from $TS0$ to $TS1$, a program that has been compiled natively ($TS0/TS0$) executes the same number of cycles when running on $TS1$ (if $TS0 \subset TS1$, otherwise even slower). However, a program that has been compiled in the first place using $IS3$ ($IS2$) runs 27% (16%) faster than on the original machine – no recompilation needed. This is reflected by comparing $TS1/IS3$ ($TS1/IS2$) vs. $TS0/TS0$.

Another observation is that among abstract ISAs, higher abstraction usually exhibits better performance, as shown by comparing $TS0/IS3$ vs. $TS0/IS2$ (13%) and $TS1/IS3$ vs. $TS1/IS2$ (13%). When comparing the results of $TS0/IS2$ or $TS0/IS3$ with $TS0/TS0$, the execution time, almost always, is increased (by 24% and 8% for $TS0/IS2$ and $TS0/IS3$ as compared to $TS0/TS0$, respectively).

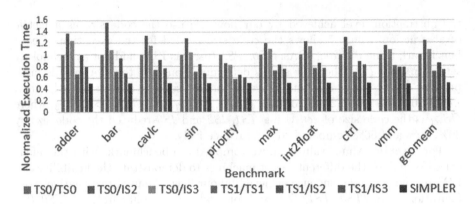

Fig. 6. Normalized execution time with respect to *TS0/TS0* for the different target machines and ISAs.

However, in the *priority* benchmark, the execution time is decreased. On one hand, it is expected that the execution time will increase since using basic instructions allows finer granularity. On the other hand, when the number of instructions is reduced, so does the number of initialization cycles. The two opposite trends cause different benchmark behaviors. Comparison of technology *TS1* and different ISAs shows the same effect.

The flexibility and code size reduction advantages of abstractPIM come with a cost. Using MAGIC technology, in every execution cycle, one write operation is performed every clock cycle, and therefore, the number of execution cycles is also the number of write operations. The additional execution cycles per benchmark result in proportional additional energy consumption and lower effective lifetime. We believe that higher abstraction is worth the cost of these limitations. This is similar to the advantages of the abstraction achieved by a high-level programming language in comparison to low-level programming languages, *e.g.*, assembly.

7 Future Work

In this section, we discuss future research directions that can be explored using abstractPIM, including current limitations of the abstractPIM flow and possible solutions.

7.1 Supporting Multi-output ISA Commands

AbstractPIM supports multi-output instructions (in this work, these instructions are demonstrated as part of ISA and not supported by the target machine, since there are no multi-output MAGIC operations), but not all kinds of multi-output instructions can be used in it, since some may lead to *bogus dependencies* that hinder the execution mapping. Figure 7 demonstrates these bogus dependencies. In the case demonstrated in Fig. 7, the input is the function code:

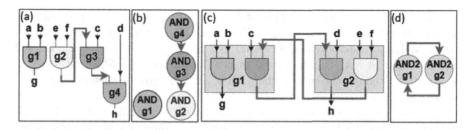

Fig. 7. Compilation with multi-output instructions which creates a circular dependency. (a) Generated netlist using single output gate synthesis. (b) Generated netlist using multi-output gate synthesis. (c) The graph that represents netlist (a), which is a DAG and can be used for the mapping algorithm. (d) The graph that represents netlist (b), which includes a cyclic dependency. (Color figure online)

$g = ab$, $h = cdef$. In Fig. 7(a), the code is compiled using single-output instructions (AND2 instruction), whereas in Fig. 7(b), it is compiled using multi-output instructions (an instruction which computes two AND2 operations, marked in blue). Figures 7(c) and 7(d) show the graphs corresponding to the netlists in Figs. 7(a) and 7(b), respectively. Whereas the graph in Fig. 7(c) is a DAG, the graph in Fig. 7(d) is not a DAG. While there is no combinational loop in both netlists and the synthesis product is valid, a circular dependency was created between the two 2-output AND2 cells. AbstractPIM relies on the graph acyclic structure (since it uses the SIMPLER mapping algorithm), and therefore instructions which might cause cyclic dependency cannot be used.

A sufficient condition that guarantees no such loops will be created, is to use only cells in which all the outputs depend on all the inputs, *e.g.*, half adder, which implements the functions $S = a \oplus b$ and $C = ab$. However, in the case of a 32-bit adder, which is a common combinational block, the first output bit S_0 is given by $S_0 = A_0 \oplus B_0 \oplus C_{in}$, where A_0 and B_0 are the least significant bits of the added numbers, and C_{in} is the carry in. As can be concluded from the S_0 calculation, it is not dependent on the other inputs and can therefore cause a cyclic graph. Future work will ensure support of any multi-output instruction, thus enabling more flexibility in planning the ISA.

7.2 Architecture-Targeted Compilation

When using the compilation method proposed in this chapter, the code is compiled to support different logic families, *e.g.*, MAGIC NOR. This flexibility comes with a cost: the compilation does allow technology backward compatibility and execution of the code on different machines without re-compiling the code, but the compiled instruction stream is not necessarily optimized for a desired specific logic family. For example, assume a code containing a XOR logic is compiled to an ISA consisting of two instructions only: NOR and NAND. A XOR logic can be implemented, *e.g.*, using either 4 NAND gates or 5 NOR gates. If the compiler is not aware of the exact target machine, it will likely compile the XOR logic into the shorter sequence consisting of 4 NAND gates. If this code is eventually run on a target machine consisting of NOR operations only, that machine implements NOR in 1 clock cycle and NAND in 4 clock cycles, so the execution will take 16 cycles (4 NAND gates) total rather than 5 cycles (5 NOR gates) total. As a result, although the code is compatible with the given target machine, it is not latency-optimized to it.

When the code is compiled for a specific stateful logic family, it can be optimized for this specific technology, *e.g.*, achieving the lowest latency possible using our flow for the used technology, while maintaining backward compatibility. The optimization can be done in the first component of abstractPIM (intermediate representation), both as part of the synthesis and as part of the mapping tool. The optimization is based on technology parameters, *i.e.*, the second component (microcode generation).

In this chapter, we discuss the optimization both as part of the synthesis and as part of the mapping tool. First, we discuss the optimization as part of the synthesis. In abstractPIM, every instruction in the ISA, which is represented by a cell in a synthesis standard library, is defined with the same area. The synthesis minimizes the area, which is equivalent in this case to minimizing the number of instructions needed for execution. However, to achieve architecture-targeted compilation, different area values can be defined for the cells in the synthesis standard library based on technology parameters. In this manner, various factors can be optimized in the synthesis. In the above NOR and NAND example, the compiler will be informed that a NAND instruction costs twice as much as a NOR instruction, and will compile the code accordingly by prioritizing the different cells in the synthesis standard library. In that sense, it is important to mention that in the case of architecture-targeted compilation, the intermediate representation and microcode generation components are no longer independent of each other. Particularly, in the case of latency optimization, the latency of each instruction, which is architecture dependent and acquired in the microcode generation component, should be embedded in the compiler. Similarly, the compiler can optimize the instruction stream considering other factors such as minimizing the number of write operations to the memristive crossbar array, prioritizing instructions with less inputs (*e.g.*, prioritizing NOR2 instruction over NOR3 instruction), *etc.*

Furthermore, the optimization of the aforementioned factors can be considered not only in the synthesis, but also in the mapping tool. For example, in our flow, we used SIMPLER as a mapping tool. As discussed in Sect. 2.2, SIMPLER builds a DAG which determines an efficient gate execution order using heuristics based on different node parameters, *e.g.*, CU (cell usage). The CU values (Eqs. 1 and 2) can be modified according to the instructions number of outputs and number of temporary computation cells.

As previously mentioned, the SIMPLER mapping tool can be replaced with any other mapping tool in the abstractPIM flow. Different mapping tools optimize different factors (*e.g.*, latency, area, or throughput), and therefore the choice of the mapping tool depends on the architecture demands. Our flow enables to easily switch between the different mapping tools and compare them to discover the best mapping tool for a specific technology and optimization factor.

7.3 High-Level Compilation

In abstractPIM, the input to our tool is a Verilog code. This code is synthesized using a synthesis standard library that includes the ISA commands, and is eventually computed on the hardware. However, the synthesis tools used in this work are CMOS-oriented, and they are aiming for maximizing the parallelism using such a technology. These tools are not optimal for execution on a single-row memristive crossbar array with cell reuse. While abstractPIM establishes foundations for a PIM compiler, it still remains in the synthesis domain. In its current shape, abstractPIM can be used to implement instruction hierarchy in PIM architectures, but there is still work to do in order to make it a software compiler. A natural research direction is to replace the synthesis tool ("silicon compiler") with a traditional compiler ("software compiler") that compiles a high-level software code (*e.g.*, Python code), into a sequence of ISA commands that can be analyzed using similar methods to those used in this chapter.

7.4 Supporting Input Overwriting

As demonstrated in FELIX [24], single-cycle operations of different Boolean functions (and not only a NOR operation) can be implemented using MAGIC gates. The MAGIC gate inputs can be overwritten to save the utilized number of cells, to improve the effective lifetime of the system and to enhance its performance. To use such logic gates in abstractPIM, the algorithm used for the mapping should be modified to support input overwriting, as done in X-MAGIC [25]. Figure 8 demonstrates the modifications made in the X-MAGIC DAG, which should be applied in the abstractPIM flow for overwriting support. These modifications include the definition of different edges in the DAG, each of which represents different dependency between the nodes. The first edge type is a *regular edge*, which represents a non-overwriting dependency. The second edge type is an *overwriting edge*, which represents a case where the output of the child node is overwritten by the parent operation.

Figure 8(a) shows an example netlist that consists of three XOR logic gates, and Fig. 8(b) shows its corresponding X-MAGIC DAG. Gates *g2* and *g3* use gate *g1* output, and therefore are connected to it via an edge. Assume gate *g2* overwrites gate *g1* output, while gate *g3* does not overwrite gate *g1* output. If gate *g2* is executed before gate *g3*, the output of gate *g1* will be overwritten as part of gate *g2* execution, and gate *g3* will not operate properly. Therefore, regular, non-overwriting dependency (marked in black) and overwriting dependency (marked in green) are marked accordingly in the DAG. To ensure that the overwriting node is the last one executed, a sequencing dependency (marked in red) between gate *g2* and gate *g3* is added to the DAG.

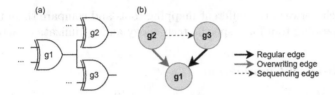

Fig. 8. X-MAGIC DAG Example. (a) An example netlist of three XOR logic gates. (b) The X-MAGIC DAG corresponding to the netlist in (a). A regular edge is marked with black, an overwriting edge is marked with green and a sequencing edge is marked with red. (Color figure online)

8   Conclusions

This chapter presents a hierarchical compilation concept and method for logic execution within a memristive crossbar array. The proposed method provides flexibility, portability, abstraction and code size reduction. Future research directions that can enhance the abstractPIM flow, *e.g.*, architecture-targeted compilation and input-overwriting support, are also presented in this chapter. The abstractPIM flow lays a solid foundation for a compiler for a memristor-based architecture, by enabling automatic mapping and execution of any logic function within the memory, using a defined ISA.

Acknowledgment. This research is supported by the ERC under the European Union's Horizon 2020 Research and Innovation Programme (grant agreement no. 757259).

References

1. Pedram, A., Richardson, S., Horowitz, M., Galal, S., Kvatinsky, S.: Dark memory and accelerator-rich system optimization in the dark silicon era. IEEE Des. Test **34**(2), 39–50 (2017)
2. Hamdioui, S., et al.: Memristor for computing: myth or reality? In: DATE, pp. 722–731, March 2017
3. Ielmini, D., Wong, H.-S.P.: In-memory computing with resistive switching devices. Nat. Electron. **1**, 333–343 (2018)
4. Lastras-Montaño, M.A., Cheng, K.-T.: Resistive random-access memory based on ratioed memristors. Nat. Electron. **1**, 466–472 (2018)
5. Wong, H.S.P., et al.: Phase change memory. Proc. IEEE **98**, 2201–2227 (2010)
6. Woods, W., Teuscher, C.: Approximate vector matrix multiplication implementations for neuromorphic applications using memristive crossbars. In: IEEE/ACM NANOARCH, pp. 103–108, July 2017
7. Deng, L., et al.: Model compression and hardware acceleration for neural networks: a comprehensive survey. Proc. IEEE **108**(4), 485–532 (2020)
8. Kvatinsky, S., et al.: MAGIC-memristor-aided logic. IEEE TCAS II **61**, 895–899 (2014)
9. Borghetti, J., et al.: 'memristive' switches enable 'stateful' logic operations via material implication. Nature **464**, 873–876 (2010)

10. Testa, E., et al.: Inversion optimization in majority-inverter graphs. In: NANOARCH, pp. 15–20, July 2016
11. Tenace, V., et al.: SAID: a supergate-aided logic synthesis flow for memristive crossbars. In: DATE, pp. 372–377, March 2019
12. Ben Hur, R., et al.: SIMPLE MAGIC: synthesis and in-memory mapping of logic execution for memristor-aided logic. In: IEEE/ACM ICCAD, pp. 225–232, November 2017
13. Ben-Hur, R., et al.: SIMPLER MAGIC: synthesis and mapping of in-memory logic executed in a single row to improve throughput. In: IEEE TCAD, July 2019
14. Bürger, J., et al.: Digital logic synthesis for memristors. In: Reed-Muller, pp. 31–40, January 2013
15. Linn, E., et al.: Beyond von Neumann - logic operations in passive crossbar arrays alongside memory operations. Nanotechnology 23, 305205 (2012)
16. P6 family of processors hardware developer's manual. http://download.intel.com/design/PentiumII/manuals/24400101.pdf
17. Eliahu, A., et al.: abstractPIM: bridging the gap between processing-in-memory technology and instruction set architecture. In: 2020 IFIP/IEEE 28th International Conference on Very Large Scale Integration (VLSI-SOC), pp. 28–33 (2020)
18. Reuben, J., et al.: Memristive logic: a framework for evaluation and comparison. In: PATMOS, pp. 1–8, September 2017
19. Yadav, D.N., Thangkhiew, P.L., Datta, K.: Look-ahead mapping of Boolean functions in memristive crossbar array. Integration 64, 152–162 (2019)
20. Thangkhiew, P.L., Zulehner, A., Wille, R., Datta, K., Sengupta, I.: An efficient memristor crossbar architecture for mapping Boolean functions using Binary Decision Diagrams (BDD). Integration 71, 125–133 (2020)
21. Brayton, R., Mishchenko, A.: ABC: an academic industrial-strength verification tool. In: Touili, T., Cook, B., Jackson, P. (eds.) CAV 2010. LNCS, vol. 6174, pp. 24–40. Springer, Heidelberg (2010). https://doi.org/10.1007/978-3-642-14295-6_5
22. Kurup, P., et al.: Logic Synthesis Using Synopsys, 2nd edn. Springer, Heidelberg (2011)
23. Amarù, L., Gaillardon, P.-E., De Micheli, G.: The EPFL combinational benchmark suite. In: IWLS (2015)
24. Gupta, S., Imani, M., Rosing, T.: FELIX: fast and energy-efficient logic in memory. In: 2018 IEEE/ACM International Conference on Computer-Aided Design (ICCAD), pp. 1–7 (2018)
25. Peled, N., et al.: X-MAGIC: enhancing PIM using input overwriting capabilities. In: 2020 IFIP/IEEE 28th International Conference on Very Large Scale Integration (VLSI-SOC), pp. 64–69 (2020)

Author Index

Printed in the United States
by Baker & Taylor Publisher Services